MARK BAILEY is Research Fellow, Gonville and Caius College, Cambridge.

D1474003

Cambridge studies in medieval life and thought

A MARGINAL ECONOMY?

Cambridge studies in medieval life and thought
Fourth series

General Editor:

J.C. HOLT
Professor of Medieval History and
Master of Fitzwilliam College, University of Cambridge

Advisory Editors:

C.N.L. BROOKE
Dixie Professor of Ecclesiastical History and
Fellow of Gonville and Caius College,
University of Cambridge

D.E. LUSCOMBE
Professor of Medieval History, University of Sheffield

The series Cambridge Studies in Medieval Life and Thought was inaugurated by G.G. Coulton in 1920. Professor J.C. Holt now acts as General Editor of a Fourth Series, with Professor C.N.L. Brooke and Professor D.E. Luscombe as Advisory Editors. The series aims to bring together outstanding work by medieval scholars over a wide range of human endeavour extending from political economy to the history of ideas.

Titles in the series

1 The Beaumont Twins: The Roots and Branches of Power in the Twelfth Century   D.B. CROUCH
2 The Thought of Gregory the Great   G.R. EVANS
3 The Government of England under Henry I   JUDITH A. GREEN
4 Charity and Community in Medieval Cambridge   MIRI RUBIN
5 Autonomy and Community: The Royal Manor of Havering, 1200–1500   MARJORIE KENISTON MCINTOSH
6 The Political Thought of Baldus de Ubaldis   JOSEPH CANNING
7 Land and Power in Late Medieval Ferrara: The Rule of the Este, 1350–1450   TREVOR DEAN
8 William of Tyre: Historian of the Latin East   PETER W. EDBURY and JOHN GORDON ROWE
9 The Royal Saints of Anglo-Saxon England: A Study of West Saxon and East Anglian Cults   SUSAN J. RIDYARD
10 John of Wales: A Study of the Works and Ideas of a Thirteenth-Century Friar   JENNY SWANSON
11 Richard III: A Study of Service   ROSEMARY HORROX
12 A Marginal Economy?: East Anglian Breckland in the Later Middle Ages   MARK BAILEY

A MARGINAL ECONOMY?

East Anglian Breckland in the
Later Middle Ages

MARK BAILEY

Research Fellow, Gonville and Caius College, Cambridge

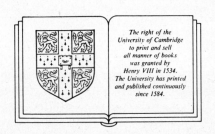

The right of the
University of Cambridge
to print and sell
all manner of books
was granted by
Henry VIII in 1534.
The University has printed
and published continuously
since 1584.

CAMBRIDGE UNIVERSITY PRESS

CAMBRIDGE

NEW YORK   NEW ROCHELLE   MELBOURNE   SYDNEY

Published by the Press Syndicate of the University of Cambridge
The Pitt Building, Trumpington Street, Cambridge CB2 1RP
32 East 57th Street, New York, NY 10022, USA
10 Stamford Road, Oakleigh, Melbourne 3166, Australia

First published 1989

Printed in Great Britain at the University Press, Cambridge

British Library cataloguing in publication data
Bailey, Mark.
A marginal economy?: East Anglian
Breckland in the later Middle Ages.
(Cambridge studies in medieval life and
thought. Fourth series: 12).
1. East Anglia. Breckland region.
Economic conditions, 1154–1485
I. Title.
330.9426; 1403

Library of Congress cataloguing in publication data
Bailey, Mark.
A marginal economy? : East Anglian Breckland in the later Middle
Ages / Mark Bailey
p.   cm. – (Cambridge studies in medieval life and thought:
4th ser., 12)
Bibliography.
Includes index.
ISBN 0 521 36501 5
1. Breckland (England) – Economic conditions.   2. Agriculture –
Economic aspects – England – Breckland – History.   I. Title.
II. Series.
HC257.B73835 1989
330.9426'14 – dc19   88-31140 CIP

ISBN 0 521 36501 5

To my parents

CONTENTS

Contents

MAPS

TABLES

Tables

Tables

ACKNOWLEDGEMENTS

This book would not have been possible without the help and support of many people, and it is a pleasure to be able to acknowledge their contribution in this small way. The research began as a doctoral dissertation submitted to the University of Cambridge, and it was during this period that most of my debts were incurred. The skills of reading and locating documents are vital to a budding medievalist, and Dorothy Owen guided my first, stumbling attempts at palaeography with kindness and expertise. Margaret Statham shared with me her considerable knowledge of the Bury abbey archives, and became a frequent advisor during many happy hours spent at the West Suffolk Record Office. At other record offices and repositories I received patient and cheerful assistance.

Christopher Dyer and Richard Smith pointed me towards certain Brandon material, and Rodney Hilton permitted me to view the ESRC's computer print-outs of the early Lakenheath court rolls. Whilst at Birmingham, Helena Graham generously allowed me to read drafts of her earlier work on the Lakenheath land market, subsequently omitted from her thesis. The examiners of the doctoral dissertation, Edward Miller and Richard Britnell, encouraged me to seek publication and highlighted those aspects which needed further attention. Richard Britnell also commented extensively on an early draft of chapter 1, and kindly allowed me to make use of his unpublished research. Bruce Campbell shared with me his wide knowledge of medieval East Anglia, and I benefited from his expert comments on drafts of chapters 1 and 2. I am further indebted to him for supplying me with detailed statistics about demesne farming on some of the Norfolk Breckland manors, and for revealing the preliminary findings of his important, forthcoming book.

Financial assistance from various bodies has allowed me to study in comfort during the last six years of research. As a postgraduate, the ESRC, the Master and Fellows of Corpus Christi College, and the University of Cambridge (Ellen McArthur studentship) all provided me with generous support. As a Research Fellow at Gonville and Caius College, I have been able to concentrate on completing the work in an ideal academic environment. I am also grateful to the editors of the *Medieval life and thought* series, Jim Holt, David Luscombe and Christopher Brooke, for their comments and advice. In the later stages, Julie Noy devoted much time and effort to checking the proofs.

Duncan Bythell first encouraged me to embark upon historical research, and has read all of this work in draft form. He has constantly emphasised the need to write for an audience wider than the mere specialist, and if the book achieves this aim, then it is to his credit. John Hatcher was an excellent supervisor of the doctoral dissertation, patient, supportive and highly stimulating. He has continued to provide valued criticism, and has commented extensively on most parts of the book. The inadequacies which remain are my responsibility alone.

The greatest debt is to my parents, Ron and Maureen. They have always stimulated my historical curiosity, and have trekked to various corners of East Anglia on cold winter days as readily as they have listened to my latest ideas. Their selfless help and tolerance throughout many years has been simply immeasurable.

ABBREVIATIONS

Ag.H.R.	*Agricultural History Review*
Bacon	Bacon collection, University of Chicago
BL	British Library
Blomefield	F. Blomefield, *An essay towards a topographical history of the county of Norfolk*, 5 vols. (London, 1739–75)
CPR	*Calendar of the patent rolls*
CUL	Cambridge University Library
Ec.H.R.	*Economic History Review* (second series unless stated)
IESRO	Ipswich and East Suffolk Record Office
NRO	Norwich and Norfolk Record Office
PRO	Public Record Office (Chancery Lane)
P.S.I.A.	*Proceedings of the Suffolk Institute of Archaeology and History*
V.C.H.	*Victoria county history*
WSROB	West Suffolk Record Office, Bury St Edmunds

The following distinguish different manors in the same village:

Downham (IP)	Manor of Ixworth priory
Downham (S)	Shardelowe's manor
Feltwell (E)	Bishopric of Ely
Feltwell (EH)	East Hall
Fornham (A)	Abbot's manor
Fornham (C)	Cellarer's manor

Chapter 1

AT THE MARGIN

THE MARGIN AND THE MEDIEVAL ECONOMY

The causes and the extent of economic change in medieval England remain matters of controversy. In the quest to understand the dynamics of the economy, historians have considered the relative influence of such factors as technological innovation, class structures and relations, demographic trends, and contemporary economic attitudes.[1] Nevertheless, while subject to sustained assault in recent years, the current weight of historical scholarship still suggests that the changing balance between land and labour was the most important influence behind economic change. The basic principles of this 'population-resources' model were first outlined in a series of seminal articles by the late Michael Postan, and have influenced the work of many later scholars.[2] In recent years, more sophisticated analysis of manorial records has yielded detailed evidence about medieval agriculture and demography which has

---

An amended version of this opening section can be found as M.D. Bailey, 'The concept of the margin in the medieval economy', *Ec.H.R.* 42 part 1 (1989).

[1] The literature on this topic is extensive, but see J.D. Chambers, *Population, economy and society in pre-industrial England* (Cambridge, 1972); M.M. Postan, *The medieval economy and society: an economic history of Britain in the Middle Ages* (Harmondsworth, 1975); J.L. Bolton, *The medieval English economy* (London, 1980); and T.H. Aston and C.H.E. Philpin, eds., *The Brenner debate: agrarian class structure and economic development in pre-industrial Europe* (Cambridge, 1985).

[2] These articles have been collected and published as M.M. Postan, *Essays on English agriculture* (Cambridge, 1973). His later views are best expressed in M.M. Postan, 'Agrarian society in its prime: Part 7, England', in *The Cambridge economic history of Europe*, vol. 1 *The agrarian life of the Middle Ages*, ed. M.M. Postan (second edition, Cambridge, 1966), pp. 548–632. See also J.Z. Titow, *English rural society 1200–1350* (London, 1969); E. Miller and J. Hatcher, *Medieval England: rural society and economic change 1086–1348* (London, 1978); J. Hatcher, *Plague, population and the English economy 1348–1530* (London, 1977).

demanded some refinement of the model.[3] Yet one central constituent that has been accepted almost without question is its concept of 'the margin'.

The model postulates that population increase in the twelfth and thirteenth centuries resulted in both the expansion of cultivation and the general growth of the economy. However, by around 1300 the population had outstripped the ability of agriculture to maintain it and there followed at least a century of demographic and economic decline. The two centuries after Domesday are regarded as a period of progressive land shortage, when the pressure of rising population forced society to colonise lands which in more propitious times would have been regarded as unfavourable for cultivation. Cumulatively, the 'journey to the margin' involved the cultivation of hundreds of thousands of previously under-utilised acres. Woods and pastures on the peripheries of anciently settled villages were converted to arable land, and, where more land was available, tracts of heath and moorland were ploughed up for grain production.

It is not surprising that so many of the acres newly won in the twelfth and thirteenth centuries should have been marginal not only in location but also in quality . . . the thin and hungry heathlands of Norfolk breckland or Suffolk 'Fielding' where no or almost no grain was to be grown in any other period of English history bar our own, or on the southern slopes of Dartmoor . . . or on the skin-deep overlays of Longbarrow warren above Winchester . . . these are not lands on which society would draw except in times of real land hunger.[4]

The development of these marginal regions was an important safety-valve in the conditions of the thirteenth century, but was no longer necessary when the pressure on land was released by demo-

---

[3] See, for example, Z. Razi, *Life, marriage and death in a medieval parish* (Cambridge, 1980), and the review by R.M. Smith in *Journal of Historical Geography* 8 (1982), pp. 305–6; B.M.S. Campbell, 'Agricultural progress in medieval England: some evidence from eastern Norfolk', *Ec.H.R.* 36 (1983), pp. 26–45.

[4] Postan, 'Agrarian society in its prime', pp. 551–2; W.G. Hoskins, *The making of the English landscape* (London, 1955), pp. 103–6; E. Miller, 'The English economy in the thirteenth century: implications of recent research', *Past and Present* 28 (1964), pp. 23–5; Miller and Hatcher, *Rural society and economic change*, p. 56, assert that 'arable villages were established . . . on Domesday sheep pastures in the Norfolk and Suffolk Breckland'; R.A. Donkin, 'Changes in the early Middle Ages', in *A new historical geography of England before 1600*, ed. H.C. Darby (Cambridge, 1976), pp. 98–106; D.B. Grigg, *Population growth and agrarian change* (Cambridge, 1980), p. 65.

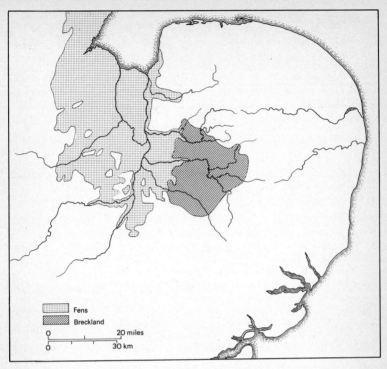

Map 1. East Anglia showing Breckland

graphic contraction in the fourteenth and fifteenth centuries. Consequently, land was abandoned and arable shrank, occasionally to
the point that whole villages were deserted, and it is assumed that
the margin led the general retreat of settlement. This 'downturn in
internal colonisation' pre-dated the arrival of plague in 1348–9 in
upland areas of Oxfordshire and Yorkshire, and Saltmarsh writes
of having visited ruined churches in Breckland 'built by the latest
pioneer settlers of the high Middle Ages, never enlarged and early
abandoned'.[5] This interpretation of the immediate pre-plague

[5] K.J. Allison, M.W. Beresford and J.G. Hurst, 'The deserted villages of Oxfordshire',
Occasional papers, Department of Local History, Leicester University 17 (1965), pp. 5–6; J.
McDonnell, 'Medieval assarting hamlets in Bilsdale, north-east Yorkshire', *Northern
History* 22 (1986), p. 276; J.A. Saltmarsh, 'Plague and economic decline in England in the
late Middle Ages', *Cambridge Historical Journal* 7 (1941), p. 24.

period has not stood unchallenged,[6] but few historians doubt that the demographic decline of the later fourteenth century resulted in a fall in land values and an abandonment of some arable. This contraction was most evident at the margin; 'villages on the furthest frontiers of cultivation ... contracted, some of them to the brink of demise'. This belief is explicit in the works of many historians. Hoskins states that

the retreat from marginal lands was most evident in the sandy Breckland of south-western Norfolk and north-western Suffolk ... it was the vast mortality of the successive epidemics that led to the piecemeal abandonment of these villages and hamlets on marginal land. On and around the edges of the Breckland there are no fewer than twenty-eight deserted villages. Most of them were small and poor, and the desertions were gradual, extending over two, three or four generations, so that most instances of final abandonment occur during the fifteenth century.[7]

Hence there are important general implications to be drawn from the performance of the margin. Because the economic development of marginal areas is assumed to be determined solely by changes in demographic pressure, historians regard them as highly sensitive indicators of population change. The contraction of arable at the margin is taken as a firm indication that population in England had begun to decline before the Black Death. Furthermore, it is argued that the productivity of marginal soils was itself an important factor in inducing overall population change. Much of England's better arable lands are assumed to have suffered from soil exhaustion in the thirteenth century as agriculture strained to feed a larger number of mouths, and so to some degree the cultivation of new lands merely represented a replacement of the old and not a net addition to it.[8] Given that these newest lands were also responsible for sustaining the latest increments of population, then their performance and fertility assume considerable importance for society's well-being: crop failure at the margin would exacerbate the state of over-population. Yet it was inevitable that the margin would fail, for most of these soils were

[6] B.F. Harvey, 'The population trend in England between 1300 and 1348', *Transactions of the Royal Historical Society*, fifth series 16 (1966), pp. 23–42.
[7] Hoskins, *English landscape*, pp. 120–1. See also Postan, *Medieval economy*, p. 39; P. Zeigler, *The Black Death* (Harmondsworth, 1969), p. 175; M.W. Beresford and J.G. Hurst, *Deserted medieval villages* (London, 1972), pp. 6–7.
[8] J.Z. Titow, *Winchester yields: a study in medieval agricultural productivity* (Cambridge, 1972).

thin and hungry . . . worth cultivating only for short periods. Before long the stored fertility of the soil would be mined out, and the land would lie exhausted. This may well have been the natural history of the East Anglian Brecklands or the Hampshire and Wiltshire chalklands and some of the Cotswold uplands . . . [lands] most likely to suffer from insufficient manuring and . . . abandoned by the plough.[9]

The failure of the margin is regarded as a major cause of the crisis of over-population in England around 1300:

It will not be too fanciful . . . to see in the falling production of the later centuries a natural punishment for earlier over-expansion . . . after a time the marginal character of marginal lands was bound to assert itself, and the honeymoon of high yields was succeeded by long periods of reckoning when the poorer lands, no longer new, punished the men who tilled them with failing crops.[10]

Implicit in this interpretation is the idea that a marginal region is one which is exploited as a necessary increment only when the strain of population on resources becomes perilously high. It also assumes that neither medieval agrarian technology nor the economy itself was sufficiently developed to make productive use of poor soils. In the medieval context, these regions would have been under-developed before the twelfth and thirteenth centuries, an argument which appears plausible enough. But exactly what characteristics constitute a marginal region in the population-resources model? Because grain production is regarded as the prime objective of pre-industrial economies, it is assumed that all regions inherently unsuited to arable farming are therefore marginal. Hence Postan defines marginal soils as those with low physical productivity, those 'incapable of producing per acre of land, or per bushel of seed, or per plough-day of cultivation as much as other or better land'.[11] All he is really describing are poor soils, although strictly speaking poor soils become marginal soils only when they are *proved* to have been exploited as an increment in the thirteenth century. However,

---

[9] Postan, 'Agrarian society in its prime', pp. 558–9; Postan, *Medieval economy*, pp. 63–73; Titow, *Rural society*, p. 93–5.

[10] Postan, 'Economic foundations of medieval society', in *Essays on English agriculture*, p. 14.

[11] M.M. Postan, 'Note', *Ec.H.R.* 12 (1959–60), p. 89. In *Medieval economy*, p. 20, he explicitly admits that 'most of these lands were marginal simply because they were, to use a humdrum adjective, poor'. Grigg, *Population growth*, p. 65 writes, 'marginal land had to be brought into cultivation, poorer soils, from which only very low yields could be obtained'.

Postan equates marginal soils with all poor soils because he accepts the Ricardian view that cultivation will first be concentrated on good land, and that poorer land will only be utilised intensively when the tension between population and resources rises above a certain level. This explains why historians have come to regard poor soils as synonymous with marginality, so that Breckland, for example, is designated marginal, not because it is proved to have been late colonised as an incremental region, but because its soils are exceptionally poor and so could only have been exploited according to the chronology outlined above.

This definition of marginality has also been extended to include other regions where the production and marketing of grain is assumed to be difficult. As Abel writes, 'a hard climate and remoteness from trading centres were [other] conditions unfavourable to farming', and such areas would also remain largely under-developed so long as population and resources were reasonably balanced.[12] Their colonisation would be assured when the pressure of population on resources began to mount significantly, only to bear the brunt of subsequent demographic decline: 'nothing was more natural than that the occupiers [of these lands] . . . should leave their old farms to start afresh under better natural conditions'.[13]

The argument that all regions of poor soil, harsh climate and remote location are therefore marginal has its roots in the theory of economic rent. Economic rent, as opposed to contract rent, is a difficult and often confusing concept, but basically represents a 'return due to the land alone as a factor of production'.[14] Ricardo argued that a colonising society would initially settle on an area of 'rich and fertile' land, for which no rent would exist. Yet, in order to feed a growing population, society would be forced to cultivate 'second and third' quality land, and rent only exists when this differential is apparent. In other words, the necessity of cultivating inferior land is the cause of rent on the superior land: as the population increases, and as grain prices rise, so the margin of cultivation is extended and the rent level at the intensive margin increases.[15]

---

[12] W. Abel, *Agricultural fluctuations in Europe from the thirteenth to the twentieth centuries* (London, 1980), pp. 88–9; G. Duby, *Rural economy and country life in the medieval west* (London, 1968), p. 301.   [13] Abel, *Agricultural fluctuations*, p. 89.
[14] D. Grigg, *An introduction to agricultural geography* (London, 1984), p. 49. See this, and other basic economic textbooks, for a more detailed discussion of economic rent.
[15] For Ricardo, see E.C.K. Gonner, ed., *Ricardo's economic essays* (London, 1923); M. Blaug, *Economic theory in retrospect*, third edition (Cambridge, 1983), pp. 91–152.

A similar concept underlies the notion that remote regions are marginal for grain production. If corn is sold at a fixed price, and if soil quality is assumed constant, then economic rent will decline with distance from the market. When economic rent reaches zero, cultivation for the market will cease, although subsistence agriculture will continue.[16] However, if the price of corn was to rise, the margin of cultivation would move and new lands would be brought under the plough: if the price was to fall, the opposite would be true. In both of these theoretical models, the 'margin of cultivation' is a constantly moving and highly specific point. This is somewhat different from the blanket use of the term by some medieval historians, who simply describe all regions of harsh climate, poor soil and geographical remoteness as marginal for cultivation.

It is not disputed that regions where economic rent approximates to zero should be designated as 'marginal for cultivation'. However, this book contends that the classical theory of rent has been adapted too crudely by the population-resources model to the conditions of the medieval economy. Ricardo assumed that the extensive margin of cultivation comprised 'inferior' – meaning poor quality – land, although this could also include 'less advantageously sited' land. It is important to appreciate that this theory of differential rent was not developed as a theory of land colonisation *per se*. Yet, despite this, subsequent writers have referred to a Ricardian view of land colonisation, where the most fertile lands are settled first. This is firmly embodied in the population-resources' definition of a 'marginal economy': all regions with disadvantages in grain production were, *ipso facto*, the 'marginal economies' of medieval England. *All* areas of poor soil and geographical remoteness were therefore late cultivated and early abandoned in the Middle Ages, and hence sensitive indicators of demographic change. They were developed only as incremental regions and therefore backward in technological and economic developments affecting the economy at large. And they were essentially dependent upon demand for bread grains (and by extension demographic fluctuations) for their economic utilisation.

This view of the margin is partly derived from the classical theory of economic rent, but is also based upon a number of prior assumptions about the nature of the medieval economy. It assumes

[16] Grigg, *Agricultural geography*, pp. 49–53.

that 'fertility' was an exhaustible, stored-up component of the soil, which was somehow graded by society for settlement purposes at an early date. It assumes that agrarian technology was primitive and unchanging, so that poor soils were doomed to exhaustion after a few years' cropping. It assumes that a region's ability to grow grain was the main determinant of its wealth and economic success. How tenable are these suppositions?

Soil fertility and agrarian technology

As a general term, 'fertility' refers to the crop-growing capacity of land, to its physical productivity. This is largely determined by the soil's natural properties, but also by prevailing farming techniques. The population-resources model assumes that agrarian technology was poorly developed throughout the Middle Ages, and so the effect of farming systems on soil fertility was likely to be deleterious rather than favourable. With little capacity for raising the land's natural fertility, it is argued that the early Saxon settlers sought out and cultivated the better lands. Hence land with the highest physical productivity had been largely colonised by 1086, whilst the remaining 'inferior' lands awaited progressive colonisation until the barren – or 'sub-marginal' – lands were reached.[17]

Such a view of soil fertility is too simplistic, even by the standards of medieval agriculture. There are both theoretical and empirical grounds for supposing that fertility was not merely a stored-up and exhaustible component of the soil, but could be altered by factors both exogenous and indigenous to the economy. In the first place, long-term climatic and environmental change could significantly alter the fertility of upland areas, and render once barren lands suitable for cultivation. The data are not ideal, but both Lamb and Parry have argued that a climatic optimum occurred in Europe between 1100 and 1250, followed by two centuries of cooling.[18] The effect of these changes on agriculture was considerable, for apparently small changes in mean temperature and rainfall over long periods could have an exponential effect on both the performance and viability of arable farming. Put simply, the warmer weather increased the area of potentially cultivable land, indepen-

[17] Postan, *Medieval economy*, pp. 17–20. See also H.C. Darby, 'Domesday England', in *New historical geography of England*, pp. 45–7.
[18] M.L. Parry, *Climatic change, agriculture and settlement* (Folkstone, 1978), p. 97; H.H. Lamb, *Climate history and the modern world* (London, 1982), p. 193–4.

dent of economic trends, and the colder weather had the reverse effect.[19] It would be premature to conclude that climatic change could itself be a prime cause of expansion or contraction at the margin, although by changing the parameters of cultivation in upland areas it certainly accentuated the effects of economic changes. It would thus appear that fertility – and by extension the performance of marginal regions – could be significantly altered by the action of exogenous variables.

Secondly, it is not impossible that soil fertility could be maintained or even improved through adaptation and technical progress, in other words by changes indigenous to the economy. To establish this requires a brief analysis of the factors affecting technical change in the Middle Ages, itself a complex and contentious issue. However, if such changes were discernible, then it would demand some revision of the view that soil exhaustion was an inevitable feature of cultivation at the margin. Proponents of the population-resources model argue, with some plausibility, that the spread of innovation in agriculture was inhibited by the strict communal organisation of open-fields, and that agrarian investment was stifled by the manorial system.[20] Agrarian technology was static, and the very fact that marginal regions had to be brought into cultivation in the twelfth and thirteenth centuries indicates the failure of medieval agriculture to increase productivity sufficiently on existing lands.[21] And if it was not possible to improve agrarian techniques on the inherently more fertile lands of England, it would surely have been impossible in marginal regions.

---

[19] Lamb, *ibid.*, p. 170, argues that by 1250 it had become possible to cultivate up to 1,300 feet above sea-level on Dartmoor and to 1,050 feet in Northumberland. Parry, *Climatic change*, p. 103, believes that 60 per cent of the high land surrounding the river Tweed, which was sub-marginal in the seventeenth century, could have been ploughed before 1250. However, this theory has not passed unquestioned by historians, who are not fully convinced that the sources for medieval climatic surveys are entirely satisfactory. Indeed, the climatic factors which encouraged arable expansion and then contraction in the Middle Ages coincided almost exactly with demographic and economic changes inducing the same tendencies, which makes it perilously difficult to establish the precise contribution of climate to the fortunes of marginal regions. At present our knowledge of climate is more tenuous than our knowledge of price and population movements, and we need more certainty as to its chronology, its extent, its effect on lowlands areas and so forth. See D.B. Grigg, *The dynamics of agricultural change: the historical experience* (London, 1982), p. 86–8.

[20] Postan, *Medieval economy*, pp. 18–19, 45–62 and 112–14.

[21] Postan, 'Agrarian society in its prime', p. 560; Postan, *Medieval economy*, p. 17. See also Titow, *Rural society*, p. 72: 'the level of medieval productivity of land was extremely low'.

Implicit in this interpretation is the view that population increase and the prevailing conditions of resource scarcity could not stimulate technical change in agriculture.[22] Yet such a view stands in direct contrast to other theories of technical change, which maintain that population growth will nearly always result in technological innovation. In one such interpretation, Clark argues that a rigid, unyielding system of agriculture is an historical rarity in a period of rising population, and that productivity will be raised by adaptation.[23] In another, Boserup argues that rising demographic pressure will force farmers to crop their arable land more frequently and reduce the area under fallow. This policy would rapidly result in soil exhaustion, unless the farmer simultaneously adopted other cultivation and fertilisation techniques – such as marling, better manuring arrangements, the wider use of leguminous crops – to offset this tendency. Hence the progressive shifts to higher cropping frequencies involve a replacement of the scarce resource, land, by the more abundant labour and capital.[24]

Neither Boserup nor Clark concerned themselves directly with the problems of medieval England, but their belief in the capacity of population growth to effect an improvement in agricultural techniques has important implications for the medieval economy. Under these conditions, 'fertility' is not regarded as some inherent, stored-up and exhaustible component of its soil, but more as a variable factor dependent upon inter-related changes in agrarian technique and population density.[25] This means that soil exhaustion need not have been an inevitable or universal feature of thirteenth-century England. It also means that lands at one time regarded as marginal could, with the advent of certain technical advances, come to be regarded as fertile lands at a later date. For example, the medieval fenlands comprised peat and silt soils of high intrinsic richness and fertility, but it required the development of more sophisticated drainage techniques to make them workable for arable cultivation. Similarly, Breckland was regarded as a region of easily worked, productive soils, until demographic and technical

[22] Indeed, central to the Malthusian and Ricardian systems is the view that population and economic growth will eventually peter out owing to the scarcity of natural resources: Blaug, *Economic theory*, p. 91.

[23] C.G. Clark, *Population growth and land use* (London, 1967), p. 253.

[24] E. Boserup, *The conditions of agricultural growth: the economics of agrarian change under population pressure* (London, 1965), pp. 13 and 58–9; E. Boserup, *Population and technology* (Oxford, 1981), pp. 5 and 95. See also Grigg, *Population growth*, pp. 36–8.

[25] Boserup, *Conditions of growth*, p. 13.

changes enabled the cultivation of richer soils in central East Anglia.[26]

Thus the growth of England's population between the seventh and thirteenth centuries did not *inevitably* result in a long-term decline in the fertility of its arable land. Nor can historians confidently grade that land as 'good' or 'bad' by some unchanging standard. Only further research can decide just how relevant are these theoretical points to the reality of medieval agriculture. However, recent work has indicated that the population-resources model was overly pessimistic in its assertions, and that it tended to underestimate medieval England's ability to improve agricultural productivity. For example, farmers in eastern Norfolk attained high levels of agrarian productivity, and managed to eliminate fallows almost entirely. They did this, not by any revolutionary methods, but by meticulous preparation of the seed-bed. This required high labour inputs, which themselves were only possible where economic rent was high enough to justify their adoption:[27] when economic rent is high, farmers will intensify production in order to maximise incomes. As the basic models of economic rent (cited earlier) consider only soil quality and distance from the market as variables, then eastern Norfolk must have possessed extremely fertile soils and excellent market access. Campbell's research confirms that this was indeed the case, for the region possessed some of the richest and most workable soils in England, and enjoyed excellent water communications with the lucrative London market.

Locational theory and the margin

The argument so far has concentrated on proving that 'fertility' is a variable determined by a number of inter-dependent factors, and not the fixed soil component as it has sometimes been viewed. The next consideration is whether inherent soil fertility was the main determinant of a region's ability to grow grain, an assumption implicit in the population-resources model. In fact, such a view is

---

[26] See below, pp. 109–10.
[27] Campbell, 'Agricultural progress', pp. 26–45. See also P.F. Brandon, 'Demesne arable farming in coastal Sussex during the later Middle Ages', *Ag.H.R.* 19 (1971), pp. 113–34. Some of these lands were described as '*possunt seminari quolibet anno*', p. 126, which was also a feature of some Kentish lands: H.L. Gray, *English field systems* (Harvard, 1915), pp. 301–2.

mainly applicable to subsistence economies, and is less relevant to farmers who produce for the market. This is clearly demonstrated in the work of Johann von Thunen.[28] He argued that distance from the market determines not only the intensity of agriculture, but also its main product. Goods which are high in bulk and low in value are unable to sustain high transport costs to market, and so are produced by farmers living near to the market.[29] On the other hand, goods that are cheap to transport relative to their value are produced some distance from the market.

Under the conditions of von Thunen's model, a poor soil region which is close to large markets could produce grain more profitably than a more distant region of better soils, because proximity to the market could compensate for the low physical productivity of the land. This is consistent with the view that all remote regions are marginal for grain farming, but it demands some revision of the argument that all poor soil regions are marginal for cultivation. Yet under Postan's strict definition of the margin (and under the conditions of Ricardo's model), the good soil region could not be marginal for grain production. At worst, the orthodox view of the margin is ill-defined and contradictory.

This imprecise definition of the margin has persisted for two reasons. At the most obvious level, it must reflect a contradictory view of the nature of the economy itself. The population–resources model does not deny the existence of commercial influences in the medieval economy, but its theoretical basis assumes a strong subsistence element, where agricultural output is governed almost wholly by the availability of land and capital, and by natural resource endowment.[30] From this flows the view that soil fertility is the prime determinant of regional economic development, and that poor soil regions equate with the margin. On the other hand, when an economy commercialises, the simple relationship between population and resource endowment is disrupted, and the value of land is no longer determined by quality alone, but also by its location, its market accessibility. Hence the view that areas of geographical remoteness also equate with the margin, regardless of their natural fertility.

[28] The best introduction to von Thunen's work is P. Hall, ed., *Von Thunen's isolated state* (London, 1966).

[29] At the time when von Thunen was writing in the 1820s, this also applied to perishable goods.

[30] See J.H. Paterson, *Land, work and resources: an introduction to economic geography* (London, 1972), pp. 31–2.

The population-resources model's definition of the margin assumes that the medieval economy was, at the same time, both subsistence and commercialised. This obviously could not have been the case: it may have contained subsistent and commercial elements, but it could not have been both at once. Part of the confusion stems from the model's adaptation of Ricardo's work. To Ricardo the important point was that rent arose from the cultivation of inferior land, and it sufficed merely to comment that land was 'inferior' because of its quality or perhaps its location. What happened when poor land was situated close to large markets, or when a fertile region was inaccessible, was unimportant to his argument. But to a model maintaining that all poor soil regions were, *ipso facto*, economically under-developed, this complication *is* important, and as it stands is unsatisfactorily resolved. The medieval economy was patently more sophisticated than the model implies, and its definition of the margin needs to be amended accordingly; meanwhile, more research on the extent and degree of commercial influences in the Middle Ages is required.

In fact, the current, somewhat contradictory, view of the margin embodies a much wider debate over the causes of agrarian differences in pre-industrial societies. It has long been assumed by historians that regional variations in agriculture are the result of environmental factors such as soil type, climate and altitude. Yet von Thunen's work suggests that regional variations are the product of economic forces, and that environment merely creates the bounds within which market forces will operate.[31] The theories of environmental and economic determinism in agriculture have been combined in a rather clumsy and simplistic manner in the population-resources model.

As it stands, the view that all geographically remote regions and all poor soil regions will be marginal for grain production (and therefore economically marginal) is unsatisfactory, because it underestimates the medieval economy's complexity. We need to establish how far the reality of medieval agriculture deviated from the theoretical economic models before we can write confidently of what constitutes the margin. For instance, the concept of economic rent enables historians to calculate the 'margin of cultivation', but only for certain theoretical and fixed conditions, and there are a number of difficulties in adapting this concept for practical

[31] Grigg, *Agricultural geography*, pp. 16–17.

purposes. Two examples will serve to illustrate this point. First, fertility is seen as a fixed and unchanging component of land in Ricardo's model, but – as we have seen – this was not necessarily the case. Secondly, von Thunen's model assumes that transport costs per unit of distance travelled are constant, but in medieval England it was far cheaper to carry grain by water than by cart. Hence eastern Norfolk produced a large grain surplus for the London market, not because it was closest to the capital, but because its transport costs were lower than those of more proximate regions who were denied good water communications. This demands a subtle but important refinement of the basic model. It is not absolute distance from the market that determines economic rent, but distance combined with the mode of transport available.

Neither Ricardo nor von Thunen fully consider whether, in practice, a farmer *wanted* to respond to the prevailing level of economic rent as determined by soil quality and location. Not all farmers are profit maximisers, and not all will choose the optimum use of land or crops. Nor do they consider whether a farmer was *capable* of responding to economic rent. In medieval England, erratic harvests, warfare, the arbitrary system of taxation, and an imperfect market mechanism could all affect a farmer's response. More importantly, feudal exactions and the strength of communal agricultural practices varied considerably throughout England, and these played a potentially crucial role in determining the profitability of grain farming. Not surprisingly, eastern Norfolk had few such restrictions, for its inhabitants enjoyed a high degree of personal freedom and minimal communal controls over agriculture, and so were burdened with low institutional costs.[32] However, it was probably an exceptional region in this respect, and other regions – to varying degrees – were constrained from exploiting their advantages of soil fertility and location by institutional rigidity. It is sometimes the case in pre-industrial economies that marketing opportunities increase faster than the ability to break down the restrictive forces of custom and communal organisation in agriculture, which serves to stifle technical progress.

What relevance does this have to our understanding of the margin? It has been assumed that intensive or progressive agricultural systems are only adopted when economic rent is high,

[32] Campbell, 'Agricultural progress', pp. 27–8.

which was patently not the case at the margin. However, if institutional factors are considered as another variable in determining economic rent, then they could be just as important in deciding the profitability of land as its inherent quality.[33] Institutional costs are apparent in two forms. First, seigneurial attitudes to rent and feudal exactions; and secondly, the built-in costs and restrictions involved in communal agricultural systems.

Ceteris paribus, as the initial profit margin in poor soil cultivation is low, then the rent cushion there is shallow, especially compared to good soil cultivation. But other things were seldom equal, not least because contract land rents could be determined as much by custom and the prevailing relationship between a feudal landlord and his tenant as by free market forces. Seigneurial attitudes to rent and other feudal dues owed by the peasantry could be crucial in deciding the profitability of arable cultivation. This is best illustrated by the case of the Royal Forests, where all forms of agricultural activity were closely regulated.[34] Particularly in the twelfth century, attempts to colonise these forests were severely restricted by special laws and courts whose main concern was to preserve the King's hunting grounds. A forest may possess fertile soils and good access to markets, but the right to cultivate it was secured only at a price, thus raising production costs independent of the normal variables and creating a marginal region.[35]

Demographic decline in the later Middle Ages reduced the value of land relative to labour, weakening the basic economic position of feudal landlords and ultimately undermining their coercive power too. The changing socio-economic relationship between landlords and peasants was a complex and varied process, but the improved bargaining position of peasants progressively favoured a reduction in rents and feudal obligations in accordance with free market forces. Yet, despite this, some landlords, when faced with declining incomes, staged a 'seigneurial reaction' in the late fourteenth century and attempted to reimpose rents and dues at pre-

---

[33] Certainly, in von Thunen's model, production costs on the farm are held to be largely constant, and there is no real consideration whether institutional costs in farming were a significant variable in determining overall land-use and profitability, Hall, *Isolated state*, pp. xxv–xxvi. This obviously has greater relevance for medieval farming than for the farming systems of von Thunen's time.
[34] J. Birrell, 'Common rights in the medieval forest', *Past and Present* 117 (1987), pp. 22–49.
[35] Miller and Hatcher, *Rural society and economic change*, pp. 34–5.

Black Death levels.[36] Land burdened with artificially high rents, onerous labour services and an oppressive landlord might still have been profitable in the century after 1348–9, but it was less likely to attract peasants for whom a wider range of rental opportunities and options was now available.

The implication is that seigneurial attitudes to rent and other feudal exactions could also be important factors in determining the profitability of arable land after the mid-fourteenth century. Areas of good soil where the hand of seigneurial oppression lay heavy could, in certain circumstances, have been less attractive to farmers than more remote or poor soil regions without such burdens. Indeed, the attitude of landlords could be a cogent depopulating force. Abel found that feudal oppression was so severe in Magdeburg in the 1360s that over 3,000 farmers abandoned their holdings.[37] Comparable examples from England are unlikely to have been on the same scale, but nevertheless the principle still holds. Hardly any of the deserted villages studied by Dyer in the west midlands were on marginal land, but most were characterised by a high proportion of unfree peasants, those most burdened by feudal exactions.[38]

Most of the classic marginal regions, as envisaged by Postan, lay in the north and west of England, away from the core of communal agricultural systems. As farmers brought these lands under cultivation, they were unlikely to import a three-field system lock, stock and barrel: assarts often proceeded piecemeal, and colonisers were much more likely to adopt a flexible, less rigid system which was highly adapted to the land's specific needs, such as the celebrated infield–outfield system. Similarly, it would be more practical and sensible to cultivate successive intakes from the waste, particularly in upland areas, individually and free from the dictates of some communal farming system.[39] The farming systems adopted in 'marginal' areas were often sensitive to the specific demands of the soil, and their extensive pastures ensured an abundant supply of manure: it was the classic three-field systems which were most likely to suffer from manure shortages.

---

[36] For this 'reaction', see R.H. Hilton, *The decline of serfdom in medieval England*, second edition (London, 1983), pp. 42–4; C.C. Dyer, 'The social and economic background to the rural revolt of 1381', in *The English rising of 1381*, eds. R.H. Hilton and T.H. Aston (Cambridge, 1984), pp. 23–6.   [37] Abel, *Agricultural fluctuations*, pp. 89–90.
[38] C. Dyer, *Lords and peasants in a changing society* (Cambridge, 1980), pp. 257–63.
[39] Communal farming methods were most prominent in the midlands, where the

The rigid dictates of communal farming methods undoubtedly added to total cultivation costs in medieval agriculture, and so regions which were relatively free from such constraints possessed some cost advantage. In marginal regions, such advantages would begin to reduce their inherently high unit costs of cultivation to a level lower than many historians have assumed. The difficulties of producing grain in marginal regions necessitated the adoption of techniques different from those used in the old-settled, fertile areas, techniques which could in themselves be regarded as a form of agricultural improvement. Hence a recent study of another classic marginal region, the Chiltern hills, concluded that 'far from being a backward area in which cultivation was subservient to a woodland or grazing economy, as has sometimes been suggested, the Chiltern hills was a region of fairly advanced agrarian practices during the Middle Ages'.[40] Output per acre here was still lower than in a region of good soils maximising *its* resources, such as eastern Norfolk, but this does not mean that agriculture in the Chilterns was therefore inefficient and unprofitable. Nor were agricultural techniques primitive in other marginal regions. Much of the arable land in Devon and Cornwall was of low quality and divided into thousands of separate enclosures. The very fact that these intakes from the waste had not been integrated into some form of communal farming system allowed them to be exploited in an individualistic and experimental manner. Overall this could not compensate for their locational and environmental disadvantages in grain farming, but in relative terms their agriculture could be quite successful, and not necessarily condemned to soil exhaustion.[41]

It remains possible that further research may prove this analysis of institutional factors, and their impact on agricultural performance, to be unfounded. But it still illustrates a major point which

manorial system was notably strong and rigid. The uplands of the north and south-west possessed a weaker and more fragmented manorial structure, which may well have encouraged the adoption of less rigid forms of communal farming. For a summary of the general differences in manorial structure and agricultural systems in England, see Bolton, *Medieval English economy*, pp. 13–32.

[40] D. Roden, 'Demesne farming in the Chiltern hills', *Ag.H.R.* 17 (1969), p. 9.

[41] J. Hatcher, *Rural economy and society in the Duchy of Cornwall 1300–1500* (Cambridge, 1970), pp. 10–14; H.P.R. Finberg, *Tavistock abbey: a study in the social and economic history of Devon* (Cambridge, 1951), pp. 114–15, writes 'the monks of Tavistock raised crops well up to the highest standards of their contemporaries. They possessed little first-rate soil . . . but the abuse of continuous cropping . . . was largely counteracted by repeated applications of sea sand, dung and ashes. This intensive and costly manuring enabled them to achieve results which by contemporary standards may fairly be called brilliant.'

merits reiteration: there are different types of 'margin', and historians must be more precise about which they are referring to. There is an intensive margin, an extensive margin, and an institutional margin. There is an environmental margin in all grain production, and there is a locational margin in commercial grain farming. Parts of Wales, Ireland, and northern England were marginal in political terms for long periods of the Middle Ages. Moreover the lack of precision when historians have written about the margin has given rise to one particularly contentious assumption about the medieval economy: that regions which are marginal for grain production are therefore marginal in economic terms.

The population-resources model assumes that because medieval England was principally a corn-based economy, each region's success in grain production determined its overall wealth and economic success. This assumes that grain production was the only significant source of wealth, and, by implication, that other forms of land-use were not substantially profitable.[42] Hence at the time of the Domesday survey, the sparsely populated uplands of the north and west were regarded as economically under-developed in comparison to the densely populated, fertile lowlands of the south and east. Similarly, areas of poor soil in the south, such as Breckland, stood out from the surrounding wealth and prosperity.[43]

Grain-growing capacity is only synonymous with economic capacity in predominantly subsistence economies. But it would be misleading to assume that the medieval economy was solely subsistence, for it manifestly underwent a major degree of commercialisation in the two centuries after Domesday. The volume of trade inevitably increased with the population size, but there are also indisputable signs that the structure and nature of trade became more complex and efficient. Thirteenth-century agriculture still retained subsistence tendencies, but production in certain areas, particularly in south-east England, appears to have become influenced by market forces to a much greater extent. Just how far this

---

[42] To a large extent, this assumption stems from a concept which is unique to the Ricardian system. Ricardian economics considers only one kind of rent, that for agricultural produce as a whole. There is no assessment of the differential rents which arise from different and competing forms of land-use: 'land used for tillage is thought to have no competing uses for grazing . . . which explains the presence of the extensive margin in classical rent theory: land is supposed to be taken up freely when needed, not from some other rent-paying alternative but from non-paying idleness': Blaug, *Economic theory*, p. 84

[43] Postan, 'Agrarian society in its prime', pp. 548–52; Postan, *Medieval economy*, pp. 17–20.

tendency percolated down the social scale has yet to be established, but there is sufficient evidence to suppose that some areas had developed a stronger commercial bias.[44]

If a more sophisticated market economy evolved in the two centuries after Domesday, it must have nurtured greater regional intercourse and inter-dependence, and in its most advanced state this process would break down subsistence tendencies within a region and encourage it to specialise in those activities to which its particular environment was best suited. Under these circumstances, greater specialisation could be practised, division of labour would become more pronounced, economic efficiency increased and income per capita raised.

As locational theory has already shown, this argument has important implications for areas of poor soil, because their development could be favourably affected by the commercialisation of neighbouring regions.[45] Thus if a region of poor soil was surrounded by highly specialised areas concentrating on specific branches of agriculture or industry, then that region might also develop a specialised economy to complement the requirements of the wider economic nexus. For instance, surrounding regions of specialised industry and grain production may rely upon proximate areas of poorer soils to supply their meat and wool, and so there may be only limited pressure to convert these poorer soils to arable farming. Equally, economic contraction in the marginal region might be related only indirectly to population decline, but directly to the fortunes of those other economies and the continued interdependence of the nexus. This pattern of complementarity would also mean that any lack of local capital for project initiation within marginal regions need not be a problem, because the necessary resources could be introduced from surrounding areas in a gradual process of inter-development.

This reassessment of the margin rests on the assumption that elements of regional intercourse and specialisation were discernible in the medieval economy, but unfortunately the extent and chro-

---

[44] For commercialisation in the medieval economy, see J. Langdon, *Horses, oxen and technological innovation: the use of draught animals in English farming from 1066 to 1500* (Cambridge, 1986), pp. 270–6.

[45] In von Thunen's system, grain production is but one competing form of land-use amongst many. At certain distances from the market, the prevailing level of economic rent would militate against grain production, but encourage sheep rearing, forestry or dairy farming instead; see Grigg, *Agricultural geography*, pp. 50–3. Compare this concept of alternative land-use with the Ricardian system described above, n. 42.

nology of this integration is poorly documented, mainly because the relevant sources yield hardly any exact or quantifiable evidence.[46] Certainly the potential for regional inter-development varied enormously according to a host of local social, economic and geographic factors, although the most crucial factor was the efficiency of trading links between regions. The medieval transport system was notoriously slow and expensive, and provided the main obstacle to removing subsistence tendencies within regions and hence to the development of regional specialisation. The relative costs of transporting agricultural produce by land and water are extremely difficult to evaluate, but overland haulage was far more expensive.[47] Water-borne transport was crucial to medieval trade, and regions bordering the sea possessed considerable natural advantages. Rivers, too, provided important lines of communication in inland areas, although the major navigational improvements in this sphere came mainly after the seventeenth century.[48] Whilst water transport was crucially important to the marketing of grain, recent research suggests that technological changes in overland transport in the twelfth and thirteenth centuries promoted greater commercialisation in the economy.[49] The wider use of the horse in this period resulted in a significant rise in haulage speed and so enhanced market accessibility, particularly for 'inland' villages, a trend which 'played an important part in establishing regional variations in agriculture'.[50] This change was less pronounced in north-west England than in the south, but nevertheless it had a profound economic influence because it involved all strata of rural

[46] Unfortunately, there are no clear-cut means of measuring this process, although a high degree of agrarian and occupational specialism, and high levels of per capita wealth, would be reasonable indirect indicators of regional development.

[47] There is very little statistical information about medieval transport, and so it is impossible to calculate the relative costs of sea/river/cart/packhorse haulage for various types of goods. Transport in the early modern period is better documented, but interpreting the evidence is still difficult and historians are divided over the efficiency of road transport: see J.A. Chartres, 'Road carrying in England in the seventeenth century: myth and reality', *Ec.H.R.* 30 (1977), pp. 73–94; C.H. Wilson, 'Land carriage in the seventeenth century', *Ec.H.R.* 33 (1980), pp. 92–5; and J.A. Chartres, 'On the road with Professor Wilson', *Ec.H.R.* 33 (1980), pp. 96–9. See also T.S. Willan, *The inland trade: studies in English internal trade in the sixteenth and seventeenth centuries* (Manchester, 1976), pp. 1–13.

[48] J.F. Willard, 'Inland transportation in England during the fourteenth century', *Speculum* 1 (1926), pp. 369–72; Grigg, *Dynamics of agricultural change*, pp. 135–43.

[49] J. Langdon, 'Horse hauling: a revolution in vehicle transport in twelfth- and thirteenth-century England?', *Past and Present* 103 (1984), pp. 64–6; *Horses, oxen and innovation*, pp. 270–6.   [50] *Ibid.*, p. 273.

society and not just the demesnes; indeed, 'it was just for the lesser, mainly peasant households that the benefits of horse hauling were most relevant'.[51]

So, given the presence of suitable markets and the potential to exploit them effectively, there is no reason why a region of poor soils should not maximise whatever potential for agrarian (or non-agrarian) enterprise it possesses. A region which is marginal for arable cultivation will not necessarily be marginal in all spheres of economic activity. In medieval England, this might mean that poor soil regions in the more populous south and east were likely to experience earlier and more thorough economic development than areas of better soil in the north-west, regardless of their inherent suitability for grain production.[52] Regions designated marginal due to their geographical remoteness by definition lack access to large markets and to areas of high population density, and so *are* more likely to be backward and under-developed. This was certainly true in arable farming, because high transport costs rendered distant regions eminently unsuited to producing grain for anything other than local or subsistence needs. It could be argued that, in terms of grain production, the margin may sometimes be equated with areas of poor soil but more readily with regions of geographical remoteness.

Remote regions may be marginal for grain cultivation, but they could still produce some goods or raw materials more cheaply than the better located regions. For instance, a high-value product of sufficient scarcity would certainly justify high transport costs to profitable markets. Difficulties in large-scale arable production do not preclude the ability to exploit other resources profitably, especially when accidents of geology have tended to locate mineral deposits in remote upland areas. This was obviously true for lead mining in the Derbyshire peaks and tin mining in Devon and Cornwall, whose products were sent as far as France and Italy as early as the twelfth century. Similarly, coal from the area around Newcastle found its way to London and many parts of southern

[51] Langdon, 'Horse hauling', p. 65.
[52] For the influence of London on farming practices and land utilisation in the south-east in the early modern period, see A. Everitt, 'The marketing of agricultural produce', in *Agrarian history of England and Wales*, vol. IV, ed. J. Thirsk (Cambridge, 1967), pp. 507–16; and E.A. Wrigley, 'A simple model of London's importance in a changing English society and economy', in *Towns in societies: essays in economic history and historical sociology*, eds. P. Abrams and E.A. Wrigley (Cambridge, 1978), pp. 226–43.

A marginal economy?

England by the early thirteenth century.[53] The extraction of high-
quality building stone from upland areas of midland and south-
western England was also important throughout the Middle
Ages.[54] The construction of Exeter Cathedral alone kept busy at
least eleven large quarries for over seventy years.[55] Birrell has
commented on the diversity of occupations available in the Forest
of Dean, a 'marginal' area in both soil and location. Extensive
woodland such as this provided peasants with pasture, iron-
working, woodworking, glassmaking, and possibly even pottery
making. She concludes that forest dwellers were 'often reasonably prosperous by peasant standards . . . the forest economy and
the peasant economy of forest regions were more complex than has
sometimes been supposed'.[56] It is by no means certain that such
regions were *economically* marginal.

It might be reasonable to suppose that peasants living in any
region possessing inherent difficulties in grain production may, as a
direct result of those difficulties, have to rely upon the development
of ancillary employment for their livelihood.[57] This was certainly
the case in remote parts of Ireland in the seventeenth century.[58] It
could even be argued that these regions were most likely to develop
non-arable pursuits precisely because arable farming was so difficult. Even if meagre subsistence farming was predominant, and if
arable production did expand rapidly in the thirteenth century,
there is no reason why other forms of industrial or semi-industrial
employment could not also be established on the margin. Many
upland areas were traversed by fast-flowing streams, ideal for
driving fulling mills, and it is not coincidental that the marginal

---

[53] Donkin, 'Changes in the early Middle Ages', pp. 107–9; E. King, *England 1175–1425*
(London, 1979) pp. 79–83; Miller and Hatcher, *Rural society and economic change*, p. 82.

[54] G.P. Jones, 'Building in stone in medieval western Europe', in *The Cambridge economic
history of Europe*, vol. II: *Trade and industry in the Middle Ages*, eds. E. Miller, C. Postan and
M.M. Postan (Cambridge, 1987), pp. 768–74.

[55] A.E. Erskine, 'The accounts of the fabric of Exeter Cathedral, 1279–1353', part II, *Devon
and Cornwall Record Society* 26 (1983), pp. xiii–xv.

[56] J. Birrell, 'Peasant craftsmen in the medieval Forest', *Ag.H.R.* 17 (1969), p. 106.

[57] J. Thirsk, 'Seventeenth-century agriculture and social change', in *Land, church and
people: essays presented to H.P.R. Finberg* (Reading, 1970), pp. 157–8, 172–5.

[58] In terms of both location and environment, Magilligan (Ulster) was marginal for grain
production. The villagers therefore developed alternative sources of income, notably in
distilling, rabbit rearing, fishing, honey production, kelp burning and smuggling: G.
Kirkham, 'Economic diversification in a marginal economy: a case study', in *Plantation
to partition: essays in Ulster history in honour of J.L. McCracken*, ed. P. Roebuck (Belfast,
1981), pp. 64–81. I am grateful to Dr Bruce Campbell for this reference.

Pennines and central Devon harboured nascent textile industries in the fourteenth century.[59]

The existence of such opportunities would attract capital for development and create local demand for agrarian produce, as happened with the Derbyshire lead industry.[60] Nor does it follow that industry would prosper and decline with the demographic trend. If a marginal region was potentially well equipped to produce non-essential goods on a large scale, then the scope of that industry may well have been restricted by depressed real wages in the thirteenth century. By inflating wages relative to the price of grain, population decline could actually place those non-essential goods within the financial means of more people and thus stimulate growth at the margin. It is arable-based economies that are most at risk when population declines because demand for bread grains is so closely linked to population size. Regions where alternative employment is available possess a wider economic base and hence greater resilience in the face of demographic fluctuation. This seems to have been the case in Cornwall and in neighbouring Devon, counties which were both marginal for grain farming in location and, in places, soil.[61] The rural cloth industry of Devon continued to expand until around the mid-fifteenth century, and the economy was further bolstered by tin mining. Its relative prosperity at this time was reflected in the construction of numerous parish churches, a movement which also created employment in the quarries. Mid-fifteenth-century tax reliefs from Devon reveal a fall in overall wealth and economic activity as a result of demographic decline, but on the whole it appeared less depressed than the purely agricultural counties of the Midlands, where soil quality was higher but employment opportunities less diverse.[62]

Nor should the potential wealth of marginal regions be underestimated. Tax assessments provide the basis for computations of medieval regional wealth, and when these are expressed as a function of area then the margin features poorly. This is hardly surprising, for we are only too aware that the resource base on the

[59] A. Baker, 'Changes in the later Middle Ages', in *New historical geography of England*, ed. Darby, p. 224.

[60] I.S.W. Blanchard, 'The miner and the agricultural community in later medieval England', *Ag.H.R.* 20 (1972), pp. 101–2.

[61] J. Hatcher, 'A diversified economy: late medieval Cornwall', *Ec.H.R.* 22 (1969), pp. 208–27.

[62] W.G. Hoskins, *Old Devon* (Newton Abbot, 1966), pp. 167–82.

margin is limited and there are consequently fewer people living there to generate wealth. Historians tend to measure regional development by contrasting levels of wealth generated per unit of area, but this is surely not a yardstick with which the population-resources model should be content to work.[63] The model is patently concerned with the *dynamic* relationship between population and resources, in other words with the balance between the land and those dependent on it. So are computations of wealth per capita not more salient indicators of a balanced, efficient and prosperous economy than calculations per unit of area? Whilst marginal regions cannot be expected to generate high levels of aggregate wealth (and computations expressed per area certainly illustrate this), if their economies are geared towards specialist production of primary goods for the market rather than for subsistence, then levels of per capita wealth there may be much higher than we might otherwise have imagined.

This preliminary discussion has deliberately raised more questions than it has answered. Only more research can resolve the most important issues: how large a part of the population did true commercialisation reach: what proportion of the total product was traded and what proportion was consumed directly by those who produced it? Only then can historians make definitive statements about what constitutes the margin. The purpose of this book is to trace the performance of one 'marginal region' during the later Middle Ages, and to consider both the accepted views on the margin and the objections suggested above in the light of the evidence. The Breckland region of north-west Suffolk and south-west Norfolk has often been cited as a classic marginal region by proponents of the population-resources model, and so would appear to be an ideal test-case. It was not marginal in a political or locational sense, but it was – and still is – undoubtedly marginal for grain production in an ecological sense.

This study will examine the types of agrarian practices adopted in medieval Breckland. How well suited were they to the poor soils, how strong were communal controls, and how flexible were they? Did the area under cultivation expand rapidly in the two centuries after Domesday, and did the soil become exhausted in the process? More important, was Breckland subjected to strong commercial pressures in this period, and was it able to develop a

[63] See, for example, the analyses in Darby, ed., *New historical geography of England*, pp. 139, 196.

specialised agricultural role? How diversified was the economy, how reliant were the region's inhabitants on arable farming? Once these issues have been addressed, it will then be possible to consider Breckland's response to the demographic decline of the later Middle Ages, and to establish how far it conformed to the pattern of development suggested by the traditional model.

THE REGION: EAST ANGLIAN BRECKLAND

By virtue of its unique physical characteristics, Breckland has always provoked interest and discussion. Popularly portrayed as a barren wilderness amidst the lush meadows and golden fields of East Anglia, it holds a fascination for a wide range of people from the casual visitor to the botanist and economic historian. Writings on the region reflect this diversity of interest. The popular works of the Clarkes and Cook contain a good deal of evocative description, and concentrate on its atmosphere, character, and folklore.[64] Other more detailed, but lesser known, research has analysed a variety of subjects, ranging from the region's flora to its historical geography.[65]

A feature common to all these works is an attraction to the region's peculiar landscape. Modern Breckland is smothered by a blanket of conifers, occasionally interspersed with tracts of light arable land and outcrops of wizened heath. Magnificent stately homes with landscaped parks are numerous, and evidence of a large military presence abounds. Yet landscape studies show only too clearly that the countryside is never static but in a state of perpetual, albeit gradual, change. The modern observer sees merely the twentieth-century conception of how the area can best be exploited: the forests are not indigenous but have spread since the 1920s, the military bases were introduced in World War II, whilst the spread of arable cultivation into the heaths was possible only with the advance of mechanisation and innovation in agriculture. Before the first Neolithic farmers cultivated the region's soils,

[64] W.G. Clarke, *In Breckland wilds* (Cambridge, 1926); R.R. Clarke and W.G. Clarke, *In Breckland wilds* (second edition, Cambridge, 1937); O. Cook, *Breckland* (second edition, London, 1980). See also J.R. Ravensdale and R. Muir, *East Anglian landscapes past and present* (London, 1984), pp. 204–20.
[65] E.P. Farrow, *Plant life on East Anglian heaths* (Cambridge, 1925); E. Schober, *Das Breckland* (Breslau, 1937); M.R. Postgate, 'An historical geography of Breckland 1600–1800' (M.A., London University, 1960); P.J.O. Trist, ed., *An ecological flora of Breckland* (Wakefield, 1979).

pollen analysis suggests that Breckland was covered by deciduous woodland.[66] The woods were subsequently cleared by repeated burning, and the easily tilled light soils were able to sustain sizeable populations throughout the Bronze and Iron Ages. However, this regular cultivation and concentrated grazing served to inhibit the regeneration of woodland and caused large patches of soil to become leached and barren. Thus, by the Roman occupation, its landscape was bereft of trees and wholly dominated by the ubiquitous scrub and heath. The heathland may have receded again as cultivation expanded in the early medieval period, but the late Middle Ages was an era of agrarian depression when tracts of this arable land were abandoned to the advancing heath, thus bringing a further adjustment to the landscape. Around the same time, rabbits were introduced to the region by means of artificially created rabbit-warrens. Rabbits burrowed into the sandy soil and fed upon the binding shoots of plants and protective growth, loosening the ground and increasing its susceptibility to sand blows. Villages depopulated in this period were further weakened by agrarian difficulties in the seventeenth century, leaving decaying tenements and crumbling churches. Thus the eighteenth century marked the culmination of a succession of economic and ecological changes which had served to exacerbate the wildest features of the landscape. By the end of that century, much of the land had become concentrated into fewer hands, facilitating the creation of large estates, emparked mansions and game reserves.[67]

The writings of eminent travellers, largely from the eighteenth century, convey a sense of the isolation and desolation which pervaded the pre-industrial Breckland landscape, and illustrate how strikingly barren it must have seemed. Evelyn was struck by 'the Travelling Sands about ten miles wide of Euston, that have so damaged the country, rolling from place to place, and like the sands in the Deserts of Libya, quite overwhelmed some gentlemen's whole estates'.[68] This is an obvious reference to the famous sand blow of 1668, when high prevailing winds carried loose sand from Lakenheath and Wangford warrens to the Little Ouse at Downham, obstructing navigation on the river and causing con-

---

[66] R.R. Clarke, *Ancient people and places*, vol. 14: *East Anglia* (London, 1960), p. 49; L. Chadwick, *In search of heathland* (Durham, 1982), pp. 39–41; O. Rackham, *The history of the countryside* (London, 1986), p. 286.

[67] Postgate, 'Historical geography of Breckland', pp. 195–204.

[68] J. Evelyn, *Diary*, 10 September 1677.

siderable damage to the village.[69] The eighteenth-century planting of wind breaks and the more recent afforestation have greatly alleviated the problem of shifting sand, but the open landscape of earlier times was much more susceptible to the regular movement of coarse soil over long or short distances.

Gilpen was fascinated by the warren area between Brandon and Mildenhall. In 1769 he described it as

a mere African desert. In some places this sandy waste occupied the whole scope of the eye . . . the whole country indeed had the appearance of a beaten sea-coast . . . in many places we saw the sand even driven into ridges . . . it was a little surprising to find such a piece of absolute desert almost in the heart of England.[70]

Fifteen years later, de la Rochefoucauld wrote:

as you leave the village [of Ingham] it becomes sandy and heavy on account of the large quantity of shifting sand in which the district abounds . . . covered with heather in every direction as far as the eye can see – not a shrub, not a plant . . . after Thetford our road continued across country as barren as that we had passed in the morning and still drier . . . everywhere sand, everywhere little clumps of reeds and bracken. A large portion of this arid country is full of rabbits, of which the numbers astonished me. We saw whole troops of them in broad daylight.[71]

Later Davy was to describe the area about Elveden warren as 'an open, wild waste, without a tree, and with no signs of cultivation'.[72] These colourful observations have been undeniably influential in shaping the subsequent popular image of Breckland, but they were highly subjective views concentrating on the worst aspects of the region's endowments. A more representative picture of Breckland would point to the slight but distinct variation in soil and topography within the region itself.

Although now accepted and widely used, the term 'Breckland' is comparatively recent and was coined by W.G. Clarke, who wrote 'the prevalence of heathland and large open sandy fields induced

69 Clarke and Clarke, *Breckland wilds*, p. 93.
70 W. Gilpin, *Some observations on several parts of Cambridgeshire, Norfolk, Suffolk and Essex made in 1769* (London, 1805), p. 28.
71 *Duc de la Rochefoucauld: A Frenchman in England in 1784*, translated by S.C. Roberts (Cambridge, 1933), pp. 210–12.
72 D.E. Davy, *A journal of excursions through the county of Suffolk 1823–1844*, ed. J.M. Blatchly, Suffolk Records Society 24 (1982), p. 140. In the eighteenth century a Dr Kerrick wrote of those 'horrible Brandon sands', and a Dr Stukeley described 'an ocean of sand . . . scarce a tree to be seen for miles or a house, except a warrener's here and there', G. Martelli, *The Elveden enterprise* (London, 1952), p. 25.

me in 1895 to give the district the name of Breckland'.[73] So, strictly speaking, it is anachronistic to refer to 'medieval Breckland', although the word 'breck' was certainly in use at that time. Medieval documents refer to the word in its familiar context as part of the open-fields of a village; court rolls mention 'le Brech' in fourteenth-century Herringswell and in Barnham there were six roods of land 'lienge in Brechelond'.[74] Similar references are to be found from many other villages, but the word does not occur as frequently as it does in sixteenth-century and later documents, where it often appears as 'brake'. Marshall defined a breck as 'a newly made enclosure', whilst Rainbird referred somewhat unspecifically to 'a large division of an open corn-field'. With rather more clarity, R.R. Clarke described it as a 'tract of heathland broken up for cultivation from time to time and then allowed to revert to waste'.[75] Hence the region is named after a system of cropping the land as opposed to some unique physical characteristic. Such a system was by no means peculiar to our region and appears in many areas where the soil is poor, but the most general use of the word 'breck' has been commonly associated with this area of East Anglia, where the practice is held to be an ancient one.[76]

The essential physical character of Breckland is the large pall of sand which covers the region and which is the source of its infertility.[77] In fact this sand lies predominantly over an Upper Cretaceous chalk bed and it is this combination which creates the peculiar features of the area and distinguishes it from other sandy regions of England. Chalk is the dominant formation in East Anglia, but is covered to differing degrees by a mantle of glacial drift, and so has varying influence over the character of local scenery and soil. For example, at Lowestoft it is hidden some 450 feet below sea-level, but in west Suffolk the chalk enters the county as a high ridge reaching to 400 feet and is consequently more prominent in all aspects of geography there. This ridge becomes

---

[73] Clarke, *Breckland wilds*, p. 22.
[74] R.G.C. Livett, ed., 'Some fourteenth-century documents relating to Herringswell', *East Anglian* 10 (1904–9), p. 122; WSROB HA513/30/2, under Mosseyfeld.
[75] W. Marshall, *Rural economy of Norfolk*, vol. II (London, 1787), p. 376; W. and H. Rainbird, *The agriculture of Suffolk* (London, 1849), p. 289; Clarke and Clarke, *Breckland wilds*, p. 1. See also Schober, *Breckland*, pp. 6–7 and H.A. Hughes, 'Note', in *P.S.I.A.* 23 (1937–9), p. 86.
[76] A. Simpson, 'The East Anglian foldcourse: some queries', *Ag.H.R.* 6 (1958), p. 92.
[77] Clarke, *Breckland wilds*, p. 14.

depressed between Newmarket and Swaffham forming a low plateau, mainly between 50 and 100 feet in height, from whence it rises into the west Norfolk heights and drives towards the coast around Hunstanton.[78] In this gap nestles Breckland, where the chalk escarpment rises gently eastwards from the fens to a peak of 193 feet near Barnham.

Drainage in Breckland is provided by a series of obsequent rivers flowing into the Great Ouse, which are held to be of Pliocene or earlier date.[79] The Nar, Wissey, Little Ouse, Thet and Lark eat backwards into the chalk escarpment, forming broad, shallow valleys with few tributaries. In Suffolk the Little Ouse leaves Breckland near Brandon and largely represents the county border with Norfolk. At Barnham heath it meets a rare tributary, the Black Bourn, which enters Breckland at Sapiston and gives its name to one of the county's largest hundreds. The Lark maintains a predominantly east–west course from Bury, cradling a number of villages in its valley until it enters the fens near Mildenhall.[80] It has a few small streams as tributaries: the locally known 'thetward-streme' between Culford and West Stow, two springs from Wordwell and Tuddenham, and Cavenham brook flowing due north to Icklingham. The major valleys are ill-drained and based on a sandy peat 1–2 feet deep, although the Black Bourn is sand peat on boulder clay.[81]

In stark contrast, the upland fields and heaths are notable for their absence of surface water. An occasional runnel defies the surrounding aridity – as at Caudle and Hunwell springs in Lakenheath and Barnham – but in general growth is difficult and drought a perennial problem on the porous sands. However, there are intensely local variations in levels of water retention depending on soil depth and texture, as evidenced by the region's famous 'stripes'. These are areas of heathland where different types of vegetation alternate over short distances, reflecting the changing texture of the soil.[82] Frost-cracking during the Ice Age created large fissures in

[78] P.R. Roxby, 'East Anglia', in *Great Britain: essays in regional geography*, ed. A.G. Ogilvie (Cambridge, 1930), pp. 151–2; J.A. Steers and J.B. Mitchell, 'East Anglia', in *Great Britain: geographical essays*, ed. J.B. Mitchell (Cambridge, 1962), pp. 86–8.

[79] Steers and Mitchell, 'East Anglia', p. 90.

[80] In fact, the use of the names Lark and Little Ouse are anachronistic when referring to medieval Breckland, for then they were known as the Burne and Welby. See F. Hervey, ed., *Reyce's Breviary of Suffolk* (London, 1902), p. 9, and Bacon 650 'in riparia de Walbi'.

[81] P.J.O. Trist, *The agriculture of Suffolk* (London, 1971), p. 16.

[82] For a photograph of these stripes, see Chadwick, *In search of heathland*, pp. 116–17.

the chalk mass and, when these were eventually filled by drift sand, the greater depth of soil between the surface and the sub-chalk rendered such areas exceptionally porous with dry and loose top soil. Where frost-cracking was less prominent or did not occur at all, the chalk remains much closer to the surface and so the overlying sands tend to be calcareous and of a heavier chalky texture with a higher capacity for holding water. Plant growth is easier in these chalky soils, causing a curious phenomenon where strips of thwarted and lusher growth intermingle.[83] In general, the loamier the soil, the higher level of water retention, and the more agriculturally productive it will be.

Another occasional exception to the absence of surface water on the upland heaths are the well-documented meres, particularly of Norfolk Breckland. Water accumulates in depressions in the chalk base, creating a number of small lakes in an otherwise barren landscape. Many authors have commented on the curious phenomenon whereby these meres are often full during dry periods and empty after heavy rainfall, and it appears that they are connected to deep-lying water tables and hence only indirectly to rainfall.[84] Such meres, however, are much less common in Suffolk Breckland, and that at Rymer(e), south of Barnham, is formed on an outcrop of clay.[85] Yet wherever such lakes occurred they were coveted as a valuable supply of water for grazing herds and flocks. So much so that ten medieval parishes probably converged on Rymer point and five parishes shared Ringmere.

Local differences in water retention in Breckland reflect a much wider diversity of soil quality and texture than is often realised. As noted before, the soils are the product of glacial deposits from the Pliocene period, although the exact chronology of successive tills is complicated.[86] Over most of Breckland these deposits consist mainly of sand and loamy sand over chalk which also contain some stone, especially flint. In the southern and eastern extremes, the chalk is overlain by boulder clay with sand deposited on top. This represents a western limit of boulder clay in East Anglia, which lies up to 200 feet thick over chalk in central Suffolk although in Breckland it is no deeper than 25 feet. The exact depth of sand

[83] N.H. Pizer, 'The soils of Breckland', in *Ecological flora*, ed. Trist, pp. 15–16; Rackham, *History of the countryside*, p. 284.
[84] Steers and Mitchell, 'East Anglia', p. 91; Rackham, *History of the countryside*, pp. 353–5.
[85] Information supplied by the owner of Rymer farm, Mr Nigel Rush, who has conducted a private survey.   [86] Postgate, 'Historical geography of Breckland', p. 32.

directly over chalk in the region varies markedly, but it lies thickest in the area around Lakenheath, Wangford, Elveden and Icklingham. The sand here is up to 15 feet deep and represents the most barren land in the region.[87] Towards the edge of Breckland, particularly in Norfolk, the soils are basically of similar texture, but because they are shallower and less leached, they tend to be more fertile.

The different depths and types of deposit cause variations in the quality and composition of the soil. Pizer writes that Breckland's 'soils are far from being simple in nature and distribution. Within short distances, which may be less than one metre, variation in the amount of stone, chalk, silt, and clay can result in variations in acidity, alkalinity, and moisture retention, which affect vegetation and determine the type that will grow.'[88] Postgate too was aware that 'the variety of local soil types . . . play an important role in determining the extent of reclamation and the profitability of cultivation'.[89] Where chalk lay closest to the surface and where sands possessed higher loam or clay content, then the land would be reasonably retentive of water and nutrients, and most suitable for cultivation. If the chalk was topped with a thick deposit of sand, or the sand was coarse with a little trace of loam or clay and perhaps imbued with flints, then water and nutrient retention would be low, the soil acidic, and the land would be difficult to cultivate and lie waste. In a soil analysis of Brandon heath, 50–70 per cent was coarse sand, with clay merely 0.5–1.5 per cent. In good reclaimed soil at Eriswell, fine gravel and coarse sand constituted 47.6 per cent of the sample, with clay and silt 8.7 per cent; whilst wasteland in Wangford contained 66.5 per cent and 1.6 per cent accordingly. In comparison, poor reclaimed land at Icklingham recorded 63 per cent and 2.3 per cent but unlike the wasteland contained very few stones and so by twentieth-century standards was regarded as just possible to cultivate.[90]

The apparently paradoxical transition from alkaline to acidic soils within short distances is fairly simple to explain. As sandy soils are not very retentive of water and calcium, they are subject to changes in substance. The sand often contains acid organic matter as

[87] W.G. Clarke, 'The Breckland sand pall and its vegetation', *Transactions of the Norwich and Norfolk Naturalists' Society*, 10 (1914–19), p. 138.

[88] Pizer, 'Soils of Breckland', p. 15.

[89] Postgate, 'Historical geography of Breckland', p. 38.

[90] E.J. Russell, 'The reclamation of wasteland: the scientific and technical problems', *Journal of the Royal Agricultural Society* 80 (1919), p. 118.

Table 1.1. *Chemical composition of*
some soil samples from Eriswell and
Wangford

	Composition (per cent)	
	Eriswell (good land)	Wangford (wasteland)
Nitrogen	0.121	0.056
Potash	0.22	0.05
Phosphoric acid	0.17	0.06
Lime	2.26	0.04
Carbonate	3.10	0.03

Source: Russell, 'Reclamation of wasteland',
p. 118.

a by-product of cultivation, and when rainfall seeps through this it causes the leaching of nutrients in the soil by a process known as podzolisation. The rate at which nutrients are dissolved depends upon a variety of factors, from the original calcium and loam content of the soil to local climate and vegetation. Again, deep lying, coarse sand allows rapid percolation of water, and readily becomes acidic and nutrient deficient. However, loamy sand close to its chalk base will be intrinsically high in calcium carbonate, and soil containing a higher clay content will be more retentive of moisture and prove restrictive to the percolation process.[91] Russell's research reveals the varying chemical composition of arable and heathland (table 1.1).

It is important to appreciate that although Breckland soils in general are marginal for cultivation – and at their worst wholly uncultivable – they are not homogenous but display intensely local nuance and variation. Suffolk Breckland harbours the deepest sands and hence the poorest, most acidic soils in the region, which 'defy all attempts to bring [them] into a productive state'.[92] Yet these lie alongside other soils – noticeably in the river valleys and along the fen edge – which possess higher fertility and have been readily cultivated for centuries. In Norfolk Breckland the soils tend to be

[91] Pizer, 'Soils of Breckland', pp. 15–16; A.S. Thomas, 'Chalk, heather and man', *Ag.H.R.* 8 (1960), pp. 57–66; Chadwick, *In search of heathland*, pp. 67–8.
[92] H. Rainbird, 'On the farming of Suffolk', *Journal of the Royal Agricultural Society* 9 (1848), p. 284.

shallower and less sterile, and the transition from poor to good quality soils less sudden. On soil factors alone, larger expanses of Norfolk Breckland are more suitable for arable cultivation.[93]

While soil type may vary within the region, climatic conditions do not. Its climate is another feature which distinguishes Breckland, and is an important factor in its marginality; hence whatever the inherent fertility of the various breck soils, the climate is sufficiently inclement to permit only limited success in their cultivation. The porosity of the soils is exacerbated by low rainfall. East Anglia as a whole receives lower annual rainfall than the rest of Britain, and this tendency is further accentuated in Breckland. Between 1916 and 1950 mean annual rainfall was around 20 to 22 inches, with lowest figures from the central villages; indeed, Elveden has the lowest on record, when only 13 inches fell in 1921.[94] Seasonally the driest period is the spring and the wettest is the summer, so Breckland crops receive least rain during the growing season, the very time it is most needed; Makings has emphasised that rainfall is crucial on light soils in April and May.[95] Postgate believes that average potential evaporation in the growing season is greater than precipitation in the Breckland.[96] Temperatures in the region further exacerbate the difficulties for growing crops. Winters are normally very cold and summers warm; for example, the mean monthly maximum temperature at Mildenhall is 5.8°C in January and 21.7°C in August. However, such figures fail to convey the wide range of temperatures experienced in any one day, for Breckland is especially susceptible to low night temperatures in any month of the year; Mildenhall averages a July range between 28.5°C and 6.6°C. The ground temperature is equally prone to extremes, for sandy soils possess low heat retention and tend to heat and cool quickly. Thus Breckland crops are liable to frost in any month of the year. Manly has noted that ground temperature minima in Breckland are at least 6°C lower than on gravelly loams in Cambridge.[97] In June 1962 at Grimes Graves the ground temperature fell to a record − 5.5°C and in 1967 33 frosts were recorded between April and June.[98] The combination of low rainfall and

[93] Postgate, 'Historical geography of Breckland', pp. 60–1.
[94] Schober, *Breckland*, p. 12.
[95] S.M. Makings, *The economics of poor land arable farming* (London, 1944), p. 58.
[96] Postgate, 'Historical geography of Breckland', p. 29.
[97] G. Manly, *Climate and the British scene* (London, 1952), p. 172.
[98] Trist, *Ecological flora*, p. 13–14.

temperature in the spring regularly retards and inhibits the growth of plants, thus rendering arable cultivation inconsistent.[99]

It remains to define the precise physical limits of the area under examination. Exact delimitation of Breckland has often proved difficult owing to the wide variety of soil types to be found along the northern, eastern and southern edges where Breckland meets the boulder clay of central East Anglia. 'The precise limits of the region are not easy to define, for . . . the Breck district shades imperceptibly into the regions . . . that elsewhere surround it.'[100] The village of Higham provides an excellent illustration of the problem. To the north of the parish is typical Breckland, poor and flinty sands subject to blowing and drought, yet to the south are fine, stoneless sands over loam. A succession of authors have attempted various delimitations, but the different criteria employed have inevitably produced different results. Young and Rainbird suggested extensive boundaries, whilst Farrow considered the distribution of certain plant types and advocated a more conservative limit.[101] Butcher and Mosby employed land utilisation as their criterion and produced a much smaller delimitation of the region, but which still contained the largest and most concentrated tracts of heathland remaining in 1934.[102] An innovation in this work was the introduction of a 'loam region' to encompass the transitional zone between true breck and boulder-clay country in Suffolk, and the creation of a separate 'breck-fen' region in Norfolk. Postgate confined his delimitation to parishes that contained wholly Breckland features, although he acknowledged a sizeable group of 'marginal parishes' for those displaying some Breckland characteristics (such as the large parishes on the fen-edge).[103]

It could be argued that the best definition on which to base a delimitation of Breckland must be those villages where the cropping of brecks was practised. Since modernisation in agriculture has

---

[99] An excellent example of this inconsistent crop yield can be found in Russell, 'Reclamation of wasteland', p. 119.

[100] A.S. Watt, 'The Breckland', in *The Cambridge region*, ed. H.C. Darby (Cambridge, 1938), p. 208.

[101] A. Young, *A general view of the agriculture of the county of Suffolk* (London, 1804), p. 5; A. Young, *A general view of the agriculture of the county of Norfolk* (London, 1804), p. 12; Rainbird and Rainbird, *Agriculture of Suffolk*, p. 4; Farrow, *Plant life on East Anglian heaths*, p. 3.

[102] R.W. Butcher, *Report of the land utilization survey*, parts 72–3: *Suffolk* (London, 1941), fig. 11. J.E.G. Mosby, *Report of the land utilization survey*, part 70: *Norfolk* (London, 1938), p. 78.　　[103] Postgate, 'Historical geography of Breckland', pp. 21–5.

rendered this practice archaic in the twentieth century, such a delimitation would be strictly historical and therefore highly suitable. Unfortunately, the documentary evidence is simply inadequate to recreate a complete picture of such a region. Another objection is that brecks have been employed elsewhere in East Anglia and are not exclusive to this corner of Norfolk and Suffolk; for example an early thirteenth-century grant from Mells (near Wenhaston in east Suffolk) concerns two acres known as *'Prestesbreche'*.[104] Other criteria have similar limitations for the purpose of this study. Butcher's survey is based on inter-war land utilisation and techniques, making it difficult to adapt for historical purposes as land use tends to change over time. Thus heathland converted to permanent tillage with the advent of modern drainage techniques and fertilisers lies outside his Breckland limits, but in the Middle Ages this very land was considered too barren for any use other than rough pasture or occasionally cropped breck. Arable land now occupying the south-east corner of Timworth parish still bears the name Timworth heath, and there are 'heath' elements in arable field names between Risby and Lackford.[105]

The specific demands of this study require not so much an interest in Breckland *per se*, but in Breckland as a region of poor soils. Thus, for the purposes of this analysis, the region's boundaries are determined by soil quality. Where more than half the land in a parish is designated as Grade 4 or Grade 5 land by the Agricultural Land Classification Survey, then it is classified as a 'central' village:[106]

Central parishes

Ampton, Barnham, Bodney, Brandon, Breckles, Bridgham, Brettenham, Buckenham Tofts, Cavenham, Colveston, Cranwich, Croxton, Culford, Didlington, Downham, Elveden, Eriswell, Euston, Fakenham Magna, Herringswell, Hilborough, Hockham, Ickburgh, Icklingham, Illington, Ingham, Kilverstone,

[104] C. Harper-Bill, ed. *The cartulary of Blythburgh priory*, vol. II, Suffolk Charters Series 3 (1980), p. 185.
[105] For example, Risby Poor's heath. What is now arable land between Risby and Lackford was extensive pasture at the end of the sixteenth century, WSROB 2753/17/16 f.40.
[106] Grade 4 land is 'land with severe limitations due to adverse soil, relief or climate, or a combination . . . generally only suitable for low output enterprises'. Grade 5 land has 'very severe limitations . . . generally under grass or rough grazing . . . the heathland grazing is of very low quality'.

Knettishall, Lackford, Lakenheath, Langford, Livermere Parva, Lynford, Mundford, Riddlesworth, Roudham, Rushford, Santon, Snarehill, Stanford, Sturston, Thetford, Thorp, Tottington, Troston, Tuddenham, Wangford, Weeting, West Harling, West Stow, West Tofts, Wordwell, Wretham.

The transition from Breckland's coarse sands to the fertile soils of central East Anglia is reasonably well-defined in Suffolk, but is more complex on the fringes of Norfolk Breckland. This transition is represented by a separate category of 'peripheral' villages, which abut the central parishes and consist predominantly of land rated at Grade 3 or higher, but which contain outcrops of Grade 4 or 5 land:

Peripheral parishes

Barton Parva, Chippenham, Coney Weston, Cressingham Magna, Cressingham Parva, East Harling, Fakenham Parva, Feltwell, Flempton, Fornham All Saints, Fornham St Genevieve, Fornham St Martin, Foulden, Freckenham, Gasthorpe, Hargham, Hengrave, Higham, Hockwold, Honington, Hopton, Ixworth Thorpe, Kennett, Kentford, Larling, Livermere Magna, Merton, Methwold, Mildenhall, Northwold, Oxborough, Quiddenham, Risby, Sapiston, Shropham, Snetterton, Stow Bedon, Thompson, Threxton, Timworth, Wilby, Wilton, Worlington.

By this method, the northern limits of Breckland are shorter than in many delimitations. The famous heaths and warrens around Beachamwell, Cockley Cley, Narford, and Swaffham are situated on blowing sands, but these are sands with a higher capacity for water retention, and so merit classification as Grade 3 land. Nor has there been any attempt to create a separate 'breck-fen' category, on the grounds that the groups are principally based upon an assessment of soil quality and not of the wider resource base. So, although more than half of the parishes of Brandon, Eriswell, Lakenheath and Wangford comprise peat fen, they are included amongst the central villages because their medieval arable fields were confined to the sandy soils of Breckland and did not penetrate the fenland. Elsewhere along the breck-fen edge, the transition from the coarse, Grade 4 land to the watery fens was less pronounced, and there were large outcrops of better quality soils; hence all of the other breck-fen villages have been categorised as peripheral.

SOURCES

Much of the manorial evidence which has survived from the Middle Ages relates to the estates of religious houses. Not only were ecclesiastical bodies among the greatest landowners in medieval England, but their administrative continuity fostered the accumulation of detailed and extensive archives. Lay estates, on the other hand, descended by an inheritance which could not always be guaranteed, and this lack of continuity militated against the survival of long series of records. However, the largest lay estates, particularly those of the higher nobility, possessed a strong centralised base and have consequently left a substantial archive. Records from the many small lay manors and estates are much rarer and more fragmentary.

Breckland lay midway between two of England's wealthiest monasteries, the Benedictine houses of Bury and Ely. The abbey of St Edmund at Bury had a considerable landed interest in the southern area of the region. The abbot held manors in Coney Weston, Culford and Fornham All Saints, and the cellarer in Barton Parva, Downham, Elveden, Fornham St Martin, Herringswell, Ingham, Mildenhall, Risby and Timworth. The prior and convent of Ely held the manor of Lakenheath, and the Bishopric of Ely held Brandon, Bridgham, Feltwell and Northwold. Both houses were archivally rich, and their records provide the basis for this study. Yet our picture of medieval Breckland is not viewed exclusively through ecclesiastical eyes, for this evidence is augmented by a refreshingly wide range of lay material. The most numerous documents in this category are drawn from the Duchy of Lancaster's manors at Methwold and Thetford, and from the Earldom of Norfolk's manors at Kennett and Hockham. More fragmentary, but no less important, are the range of documents from the smaller lay estates at Icklingham, Hilborough, Lackford and Langford.[107]

The range of extant manorial account rolls is thus sufficiently wide to enable a detailed investigation of the region, but it is not ideal. There is hardly any documentation before the 1300s, and no one manor provides a long and continuous series of accounts. There is consequently not enough material to test the soil exhaustion

---

[107] A breakdown of archives used in this study can be found in the bibliography.

hypothesis properly, nor to monitor closely the effects of thirteenth-century population pressure on Breckland's economy and agriculture. Most accounts are concentrated in the period 1330–1450, leaving an imperfect picture of both the 1315–22 agrarian crisis and the economic recovery of the early sixteenth century. On a few manors, the absence of extant material before 1380 is particularly noticeable, and results almost entirely from the destruction of manorial documents in the uprising of 1381. Hardly any pre-1381 accounts or court rolls have survived from Mildenhall, Methwold or Thetford, all manors which featured prominently in the revolt.[108]

Surviving court rolls are also confined mainly to the fourteenth and fifteenth centuries. The most complete series relate to the Ely manors of Brandon and Lakenheath, but there are gaps in the Brandon rolls and many of the post-1350 Lakenheath rolls are in a bad condition. Of all the Breckland material, these would be the most suitable for attempting a detailed demographic analysis of the type undertaken by Razi at Halesowen.[109] Unfortunately, such a survey was not practicable within the bounds of the present study, although the courts have been fully utilised in every other way. Some East Anglian court rolls contain information about tithing payments or capital pledges, from which historians have extracted demographic data. However, this is not possible with Breckland courts, because tithing payments are inconsistently recorded, and the number of capital pledges was often fixed and constant whatever the male population of the manor. At Brandon, Methwold and Northwold, for instance, there were nearly always twelve throughout the Middle Ages. Because the direct evidence is so limited, there has been little attempt to analyse Breckland's demography in detail, and throughout the book population trends are viewed through indirect indicators.

This research has drawn upon the full range of court material, but it has not always used it exhaustively. The remarkable complexity and activity in the land market at Lakenheath in the half century before the Black Death merits a thesis in itself, and an ESRC project under Rodney Hilton at Birmingham is currently

[108] Methwold featured prominently in the rising of 1381, *CPR*, 1381–5, p. 144, and a survey of Methwold manor in 1388 noted that '*les rentales et extentz customers et evidences perduz et artz par rebelles en temps du Rumore*', PRO DL29.728/11975. The manorial documents of Methwold and Thetford were obviously kept in the local manor house rather than centrally based.   [109] Razi, *Life, marriage and death*.

compiling and assessing this data. Similarly, the voluminous Hockham and Northwold rolls have been used largely to illustrate general points and trends, and would reward more detailed analyses.[110] On the whole, this book uses manorial courts to furnish details about Breckland's agriculture and industry, and its overall economic performance. Because its focus is on the concept of 'marginality', it is less concerned with the function of manorial courts *per se*, or with local differences in manorial control and jurisdiction, changing lord/peasant relationships, and the operation of the land market. Such problems, whilst important, are not central to the questions posed earlier in this chapter and await further research.

There are two main reasons why quite plentiful, but inevitably patchy, documentation has survived from medieval Breckland. First, the Ely and Bury manors were geared towards providing a continuous supply of food and ready cash for their respective monastic communities, and as a consequence were carefully and directly managed for much of the later Middle Ages. Given also the administrative continuity which these estates enjoyed, then there were powerful incentives to compile exhaustive and meticulous records about all aspects of farming and rental income. Parts of these monastic estates were broken up and dispersed at the Dissolution of the monasteries, but a sizeable proportion remained intact and fell into the hands of substantial families, such as the Bacons and the Kitsons. As a consequence, much of the manorial documentation which accompanied this land was kept together at a time when material from many other ecclesiastical institutions was lost or destroyed. The second reason for the survival of this material, and of material from smaller, miscellaneous lay estates, is the pattern of landholding in Breckland after the Middle Ages. As chapter 2 demonstrates, much of Breckland's land was systematically accumulated into fewer hands between the fourteenth and eighteenth centuries, which resulted in the creation of large estates and stately homes. Not only did this facilitate the concentration of archive material, but it often presented a ready-made repository for its safe-keeping: hence collections from Hengrave, Hilborough, Elveden and Euston Halls, and from the Bacon family archives, provide the basis of this study.

---

[110] Alan Davison is currently undertaking such a study of the Hockham material.

Chapter 2

FIELD SYSTEMS AND
AGRARIAN TECHNIQUES
IN MEDIEVAL BRECKLAND

FIELD SYSTEMS AND THE STRUCTURE OF LANDHOLDINGS

Much work remains to be done on the pre-industrial field systems of England, although historians are aware that broad regional differences existed in both field arrangements and agrarian techniques.[1] Research on the seventeenth and eighteenth centuries has already shown that the field systems of Breckland contributed to its regional distinctiveness.[2] No work on the medieval period has been previously undertaken, but such a study would be valuable nonetheless. First, it would provide an opportunity to plot the evolution of a regional field system from the thirteenth century right through to Parliamentary enclosure in the nineteenth century, and to examine the forces instigating such changes; and secondly, it would offer an interesting example of how medieval farmers adapted their limited range of agrarian techniques to the specific demands of poor soils.

An analysis of the Breckland system is best understood in the context of East Anglian agrarian techniques in general, which bore little resemblance to the classic three-field system prevalent in the Midlands.[3] The organisation of small pieces of village arable land

---

[1] See, for example, J. Thirsk, 'The common fields', *Past and Present* 29 (1964), pp. 3–25; and G.C. Homans, 'The explanation of English regional differences', *Past and Present* 42 (1969), pp. 18–34.

[2] M.R. Postgate, 'Field systems of the Breckland', *Ag.H.R.* 10 (1962), pp. 80–101.

[3] Familiarity with East Anglian field systems is highly recommended if Breckland is to be understood in its proper context. The best general introductions are Gray, *English field systems*; M.R. Postgate, 'Field systems of East Anglia', in *Studies of field systems in the British Isles*, ed. A.R.H. Baker and R.A. Butlin (Cambridge, 1973), pp. 281–324; and the works of Bruce Campbell, notably 'Population change and the genesis of commonfields on a Norfolk manor', *Ec.H.R.* 33 (1980), pp. 174–92; 'The extent and layout of commonfields in eastern Norfolk', *Norfolk Archaeology* 38 (1981), pp. 18–20; and 'The regional uniqueness of English field systems? Some evidence from eastern Norfolk', *Ag.H.R.* 29 (1981), pp. 16–28.

into three regular fields, and the imposition of a strict three-course rotation of winter-sown crops, spring-sown and then fallow, was characteristic only of the western extreme of East Anglia. Over most of Norfolk, Essex and Suffolk arable land was rarely segregated into a set field pattern, and any divisions of that land were complex and varied.

Like many areas of East Anglia, medieval Breckland was a region of 'open-fields' in the sense that its arable land lay open and not enclosed by hedges. This much it had in common with Midland villages, although here the similarities end. In Breckland, fields as cropping units were unimportant, and consequently their number varied from village to village: there were twelve fields in Brandon, four in Lakenheath, seven in Kennett, and at least six in Methwold.[4] In some places it was not considered necessary to delimit fields at all, which explains their absence from many detailed village surveys. When surveyors needed to identify certain areas of the village arable more precisely, they subdivided it into units known as *quarentenae* or furlongs. Each *quarentena* would also be delimited on the ground by stone markers or grass mounds, but again they were merely convenient subdivisions of the open-fields and had no real agricultural significance. They differed from the classic Midland furlongs by containing pasture grounds as well as arable land, and also by varying in size and displaying little uniformity.[5] At Wangford in 1542, 'Downdale' contained 86 acres 1 rood, whilst 'Thanklesfurlong' contained 114 acres. 'Le Hamme' in Culford comprised 16 acres 2 roods of arable and 7 roods of pasture in 1435, and yet 'Mekelewong' was much bigger at 63 acres 1 rood. The tendency was to name *quarentenae* after a variety of local features, such as 'Stonhill' or 'Smallway', although a little imagination was sometimes employed, as, for example, in Barnham's 'Deadwomansfurlong'.[6] These units were themselves divided into *peciae*, which were common throughout East Anglia and were comparable to the selions of the Midlands, probably representing a basic unit of ploughland.[7] The need for ploughteams to take periodic rests dictated that *peciae* were approximately a furlong in

[4] Brandon, IESRO v.11/2/1.1; court rolls from Lakenheath mention northfeld, suthfeld, middelfeld and windmelnefeld; the Kennett field book of 1563 mentions north, south, east, and west fields, foxhole, castle and carraps fields, WSROB 339/5 pp. 2–6, and 45–7; Methwold, PRO DL43.7/29b.

[5] Postgate, 'Field systems of East Anglia', p. 291.

[6] NRO Ms 4071 ff.8–9 and 16–18; BL Add.Ms 42055 ff.25 and 45–7; WSROB HA513/30/2.   [7] Postgate, 'Field systems of East Anglia', pp. 291–2.

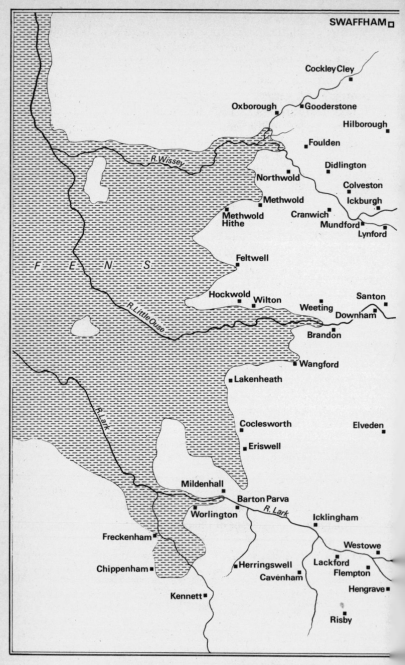

Map 2. Breckland in the Middle Ages

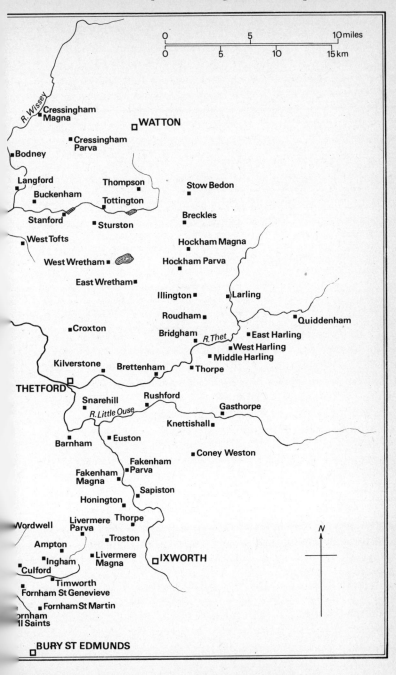

R. Wissey

Cressingham Magna

□ WATTON

Cressingham Parva

Bodney

Langford
Thompson

Buckenham
Tottington

Stanford

Sturston

West Tofts

West Wretham

East Wretham

Stow Bedon

Breckles

Hockham Magna

Hockham Parva

Illington
Larling

Roudham
Quiddenham

Croxton
Bridgham
R. Thet
East Harling
West Harling
Middle Harling

Kilverstone
Brettenham
Thorpe

THETFORD

Snarehill
Rushford
Gasthorpe

R. Little Ouse
Knettishall

Barnham
Euston

Coney Weston

Fakenham Parva

Fakenham Magna

Sapiston

Honington

Wordwell
Livermere Parva
Thorpe

Ampton
Troston

Ingham
Livermere Magna
□ IXWORTH

Culford

Timworth

Fornham St Genevieve

Fornham St Martin

ornham
ll Saints

□ BURY ST EDMUNDS

0   5   10 miles
0   5   10   15 km

N

length and two roods in area. Half-acre *peciae* were common in Breckland, so that, for instance, 'Dowbank' furlong in Wangford comprised 155 separate *peciae*, of which 80 were two roods.[8]

The exact layout of Breckland's open-fields merits closer examination, because it varied perceptibly from central to peripheral parishes as overall soil quality improved. In the central villages, abuttals with the arable land of neighbouring communities were less frequent. The villages on the fen edge were hemmed in by marsh and heath on their western and eastern borders respectively, but their fields abutted to the north and south. In Barnham the arable was separated from that of Euston by grass 'heads' to the east, but elsewhere gave way to heathland and the meadows of the Little Ouse valley.[9] The fields of Elveden were an island in a sea of heath. Layout in the peripheral parishes was somewhat different, not least because villages simply lay closer together. To the east of the region, these villages represented a transitional zone between Breckland proper and the heavier soils of central East Anglia. In the parishes of Fornham St Genevieve, Fornham St Martin, Barton Magna, Culford, Ingham, Ampton and Timworth there was an uninterrupted maze of open-fields and pastures which crossed village boundaries freely. Nor were the differences confined solely to layout. Although the strips of peasant and demesne land lay intermingled and widely spread throughout the open-fields of both central and peripheral parishes, table 2.1 reveals that demesne *peciae* were larger than those belonging to peasants, and were larger still in peripheral villages. Other, unquantifiable evidence from peripheral parishes reinforces the tendency towards larger demesne *peciae* there. At Mildenhall in 1382, corn was sown on 15 acres 'in one pecia at Smethysholmes', 22 acres in one block at Littley was leased to a local peasant, and in Worlington there were 15 acres of demesne in one *pecia* at Thistelborgh.[10] Compare these with Brandon and Wangford, where the largest demesne *peciae* were 12 and 4.5 acres respectively.[11] The explanation for these differences probably lies in changes in soil quality and manorial structure, but their chief practical importance lay in their impact on farming methods.

The complicated layout of Breckland's open-fields was coupled

[8] NRO Ms 4071 ff.20–2.   [9] WSROB HA513/30/2.
[10] BL Add.Roll 53116; PRO DL43.14/3 f.27.
[11] The largest *pecia* in Brandon was in Bridhithfeld, IESRO v.11/2/1.1. The 4.5 acre *pecia* was common in Wangford, NRO Ms 4071.

Table 2.1. *'Pecia' size in some Breckland villages*

Year	Village	Status of land	Area (acres)	Number of *peciae*	Main *pecia* area (roods)
1348	Culford	Customary	273	554	1.97
1542	Wangford	Tenant*	768	1,460	2.10
1566	Brandon	Tenant*	1,218	1,604	3.04
1442	Fornham	Leasehold	154	133	4.63
1290	Rushford	Demesne	193	85	9.08
1357	Culford	Demesne	255	47	21.70
1542	Wangford	Demesne	468	300	6.23
1566	Brandon	Demesne	460	91	20.22
1442	Fornham	Demesne	300 +	33	36.36
1343	Ingham	Demesne	330	37	35.67

Note:
* Including glebe land.
+ Not including Heynesmerewong, Syklondclos, Hodding or Bendych, where *peciae* not stated.
Sources: Culford, BL Add. Ms 42055 ff.8–22, and Add. Ms 14849 f.23; Wangford, NRO Ms 4071; Brandon, IESRO v.11/2/1.1; Fornham (a), BL Add. Ms 34689 ff.26–7 and 37–41; Rushford, NRO Ms 15170; Ingham, CUL Add. Ms 4220 f.88.

with a complex manorial system. East Anglia has long been noted for the fluidity of its manorial structure, which contrasts starkly with the more rigid manorialism of the Midlands. In the Midlands there is a strong tendency for the manor and village to coincide, but 'in the east of England the vill and the manor represent systems even less closely connected'.[12] In Breckland, manors and villages were not coterminous but persistently traversed and subdivided each other's boundaries. Feltwell contained seven manors and Knettishall three, and the main manor in Hockham extended into four neighbouring villages.[13] In peripheral villages, where settlements lay closer and open-fields overlapped frequently, the relationship was even more confused. Culford was split between one main manor belonging to the abbot of Bury St Edmunds and a small lay manor called Easthall. Yet within the village's open-fields were land parcels which also pertained to the manors of Wordwell, Ingham, Fornham St Genevieve, West Stow and Timworth.[14]

[12] E.A. Kosminsky, *Studies in the agrarian history of England in the thirteenth century* (Oxford, 1956), p. 74.
[13] Blomefield, vol. I, pp. 314 and 497–502; W.A. Copinger, *The manors of Suffolk*, vol. I (London, 1905), pp. 338–42.   [14] BL Add.Ms 42055 ff.28, 30, 35, 42–3 and 45.

Such fragmented lordship must have undermined the strength of communal village regulations in agriculture.

This complex manorial structure coexisted with a fluid tenurial structure. Medieval peasants held land from a manorial lord according to free or unfree (also called servile or customary) status, with free peasants enjoying greater privileges and hence freedom. At Domesday, East Anglia was noted for its unusually large proportion of free and semi-free peasants, who possessed the right to alienate their land at will and divide it between their heirs at death (partible inheritance). These privileges ensured a buoyant land market, but were traditionally denied to unfree peasants. Yet the southern end of Breckland was an exception to this general picture of freedom, for freemen comprised only 12.9 per cent of the population of Lackford hundred in 1086; over much of the rest of the region, they comprised around 30–39 per cent.[15] This is probably explained by the high proportion of ecclesiastical manors in the area, for Bury and Ely abbeys proved conservative landlords keen on maintaining servile workforces to exploit their demesnes cheaply. Theoretically, the emphasis on unfreedom should have restricted the development of Breckland's land market and its tenurial structure compared to the rest of East Anglia, but late thirteenth-century evidence shows these elements to be at least as complex as elsewhere.

The East Anglian land market has received considerable attention from historians in recent years, and their research indicates that servile peasants were more actively engaged in the land market than those of similar status in more feudalised areas.[16] Some servile holdings came to be inherited partibly, and transfers of land *inter vivos* were permitted on payment of a suitable fee in the manorial court. Both practices were evident in Breckland by 1300, and servile peasants were also alienating small pieces of land temporarily through sub-letting. In one court at Langford, five men were found to have sub-let a total of 15 acres without informing the court officials.[17] Individual status became clouded by an increasing

---

[15] B. Dodwell, 'The free peasantry of East Anglia in Domesday', *Norfolk Archaeology* 27 (1939), pp. 145–57.

[16] See the chapters by Smith, Campbell and Ravensdale in R.M. Smith, ed., *Land, kinship and life-cycle* (Cambridge, 1984).

[17] NRO NCC(Petre) Box 8/21, July 1397. For sub-letting elsewhere in East Anglia, see J.A. Raftis, *Tenure and mobility: studies in the social history of the medieval English village* (Toronto, 1964), pp. 74–81.

tendency to hold both free and unfree land, although courts were
keen to restrict this process. Isabella Dowe of Lakenheath and
Thomas Curteys of Fornham are expressly recorded as holding
both, and Henry le Huxtere of Culford was a customary tenant
who also held a free messuage and a pightle formerly belonging to
John de Ely.[18] The absence of a simple distinction between free and
unfree status is evident in those manorial surveys which record the
existence of men bearing an intermediate personal and tenurial
status, such as the 'mollmen' of the Ely customals.[19] At Lackford in
the early fourteenth century there were 8 freemen and 35 'customary tenants of mollond', and there was a large class of mollmen at
Fornham All Saints.[20] The distinction became further blurred after
the Black Death, so that fifteenth-century Lackford rentals no
longer recorded any form of personal or tenurial status, a movement paralleled elsewhere in East Anglia.[21] Indeed, later
Mildenhall court rolls regularly describe lands and tenants as of
'unknown status'.[22]

The infertility of Breckland ensured that there would be great
pressure upon such land as was cultivable, and this, combined with
the active land market, resulted in much subdivision and alienation
of holdings when demographic pressure was rising in the twelfth
and thirteenth centuries. This was particularly true amongst those
with easiest access to the land market, the freeholders, whose
holdings could become very fragmented and complex. The process
became so advanced that, as Kosminsky succinctly comments,
'inhabitants of a village held their lands not from the chief lord, but
from his tenants and often from the tenants of his tenants'.[23] At
Rushford in the early fourteenth century it was noted that John

[18] WSROB E.3/15.9/1.1 m.7; BL Add.Ms 42055 f.9. E. Miller, *The abbey and bishopric of Ely*
(Cambridge, 1951), pp. 148–9, comments that some peasants 'had gone on buying and
selling both free and villein land, so that by the fourteenth century it became very hard
to speak of a man's land without specifying it was both bond and free'.

[19] Miller, *ibid.*, p. 114. The unusual social structure of medieval East Anglia has attracted
much literature. See D.C. Douglas, *The social structure of medieval East Anglia* (Oxford,
1927); G.C. Homans, 'The Frisians in East Anglia', *Ec.H.R.* 10 (1957–8), pp. 189–206; B.
Dodwell, 'Holdings and inheritance in medieval East Anglia', *Ec.H.R.* 20 (1967), pp. 53–
66.   [20] WSROB E.3/15.12/3.7; BL Add.Ms 14849 f.26.

[21] WSROB E.3/15.52/3.1 and 3.2a. At Rickinghall (Suffolk) in the fourteenth and fifteenth
centuries, 'the significant difference between free and customary lands disappeared', Y.
Miyoshi, *A peasant society in economic change: a Suffolk manor 1279–1437* (Tokyo, 1981),
pp. 262–5. For a discussion of the general process, see F.G. Davenport, 'The decay of
villeinage in East Anglia', *Transactions of the Royal Historical Society*, second series 14
(1900), pp. 123–42.   [22] WSROB E.18/451/6, court held October 1476.

[23] Kosminsky, *Studies in agrarian history*, pp. 79–80.

Palmer held 6 roods of arable from four other freemen, and therefore he owed no rent to the lord of the manor directly.[24] Furthermore, the manorial symmetry was upset by freemen holding land from lords of different manors, thus creating composite holdings on an inter-manorial basis. At West Stow in the late thirteenth century, Isabella de Horningsheath held a messuage and 60 acres from Bury abbey, but she in turn had six other tenants holding from her, of whom two had further alienated their holdings.[25] In Fornham St Genevieve a number of freemen had constructed holdings from land held simultaneously from the abbot, the cellerar and Easthall manor, and in All Saints Robert de Ickworth created a holding of 4 acres from lands held from three other freemen. At Mildenhall, marketing opportunities stimulated an even more active land market, and hence an even more complex structure.[26]

It was not just the free lands which became fragmented, and as transfers of unfree land became more frequent so these holdings suffered subdivision too. This process is clearly illustrated by the disintegration and alienation of ancient *tenementa*. The *tenementum* was the basic unit of landholding in medieval East Anglia, and served as a fiscal division for the purpose of apportioning rents, services and manorial offices. As these were predominantly the features of personal unfreedom, documents normally refer to *tenementa* in association with unfree holdings. The exact nature, origin and size of *tenementa* have been the subject of considerable literature, and much research is still needed. The Breckland evidence tends to confirm rather than contradict the state of existing knowledge.[27] Exactly when *tenementa* were introduced is uncer-

---

[24] NRO Ms 15170   [25] *Pinchbeck register*, vol. II, pp. 238–9.

[26] *Ibid.*, pp. 128–31, 175–6 and 243–55; for sub-tenancy, see also CUL Add.Ms 4220 f.126.

[27] Research into the *tenementum* has advanced greatly since Gray's early work, Gray, *English field systems*, pp. 334–41. See the works cited in n. 19 above, and P.M. Warner, 'Blything hundred: a study in the development of settlement, 400–1400' (Ph.D., Leicester, 1982), ch. 8. Also R.M. Smith, 'Families and their land in an area of partible inheritance: Redgrave, Suffolk 1260–1320', in Smith, ed., *Land, kinship and life-cycle*, pp. 139–49, and J. Williamson, 'Norfolk: thirteenth century', in *The peasant land market in medieval England* ed. P.D.A. Harvey (Oxford, 1984), pp. 31–106. Many of the Breckland *tenementa* were of the 10-, 15-, 20- and 30-*ware* acre size noted by Dodwell, 'Holdings and inheritance', p. 68, although these referred to units of assessment rather than statute acres. In other words the actual physical area of *tenementa* could vary quite markedly, and, for example, the standard 20-acre *tenementa* at Culford concealed a variety of sizes. The *tenementum* belonging to Adam Finch contained a messuage and 19 acres, whilst that of John son of Robert comprised 4 cottages and 28 acres, BL Add.Ms 42055 ff.8–23.

tain, but they appear to have been artificially imposed upon the open-fields sometime in the late twelfth century, and for purposes of identification were named after the tenants who then held them. Many large estates underwent reorganisation in the late twelfth and early thirteenth centuries, as landlords switched from leasing their demesnes to direct exploitation. This change to direct farming often resulted in the reimposition of labour services, and so it is tempting to view in the creation of these *tenementa* a means of restructuring rents and labour services on customary holdings.[28]

Although the original *tenementa* were composite holdings held by just one tenant, the continuing rise in population and economic expansion of the thirteenth century resulted in their systematic disintegration. By the late thirteenth century, the buoyant land market had split a holding in Redgrave (Suffolk) between 34 tenants, and one at Coney Weston between 6 tenants.[29] Some of this subdivision was caused by the action of partible inheritance, but in Breckland the process was due largely to sales and alienation *inter vivos*. At Lakenheath it was customary for unfree and molland holdings to be inherited impartibly, although in practice small pieces of land were subsequently redistributed by the heir.[30] There are 178 cases of *inter vivos* peasant land transactions recorded in the Lakenheath courts between 1325 and 1335, of which 80 per cent concern parcels of under 5.5 acres and only 11 per cent involved members of the same family.[31] This process explains why the *tenementum* formerly held by Richard Cut in Timworth, amounting to 14 acres 3 roods, had become divided between 11 tenants by 1348, none of whom appeared to be related.[32] Yet the action of partible inheritance is discernible in some villages, for at Culford the *tenementum* formerly held by Henry Acke had become split between ten tenants, of which John Acke held 4 acres 1 rood, and

28 Not all landholdings were grouped into *tenementa* in Breckland. On the Ely estates land was assessed in virgates, despite the fact that these were not a common East Anglian form. At Lakenheath the virgate probably comprised 15 acres, although the 'full-land' used at Brandon, Bridgham, Feltwell and Northwold comprised 40 acres. See Douglas, *Social structure*, pp. 24 and 37–40, and Dodwell, 'Holdings and inheritance', p. 57.
29 R.M. Smith, 'English peasant life-cycles and socio-economic networks: a quantitative geographical case study' (Ph.D., Cambridge, 1975), p. 181; Bodleian Ms Gough Suffolk 3 f.60, *tenementum* of William Adekyn. The split or 'decay' of the original *tenementa* is a well documented phenomenon; for instance, Miller, *Bishopric of Ely*, pp. 130–4; Dodwell, 'Holdings and inheritance', pp. 58–63.
30 This was also the case at Brandon: the practice was common enough in areas of impartible inheritance in East Anglia, Williamson, 'Thirteenth century', pp. 91–4.
31 CUL EDC 7/15/II/Box 1/6–10.   32 CUL Add.Ms 4220 f.85.

49

Laurence and William Acke jointly held 19 acres 2 roods. That heirs were prepared to hold land jointly rather than subdivide it indefinitely into small, unmanageable pieces is further indicated by a reference to the 'heirs of Galfred le Reve' holding half a rood in the same *tenementum*.[33] Landlords were prepared to tolerate subdivision as long as the manorial court was notified of land transfers and a suitable fee rendered, and as long as rents and services were forthcoming.[34] It is for this reason that later rentals still refer to the original holding, in order to keep track of rents and services due in the wake of subsequent subdivision. It is unlikely that these dues were systematically divided and apportioned as the original unit disintegrated, but instead the main holder and his co-holders ('*sui parcenarii*') were collectively responsible. This is not to say that tenants could always agree on their contribution, and at Lakenheath a holding remained in the lord's hands whilst its co-holders decided upon the partitioning of its services amongst themselves.[35] Such problems were avoided by the commutation of services for cash, which partly explains the popularity of this process in East Anglia from the late thirteenth century.

Gray argued that the original *tenementum* was a relatively compact area, and that the *peciae* which comprised it tended to lie in close proximity, in contrast to the Midlands where holdings were spread equally throughout the village fields. The work of both Douglas and Allison, whose evidence was largely drawn from the Norfolk Goodsands, confirmed this observation. However, Postgate was unable to find a similar pattern in seventeenth-century Breckland,[36] and it seems not to have existed in the Middle Ages. For instance, Thomas de Gunton held 132 acres 3 roods spread across 17 *quarentenae* in Methwold,[37] whilst table 2.2 shows that most tenant holdings were very evenly spread throughout the

[33] BL Add.Ms 42055 ff.8–23.

[34] Smith, 'Families and their land', pp. 141–2, and 194–5.

[35] CUL EDC 7/15/II/Box 2/13 m.2, court held March 1338. See also F.G. Davenport, *The economic development of a Norfolk manor 1086–1565* (Cambridge, 1906), pp. 50–1. Problems such as these rendered some landlords positively hostile to the fragmentation of holdings on their estates, B.F. Harvey, *Westminster abbey and its estates in the middle ages* (Oxford, 1977), pp. 299–307. In a rental of the Bury abbey manor of Barton Magna (Suffolk), a list of lands is headed '*de terris alienatis*', where the services due were no longer known, BL Harl. 3977 f.88.

[36] Gray, *English field systems*, pp. 338–40; Douglas, *Social structure*, p. 22; K.J. Allison, 'Sheep corn husbandry of Norfolk', *Ag.H.R.* 5 (1957), p. 20; Postgate, 'Historical geography of Breckland', pp. 110–12.

[37] NRO Ms 9973, undated, fifteenth century.

Table 2.2. *Location of four holdings in the fields of Brandon in 1566*
(acres)

Tenant	1	2	3	4	5	6	7	8	9	10
W. Humberstone	6.75	7.5	14.0	7.5	8.0	3.0	5.25	9	5.75	5.75
H. Buxton	7.75	11.5	9.0	6.0	9.75	7.75	6.0	7.5	4.75	6.25
J. Canham	5.25	4.5	4.0	3.5	3.5	5.0	1.5	7.25	4.5	3.5
E. Anger	3.75	2.5	3.5	2.5	2.0	3.75	3.75	2.75	1.5	2.0

Note:
1 = Bridhithfeld 2 = Womanlodefeld 3 = Drovesfeld 4 = Fourhowefeld
5 = Townfeld 6 = Middelfeld 7 = Wildenhillfeld 8 = Cotteshill 9 = Dedhedlond
10 = Claypittfeld

town fields in sixteenth-century Brandon. Why should Breckland be different in this respect from other East Anglian villages? The reason is probably due to the infertility of its soils, so that holdings were scattered as a form of risk aversion, a common practice in marginal regions of the Third World.[38] Indeed, this would also explain why demesne *peciae* were smaller in central parishes than in the peripheral villages, where soil quality was better.

Hence, on the eve of the Black Death the structure of land tenure in Breckland was in a state of high activity and flux. Population decline after the mid-fourteenth century halted the process of fragmentation, and resulted in a gradual rise in holding size and the accumulation of land into fewer hands. The spread of leasehold tenures, where free and particularly unfree lands were farmed out to tenants for a specific money rent without labour services and other onerous feudal dues, precipitated the demise of *tenementa* as working units on some manors. Yet fifteenth-century documents still recorded the original tenures, describing dozens of small land parcels at leasehold as 'belonging to the *tenementum* of x, formerly held by y and lately by z'.[39] As the ancient *tenementa* effectively dissolved, ambitious peasants began to construct large farms from lands held on a mixture of copyhold, leasehold and freehold.

The accumulation of land into fewer hands did not stop in the fifteenth century, but continued for another three centuries. The

[38] D. McCloskey, 'English open fields as behaviour towards risk', in *Research in Economic History* 1 (1976), ed. P.J. Uselding, pp. 154–62.
[39] For instance at Culford in 1435 the heirs of Walter Long held one acre *'quondam Johanni Hoketon et nuper Johanni Penbrook'*, BL Add.Ms 42055 f.33.

pace of this movement varied from village to village, but it was evident everywhere. Not only did it simplify the tenurial structure, but it also rationalised the manorial system. From the late fifteenth century, and gathering pace in the sixteenth, manorial lords purchased smaller manorial units to bring villages under single ownership. Along the Lark valley, first the Lucases and then the Kitsons were prominent in purchasing primary and secondary manors in adjacent townships.[40] The Bacon family acquired Bury abbey's manor at Culford at the Dissolution, and in 1586 purchased Easthall to complete their grip on the village.[41] It was this concentration of lordship which enabled the adoption of the socially disruptive farming practices described by Allison.[42]

Local variations in the pace and extent of the concentration of landownership did occur, but in general the process was more pronounced in the century before 1750 than in the fifteenth century. Low prices for staple agrarian produce, coupled with an increasingly onerous land tax, made this a difficult period for agriculture, and in such conditions smallholders particularly felt the burden of high unit costs of cultivation.[43] The problem was exacerbated on poor soils where profit margins were low in any event, and many small-scale farmers lacked the financial resources to survive the depression. Thirsk saw in this distress a need for long-term adjustment, and the response in the sheep-corn regions of England, such as the light soils of East Anglia, was to produce more and to develop new production techniques. Such technical economies were only possible in large-scale cereal production, and so landlords sought to purchase inefficient smallholdings whenever possible to make their own farms more compact.[44] They were so successful that the smallholder was driven to the brink of extinction in many villages, and by the mid-eighteenth century Breckland

---

[40] Copinger, *Manors of Suffolk*, vol. vi, pp. 268 and 271 (Fornham St Genevieve and St Martin); vol. vii, pp. 21, 24, 50, 81, 91 and 93 (Flempton, Fornham All Saints, Hengrave, Lackford, Risby and Risby Charman's).

[41] *Ibid.*, vol. i, p. 286. He also secured the manors of Timworth and Ingham, p. 329 and vol. vi, p. 346.

[42] See below, p. 293. Some observers have regarded the streamlining of the manorial system as an important prerequisite of 'improved' farming, J. Spratt, 'Agrarian conditions in Norfolk and Suffolk, 1600–1650', *Bulletin of the Institute of Historical Research* 15 (1937–8), p. 114.

[43] G.E. Mingay, *Enclosure and the small farmer in the age of the industrial revolution* (London, 1968), pp. 26–31.

[44] E. Kerridge, *Agrarian problems in the sixteenth century and after* (London, 1969), pp. 123–9.

Field systems and agrarian techniques

was less populated than at any time since Domesday. In the 1790s, fourteen landlords owned 54,637 acres in fifteen Breckland parishes and were leasing the land as 27 tenant farms of around 2,000 acres each.[45] In 1730 the whole village of Rushford formed only a part of one large farm, and by 1753 Roudham parish was split into four tenancy units, the biggest containing 788 acres.[46] When the last Marquis Cornwallis died in 1823 his estate covered five Suffolk parishes and 11,000 acres.[47] In the eighteenth century it was also popular to convert large areas of these estates into parkland, to the extent that parks soon comprised 6 per cent of Breckland's total area.[48]

Engrossment of this magnitude inevitably resulted in the shrinkage of villages, and taken to extreme lengths caused the disappearance of whole communities. Work on East Anglian village desertion has progressed greatly since Allison's pioneering effort,[49] and it is now apparent that many Breckland desertions date from this period rather than from the Middle Ages. Kilverstone was probably deserted by the late seventeenth century, and West Wretham and Roudham a century later.[50] West Harling remained a thriving community until its rapid depopulation in the early eighteenth century, an experienced paralleled by that of Wordwell. The village expanded in the period 1600–1650, only to be described in 1757 as

so reduced as to have no more buildings in it than the Church, the Farm or Mannor House, and one dwelling house for the Sheppard. They stand pretty near one another, and not long since the Parsonage House made one amongst them . . . but now the grass grows over the site of it . . . the Church is a very mean Fabrick and kept in a most nasty condition, 'tis almost quite untiled.[51]

Although no direct evidence exists, it is likely that Knettishall,

45 Postgate, 'Field systems of Breckland', p. 99.
46 Postgate, 'Historical geography of Breckland', p. 202; A. Davison, 'Roudham: the documentary evidence', *East Anglian Archaeology* 14 (1982), p. 58.
47 Davy, *Journal of excursions*, n. 287.
48 Postgate, 'Historical geography of Breckland', p. 196.
49 K.J. Allison, 'The lost villages of Norfolk', *Norfolk Archaeology* 31 (1955), pp. 116–62.
50 Medieval Village Research Group, 29th annual report (1981), pp. 8–9.
51 A. Davison, 'West Harling: a village and its disappearance', *Norfolk Archaeology* 37 (1980), pp. 301–3; S.H.A. Hervey, ed., *West Stow and Wordwell parish registers with notes* (Woodbridge, 1903), p. 293; C. Paine, 'Wordwell, west Suffolk', duplicated, WSROB.

Livermere Parva and Timworth suffered similar fates.[52] Yet in all
of these villages, grain production continued long after the village
had expired as a community. The new tenant farms maintained a
traditional sheep and corn husbandry, drawing their labour from
employees housed in specially constructed and conveniently sited
estate cottages, rather than from a traditional village nucleus.[53] In
other cases, villages already weakened by depopulation met sudden
deaths through emparkment: Fakenham Parva was lost with the
creation of Euston park in the late 1660s; a map of 1769 shows the
village of Fornham St Genevieve prior to its removal for
emparkment; and Livermere Parva and Didlington suffered similar
fates.[54] Other villages were more fortunate, and Culford, Elveden,
Euston and Hengrave were resited and rebuilt at a respectful
distance outside the new park gates.

CROPPING AND PASTURING ARRANGEMENTS

In common with most English villages, peasants in medieval
Breckland enjoyed communal rights over some local pastures and
marshes. Heathland dominated the region's economy and landscape, and its exploitation was closely regulated. It had two main
uses: as grazing land, primarily for sheep and rabbits, and as a
valuable source of fuel and litter. Large areas of heath were arid and
poor, so grazing was extensive rather than intensive. There were no
attempts to segregate the sheep from the rabbit pastures because the
two were compatible, sheep preferring grey lichens and mosses
avoided by rabbits: competition for food would only emerge in
years of hardship. Hence a boy was hired to shepherd lambs on
Lakenheath warren in the 1330s, and south-east of Thetford lay 'the
warren of Westwicke et a parcell of meddowe there, with ye
foldcourses and pastures for 600 hoggs there'.[55]

[52] Knettishall and Timworth are heavily depopulated, leaving isolated churches in an area
    where nucleated villages are the norm. Knettishall church now lies in ruins. A number of
    deeds of exchange and purchase indicate the engrossment of land in Timworth in the
    eighteenth century, WSROB E.3/10/18.4. Livermere Parva was emparked by Baptist
    Lee in the late eighteenth century. For an aerial photograph of its earthworks before they
    were ploughed see N. Scarfe, *The Suffolk landscape* (London, 1972), plate 33.
[53] Allison, 'Lost villages of Norfolk', p. 139; Kerridge, *Agrarian problems*, pp. 124–5.
[54] W. White, *History, gazetteer and directory of Suffolk* (Ipswich, 1844), p. 686. For Fornham,
    see WSROB map 373/23; Didlington, Allison, 'Lost villages of Norfolk', p. 146.
[55] CUL EDC 7/15/I/9; WSROB J515 f.10. My thanks to Lord Fisher of Kilverstone Hall
    for permission to view this document.

In a region almost bereft of woodland, the right to cut and remove fern and bracken was important for local peasants.[56] Bracken was extremely useful as a hot, quick-burning fuel, and access to it was carefully monitored. Lakenheath peasants could only take it after 29 August, although at Brandon it was available as required.[57] Other manorial courts regulated activity only when resources became depleted. In February 1478 all furze cutting was banned on the heath at Barton Parva, whilst sixteenth-century Lackford courts banned the use of mattocks, presumably because of the damage they inflicted on furze roots.[58] Those requiring still more bracken could always pay for the right to remove it from a specified area. At Lakenheath in 1328 the manor sold 21 acres of bracken at 4d. an acre, and 4s. 10d. was received from similar sales on Kennett warren in 1270. Occasionally peasants secured the exclusive rights to all grazing and litter on a small piece of heath-land, but at a price: it cost Peter Godwyne of Kennett 12s. for one acre in 1270, a striking example of the heath's potential value.[59]

The exact rights of litter and grazing over heathland were closely defined, but peasants were not permitted access to all heaths. Villagers in Bridgham were allowed to pasture their beasts on a specified 260-acre heath, but all other rights were restricted, or 'several', to the Bishopric of Ely. Yet on a different heath they were permitted equal rights with the bishop, as long as they did not sell bracken outside the village.[60] At Ingham, 'the lord hath a severall heathe and that the tenants can cut no fengere nor lynge ther with owt the lords licence'.[61] In practice, these formal regulations were transgressed frequently and court rolls contain many amercements for illegal exploitation of heathland. A number of Ingham villagers were amerced for collecting litter from a different heath at the wrong time of the year, whilst outsiders were reprimanded for having taken it at all.[62] Similarly, there are numerous presentments of aliens pasturing sheep on heaths where they had no rights of common, whilst commoners themselves often grazed animals when or where it was forbidden to do so. At Brandon four men

---

[56] Rackham, *History of the countryside*, pp. 295–6. Medieval documents describe furze as *whynnes* and bracken as either *fugerium* or *iampa*.

[57] G. Crompton, 'The history of Lakenheath warren: a historical study for ecologists', *Report to the Nature Conservancy Council* (1972), p. 51; CUL EDR G3/27 f.190.

[58] Barton Parva, Bodleian Ms Suffolk Rolls 1/3; Lackford, WSROB E.3/15.12/1.19.

[59] CUL EDC 7/15/I/7; PRO sc6.768/5.   [60] CUL EDR G3/27 f.146.

[61] BL Add.Ms 31970 f.89.   [62] CUL Add.Ms 4220 ff.89–90.

were so regularly amerced for 'releasing their sheep in the lord's heath' that their payments were thinly disguised licences to graze.[63] However, commoning transgressions were not confined to the peasantry, and some lords resorted to illegal methods to ensure exclusive access to heathland: in the late thirteenth century it was reported that 'Adam de Walsingham, Master of St Salvator's Hospital, appropriates for the said hospital 120 acres of several heath in the village of West Stow which ought to be common to the aforesaid village'.[64]

Cropping techniques

In the classic three-field system, villagers co-operated to sow one field with winter crops and another with spring, and to graze all their animals on the remaining fallow field. In medieval East Anglia, such communal rights over the open-fields were rare, and in places were almost non-existent. In eastern Norfolk, for example, communal grazing of the fallow was confined to a short period after harvest known as the 'shack', but thereafter lords and peasants pastured or sowed their strips of land as they pleased.[65] Farmers in these areas of such rampant individualism were often the first to take the short step and enclose their open-fields with ditches and hedges in the fifteenth and sixteenth centuries. Walsham-le-Willows, in high Suffolk, was a village of extensive open-fields in the mid-fourteenth century which underwent piecemeal enclosure over the next two hundred years. By 1577 over 75 per cent of its arable had been enclosed and communal rights on it extinguished, and this was typical of central areas of East Anglia: 'only a small amount of open field land still survived in the central and eastern districts by the end of the seventeenth century'.[66]

Breckland, along with the other light-soil regions of East Anglia, was anomalous in this general picture of early enclosure, for it maintained its open-fields until the Parliamentary enclosures of the nineteenth century. Allison attributes the survival of open-fields in these areas to the development of the peculiar 'foldcourse system' in

---

[63] See, for instance, Bacon 290/1-2. [64] *Pinchbeck register*, vol. II, p. 241.
[65] Campbell, 'Population change', pp. 174-5.
[66] K.M. Dodd, ed., *The field book of Walsham-le-Willows 1577* (Woodbridge, 1974), p. 43. For the process of enclosure in the fifteenth century, see D. Dymond. 'The parish of Walsham-le-Willows: two Elizabethan surveys and their medieval background', *P.S.I.A.* 33 (1974), pp. 204-8.

the seventeenth century.[67] The light soils of East Anglia harboured a sheep-corn husbandry, in which the grazing and rearing of sheep was crucial to maintaining the fertility of the poor soils. This system employed a flexible form of communal cropping which ensured that large, compact areas of fallow arable were accessible to the all-important sheep flocks. The unit of cropping was not the field, but the shift. A shift was basically a group of lands cropped alike in any one year, and was independent of field and *quarentena* divisions. There was no reason why lands comprising a given shift should themselves be adjacent, nor was it necessary for a whole field or *quarentena* to fall within one shift; they could be divided between two or even more. Unlike a rigid cropping system based on fields, shifts were much more flexible and adaptable to changes in demand for grain. Shifts were no more permanent than the crop rotations which they applied, and so the number of shifts operating in a village could vary according to necessity.[68]

The shift system was at its most advanced in the seventeenth and eighteenth centuries, and in this form employed differential cropping of the arable land, a feature first described by Darby and Saltmarsh at West Wretham.[69] Deposits of better soil were cropped more intensively and designated 'infield', while the larger areas of poorer soils were cropped more sparingly and designated 'outfield'. This technique is common to many areas where the soils are poor, although the exact connotation of outfield varies from one region to another. In Breckland, outfield was systematically exploited to provide a regular, annual supplement to cereal production, whilst Devon outfields were tilled in a more sporadic and irregular fashion, resembling occasional intakes from the waste rather than a permanent part of the village arable.[70]

When were flexible communal cropping and the infield-outfield system introduced to Breckland? Allison believed that infield-outfield cropping was the creation of the later seventeenth- and eighteenth-century improvers, but Simpson disagreed, argu-

---

[67] This summary is based upon Allison, 'Sheep corn husbandry', and Postgate, 'Field systems of Breckland'.

[68] For shifts, see also Postgate, 'Field systems of East Anglia', pp. 299–300.

[69] J.A. Saltmarsh and H.C. Darby, 'The infield-outfield system on a Norfolk manor', *Economic History* 3 (1935), pp. 30–44.

[70] Postgate, 'Field systems of East Anglia', pp. 300–3; H.S.A. Fox, 'Outfield cultivation in Devon and Cornwall; a reinterpretation', in *Husbandry and marketing in the south west 1500–1800*, ed. M. Havinden, Exeter papers in economic history 8 (1973), pp. 27–8. I am grateful to Dr Bruce Campbell for this reference.

ing that heathland intakes had been employed 'as long as there had been flocks to make periodic cropping possible'.[71] Recent research has helped clarify the position, for both Postgate and Williamson have discovered references to differential cropping in medieval Breckland and the Norfolk Goodsands.[72] Postgate further argued that seventeenth-century Breckland was different from other poor-soil regions because its farmers employed a tripartite system of cropping intensity, namely infield, outfield, and occasionally tilled heathland or breck. Postgate's innovation was to distinguish clearly between outfield and breck. The outfield was considered as part of the permanent arable in the same way as infield, whereas brecks were regarded more as temporary appendages to this, being cultivated for a short period and then abandoned to the heathland again.[73]

There are many difficulties involved in describing cropping arrangements in medieval Breckland. Even in the seventeenth century, when these arrangements were well developed, they were subject to variety and change. Postgate, for instance, found it almost impossible to delimit infield and outfield in any exact manner. Infield was not necessarily that nearest the village in the same way that outfield was not necessarily the farthest away. The division between infield/outfield/breck was neither constant nor finite, but often fluctuated over time: at Icklingham the same land parcels were described as infield in one survey, and outfield in another.[74] The most likely cause of such flexibility was a change in the demand for grain. As the Middle Ages incorporated periods of both very high and very low demand for bread grains, then our task must be to outline the parameters within which changes in the system occurred.

Firm evidence for communal cropping in medieval Breckland is limited. However, as the fertility of the soil was dependent upon regular manuring by sheep, then some informal co-operation on sowing procedure must have been necessary in order to leave compact areas of fallow for grazing each year. Yet the lack of evidence does suggest that the system was not as well developed as it

[71] Allison, 'Sheep corn husbandry', p. 29; A. Simpson, 'East Anglian foldcourse', pp. 87–96.

[72] Postgate, 'Field systems of Breckland', pp. 92–3; Williamson, 'Thirteenth century', p. 99.

[73] To this extent, East Anglian 'brecks' resembled the Devon 'outfields' mentioned earlier. Postgate, 'Field systems of Breckland', p. 91, and 'Field systems of East Anglia', p. 302.

[74] Postgate, 'Field systems of East Anglia', p. 301.

was in the seventeenth century. References to shifts are the best indication that a form of communal cropping was in operation. A rental of Thetford dated 1338 noted that two roods in Fautonfeld lay 'in the shift (*sesona*) of Welstugesmereschift'.[75] A fourteenth-century scribe at Brandon mentioned an 'oats shift', meaning a group of lands sown with oats in a given year, and in Barnham surveyors delimited 'fyvefurlong shifte', referring to a group of lands sown alike in a given year.[76] At Brandon after the Black Death some land was expressly leased as 'barley land' or 'rye land', with the length of lease determined by the length of the crop rotation on the shift, and Lakenheath tenants were expected to sow their land by 'reasonable courses'.[77] At Chippenham in the early fifteenth century, a peasant was fined for sowing out of turn, and William Sadler of Langford sowed his lands 'to the impediment of his neighbours and the lord's tenants', who should have had access to pasture there.[78] Such references appear less frequently than in the seventeenth century, partly due to the nature of medieval documentation, but also because the system was less clearly defined in the Middle Ages. The explanation for this must lie in the different landholding and manorial structures in the two periods. Shifts were easier to impose in the eighteenth century when seigneurial power was strong and landownership was concentrated into a few hands, and it is not coincidental that shifts assumed their most identifiable form at the time when rural depopulation was most advanced. What Campbell found in eastern Norfolk has some relevance for medieval Breckland: the subdivision of landholdings and the fragmentation of feudal power weakened attempts at communal cropping.[79]

Some form of communal cropping was found everywhere in Breckland, but it was more evident in periods of low demand for grain and in central villages. The overlapping of open-fields in peripheral villages, the fragmented lordship, and the large, consolidated blocks of demesne land would have served to complicate

75 WSROB J515 f.80.
76 Brandon, PRO sc6.1304/31; Barnham, WSROB HA513/30/2. Brandon scribes also refer to *sesona inculta* and *sesnesio de Brydefeld*, Bacon 646 and PRO sc6.1304/30. At Downham in the mid-fourteenth century, corn was sown '*ad seysonam siliginis*', WSROB 651/35/7.   77 Bacon 291/36; CUL EDC 7/15/II/Box 1/9 m.4.
78 M. Spufford, 'A Cambridgeshire community: Chippenham from settlement to enclosure', *Occasional papers, Department of Local History, Leicester University* 20 (1965), p. 19; NRO NCC(Petre) Box 8/21, court held May 1378.
79 Campbell, 'Regional uniqueness', pp. 23–4.

attempts at communal cropping compared with central parishes. Compare those rigid Brandon leases, which controlled both the crop and length of rotation to be sown, with a rather less formal custom of Ingham stating that tenants 'ought to forbere the sowynge of ther londs ther every yere where the lords shepys course or fould shall chaunce to be in the same yere'.[80] The latter implies a slightly different set of priorities, and greater flexibility over sowing patterns.

Whilst our knowledge of the relationship between soil type and shift cropping remains sketchy, it is much more certain that the system was subject to change within the medieval period. Given Postgate's evidence for the flexibility of shifts in certain economic conditions, and given the existence of periods of very high and very low demand for grain in the Middle Ages, then refinements to the system – and its breakdown in the era of high demand – seem likely. As Britnell has correctly suggested, shifts were transient and their permanence depended on the frequency with which a rotation was repeated.[81] The more a rotation was applied, the more permanent and discernible the shift, and conversely so. If farmers were introducing legumes into fallows, or were seeking special licences to fold sheep temporarily on their own lands, then they would undermine the system's rigidity, and taken to extreme lengths would render cropping an individual exercise. Evidence presented in chapter 4 would indicate that this was increasingly a feature of Breckland in the period before the Black Death. Yet in the fifteenth century, when demand for grain was low and landholding less fragmented, cropping patterns were more rigidly and systematically applied; hence the complaint by an early sixteenth-century landlord that his tenants were refusing to keep to the agreed shifts.[82]

It is also certain that medieval cropping techniques exploited some lands more intensively than others. The length of fallow between crop rotations varied from shift to shift, and consequently accounts distinguish between two types of fallow land. *Terra warecta* refers to land which is to be sown the next year, and was a standard form throughout medieval East Anglia.[83] All other

[80] BL Add.Ms 31970 f.91. The number of lords with manorial jurisdiction over land in Ingham's open-fields was much greater than in Brandon, which might also explain Ingham's less formal customs.

[81] For an excellent general survey of shifts and agrarian techniques in East Anglia in this period, see R.H. Britnell in the *Cambridge agrarian history of England and Wales*, vol. III (forthcoming).   [82] WSROB 449/3/4 m.5.

[83] I am grateful to Dr Bruce Campbell for this information.

unsown arable is described as *terra frisca*, a longer, recuperative fallow which indicates the use of convertible husbandry. Hence on the Brandon demesne in 1363, 109 acres were sown or leased, 50 acres on Fourhowefeld were *warecta* and prepared for seeding the next year, and 405 acres 1 rood were *frisca* and depastured by sheep and rabbits.[84]

There is plenty of other evidence that the arable was distinguished between infield and outfield. Again at Brandon, four fields – Womanlodefeld, Drovefeld, Fourhowefeld and Bridhythefeld – were cultivated as infield on a four-course rotation, leaving one fallow each year, whilst the remaining fields were cultivated much more sparingly, and obviously represented the outfields.[85] The south-east of Barnham contains the village's most fertile land which was described in the fifteenth century as 'le infelde', and a scribe at Risby added 'hic finit le Infelde' to a sixteenth-century rental.[86] A fifteenth-century Icklingham account described some lands as either 'everyerlond' or 'toyerlond'. A contemporary rental was more specific, labelling a furlong lying in the more fertile river valley 'everyyerlond', whilst arable above the valley slopes lying next to the heath was not labelled at all.[87] *Pecia* size tended to be smaller on the infield: being more fertile, it was in greater demand and more prone to subdivision. Leymere furlong in Icklingham (infield) contained 11 acres in 16 *peciae*, whilst Westfield furlong contained 118 acres 2 roods in 23 *peciae*, a mean size of 2.75 and 20.6 roods respectively.[88] On the lands of Edward Gasteyn and of Calthorpe manor in Barnham, 70 acres lay in 99 *peciae* in the infield (2.8 roods), and 87 acres 2 roods lay in 50 *peciae* on West Northfield (7 roods).[89] At Risby, the largest *peciae* lay next to heathland, by implication the poorer outfield land.[90] As infield only constituted a small proportion of the total village arable, it only comprised a small proportion of any one holding: for example, it contributed only 70 acres to Gasteyn and Calthorpe's combined holding of 721 acres, or 9.7 per cent.[91]

[84] Bacon 647.
[85] The rotation on the infields is implied in CUL EDR G3/27 ff.189–90; compare this with cropping in the 1360s, Bacon 647–9, PRO SC6.1304/29–30.
[86] WSROB HA513/30/2, first folio; WSROB 2753/17/16 f.27. At Thetford there was land 'layd therto by ye yere', WSROB J515 ff.70–1.
[87] NRO Ms 13201; WSROB E.3/10/9.8 and 9.9. At Ampton in 1511 the demesne lessee agreed to sow certain land for two years and then pasture it for two more – obviously outfield, Copinger, *Manors of Suffolk*, vol. VI, p. 746.
[88] WSROB E.3/10/9.9.   [89] WSROB HA513/30/2, penultimate folio.
[90] WSROB 2753/17/16 f.37.   [91] WSROB HA513/30/2.

The length of time for which any piece of arable was left *frisca*, and the proportion of total arable which was *frisca* in any one year, varied enormously according to the condition of the soil and the prevailing demand for grain. High corn prices in the thirteenth and fourteenth centuries meant that fallows of more than one year on infield would be rare, and the long recuperative fallows normally associated with outfield were probably reduced to just a couple of years duration before the next cropping sequence began. Consequently, at the peak of medieval cultivation demesnes on the poorest soils fallowed only one-third of their arable each year, an impressive performance for such poor soils.[92] Over much of England, fallow arable was an important source of summer pasture for the village livestock, and so any reduction in its area would have serious repercussions for pasturing arrangements. Yet in this context the systematic reduction of fallow in Breckland was unimportant, because the region possessed ample reserves of summer pasture. The real problem with declining fallows was how to keep the cultivated soils adequately manured. Whenever soils did become exhausted, or when the demand for grain collapsed in the fifteenth century, so cropping sequences incorporated much longer fallows, and in these conditions around 70 per cent of demesne arable could be left uncultivated each year. In these circumstances, some outfields were left *frisca* for many years and came to be used almost exclusively as rough pasture. Bracken and gorse quickly re-established themselves here, rendering the arable almost indistinguishable from the surrounding heath, and in some cases the boundaries of the old *peciae* were obliterated. This led to a dispute over ownership of land in Stonehillfeld in Brandon in 1471, when Robert Pycas ploughed 3 roods of abandoned demesne land lying *frisca* and tried to claim that he had always held them freely.[93] Similarly, jurors were uncertain as to the ownership of two long-abandoned acres in Culfordale in 1435, and in Brandon in 1566 there were 18 acres 'of land unknowne'.[94]

Although an infield–outfield pattern was central to cropping sequences on the regularly tilled arable of medieval Breckland, positive evidence for temporary intakes of heathland, or brecking, is rather more difficult to find and to analyse. There is no doubt that most of the heathland remained uncultivated, and that the arable

[92] This statement is based on the evidence contained in table 4.3.
[93] Bacon 296/17.
[94] BL Add.Ms 42055 f.37; IESRO v.11/2/1.1 in Cotteshillfeld.

area in the Middle Ages was a good deal smaller than it was at the end of the eighteenth century. Fifteenth-century extents reveal that much of Barnham parish south of the present Duke's Ride was permanent heathland, yet by 1840 large areas had become enclosed arable brecks, and the medieval heath at Euston had also been ploughed.[95] At no stage in the Middle Ages did cultivation at Culford extend north of the modern Balloon farm, yet by the nineteenth century brecks had altered this.[96] Comparison of any medieval survey with Parliamentary enclosure maps demonstrates the widespread extension of brecks over former heathland. This certainly endorses Allison's claim that the seventeenth and eighteenth centuries were the years of most productive brecking.[97]

Medieval field-name evidence is misleading, because the noun 'breck' was applied to any assart from the heath, and did not necessarily refer to a temporarily cultivated piece of heathland. Such a distinction may appear so slight as to be irrelevant, but it means that field-name evidence of brecks cannot be used to indicate the cropping practices identified by Postgate. For instance, the Rushford demesne included 30 acres on 'le Breche', but this was a distinctly permanent sector of the arable and was valued highly at 6d. per acre.[98] Valued at ½d. per acre, a 42-acre breck at Culford was decidedly poorer in quality, but was still included in the list of permanent demesne arable in 1302 and 1437.[99] All that can be inferred with any certainty from field-name evidence is that 'brecks' described late assarts from the heathland which were subsequently absorbed into the village arable.

If medieval field-names are not reliable guides to the practice of brecking in its classic sense, then cropping patterns remain the only acid test. Evidence of cropping on demesne brecks is limited to the fourteenth century, and indicates that they were fully integrated parts of the outfield. In the 1340s the Fornham (A) 'brech' was sown

[95] Compare the evidence in the medieval rentals and terriers with that in the nineteenth-century tithe map, WSROB HA513/30/1–3 and T.99/2.

[96] BL Add.Ms 42055 and WSROB T.120/1–2. By the later date, arable land had been extended up to the parish boundary at Rymer Point, although odd outcrops of the medieval heath remained, such as the 62 acres at map reference TL852742 (piece 131 on the tithe map).

[97] Postgate notes that the number of brecks actually sown in any one year varied according to demand, but the peak was probably reached during the Napoleonic wars, Postgate, 'Field systems of East Anglia', p. 302.   [98] NRO Ms 15170.

[99] BL Add.Ms 42055 f.45 and 14847 f.23. 'Le brech' in Fornham (A) was similarly assessed in the fourteenth century, and remained an integral parcel of the demesne throughout the fifteenth century, BL Add.Ms 34689 ff.6 and 27.

two years out of five, and three years out of six in the 1360s.[100] In Richard II's reign, court rolls suggest that the Fornham (C) breck near Timworth heath was similarly cultivated.[101] Of course this evidence is from a period when demand for grain was buoyant and the cultivation of outfields was more intensive, and so expediency probably elevated these brecks from occasionally cropped heathland to integral parts of the village arable. Yet, when the bottom fell out of the grain market in the fifteenth century, this land may well have reverted to heath and been subject to irregular and occasional ploughing, thus resembling a true breck; unfortunately, no details have survived to confirm this. From all extant material, unequivocal evidence of brecking is rare. The lessee of the Lackford demesne ploughed a section of Risby heath in 1403, and at Fornham St Genevieve the demesne sowed rye 'super le hethe' in 1363.[102] Land named 'Cokesbreche' in Lakenheath was held by a variety of tenants in the early fourteenth century and then abandoned at the Black Death. In the late 1350s, John de Lakenheath acquired the land (4 acres) on leasehold and cropped it for six years before abandoning it to the advancing heath. Thus it remained for over twenty years until the demesne sowed it with oats, after which it disappeared from the records entirely.[103]

The long-term changes in Breckland's landholding structure largely explain why brecking featured less prominently in medieval cropping practices than in later centuries. As larger farming units gradually replaced the smallholdings of the Middle Ages, so the later farmers gained crucial advantages over their predecessors. Lower overheads per acre enabled them to till the heaths more cost-effectively, and depopulation facilitated the extinction of ancient common rights on heathland which might otherwise have proved an obstacle to their cultivation. Furthermore, technological progress in agriculture had widened farming scope by the eighteenth century, and capital was more readily available for farmers to implement these innovations. New crops such as turnips, lucerne

---

[100] WSROB E.3/15.7/2.1–2.4, and 2.6–7; E.3/15.6/2.28, 2.30b and 2.32–3.

[101] There are no extant accounts with which to document this, but 'le brech' is mentioned constantly in court rolls when peasant livestock trampled on demesne crops of wheat, rye, barley and oats there, WSROB E.3/15.9/1.5.

[102] Lackford, WSROB E.3/15.12/1.4, court held August 1403; WSROB E.3/15.6/1.3 m.14, court held January 1363.

[103] CUL EDC 7/15/II/Box 1/4 m.1, court held December 1310; on leasehold, see CUL EDC 7/15/I/17, 20–2, and 28.

and sainfoin, and extensive marling techniques were introduced on an experimental basis and did well enough to enable the spread of cultivation over land previously regarded as sub-marginal.[104] The disappearance of the smallholder also enabled the capitalist farmers to monopolise and rationalise sheep farming, and the resultant rise in the sheep population provided the necessary manure for large-scale brecking.[105]

Pasturing arrangements

By contrast with the classic three-field system, communal rights to grazing animals over the open-fields of medieval East Anglia were not assured. In eastern Norfolk, apart from a short period after the harvest, there were no communal pasture rights over the arable land. However, the need for constant manuring on the lighter soils of East Anglia demanded a more organised system. Hence the development of the peculiar foldcourse system, whose features in the seventeenth and eighteenth centuries were described by Allison.[106] In this system, the grazing of fallow arable was restricted to the owners of specified foldcourses. A foldcourse was the exclusive right to erect a sheep-fold over a carefully defined area of ground, and a village may have been split between anything up to a dozen such courses. The owner would fence off the sown arable with wattle hurdles, and fold his sheep on whatever fallow arable lay within his designated foldcourse. Thus immediately the need for a shift, and not a field, system of cropping becomes clear. Under field-based rotations, a given foldcourse may consist of all fallow one year and all sown arable the next, whereas a shift system permits a suitable balance between fallow and sown land within each foldcourse each year and allows a certain elasticity.

Allison found that foldcourse ownership in the seventeenth century was restricted to the manorial lord or his lessee, and thus presumed that it was a seigneurial monopoly. This did not mean

104 Martelli, *Elveden enterprise*, pp. 33–6.
105 For example, it has been calculated that there were twice as many sheep in Eriswell in 1850 as in 1086, J.T. Munday, 'Eriswell Notebook', duplicated, WSROB. In Blackbourne hundred in 1908 there were 34,404 sheep (somewhat below the estimated eighteenth-century peak), compared with a recorded 17,128 sheep in 1283. Blackbourne straddled the eastern section of Suffolk Breckland, E. Powell, *A Suffolk hundred in the year 1283* (Cambridge, 1910), p. xxviii.
106 Allison, 'Sheep corn husbandry'.

that the sheep's manure – or tathe as it was known locally[107] – was confined to demesne land, for the sheep 'ranged over the open-field holdings of the lord's tenants'.[108] Nor was the foldcourse area restricted just to the arable lands, but included the heaths and, on the fen edge, marshland, both of which were vital sources of summer pasture. The number and variety of foldcourses within a township is also stressed. As foldcourses came under manorial jurisdiction, and as there was frequently more than one manor to a vill, then the number of folds in each village could be large, especially given the local practice of keeping lambs and ewes separate from other sheep. Foldcourse boundaries were rigidly fixed, thus limiting the number of sheep which each one could support. A few foldcourses traversed parish boundaries, such as one at Downham in the sixteenth century. Foldcourses at Holkham (Norfolk) were contained within the parish and between them covered all the village arable, but the four in North Creake (Norfolk) covered only part of the open-fields.[109]

The rights of tenants in this system were limited. Their animals could pasture on the harvest stubble during the period known as 'shack', but thereafter the cattle were collected together in a communal herd and allowed to share the foldcourse grounds.[110] However, their sheep-farming activities were strictly regulated by the lord. Each tenant was allowed to keep only a specific number according to his land or tenure, known as 'cullet', and these were compelled to lie within the lord's fold. Variations on cullet rights abounded: tenants were required to pay for the privilege in some villages, in others they could pay for the right to keep their sheep separate, yet elsewhere only freeholders enjoyed cullet rights and no payment was necessary.

Although an important general survey, Allison's work – through the very nature of the subject – has raised as many questions as it has answered. He concentrates upon the foldcourse system as a source of social friction and depopulation rather than

---

[107] Marshall, *Rural economy*, vol. I, pp. 33–4 comments 'tathe: a provincial term conveying a compound idea, for which we have no English word. When we make use of the term fold, as applied to the fertilising effect of sheep pent upon land, we do not mean to convey an idea merely of the faeces they leave behind them, in this case, but also of the urine, the trampling, and perhaps the perspiration and the warmth, communicated to the soil by the practice of folding.'

[108] Allison, 'Sheep corn husbandry', p. 21.   [109] *Ibid.*, p. 18.

[110] *Ibid.*, p. 19, suggests that shack commonly lasted from 29 September until 25 March in many villages. See also Campbell, 'Regional uniqueness', p. 20 for variations in Norfolk.

upon the more fundamental issues of its variety and historical evolution.[111] How different was it in the Middle Ages and why? Only more, painstaking local research can answer this question, although Campbell has already indicated its variety and flexibility across East Anglia. Local differences in soil type, strength of lordship, landholding patterns and population density could all refine the system, so that the legal right to 'liberty of fold' carried different implications from place to place.[112] Areas of fertile soils and a weak manorial structure inhibited the development of a foldcourse system, yet in north-west Norfolk, where soils were poor and lordship relatively strong, a fairly rigid and closely regulated system emerged. Breckland's soils and its structure of lordship would suggest more similarities with north-west rather than eastern Norfolk.[113] At the risk of repetition, variation over both time and place prevents any definitive description of foldcourses, even within Breckland. The immediate aim is to discuss its general features in the Middle Ages, and to consider changes *within* the period at a later stage. Not that this is an easy task. Evidence about its operation appears only when it was in dispute, and the historian must accept that some of the system's vagaries will always prove elusive. Indeed, the cases recorded in the court rolls indicate that our forefathers were themselves unclear as to certain practices: one exasperated court steward made a plea to jurors at Barton Parva to ascertain exactly 'who is occupying and pasturing flocks and how'.[114]

The overwhelming impression is of a less rigid system than in later centuries. The most fundamental difference was the diversity of foldcourse ownership, for in the Middle Ages there is little evidence to suggest that folds were confined to manorial lords. In this respect Breckland was different from other parts of medieval East Anglia, for fold rights were a seigneurial monopoly in much of north and east Norfolk.[115] In Breckland, some peasants possessed

[111] Allison, 'Sheep corn husbandry', pp. 22–7.

[112] B.M.S. Campbell, 'Field systems in eastern Norfolk during the middle ages: a study with particular reference to the demographic and agrarian changes of the fourteenth century' (Ph.D., Cambridge, 1975), p. 320.

[113] These comments are based on B.M.S. Campbell, 'The complexity of manorial structure in medieval Norfolk: a case study', *Norfolk Archaeology* 39 (1986), map 1. By calculating the number of lordships in a village, and their wealth and size from the *Nomina villarum* of 1316 and the 1334 Lay Subsidy, he found that eastern Norfolk possessed small, low value and numerous lordships, in direct contrast to those in north-western Norfolk.

[114] WSROB E.18/451/69 f.58.

[115] Campbell, 'Complexity of manorial structure', p. 249.

the right to erect their own foldcourses, expressed in documents as 'freefold' or 'liberty of fold'.[116] The vast majority of these belonged to freemen, although villeins in Barnham, Chippenham and Hilborough are also recorded as holding them.[117] So foldcourse ownership extended to lords, freemen and occasionally to servile peasants, and there were two basic forms of tenure. One was of the type described by Allison, fixed and permanent foldcourses covering specific areas and protected by inalienable rights. The other type was less common, and was secured through the purchase of a temporary licence.

By far the largest and most important of the regular foldcourses were those belonging to the demesne, although their exact number and size varied from manor to manor. The Prior and Convent of Ely had three attached to the Lakenheath demesne, as did the abbot of Bury at Fornham (A).[118] The number of peasant folds varied too: four at Timworth, and sixteen at Mildenhall, whilst 42 per cent of the Bishopric of Ely's freemen in Bridgham had their own folds.[119] However, an individual peasant seldom, if ever, owned more folds than the demesne. It is evident from the earliest records that peasant foldcourses were legally attached to specific holdings and passed down through successive generations. In the twelfth century Abbot Samson of Bury granted a *tenementum* in Fornham 'with all that pertains to it, in messuages, in arable lands, in meadows and pastures, and a fold of one hundred ewes'.[120] Later documents constantly emphasise the attachment of folds to the peasant holding. A fold in Roudham 'pertained to the lands of Henry son of John and John Horold', William Cosyn of Cavenham had 'a rodd of lond with the lyberte of a folde cours', and half an acre of freeland in Flempton carried the right to 'le Breyerefold'.[121]

[116] Documents use a variety of terms to describe fold rights, although there is no evidence to suggest that the different phrases indicate different forms of foldcourse.

[117] CUL Gg.iv.4 f.130; Spufford, 'Chippenham', p. 20.; NRO Hilborough Deposit Box T (Daleth), i, court held October 1312.

[118] Crompton, 'Lakenheath warren', p. 20; fifteenth-century Fornham accounts divide the demesne sheep into their respective flocks, WSROB E.3/15.6/2.60.

[119] Timworth, CUL Add.Ms 4220 f.89, and f.134 for Mildenhall; Bridgham, CUL EDR G3/27 ff.146–7.

[120] R.H.C. Davis, ed., *The Kalendar of abbot Samson of Bury St Edmunds and related documents* (London, 1954), pp. 94–5 and 106–7.

[121] Roudham, CUL EDC G3/27 f.147; Cavenham, PRO SC12.27/32; Flempton, WSROB 449/2/65. At Herringswell a court noted that 'the other acre and a half lies at northfeld on the hallbreyde with liberty of fold for 100 sheep', WSROB E.18/451/69 f.78. At Risby, one acre in fitenacres carried with it liberty of fold, WSROB 449/2/404. At Elveden there were 60 acres of land with freefold 'pertaining to them', CUL Add.Ms 4220 f.87.

The rights to other foldcourses were contained in special charters. In Bridgham, John son of Hugo had a fold of 200 ewes 'as shown by his charter', and Mildenhall courts occasionally insisted that these be presented for inspection.[122] In practical terms there was no difference between folds held by charter and those held by land. Both enjoyed the same security and rights as the demesne folds, as the legal preamble to a fold in Methwold emphasised.[123] And just as landholdings underwent subdivision, so did some of those folds held on land tenures. This was rare, because of the practical difficulties involved in physically dividing them, but at Freckenham William Ailbern held three roods and the liberty of half a fold in Petfeld.[124] Richard Wulman held half a fold in Northwold, whilst the remainder was held jointly by a father, his son, and their '*participes*'.[125]

All medieval foldcourses were strictly delimited. Pasture areas in Brandon were carefully defined and marked on the ground by *meta*, presumably stone markers, although dykes were used at Elveden to divide Thetford priory's foldcourse from other sheep grounds.[126] The general impression is that the lands allotted to each fold had been established from an early date, although documents seldom reveal any complete delimitation. One rare example has survived from Barnham, where a terrier begins 'all these londs lyeth within the Lyberty of the Nunns Course': 56 acres in Bradfyld, 40 acres in Mossyfeld, 12 acres in diverse crofts and another 13 acres of infield land.[127] However, the document does not indicate whether this was the full extent of the foldcourse, or whether its owner enjoyed bite on other permanent pastures, which seems likely. In Ingham,

Salamon de Ingham has his pasture from a certain place called Landmere, lengthways as far as le Wesmeden and by the pasture of Culford Easthall, breadthways as far as Canteculhenyd. And he ought to have bite [*chacia*] with his sheep from Estfeld to the said pasture and no further and he should

122 CUL EDR G3/27 f.147; CUL Add.Ms 4220 ff.136–7.
123 NRO Ms 9973 notes that the fold had pasture rights 'following those of the lord'.
124 BL Harl. Charter 49 F 44. This feature would be most prominent in periods of high population pressure. At Lakenheath, the earl of Gloucester had raised a fold on his demesne (Clare fee) in the late thirteenth century, but later leased the land to two tenants. After a while, the tenants took out separate leases and split the demesne between them, but rather than split the fold they agreed with the lord to have a complete liberty of fold each. This is a rare example, but a practical solution nonetheless. One suspects that the lord would not have been so willing had the fold been a purely peasant concern, CUL EDC 7/15/II/Box 1/19 m.2.   125 CUL EDR G3/27 f.154.
126 *Ibid.*, ff.189–90; WSROB J515 f.77.   127 WSROB HA513/30/2 f.1.

69

common with his sheep in no place in the village of Ingham except in a certain place called le Scothes.[128]

Rigid physical delimitation of foldcourses was coupled with strict numerical control, and most descriptions of folds include a statement like 'to the number of 200 sheep'. Edmund Conyn of Fakenham Magna held a fold 'to manure his own lands in the village fields, containing three hundred sheep by the long hundred'.[129] Court rolls demonstrate that fines were levied for exceeding permitted numbers, as overstocking was a debilitating practice and Breckland pastures simply could not sustain unlimited and uncontrolled grazing by sheep. Hence a Bury abbey register carefully records the exact number of sheep to be pastured each year on heathland in Fornham St Genevieve.[130] Courts kept a close check on transgressions of this nature, and overstocking and illegal grazing offences are the most common form of foldcourse trespass. The parson of Ingham church was indicted for both offences in 1319 and 1320: first, for having 120 sheep above the allotted number in his fold, and then 'because he depastured with the sheep of his fold in the lord's several pasture beyond the bounds of his foldcourse [*extra cursum proprium suum*] on numerous occasions where he ought not to pasture'. He was later noted to have kept sheep on the lord's heath 'beyond his own markers'.[131]

These regular, permanent folds contrast sharply with the second basic form of ownership. This was the temporary fold licence, valid for a short period only and granted by the manorial lord for a cash payment. In north-west Norfolk, such licences represented the peasantry's only access to foldcourse ownership.[132] They were not very common in Breckland because they inevitably disrupted existing cropping and pasturing arrangements, but they did allow more effective tathing of the arable in periods of high demand for grain. Gilbert de Kirkeby of Brandon paid to have 'one fold of four score sheep for the next year' in the 1340s, and in 1336 three Mildenhall tenants paid 2s. 4d. each for temporary folds of 100 sheep.[133] In Hockham John de Hopton paid 12d. for a licence to

---

[128] CUL Add.Ms 4220 f.90.   [129] IESRO Phillipps Collection T.4373/2 f.49.
[130] BL Add.Ms 34689 f.23.   [131] CUL Add.Ms 4220 f.89-90.
[132] J. Williamson, 'Peasant holdings in medieval Norfolk: a detailed investigation into the holdings of the peasantry in three Norfolk villages in the thirteenth century' (Ph.D., Reading, 1976), pp. 96 and 292.
[133] Bacon 291/9; WSROB E.18/459/2 court held '9 Ed.III'. The cost of licences varied over time and place. At Herringswell three tenants paid for their folds in lambs, BL Harl. 3977 f.83.

have an extra 40 sheep in his fold for just under one year.[134] Such
licences were most frequent when pressure on the land was greatest,
and must have disrupted existing sowing and pasturing patterns;
they represent both a cause and a symptom of the medieval system's
flexibility compared with later centuries. Once again, the size and
extent of these folds were carefully controlled by manorial courts,
and grants of annual folds on Lackford heath were strictly delimited, 'as appears by the boundary markers'.[135]

What is known about the exact size of each foldcourse in each
village, and what proportion was pasture or arable? Unfortunately,
examples like Ingham and Holkham are very rare, and few records
give even the merest hint. This is another dark area of our knowledge which can never be brightened. Yet it is known that each
foldcourse could have access to five distinct grazing areas: fallow
arable, pasture and meadow, heathland, fenland and the specific
right to manure one's own land.[136] Not every foldcourse possessed
all these elements, and many comprised different proportions of
each. The large demesne folds extended over most of these components. At Brandon, the Bishopric of Ely enjoyed exclusive
grazing rights on specified pieces of fen, 23 acres of pasture and on
fallow land in four named fields, although it is uncertain if more
than one foldcourse was attached to this.[137] At Barnham demesne
flocks had bite over heath as well as arable land: hence the
Calthorpe flock grazed on Calthorpe heath, and the Eastling fold
on Eastling heath.[138] Nearly all of the temporary folds had a much
smaller range of access, and in many places their bite was restricted
simply to the owner's fallows, so that grants were normally accompanied by the qualification 'in his tenementum', or 'on his own
lands'. It was probable that many of these folds lay within the
grazing area of another, permanent foldcourse, but such an arrangement was acceptable for a temporary period. Indeed, it would
allow the owner of the primary foldcourse to concentrate on
tathing his own lands rather than those of others, thus increasing the
overall area manured in that year. Hence the Duchy of Lancaster
granted a fold to a tenant of Methwold in 1367, on condition that it
'did not prejudice the lord's fold'.[139]

Thus fold ownership in medieval Breckland was not the seigneurial monopoly it was to become in later centuries. Why had

[134] NRO Ms 13848 m.1.   [135] WSROB e.3/15.12/2.2.
[136] Allison, 'Sheep corn husbandry', pp. 17–19.   [137] CUL EDR G3/27 f.189–90.
[138] WSROB HA513/30/2.   [139] PRO DL30.104/1471 m.3.

folds become alienated in Breckland, why had this not occurred in other parts of Norfolk, and what were the consequences for seigneurial power over day-to-day foldcourse jurisdiction? And how did later landlords manage to reassert a monopoly of ownership? The evidence suggests that the right to create and control foldcourses throughout East Anglia belonged to the lord, but that in Breckland they had deliberately chosen to alienate some folds.[140] That seigneurial blessing was an essential prerequisite to holding a fold is emphasised at Troston, where John le Verdon had a freefold 'from lord Reginald Pecche'.[141] The nature of the local economy and environment is a sufficient explanation as to why this should have developed in Breckland. Here was an area where large pastures abounded, and where sheep farming was both a local specialism and crucial for maintaining the arable in good heart, all compelling reasons for extending limited fold ownership to sections of the peasantry. It is impossible to trace the process of alienation exactly, but it might have dated from the years of demesne rentier farming in the twelfth century. Permanent folds probably emerged from those temporary licences which had been regularly endorsed over a number of years, and which were eventually sanctioned by custom. Such a suggestion is impossible to prove conclusively, but it is a logical progression and the documents suggest no alternative derivation. Yet the records do emphasise that permanent folds were ratified by customary forces. An inquiry at Mildenhall in 1340 noted that John de Chelmersford had purchased a fold charter from William de Pakenham, whose 'ancestors had a fold since time immemorial', and Henry de Fenhow held 'one fold pertaining to his free tenementum since ancient times'.[142]

Where medieval lords did maintain full jurisdiction was over the day-to-day operation of folds and over the creation of new ones. In 1346 the manorial lord in Downham created an extra fold for his own use, and the prior of Ely allowed William Maichel to erect a new fold in Lakenheath in 1327.[143] Landlords were certainly anxious to maintain strict control over the number of folds operat-

[140] An inquisition at Billingford (Norfolk) in 1307 concluded that 'according to the custom and practice of Norfolk, no person had a right to erect a fold in his own land, except the lord, unless for some special reason or grant from him', Blomefield, vol. IV, p. 367. At Redgrave (Suffolk), 'the lord may graunte by copye to any of his tenntes a fold course within the mannor and that none can be levyed without the lords lycence', BL Add.Ms 31970 f.77.   [141] *Pinchbeck register*, vol. II, p. 224.
[142] CUL Add.Ms 4220 f.134.   [143] WSROB 651/35/2; CUL EDC 7/15/I/6.

ing in their villages, an attitude illustrated in a forthright Mildenhall inquisition which stated 'that no-one else in this village shall have a fold, except at the will of the aforesaid abbey [of Bury] and this by its authority'.[144] Any peasant who illegally erected a fold was ordered to dismantle it by the manorial court, and failure to do so resulted in swift and effective retribution by its officials. Jurors in Barton Parva were repeatedly enjoined to identify those who had illegally erected folds, and when John de Ingham did just that in fields to the west of Ingham village in 1332, it was promptly destroyed.[145] In Mildenhall a posse of armed manorial officials marched on a fold belonging to Thomas de Cavenham which had been illegally 'erected on his lands in the village of Mildenhall, and they broke the stakes and hurdles and then carried them away', because Bury abbey claimed to have the right 'to throw down any fold thus erected'.[146]

Lordship was patently an important influence on Breckland's pasturing arrangements, but which lord assumed superiority in villages comprised of more than one manor? It seems that each village had an appointed 'chief lord of the village' who took responsibility for corporate farming arrangements and possessed supreme authority for foldcourse regulation over all the village lands. These lords, one to each vill, are listed in the *Nomina Villarum* of 1316, and the position usually corresponded with lordship of the largest manor in the village.[147] Yet where the open-fields of two villages overlapped, and where manorial jurisdiction crossed parish boundaries, chief lords could still clash with one another over foldcourse rights. In 1383, John Burgess, the Bishopric of Ely's bailiff at Northwold, ordered the destruction of a fold belonging to a Methwold peasant near the village boundary. However, the Duchy of Lancaster's court at Methwold declared this action in breach of its own jurisdiction, and promptly exonerated the peasant and amerced Burgess 16s.[148]

The right of the chief lord to co-ordinate foldcourses and fold grants was also implicitly challenged by petty landlords eager to establish some autonomy for themselves and for their tenants. In a running dispute with the abbot of Bury in the early fourteenth

---

[144] CUL Add.Ms 4220 f.135.
[145] WSROB e.7/24/1.3, court held February 1385; CUL Add.Ms 4220 f.90.
[146] CUL Add.Ms 4220 ff.134–5.
[147] I am grateful to Dr Bruce Campbell for this information.
[148] PRO dl30.104/1478 m.2.

century, lord Thomas de Battisford detained rents and tried to establish an extra fold in Fornham, and there was some dispute over fold rights between the Clare and Bury manors in Mildenhall around the same time.[149] In Lakenheath the situation was complicated by the presence of two co-holders as chief lords, namely the prior of Ely and the Honor of Clare.[150] In fact this conflict of interest was resolved in 1332 when the Clare fee was granted to Ely, but previously there had been significant clashes between the two parties over the right to erect certain folds. In 1310 the Clare bailiff had set boundary markers on the prior's land without permission, and in 1318 eight men threw down a Clare foldcourse on the express instructions of the prior. In 1327 it was said that a Clare tenant had obtained permission from the Clare steward to erect a fold, but for three successive years the Ely officials had dismantled it as often as it had been raised.[151]

The period of greatest diversity of foldcourse ownership, and of the system's greatest flexibility, was immediately before the Black Death, but thereafter a long and gradual process of change resulted in a reassertion of seigneurial monopoly over fold ownership in Breckland. The slowly changing pattern of landholding in the five centuries after 1350 inevitably encouraged the concentration of folds into fewer hands. As landlords purchased copyholds and freeholds to streamline agrarian operations, so they gradually gained control of peasant foldcourses. At Risby a fold attached to the land of a leading freeholder, Dulae de Risby, was rendered in the hands of the cellarer of Bury in 1349, and was subsequently used by the demesne.[152] Often the process took longer, and the free half-acre with le Breyerefold in Flempton was held by a variety of tenants in the fourteenth century, but by 1496 had fallen into the lord's possession where it subsequently remained.[153] Other landlords became much more aggressive in asserting their control over foldcourses, often committing overt infringements upon customary peasant rights. Renewed interest in sheep farming in the sixteenth century heightened seigneurial desire and commitment to secure control of all folds within their jurisdiction, and to rational-

---

[149] De Battisford was also indicted for rioting offences at Bury in 1327; WSROB E.3/15.7/2.2 and E.3/15.6/1.6, court held October 1345. CUL Add.Ms 4220 f.125.

[150] *Feudal aids with other analogous documents 1284–1431*, vol. v (London, 1908), p. 47.

[151] CUL EDC 7/15/II/Box 1/3 m.47 and Box 1/9 m.2.

[152] WSROB E.3/15.13/2.11, sheep account.

[153] WSROB 449/2/122. Similarly, in 1453 the Fornham (A) demesne absorbed a foldcourse formerly belonging to Thomas Taylor, WSROB E.3/15.7/2.10.

ise the existing foldcourse structure. Demesne courses were expanded, peasant folds absorbed,[154] and discretionary, temporary folds ceased. Where purchase proved slow or unsuccessful, some lords turned to violence and others to judicial tactics. At Sturston in 1597, Edmund Jermyn evicted 17 tenants, appropriated lands and seized foldcourses to accommodate his rapidly expanding pastoral activities.[155] In Eriswell around the same time, the legitimacy of a peasant fold of 300 sheep lying over part of the fallow arable was disputed by the lord's lessee, who shamelessly resurrected his seigneurial right to apportion 'liberty of foldage and the sheepcourse for 2000 sheep in the said village and fields of Eriswell', claiming that folds could only be erected 'by the licence of the lords of the manor for the time being and not otherwise'.[156] This was certainly true for temporary folds, but in this case the fold was held by tenurial right, and the defendant rejected the need for such a licence, arguing that he and his ancestors had enjoyed use of 'commoning pasture for 300 sheep in the said three fields, in each year when the said fields lie fallow and unsown as pertains to his messuage and lands, and they also have the right to erect a fold' over whichever of their own lands lie fallow.[157]

In general, the pace and extent of foldcourse reacquisition by landlords varied according to local conditions and seigneurial disposition. A stubborn tenant determined to uphold his customary right would delay a landlord seeking to monopolise fold ownership, as in the Eriswell case where the tenant's claim was in fact upheld. Most landlords were prepared to bide their time, and probably closed their grip in the period when land engrossment was at its height, around the early eighteenth century. Compare the sufferings of Sturston at the hands of Edmund Jermyn with the experience of Lakenheath. By 1597 monopoly of fold had been secured in Sturston, yet at Lakenheath in 1649, of six sheepwalks, three belonged to the manor farm, two as copyhold property to the Styward family, and one as freehold to Lady Waldegrave.[158] It was

[154] Allison, 'Sheep corn husbandry', pp. 22–3.
[155] Allison, 'Lost villages of Norfolk', p. 136.
[156] WSROB E.18/400/1.3, unmarked folio. The exact entry reads 'liberte del foldage et corse de barbits pour 2000 berbits dans le dit ville et campes de Ereswell'. Folds could only be erected 'per licence del Seniors del Manor pour le temps etant et ni allors'.
[157] 'Common de pasture pour 300 barbits dans le dit trois campes chesconeanni quant le dit campes giser [*sic.*] freshe et unsoane comme a son messwage et terres appourtent et ils auxi ont use de erect un folde'. An almost illegible addition to the folio appears to be a list of regnal years in which court rolls ratified 'fre dedes . . . per lever de foldage'.
[158] Crompton, 'Lakenheath warren', p. 20.

not until the next century that successive generations of Stywards managed to secure all fold rights in the village.

Seigneurial involvement in the pasturing arrangements of the medieval village was not confined solely to regulating foldcourse ownership. It was the chief lord's responsibility to organise pasture for the sheep of all peasants who did not possess foldage rights, although there was much variation on its precise mechanisms. On some manors, peasant sheep were incorporated into the lord's fold and tended by the manorial shepherd, as at Culford where tenants were compelled to elect a man 'to keep the sheep of the lord and the sheep of the free and customary tenants in the lord's fold'.[159] In larger villages, where there could be over 2,000 peasant sheep, it was necessary to have a separate village flock, or a *collecte* fold as it was called at Barnham, Brandon, Lakenheath and Wangford.[160] Again, shepherding these communal flocks was a seigneurial responsibility, and the Lakenheath manor paid 4s. each year to 'the village shepherd', whilst in Brandon the 'shepherd of alien sheep' was paid in kind.[161] On some manors the compulsion to fold in manorial flocks was restricted to customary peasants only, and freemen were permitted to keep sheep in other freemen's folds. Thus in 1283 Cecilia le Reeve of Sapiston kept seven sheep in the fold of Peter le Clericus of Honington.[162] On other manors, such as Gasthorpe, tenants had to pay the lord for keeping these cullet sheep, and in West Harling the rate was 1d. per year for every ten sheep.[163] However, the restrictions on cullet sheep recorded by Allison were not common in medieval Breckland, and for most of the period peasants could theoretically place an unlimited number of sheep in the lord's or the communal fold. Restrictions on peasant sheep appear to be a product of the late fifteenth and sixteenth

[159] BL Add.Ms 14849 f.22.
[160] For example, a Lakenheath court noted that niefs and bond tenants should put their sheep '*in falda domini de collecte*', CUL EDC 7/15/II/Box 1/9 m.26.
[161] CUL EDC 7/15/I/6, for instance, yet in the aftermath of the Black Death the shortage of labour meant that this shepherd had to be elected from surviving tenants, CUL EDC7/15/II/Box 2/17 m.16, court held October 1350. Brandon, PRO sc6.1304/23.
[162] Powell, *Suffolk hundred*, appendix, Sapiston entry.
[163] Blomefield, vol. I, pp. 168 and 200. In most villages it was not necessary to pay for this foldage, unless peasants specifically wanted extra pasture for their sheep. At Risby in 1340, 15s. was paid for lambs especially pastured in le Hyde woods, WSROB E.3/15.13/2.9. At Culford Walter Curteys could graze his sheep without payment, but if he required additional pasture in the lord's foldcourse beyond 'Timworthesty', then he was obliged to pay the abbot of Bury 20s., BL Add.Ms 14849 f.19.

centuries when seigneurial control over sheep farming was increasing.[164]

In some villages, peasants without folds could purchase an exemption from keeping their sheep in the designated fold, a practice common elsewhere in East Anglia. Such exemptions were known as 'outlayr' at Fakenham Magna and began after the end of shack on 2 February – in 1330, 228 sheep were thus exempt at 1d. a head.[165] On the manor of Fornham (C), customary tenants had the right to buy 'shepselver', which operated between 3 May and 1 August, and allowed their sheep 'to lie outside the fold of the lord' at a cost of $\frac{1}{2}$d. each. In 1328, the owners of 45 sheep exercised this right, although the option was not taken in 1327 and 1329.[166] Peasants at Harling Thorpe had to put their sheep in the lord's fold, but could pay at the rate of 1d. per five sheep to fold them on their own lands.[167] It is difficult to be certain why some manors had this facility and not others. Perhaps manors did this rather than grant temporary fold licences, because in practice they amounted to the same thing. Whatever the reason, the existence of temporary folds and of 'shepselver' illustrates the occasional need to allow peasants the freedom to manure their own lands. Why else would they pay to extricate themselves from a free and convenient source of summer feed?

There were two distinct phases of foldcourse operation in the course of the agrarian year, and, as these exemption payments indicate, the summer months (normally 3 February to 31 July) were the more significant. In the period after harvest known as 'shack', cattle and sheep grazed on the stubble of the unsown arable, tathing it for the coming season. One suspects that at night the sheep were folded according to their fold, but that during the day the owners could graze them as they wished. There were some areas exempt from shack, such as pastures held in severalty all year round and a few arable closes, but in general it was not until the sixteenth century that landlords began to remove large areas of land from shack grazing.[168] The main concern of court ordinances in this period was to protect the stubble and prevent peasants from cutting and carrying it out of the fields.[169] The length of shack,

[164] See below, chapter 5.   [165] BL Add.Roll 9100.
[166] WSROB E.3/15.6/2.7–2.9.   [167] Blomefield, vol. I, p. 200.
[168] See below, chapter 5, p. 294.
[169] For example on the Bury abbey estate at Fornham, WSROB E.3/15.7/1.2, court held March 1339 and E.3/15.7/1.6, court held October 1347.

alternatively known as open or common time, varied from village to village. At Mildenhall in 1431 a man was amerced for keeping a meadow enclosed between Michaelmas and 2 February 'at the time when it ought to be open' according to ancient custom.[170] In many places, shack spanned from 1 August to 2 February.[171] This did not allow villagers to release their animals into the fields immediately, for they had to wait until all the corn had been removed. Allison has shown that local climatic conditions often decided when animals were allowed into the stubble,[172] and in medieval Breckland the decision rested with the chief lord's bailiff or reeve. Short of pasture after a hard summer, all the shepherds in Brandon were amerced for putting sheep into the fields before the corn had been removed and 'against the advice of the bailiff', and ten men were amerced at Hilborough in 1311 for a similar offence.[173] In other villages, the same principle applied, in that tenants had to keep their sheep off the stubble until the lord's flocks had taken first bite, which was the case at Barton Parva.[174]

When the shack period had terminated, access to the fallow arable was restricted to the respective foldcourse owners. At Barton Parva, this was known as 'le severall tyme'.[175] The land to be used for spring crops was fenced off from the remaining fallows, and these could now only be grazed according to the foldcourse in which they lay. The village sheep were rounded up and kept permanently within their designated individual or collective folds. Thus at Hilborough in 1374–5, William Michel paid for grazing up until 2 February 'and not beyond because afterwards those sheep were placed in the lord's fold'.[176] As the area under fallow was limited by this time of year, most flocks relied on the heathland for food. The regulations concerning peasant sheep in the summer were strictly

---

[170] WSROB E.18/451/4, court held October 1431.

[171] The tendency for shack to span this period (from the feast of St Peter Advincula to the Purification of the Blessed Virgin Mary) was common throughout Breckland. One exception, however, was Fornham St Martin, where shack probably extended until 3 May, see above n. 166.

[172] Allison, 'Sheep corn husbandry', p. 19.

[173] Bacon 291/1, court held September 1327. Peasants were also amerced for releasing cattle into the stubble before the lord's animals and without the bailiff's assent, Bacon 293/13, court held September 1407. NRO Hilborough Deposit Box T (Daleth), i, court held September 1311. The Lakenheath reeve was amerced for allowing sheep to be removed from folds before completion of the harvest, CUL EDC 7/15/II/Box 1/9 m.10.

[174] John Knyt was amerced for failure to comply with this by-law in 1379, WSROB E.7/24/1.3, and in 1523 the court ordered that no-one should place sheep in the stubble 'before the lord's flocks', E.18/451/69 f.45.   [175] WSROB E.18/451/69 f.67.

[176] NRO Hilborough Deposit Box T (Daleth), vii m.2.

observed and enforced. At Herringswell a tenant who continued adhering to his shack rights was amerced for grazing sheep 'in the period that he ought not', and a Methwold man pastured his sheep in Northfield 'beyond the customary time'.[177] Indeed, a sixteenth-century Elveden inquisition established that after shack, inhabitants 'had no libertye of feedinge within the same parcell of foldcourse'.[178]

The operation of foldcourses amongst all this sown land was only possible with the use of mobile fences and hurdles to protect the crops from wandering sheep, although numerous damage presentments in court rolls show that this was only partially successful. Documents often refer to people 'raising folds', which describes the physical act of staking wattled fencing into the ground. A frequent condition of servile tenure was to carry hurdles for the lord's foldcourse, although in some areas of East Anglia this service had been commuted for a cash payment by the late thirteenth century.[179] At Bridgham this rent amounted to 74 hurdles each year, and these were carefully recorded as part of the stock of the manor.[180] Holders of full-lands at Brandon had to provide eight hurdles a year with stakes to keep them upright, and were compelled to move the bishop's fold as required.[181] The service rankled with some tenants, for courts consistently amerced them for failure to comply. At Fornham (A), John de Hinderclay paid 1d. for 'contempt because he refused to carry the lord's fold', two Hockham men were amerced for not erecting 'foldgates' in specified places, and Bartholomew Clement of Brandon 'detained 12 fold hurdles in rent'.[182] Most Breckland manors bought sedge and wood so that their shepherds could wattle more fences for extra cash, a practice which would have won approval from the author of a well-known treatise on farm management.[183] On other occa-

---

177 WSROB E.18/451/69 f.112, court held July 1532; PRO DL30/104/1471 m.3, court held July 1367.   178 WSROB J515 f.77.
179 Harper-Bill, *Blythburgh priory*, no. 285.   180 PRO SC6.1132/10.
181 CUL EDC G3/27 f.191. At Coney Weston customary tenants had to carry the lord's hurdles twice annually, Bodleian Ms Gough Suffolk 3 f.35. Other tenants of Bury abbey were similarly burdened: for Ingham, see CUL Add.Ms 4220 f.84, for Culford see BL Add.Ms 14849 ff.20 and 28.
182 WSROB E.3/15.6/1.5, court held June 1345; NRO Ms 13848, court held May 1373; Bacon 289/24.
183 Accounts abound with such payments to shepherds. The author of the Seneschaucy advocated that 'each shepherd . . . ought to cover, enclose, repair and do hedging, fences and hurdles', D. Oschinsky, ed., *Walter of Henley* (Oxford, 1971), p. 287. For an example of purchases, see the Downham court roll of 1345–6 WSROB 651/35/2.

sions, they were purchased complete from the markets at Bury and Mildenhall.

The various permanent pastures would also be cleared of grazing animals after shack, and then exploited according to foldcourse dictates. The peasant great cattle – their oxen and cows – were herded together and tended by an elected official. The herd grazed at the bailiff's direction, but had access to the fallows. Any other peasant livestock was kept in their owners' enclosures, or on roadsides, but particularly on communal greens which were normal features of Breckland villages.[184] The importance of permanent summer pastures for sheep is emphasised by the number of disputes in which they feature. In modern times on Lakenheath warren, it requires around 150 acres of pasture to sustain 100 sheep for seven months, and even a rough calculation indicates that the pressure of animals on the medieval heaths was considerable.[185] In the search for suitable pastures, shepherds would herd their flocks into neighbouring parishes, and courts at Langford were constantly fining men from Bodney, Buckenham Tofts, Cressingham, Didlington, Ickburgh and Stanford for illegal grazing with sheep on its heathland.[186] Meanwhile, lords and their tenants wrangled for more permanent rights to pastures. In 1288–9 the Queen's mother, in right of ward, was in dispute with 100 inhabitants of Icklingham who all grazed on a common pasture in the village which she claimed to hold in severalty.[187] A different Icklingham pasture, this time on the Elveden road, was the source of an inquiry after it had been claimed 'that all commoners of the said village of Icklingham are allowed to place and have in the said pasture commoning for their sheep, that is after the lord's sheep'. The qualification *after* or *behind* the lord's sheep suggests that the lord was denying them access to the pasture at the beginning of shack, a suggestion substantiated by the jury's acceptance that the lord 'ought to have his bite in the said pasture with his sheep without obstruction from others. And if other sheep are in the said pasture

---

[184] Evidence of village greens abounds. Mildenhall, together with its outlying breck-fen hamlets, had a number, such as 'le commen grene apud Halywell', WSROB E.18/454/1.3 f.79; manorial accounts refer to many others, greynesgrene, messagesgrene, beksgrene and so on. Coney Weston clustered to the north and east of 'south green', Bodleian Ms Gough Suffolk 3, and there was a Countessgrene in Northwold, NRO Ms 18630 m.30. For Ampton, see CUL Add.Ms 4220 f.82.

[185] I am grateful to Robin Watson of North Farm, Barnham for this information.

[186] NRO NCC(Petre) Box 8/21.

[187] J. Gage, *A history of Thingoe* (Bury St Edmunds, 1838), p. 35.

before the sheep course of the lord . . . [then] it is permitted for the shepherd of the lord to drive those sheep out of the course as he has done so before'.[188] This can only refer to the lord exploiting the pasture as part of his foldcourse during the summer months. The tenants' claim was upheld.

The overlapping manorial structure sometimes resulted in the development of intercommoning, where certain pastures were shared by communities or foldcourses. An agreement existed between manorial lords whereby these pastures, often on parish boundaries or where foldcourses abutted, were to be grazed by their respective flocks. In Culford, Bury abbey agreed with the lord of Easthall manor that the abbey should have twice as many sheep on a certain pasture in the village, so that if the abbot 'had 600 ewes in this pasture, the lord of Easthall ought to have 300 ewes'.[189] A large pasture provided bite for three flocks between Risby, Flempton and Hengrave, and to the west of Risby two pastures totalling almost 25 acres were 'used both with ye flocks of ye lord of Risby et flock of ye lord of Hyham'.[190] Areas of intercommon have also been identified on heathland between Troston and Honington, Barnham and Thetford, and Ickburgh and Stanford.[191]

Allison stressed that all these complex pasturing and cropping arrangements were designed to ensure effective manuring of the poor soils, and manorial accounts occasionally indicate the high value placed on tathe by lord and tenant alike. In Feltwell in the early fourteenth century, land lying *warecta* was valued at 4d. per acre, but the same land composted by carts was rated at 24d.[192] On the Coney Weston demesne, the tathing potential of the lord's fold was carefully analysed and recorded; 'the lord's fold is able to manure each year 60 acres of land and the manure is valued at 12d. per acre'.[193] At Fornham (A) immediately prior to the Black Death

188 NRO Ms 13187, court held November 1386: '*quod omnes communarii predicte ville de Ikelingham licite possunt et debent in predicta pastura cum bidentibus eorum communicare quotiens illis placet videlicet aretro bidentes domini . . . debet habere annchaciam [sic] suam in pastura predicta cum bidentibus suis sine impedimento aliorum. Et si alicuius bidentes sunt in dicta pastura ante cursum bidentium domini . . . licitum est bercarium domini qui pro tempore fuit illas bidentes extra cursum predictum abfugare'.*   189 BL Add.Ms 42055 f.8.

190 WSROB 2753/17/16 ff.37 and 40.

191 WSROB HA513/30/13; T.99/2; NRO NCC(Petre) Box 8/29. This practice was of some antiquity, as Darby has identified it on the light soils of east Suffolk at Domesday, H.C. Darby, *A Domesday geography of eastern England* (Cambridge, third edition, 1971), p. 174; see also D. Dymond, 'The Suffolk landscape' in *East Anglian Studies*, ed. L. Munby (Cambridge, 1968), pp. 41–2.   192 PRO SC6.931/20.

193 BL Harl. 230 f.155.

the value reached 24d. per acre.[194] But who received the benefit of this valuable tathe, and was it applied equally across all of the open-fields? Allison commented that some areas of arable lay outside foldcourse jurisdiction:[195] if this were so in medieval Breckland, then how would they be manured and cropped?

There were two basic methods of tathing arable land: by direct folding of sheep, which was the most important method, or by collecting dung deposited elsewhere in carts and then spreading it on the appropriate land. It is certain that the permanent and temporary peasant foldcourses grazed primarily over peasant land, but what of the large demesne and collected folds? There are strong *a priori* grounds for assuming that demesne arable was the main recipient of this manure. First, the obvious rationale behind sei-gneurial insistence that all sheep be collected into his fold was to provide the demesne with sufficient manure, although this would be contrary to Allison's observation that tathe was dissipated throughout the open-fields without tenurial distinction.[196] Yet why should the lord assume responsibility for the shepherding and pasturing of peasant sheep without some positive incentive, and what greater reward than exclusive use of the dung for his infertile soils? Secondly, as demesne arable lay in larger blocks than did tenant land, then presumably selective and confined tathing there by manorial flocks would be more viable, especially in peripheral manors. Indeed, this would comply with the trend towards less formal regulations suggested for peripheral manors. What evi-dence is there to substantiate these suggestions?

Indirect evidence suggests that demesne and collected folds possessed bite over both tenant and demesne arable in central villages, so that the open-fields were tathed regardless of owner-ship. Nevertheless, whilst some tenant land might occasionally have gone short of manure, one suspects that the demesne seldom did. On such meagre soils it was not in the lord's interest to demand a monopoly on tathe, for depriving tenant land of dung would induce progressive soil exhaustion and ultimately land abandon-ment. Fewer tenants would mean lower rent income and a shortage of labour to work the demesne cheaply, particularly through labour services. Furthermore, the small size of *peciae* in central manors would have rendered selective demesne grazing difficult and inefficient. What little evidence exists, tends to confirm this

---

[194] WSROB E.3/15.7/2.2a.   [195] Allison, 'Sheep corn husbandry', p. 16.
[196] *Ibid.*, p. 15.

belief. The Nunns Course in Barnham, noted earlier, grazed on 56 acres in Bradfyld, yet a contemporary rental reveals that the same nuns held only 30 acres there.[197] The Bishopric of Ely's flocks enjoyed bite on four fields in Brandon, but there is no indication to suggest their confinement to demesne land, and peasant cropping was strictly regulated to accommodate the foldcourse(s).[198] Peasant lands were well manured in Lakenheath, because the demesne often paid for the right to some manure from the village fold.[199] At Icklingham too, villagers complained in the sixteenth century that the lord had illegally moved flocks from the town lands against the custom, thus rendering them barren.[200]

Whilst there is no reason for supposing that the area covered by the demesne foldcourses in peripheral manors excluded peasant arable, there are suggestions that some flocks concentrated their tathe more on the demesne. In terms of agrarian practices, these villages represented a transitional zone between the flexible communal arrangements in Breckland proper and the individualism of central East Anglia, and consequently contained elements of each. The transition was gradual, so that arrangements altered by nuance rather than by essence between central and peripheral villages. The Fornhams probably represent the most extreme deviation from central villages on both soil quality and agrarian practices, and so can be used as an example of the possible extent of changes over space. All available evidence from these three villages indicates that the demesne folds did concentrate on demesne arable. The lessee of Fornham (C) was covenanted to keep all manure from the cellarer's flock on the demesne arable and not to dissipate it elsewhere, and Reginald Walkard of Fornham All Saints 'has 60 sheep in the lord's fold to manure the land of the lord'.[201] Such a policy would have encouraged tenants with land lying under the jurisdiction of these foldcourses to apply for temporary folds on their own fallows. All this would encourage greater individualism, but not to the extent that some form of communal control over cropping was entirely absent. Adam Merk was amerced for impeding a foldcourse, presumably by sowing out of shift, and at All Saints in 1360–1, 19

[197] WSROB HA513/30/2 ff.1 and penultimate.
[198] CUL EDR G3/27 ff. 189–90. Also see p. 59.
[199] CUL EDC 7/15/I/13, where this manure was rated at 18d. an acre.
[200] H. Prigg, ed., *Icklingham papers* (Woodbridge, 1901), p. 58.
[201] WSROB 449/2/285; E.3/15.6/1.13. In another peripheral manor, Mildenhall, the lessee of Aspal's foldcourse was not to dissipate the tathe over any other land, CUL Add.Ms 4220 f.134.

acres 1.5 roods of tenant land were leased 'for sowing', whilst a further 28.5 acres could not be leased because they lay 'in the common fields'.[202]

Other factors could have served to obstruct the creation of compact fallows and hence the imposition of foldcourse regulations, notably in peripheral villages. It is difficult to comprehend how small, adjacent arable strips, lying in areas where different manorial and township jurisdiction intermingled, could be subjected to one set of communal sowing and cropping patterns other than shack. Of course, these overlapping areas between villages were the exception rather than the rule, and some special expedient of which we are unaware may have been developed to reconcile the conflicting interests. This apart, the only possible conclusion can be that such lands lay outside the bounds of larger foldcourses or were permitted folding by the tenants' own sheep, both of which would release them from sowing according to communal shifts (although shack regulation would still apply), and allow more individualistic arrangements.[203] Perhaps this explains why two acres in Fornham St Martin were specifically sub-let to Hilda Wynnegold 'without manuring', so that after shack she could presumably crop or pasture them as she pleased.[204] Such individualism is evident in other sub-leases, and when Basil Piryna leased one acre at Merelond to Radulph Oter, 'the aforesaid Radulph manures the said land once during the said term'.[205] There were also areas of the open-fields in central villages which did not lie in the jurisdiction of any foldcourse, which would have absolved these lands from the responsibility of communal cropping. For example, there were at least five folds in Barnham which possessed feed over 45.5 acres of infield land, and yet there were at least 109 acres of infield in the

---

[202] WSROB E.3/15.6/1.5, court held April 1345; E.3/15.6/2.28. The description 'in the common fields' is somewhat confusing, and cannot mean that they were grazed communally throughout the year. Rather, it means that these fields were subject to common rights, or subject to shack until 2 February and then grazed by the foldcourse owner's sheep; evidently, this land was due to lie within a fallow shift for foldcourse grazing this year. There is a similar reference to common fields at Worlington, implying a similar mechanism, PRO C134.89/21.

[203] The suggestion that some lands were exempt from communal sowing regulations is certainly not alien to the sheep-corn districts of East Anglia. Simpson, 'Foldcourse system', p. 89 quotes a claim made by residents of Harthill (Norfolk) in 1634 to be able to sow 'at therre will and pleasuer'.

[204] WSROB E.3/15.9/1.1 m.19, court held in 1276.

[205] WSROB E.3/15.9/1.2 m.5.

village.[206] Were the remainder free of foldcourse jurisdiction, or were there other folds about which the documents are silent?

AGRARIAN TECHNIQUES IN MEDIEVAL BRECKLAND

The discussion in chapter I highlighted the extent of potential and actual differences in agrarian success and productivity from one region to another in medieval England, although the difficulty of measuring and comparing these differences quantitatively was stressed. Such variations were explained not by reference to regional differences in technical knowledge, but to the ability to apply that knowledge successfully. Factors likely to restrict the development of agrarian techniques in marginal regions are the lack of capital and marketing opportunities, and the intrinsic infertility of the soil. In Breckland, soil and climatic factors rendered high-intensity arable farming impossible, and its consistently low grain yields would seem to indicate low agrarian productivity and, by implication, technological backwardness.

When searching for signs of agricultural progress, historians sometimes point to the widespread introduction of leguminous crops, and the more careful preparation of seed-beds.[207] Legumes are important to increasing output because they add nitrogen to the soil, but they struggled to make any impact on Breckland's poor soils and were little used. Yet legumes featured more prominently in sowing schedules a few miles to the east of Breckland on the heavier loams, indicating that their qualities must have been known to Breckland farmers but that a conscious decision had been made not to use them.[208] Preparation of the seed-bed in the Middle Ages was generally limited, and so more assiduous care over ploughing, weeding and then harrowing would air and cleanse the soil, and ultimately raise yields.[209] Such techniques were heavily labour intensive, but were applied with some success in response to high grain prices in eastern Norfolk.[210]

---

[206] WSROB HA513/30/2 f.I.   [207] Grigg, *Population growth*, pp. 36–8.

[208] For the proportion of legumes sown on Breckland demesnes see table 3.12, and see tables 3.10 and 3.11 for comparisons with the loamy high Suffolk element of Blackbourne hundred.

[209] Some authorities believe that the dirtiness of the soil was the major obstacle to higher yields in medieval England, W.H. Long, 'The low yields of corn in medieval England', *Ec.H.R.* 32 (1979), pp. 459–69.

[210] Campbell, 'Agricultural progress', pp. 36–8.

The ploughing of *warecta* land in the summer was an important method of airing and cleansing the soil. It was assiduously practised in eastern Norfolk, where there were often between four and six such ploughings in the late fourteenth century, although Walter of Henley advocated just two.[211] Breckland manors were not exceptional in this respect. A total of 392 acres lay *warecta* at Cressingham between 1362 and 1381 (6 accounts), of which 27 per cent was ploughed once, 29 per cent twice, 22 per cent thrice, and the remainder four times; of 250 acres at Brandon in the 1360s (4 accounts), 31 per cent was ploughed once and the rest twice.[212] Weeding was a customary service on many Breckland manors, but it was still not possible to weed any more than just a small proportion of the sown area by these means. Some demesnes occasionally hired workers for harrowing and '*in sulcis spargendis*', both of which served to cover and protect the sown corn and thus enhance yields. There is also evidence of labour being contracted to break with mattocks the earthen clods remaining after the ploughing of *frisca*. However, this practice was not widespread but largely confined to the peripheral manors, whose better soils would be more responsive to intensive techniques, although even there the proportion of land affected was not high.[213]

If the use of legumes and certain labour intensive techniques were not widespread, do we then condemn Breckland as a good example of backwardness and of limited progress in medieval agriculture? If we do, then it only appears so in comparison with regions of inherently better soils which could sustain and justify such techniques. In fact, judging Breckland's agrarian performance by its failure to adopt certain intensive farming methods on soils where such techniques were inappropriate is misleading; such a test is relevant to good soils, but not to poor. Given the absolute limitations upon medieval agrarian technology, it would be very difficult to increase yields per acre in Breckland, and so why should its farmers have attempted such a feat? On the contrary, their

---

[211] Britnell, contribution to *Agrarian history of England*, vol. III (forthcoming).

[212] NRO DCN Supplement (R187A); Bacon 647–9 and PRO SC6.1304/30.

[213] For instance, see the cellarer of Bury's manor at Risby, where in 1340 a 'harrower and furrow spreader' had been employed between 29 September and 3 May, WSROB E.3/15.13/2.9. In 1398–9 this task was performed by hired labour, since labour services had been annulled: one man was hired for 12 days for '*sulc' sparg' et corn' fug*'' at the wheat sowing. A further 32 days' work were also required for the same task at the sowing of spring crops, E.3/15.13/2.21. The wages paid were low, around 1d. per day, which might indicate the use of child labour.

refusal to increase capital/labour inputs to the levels reached in eastern Norfolk makes good economic sense, because diminishing returns appear at lower levels of input on poor soils. Similarly, maximum profit per acre and maximum profit per unit of inputs were achieved with much less intensive use of labour and capital than on good soils. So if Breckland farmers were to employ the same input levels as their counterparts in eastern Norfolk, then it would amount to a costly over-utilisation of resources.

The example of Breckland reveals the potential dangers of applying such terms as 'backwardness' and 'advance' to medieval agriculture. Both Breckland and eastern Norfolk produced grain for the market, although eastern Norfolk did so on a larger scale and under a more intensive agricultural system. Von Thunen's model would explain the adoption of more intensive agriculture in terms of eastern Norfolk's better access to large markets: in Ricardian terms it was due to its higher soil fertility. Both theories would propose that eastern Norfolk derived a higher economic rent from barley production than did Breckland. It is the difference in economic rent which explains the differing intensities of agrarian techniques between the two regions, and not because one region was 'backward' or 'advanced'.[214] To evaluate the extent of agrarian progress in 'marginal' regions, we should best consider their capacity to overcome the constraints of their environment and location rather than condemn their refusal to adopt farming techniques and methods which were simply unprofitable in that environment and location.

Intensifying production in order to raise yields per acre is only one facet of progressive agriculture, and there are other indicators of progress. The cropping and pasturing arrangements employed in Breckland were remarkably sophisticated and flexible for an open-field system on poor soils, and represented an advanced and complex variation of the basic infield-outfield model. If this does not constitute agrarian progress at the margin, then what does? When market opportunities to increase output presented themselves, these arrangements possessed the facility, not to raise output per acre, but to allow larger areas of poor land to be cropped for longer periods. Breckland raised output by extensive methods, by tilting the balance of convertible husbandry towards arable

---

[214] Hence a 'backward' region might be one which retains an extensive agrarian system when the prevailing level of economic rent merits a more intensive one.

cultivation. Extensions of this kind did not require inputs designed
to raise yields, but inputs designed to maintain them, inputs which
would offset the soil deterioration that inevitably accompanied
reduced fallowing.[215]

Agrarian progress in Breckland is also reflected in the extensive
use of marl and manure. The use of marl is a well-documented
method of conditioning poor soils in many places and periods, such
as in south-west England and parts of Scotland, where acidity was
mitigated with some success by liming and the application of sea-
sand rich in calcium carbonate.[216] Sanding would obviously be
unsuitable in Breckland, and the addition of clay was far more
appropriate because it helped to bind the soil together and raise its
capacity for retaining water. Liming was also important, because it
offset the acidity common in Breckland's soil. Unfortunately there
are few direct references to marling in Breckland accounts, presumably because the task was undertaken by the full-time demesne
workers (the 'famuli') and by unspecified labour services.[217] Yet
indirect evidence for marling abounds. When blasted in kilns, chalk
was ready for direct application to the land as 'burnt lime',
and there were limekilns on the demesnes at Fornham and
Mildenhall.[218] Peasants, too, were active in liming activities, as
illustrated by their leasing of demesne kilns and by their blasting of
chalk at Thetford.[219] In addition, documents frequently refer to
pits being dug through the topsoil to reach the chalk below. Bury
abbey held a 'gravelpet' in Culford and they were also known in

[215] Such inputs were certainly evident when land pressure was greatest, see below, chapter 4, pp. 208, 216–18.
[216] Finberg, *Tavistock abbey*, pp. 88–91; Hatcher, *Duchy of Cornwall*, pp. 12–13. For Scotland see R.A. Dodgshon, 'Land improvement in Scottish farming: marl and lime in Roxburghshire and Berwickshire in the eighteenth century', *Ag.H.R.* 26 (1978), pp. 1–14.
[217] The Mildenhall account of 1408–9 notes that 43 cartloads of clay (*argillum*) were dug and laid on the land, BL Add.Roll 53125. The reference appears because of a temporary shortage of famuli due to illness, and the demesne was clearly forced to rely on hired labour to complete a job normally performed by the famuli. Compare this with the extent of marling in the eighteenth century: a tenant of Wilby was required to put 200 loads of clay on his farm each year, A. Davison, 'Some aspects of the agrarian history of Hargham and Snetterton', *Norfolk Archaeology* 35 (1970), p. 353.
[218] WSROB E.3/15.6/2.58, and perhaps also a peasant limekiln, BL Add.Ms 34689 f.32. Mildenhall accounts regularly refer to lands 'lying near the limekiln'; in 1400 Richard Brenard leased two acres of Holmes' *tentmentum* 'north of the limekiln', WSROB E.18/455/2.
[219] In 1435–6 the Fornham kiln was leased for 30s. 6d., WSROB E.3/15.6/2.57. For Thetford and Brandon see below, chapter 3, p. 166.

Brandon, whilst 'calkepets' abounded in Barnham and Fornham, and there was a 'calkepetwong' in Coney Weston and a 'calkewellehelle' in Cranwich.[220] Rymer Point was peppered with claypits belonging to nine parishes, and there were loam pits (lampetts) and 'lampelonds' in Quiddenham, Cranwich, Mildenhall, Icklingham and Fornham.[221] Less specifically, there were 'marlepetfurlonges' in Culford and Flempton, a 'marlepetwong' in Bridgham, a 'marledwong' in Hockham, a 'marlydlond' in Coney Weston, and a 'marlpet' in Lakenheath.[222] Court rolls clearly demonstrate that peasants exploited these deposits, although on occasions they did so illegally. Three men dug 'cleypittes' in Hockham, six Lakenheath men dug at 'calkesherne', and numerous Tuddenham and Mildenhall men were amerced for extracting clay from Courbehynmell in Barton Parva.[223]

Undoubtedly, the main method of maintaining the fertility of the soil was the application of animal manure, either directly or by transferring it from courtyards to fields in *tumberella*, carts specifically designed for the purpose. The direct folding of sheep on arable land was normally undertaken at night. One Fornham court roll noted how a flock was shepherded on permanent pasture and in woods 'until a certain hour of the day'.[224] This time would likely be the evening, when shepherds drove flocks to their nocturnal resting places. That landlords were anxious to stop flocks from wandering freely across pastures at night is reflected in an order which banned sheep from Mildenhall fens at night, and in a case at Hockham where John Fytte illegally left his flock on the Countess

---

220 Culford, BL Add.Ms 42055 ff.28 and 31 where a freeman held one gravelpit; Brandon, Bacon 295/43; Barnham, WSROB HA513/30/2; Fornham, WSROB HA528 Hengrave Hall deposit 114 f.41; Coney Weston, Bodleian Ms Gough Suffolk 3 f.1; Cranwich, Hilborough Deposit Box T (Daleth), vii m.8.

221 Quiddenham, NRO Phi/493; Cranwich, Hilborough Deposit Box T (Daleth), vii m.8; they appear frequently in the Mildenhall leases, for instance BL Add.Roll 53116; Icklingham, WSROB E.3/10/9.8; Fornham, WSROB HA528/114 f.30.

222 Culford, BL Add.Ms 14849 f.19; Flempton, WSROB 449/2/99; Bridgham, CUL EDR G3/27 f.146; Hockham, NRO Ms 13854; Coney Weston, Bodleian Ms Gough Suffolk 3 f.1; Lakenheath, CUL EDC 7/15/I/34. There was a 'marlhow' furlong in Freckenham, BL Add.Charter 9118. Demesne lands of the abbey of St Edmunds were often well provided with marl, BL Harl. 230 ff.184–7.

223 Hockham, NRO Ms 13848, court held May 1373; Lakenheath, CUL EDC 7/15/II/Box 1/8 m.19, court held May1328; Barton, WSROB E.7/24/1.3, court held October 1381. In eighteenth-century Tottington, it was customary for tenants to have free access to a claypit, presumably a right of some antiquity, NRO WLS XXXVII/16. There was also a claypit in Timworth, BL Add.Ms 7096 f.33.   224 WSROB E.3/15.9/1.1 m.16.

of Norfolk's heath at night.[225] The importance of night tathing is evident from many direct references. In Culford, 'if the tenants (of Easthall manor) have a fold of their own, then the sheep of these tenants ought to lie in the fold of the lord abbot [of Bury] for two nights, and in their own folds for one night'.[226] At Langford, three men were amerced for keeping their sheep from the lord's fold at night, and John Chapman of Northwold was amerced because sheep 'lying outside his fold at night' caused damage to crops.[227]

If the area of fallow arable was limited, or during spells of exceptionally cold weather, the sheep would be folded in sheepcotes standing isolated on the permanent pastures rather than on arable.[228] At Fornham St Martin a large new cote was built for the cellarer of Bury abbey in the late fourteenth century, whilst the abbot's flocks used one on heathland south of All Saints and another at Sykeland near Timworth heath.[229] Every flock had one of these on permanent pasture within the foldcourse, so that Lakenheath accounts mention three cotes, each corresponding with the demesne folds. Large flocks required large constructions, and that at Icklingham in 1335 was built with 27,000 sedges and cost a total of £9 9s. 2d.[230] These cotes would be regularly mucked out with straw, and the compost then carted to the arable fields for spreading before or after seeding. This was supplemented by manure from other animal houses and the manorial courtyard, and accounts often record payments to the men undertaking this unpleasant but invaluable work. At other times, labour services were used.[231] Peasants themselves would collect household refuse from their own yards, supplemented with the waste of domestic animals and pigs,

---

225 WSROB E.18/451/69 f.80, court held March 1528; NRO Ms 2522 m.9, court held September 1382. At Hilborough in October 1311, William Ferthing was amerced for leaving his hoggs in the common heath at night, Hilborough Deposit Box T (Daleth), i.

226 BL Add.Ms 42055 f.8. Marshall, *Rural economy*, vol. II, p. 14, commenting on an experiment to ascertain the value of night folding to barley, writes 'the vestiges of the fold are discriminable to an inch. The crop is thicker upon the ground . . . the ears fuller and much longer'.

227 NRO NCC(Petre) Box 8/21, court held July 1391; NRO Ms 18630 m.27, court held December 1436.   228 M.L. Ryder, *Sheep and man* (London, 1983), pp. 682–5.

229 WSROB 449/2/285; BL Add.Ms 34689 ff.33 and 39.

230 Lakenheath, CUL EDC 7/15/I/4; Icklingham, NRO Ms 13192; in 1342 further expense was incurred on wattles 'to keep out the wind and the cold', BL Add.Roll 25810.

231 Some labour services specifically related to dung spreading. Mollmen at Fornham were required to carry one cartload of manure each year in their own carts, BL Add.Ms 14849 ff.27–8. In 1313 the Risby demesne used ten summer works to cart dung from the manorial courtyard and another fifteen to spread it on the land, WSROB E.3/15.13/2.6. The carriage and spreading of dung were both customary services at Quiddenham, NRO Phi/493.

to add to their own lands. There is no evidence that sheep were allowed to be impounded in courtyards for this purpose, and in fact Richard Walcard of Fornham All Saints was amerced for placing 'his sheep in his enclosure during the summer months'.[232]

Documents seldom indicate the exact amount of land tathed each year, although this depended on the constantly changing relationship between manure available and the area under cultivation. The concern that manure supplies dwindled as pastures were ploughed for arable has little relevance in Breckland because any growth in cultivated area represented only a small proportion of the available pasture: for instance, a 25 per cent increase in the arable area of Eriswell would have resulted in only an 8 per cent drop in the area of heathland. The proportion of the sown area manured on fifteen eastern Norfolk demesnes averaged 27.9 per cent in the late fourteenth century (a range of 12.6 per cent to 44 per cent), and Breckland demesnes appear favourably in comparison.[233] Many accounts record merely the amount of *warecta* land manured in any one year, such as the 52 per cent at Brandon between 1362 and 1367.[234] However, two rare examples from Lakenheath and Cressingham provide a rough indication of the total sown area manured, and the relative importance of direct and cart manuring. Table 2.3 reveals that even in a period of high grain prices Breckland landlords might expect at least one-third or half their lands to be tathed, a better figure than in areas renowned for their progressive agriculture, and a further indication of the integrated nature of arable and pastoral farming in the region.

These statistics, however, conceal the fact that manuring practices were discriminate. Land sown with legumes or poorer cereals (notably drage and oats) were rarely treated with dung, and the tathe was concentrated on land bearing the important cash crops of barley, rye and wheat. Thus at Lakenheath in 1327–8, 192.5 of the 225 acres sown with wheat, rye and barley were manured (86 per cent), and the tendency to forego manuring on oats land is evident at Fornham All Saints.[235] Both these examples also reveal that barley land alone was manured by the use of carts, and not that devoted to the winter crops. Presumably this was because sheep could be folded freely during the shack period prior to the sowing

---

[232] WSROB E.3/15.6/1.12. At Barton Magna (Suffolk), however, a peasant could pay at the rate of 1d. for six ewes to keep them 'at his house' (*ad domum suum*).

[233] Campbell, 'Agricultural progress', p. 36.

[234] Bacon 647–9 and PRO sc6.1304/30.   [235] BL Add.Ms 34689 f.11.

Table 2.3. *Area of demesne arable land manured at Lakenheath and Cressingham (acres)*

Year	Area sown (acres)	Area manured		Proportion of sown area manured (%)
		by fold	by cart	
Lakenheath				
1320–1	382.25	*c.* 230		60.2
1326–7	321.0	164.0	33.0	61.4
1327–8	321.0	162.5	30.0	60.0
1329–30	346	122.0	21.0	41.3
				Mean 55.7
Cressingham				
1362–3	198.0	70.0	16.0	43.4
1363–4	233.0	60.0	10.0	30.0
1365–6	207.5	57.0	23.0	38.6
1373–4	195.5	35.0	18.0	27.1
1375–6	195.0	44.0	18.0	31.8
1376–7	193.75	50.0	12.0	32.0
1380–1	205.0	44.0	10.0	26.3
				Mean 32.7

Sources: CUL EDC 7/15/I/4, 6–8; NRO DCN Supplement (R187A).

of wheat and rye, whereas land awaiting a barley crop remained fallow for longer, sometimes up to four months after shack had terminated. The logistical difficulties of driving flocks onto barley land amidst sown parcels of other crops after shack, plus the dictates of individual foldcourses, must have rendered carts the most practical method of treating it, and the sheep themselves were probably concentrated on the compact fallows instead. Hence straw became an important commodity to lord and peasant alike, for it absorbed and bound the dung from stalled and penned animals and facilitated its transfer to the valuable barley lands. The Downham, Langford and Risby demesnes sold reasonably large quantities of straw to willing peasants.[236] The importance of manure to peasants is

---

[236] Downham, WSROB 651/35/7; Langford, NRO NCC(Petre) Box 8/22; Risby, WSROB E.3/15.13/2.9. The value of straw is stressed by H.S. Bennett, *Life on the English manor: a study of peasant conditions 1150–1400* (Cambridge, 1937), p. 86.

demonstrated in court rolls, where it was sometimes seized as security in pleas of debt.[237] Lakenheath courts also record sales of dung between peasants, the lease of cows specifically for their excreta, and amercements for building dunghills in communal places.[238] Indeed, preparations for the vital barley crop were thorough and highly adapted to local conditions. Most parts of the country sowed barley in April, but some Breckland farmers habitually delayed seeding until early June.[239] Not only did this allow extra preparation and manuring – a crucial consideration on poor soils when barley was to be sown thickly – but it avoided the driest months of Breckland's farming year and gave seedlings the benefit of the year's most consistent rainfall. Furthermore, because barley has a shallower root than winter grains, it was more likely to benefit from any nitrogen artificially added to the soil.

The crucial question is whether manure supplies were sufficient to maintain the arable in good heart, particularly when the area under cultivation was rising. Such a concept is very difficult to quantify, although Titow has devised a crude method of calculating the stock of animals (and hence manure supplies) relative to the area under cultivation. On the Winchester estates before the Black Death the mean animal ratio was 72.7, which he regards as insufficient manuring.[240] In comparison, the Breckland mean of 39.6 (1300–49) seems woefully low for a region of such poor soils.[241] Yet demesnes in eastern Norfolk which possessed an even lower animal ratio were renowned for their high agrarian productivity, which suggests that animal ratios are not always a reliable test of

---

237 Compost valued at 5d. was seized from Alice le Newcomere in Mildenhall and she was ordered to respond to Thomas Hammond in a plea of debt, WSROB E.18/451/2, court held December 1327.

238 In November 1329 Payn Jakes sold a manure heap lying outside his house to John de Wangford, but later helped himself to six cartloads of manure without John's permission, CUL EDC 7/15/II/Box 1/8 m.13. Ranulf le Gardener leased a cow to Adam Outlawe for 6d. between November 1332 and Easter 1333, specifically for its lactage and its dung, Box 1/9 m.25. In June 1335 ten men were amerced for illegally maintaining dung heaps on common land, Box 1/9 m.38.

239 At Eriswell in 1600, barley was sown on 1 June, WSROB E.18/400/1.3, unmarked folio in centre of Ms. Barley was certainly sown later than other spring crops as a matter of course. All the spring crops except barley had been sown at Icklingham by April 1340, NRO Ms 13194.

240 Titow, *Winchester yields*, appendix L. In this calculation, demesne cattle are equivalent to one manure unit each and demesne sheep to one-quarter unit, and the total number of units is then expressed as a function of every hundred sown acres.

241 See table 4.7.

agrarian efficiency.[242] The same is almost certainly true of Breckland, where the practice of manuring land discriminately, of stocking foldcourses with the sheep of others, and of creating new folds as the occasion demanded, all made for a complex system of manuring to which Titow's simplistic calculation cannot do justice.

The widespread use of horses has been taken as a sign of progressive agriculture and high productivity.[243] The ox was stronger, but on light soils the horse was faster and so raised ploughing capacity, which in turn raised productivity.[244] Stotts and affers, small plough horses used throughout East Anglia, were prominent on Breckland demesnes, although some ecclesiastical estates continued to use oxen as well.[245] All the indications are that Breckland peasants kept an even higher proportion of horses than did their lords. Court rolls often describe peasant animals which had wandered illegally into sown areas, and at Downham 42 per cent of such trespasses concerned horses and only 2 per cent oxen, while at Brandon the figures were 40 per cent and 1 per cent. In fact, recent research has suggested that horses were important in saving costs in agriculture rather than raising yields.[246] The main advantage of the horse was its versatility, and costs of upkeep were kept to a minimum by careful feeding – straw and pasture were used during periods of low exertion, and vetches and oats were only provided during more strenuous times.[247]

The absence in Breckland of certain agrarian techniques normally associated with technical progress is not surprising given its unreceptive soils, but this does not then mean that the region stagnated in a technological backwater. Attempts to raise output by intensive methods were largely futile on such poor soils and were

---

[242] Campbell, 'Agricultural progress', p. 30, estimates the mean animal ratio of 30 demesnes to be a mere 34.8.

[243] Hallam, *Rural England 1066–1348* (London, 1981), p. 248.

[244] Roden, 'Demesne farming', p. 14; Campbell, 'Agricultural progress', pp. 36–7. Walter of Henley recognised that the horse worked best on light, stony ground, Oschinsky, *Walter of Henley*, p. 319.

[245] The Bury abbey estates certainly used mixed ploughteams, although nowhere did oxen outnumber horses. At Downham, Icklingham, Hilborough, Hockham, Langford, Methwold and Quiddenham, the ox was almost entirely absent. Horses required stall feeding and so demesnes grew oats mainly for this purpose, and accounts reveal that it was common for them to be stall fed with both threshed and unthreshed oats each night between 29 September or 1 November and 3 May.

[246] Langdon, *Horses, oxen and innovation*, pp. 265–8.

[247] J. Langdon, 'The economics of horses and oxen in medieval England', *Ag.H.R.* 30 (1982), pp. 39–40.

simply not cost-effective, so it would be unreasonable to attaint the absence of such techniques: they might just have increased yields per acre, but they would certainly have raised costs and lowered farmers' incomes. Assiduous application of marl and manure was the most cost-effective method of combating the perennial problem of soil exhaustion, and extremely flexible and elaborate cropping and pasturing arrangements were evolved in order to maximise the area of land manured each year. Breckland farmers were encouraged to adopt these techniques because market opportunities were sufficiently attractive. In periods of high demand for grain, the basic infield-outfield system became more sophisticated, and expedients were adopted which were designed to facilitate tathing of the arable, developments which can only be construed as technological advance at the margin. Whether farmers were completely successful in offsetting soil deterioration in the periods of greatest pressure is difficult to establish precisely, although the indications are that they fought a losing battle. However, any failure is more suitably explained by reference to the limitations of medieval agrarian technology in general and to the overall level of grain prices, which was not high enough to encourage the adoption of more progressive techniques. There is no evidence to suggest that Breckland farmers were wilfully ignorant or primitive.

Within the bounds of medieval agrarian technology, farming practices in Breckland represented an innovative and highly adapted method of exploiting meagre soils. The heathland provided an insuperable obstacle to extensive arable cultivation, but was otherwise a fully integrated component of the agrarian system. The heath plants sustained large flocks of sheep whose manure warded off soil deterioration on the open-fields, an interdependence of considerable antiquity.[248] Breckland therefore reinforces the view that, outside the rigid communalism of the Midland system, agricultural techniques in marginal regions could be flexible and innovative. The explanation as to why such a complicated system developed in Breckland lies in the wider debate on the evolution of field-systems, but manorial structure, soil

---

[248] S. West, 'West Stow: the Anglo-Saxon village', vol. 1, *East Anglian Archaeology* 24 (1985), p. 169. For a comparable development on the Suffolk Sandlings, see P.H. Armstrong, 'Changes in the land-use of the Suffolk Sandlings; a study in the disintegration of an ecosystem', *Geography* 58 (1973), pp. 1–8.

quality and market forces all played a part.[249] As Kosminsky wrote of medieval East Anglia, 'here we have the core of the population of England, and a series of important centres of industry and trade, and here consequently were the prerequisites for the development of agriculture'.[250]

[249] Campbell, 'Population change', p. 174.
[250] Kosminsky, *Studies in agrarian history*, p. 142.

Chapter 3

EAST ANGLIAN BRECKLAND: A MARGINAL ECONOMY?

A MARGINAL ECONOMY

If the level of peasant incomes and the timing of regional development in the Middle Ages did depend upon inherent crop-growing capacity, then there is no doubting Breckland's marginal status. At Domesday the concentration of ploughteams – which roughly measures the area cultivated – was low, and in central districts rarely exceeded two ploughteams per square mile. Lackford and Grimshoe hundreds harboured the worst tracts of land and consequently returned the lowest figures in either Norfolk or Suffolk (table 3.2). Even the land which was cultivable was among the poorest in East Anglia. Pre-Black Death valuations of demesne arable land in eastern Norfolk were sometimes as high as 36d. per acre, yet at Sedgeford on the Goodsands it reached only 8d.[1] Table 3.1 provides some Breckland valuations.

In 1302 only 40 per cent of Culford parish was given over to arable land, and at Elveden the proportion was substantially less, around 20 per cent.[2] In peripheral parishes, this figure would have been progressively larger. But the heathland pasture which dominated Breckland parishes was also of poor quality. In 1086 the region had one of the lowest concentrations of meadowland in East Anglia, and late thirteenth-century valuations reflect its scarcity. The Coney Weston demesne had 335 acres 3 roods of arable and only 3 acres 1 rood of meadow at 48d. an acre; meadow in Culford was valued at 18d. and at 36d. in Fornham (A) with a range of 20d. to 60d.[3] The soils were too porous to support decent meadow

---

[1] Campbell, 'Agricultural progress', p. 28; Williamson, 'Peasant holdings', p. 227.

[2] Culford calculation made from the extent of 1302, BL Harl. Ms 230 f.147; the parish consists of 2,229 acres. At Elveden in 1646 there were 1,430 acres of arable land in a parish of 7,128 acres, Postgate, 'Historical geography of Breckland', p. 75.

[3] Figures taken from the sources cited in table 3.1.

Table 3.1. *Demesne arable valuations in Breckland before the Black Death (pence per acre)*

Demesne	Year	Value (d.)	Range
Barton Parva	?	6.3	3–6
Brettenham	1324–5	4.4	—
Bridgham	1251	8	—
Cavenham	1348	4	—
Coney Weston	1302	6	—
Cressingham Mg.	1283	10	—
Culford	1348	2	0.5–6
Euston	1283	1	—
Fornham (A)	?	4.7	2–16
Hengrave	1334	4	—
Hilborough	1256	2	—
Methwold	1347	2	—
Northwold	1251	4	—
Risby	?	4	—
Rushford	1271	2	—
Worlington	1322	3	—

Sources: CUL Gv.iv.4 f.108; NRO Ms 15170; CUL EDR G3/27 f.146; PRO C135.87/27; BL Harl. 230 f.155; Blomefield, vol. III, p. 426; BL Add. Ms 14849 f.19; Powell, *Suffolk hundred*, p. 83; BL Add. Ms 34689 f.6; CUL Hengrave Hall Ms 1 (1), p. 27; Blomefield, vol. III, p. 437; *ibid.*, vol. I, p. 507; CUL EDR G3/27 f.153; CUL Add. Ms 4220 f.334; NRO Ms 2680; PRO C134.89/21.

grounds, and what meadow existed was confined to the river valleys, thus increasing their susceptibility to flooding. Some of the best meadowland was on the breck-fen edge, where damper conditions encouraged lusher growth.

Poor resources prevented Breckland from supporting a large population, in sharp contrast to much of East Anglia where population was up to three times as dense in 1086 (table 3.2). Nevertheless, although Breckland does not compare favourably with many areas of lowland southern England, it was patently better developed than other 'marginal' regions at this time. In the whole of Yorkshire's North Riding the highest ploughteam density was 1.8 per square mile and in many wapentakes the figure was under 1 (0.3 was

Table 3.2. *Population and ploughteam density in Breckland at Domesday*

Hundred	Population per square mile	Ploughteams per square mile
Lackford	5.4	1.7
Blackbourne	8.0	2.1
Cackclose	12.8	1.6
Grimshoe (west)	5.3	1.1
(east)	6.5	1.3
Shropham (west)	7.5	1.7
(east)	12.5	2.4
Guiltcross	10.8	2.4
South Greenhoe	9.3	1.8

Source: Darby, *Domesday geography of eastern England*, pp. 113, 117, 167 and 173. For greater detail, Darby subdivided hundreds whenever they contained significant variations in density. Only the Breckland elements are given here.

common), and population density did not exceed four.[4] In places this could have been due to the devastation of the north by the Normans, but it also reflects the fact that Breckland, situated in an old-settled part of England, had been colonised earlier than north Yorkshire. Breckland was marginal through soil factors alone, whilst north Yorkshire possessed much higher ground and was also geographically remote from the large grain markets.

Where the production of grain was possible in Breckland, its general performance reflected the constraints imposed by soil and climate. The range of crops which could be grown effectively was restricted to rye, barley and oats, and as soil quality deteriorated so rye and oats assumed greater prominence. Medieval yield data is largely culled from demesne evidence, and the range of Breckland material is disappointingly narrow. In general though, mean yields, particularly those per acre, were significantly below those from regions of better soil. Beveridge estimated that for medieval England the mean yield of wheat was 9.36 bushels per acre, of barley 14.32 bushels and of oats 10.56 bushels.[5] Yields in East Anglia could be high, and demesnes in eastern Norfolk sometimes returned 20

[4] H.C. Darby and I.S. Maxwell, *A Domesday geography of northern England* (Cambridge, 1962), pp. 117 and 121.
[5] W. Beveridge, 'The yield and price of corn in the Middle Ages', in *Essays in Economic History*, vol. I, ed. E.M. Carus-Wilson (London, 1954), p. 16.

bushels to the acre for wheat, barley and oats.[6] Table 3.3 confirms Breckland's poor performance in intensive grain production, and illustrates how it suffered from inconsistent yields. Barley showed the most respectable record, mainly because it was sown twice as thickly as other crops. Oats did quite poorly on land where it might have been expected to flourish. However, the calculated oats yield might not be representative of the actual yields, as many manors fed oats unthreshed to animals, and the quantity thus disposed might have been under-recorded or sometimes not recorded at all. Certainly the evidence from court rolls indicates that oats bore the brunt of damage caused by marauding rabbits and cattle.[7] Table 3.4 demonstrates that seeding rates in Breckland were low, and in absolute terms were well below those in other areas of better soil and high productivity. In eastern Norfolk during the same period, for instance, all crops were commonly sown twice as thickly as on Breckland manors.[8]

The limited potential for intensive agriculture in Breckland is reflected in its low valuations of taxable wealth in relation to its area. In the Lay Subsidy of 1334 it was assessed at between ten and twenty shillings per square mile, which was below average for Suffolk and Essex, and much lower than many parts of Norfolk where wealth was up to three times greater.[9] A similar distinction had been evident in the 1327 subsidy in Blackbourne hundred, which straddles the clays of High Suffolk and the sands of Breckland. The Breckland parishes of Blackbourne were taxed at a mere 18s. 4d. per thousand acres, whilst the high Suffolk component was twice as wealthy at 37s. 5d.[10] All these features serve to emphasise Breckland's status as a region whose resource endowment rendered it far less suitable for agrarian operations – particularly cereal production – than other, better endowed regions. But did this necessarily mean that Breckland was exploited according to the chronology outlined in the population–resources model, or

[6] Campbell, 'Agricultural progress', p. 38.
[7] The extent of the damage to demesne corn by peasant animals is difficult to assess in any given year. However in an exceptional example at Methwold, in August 1381, there were 49 separate indictments for damage to 52 acres of demesne corn, PRO DL30.104/1476.
[8] Campbell, 'Agricultural progress', p. 31.
[9] R.E. Glasscock, 'The distribution of wealth in East Anglia in the early fourteenth century', *Transactions of the Institute of British Geographers* 32 (1963), pp. 114, 117–18.
[10] S.H.A. Hervey, ed., *Suffolk in 1327: being a subsidy return*, Suffolk green books 9, vol. II (1906); the Breckland parishes covered 26,136 acres and were assessed at 479s. and the high Suffolk parishes 40,485 acres at 1,515s. 10d.

Table 3.3a. *Grain yields on Breckland demesnes, net of tithes* (bushels per seed)

Year	Wheat	Rye	Barley	Peas	Large oats	Small oats
Brandon						
1346		3.99	3.71	1.70		2.62
1347		2.85	3.83	2.71		2.99
1354					2.42	
1365		4.14	3.66*		2.00	3.30*
1367			5.52			5.19
1368		1.65	1.65			1.16
1369		2.72	2.68		1.98	1.67
1370		3.55	4.96		1.46	6.37
1371		2.07	4.08			2.38
1372		4.22	4.26			2.76
1386	5.00	5.67*	3.87			4.96
1389		3.38	5.12			3.67*
1390		3.91	4.18			4.30
1391		5.55*	5.31			4.23
1392		4.39	4.54			5.30
1393		2.50	3.91			2.58
1394		4.73	3.21			1.62
1395		4.38	3.41			4.09
Hilborough						
1412		2.07	3.59			
Icklingham						
1330			3.71	1.75		5.23
1331		1.99	1.48	1.67		2.61
1332		2.84	3.39	0.79		4.69
1333	6.21	4.99	6.52	0.73		2.52
1334	4.83	2.27	2.12			
1335	5.50		3.14	7.00		4.98
1340	2.29	1.66	2.95	2.00		2.39
1343	4.18	3.58	5.12	2.89		2.58
Lakenheath						
1356	2.44	2.32	2.30	2.27		2.80
1394	1.88	2.14	1.95	1.67		
1451	1.15	3.94	3.84			3.75
1459		3.45	3.07			
1460		2.48	4.39			
West Harling						
1328–36 (mean)		3.00	2.45	1.60		3.40

Table 3.3a. (cont.)

Year	Wheat	Rye	Barley	Peas	Large oats	Small oats
1367–77 (mean)	3.20	4.25	3.60	4.20		2.70
Wretham						
1302–39 (mean)	7.30	3.10	2.50	3.60		2.60
Barton Parva						
1289	2.13	2.45	5.59	6.65		2.26
1294	2.92	2.05	3.27	2.33		2.02
1297	4.75	3.02	2.46	1.00		2.25
1298	2.75	3.06	3.37	3.17		2.06
1299	2.78	1.99	3.67	4.41		
1300	2.73	2.54	3.10	4.38		
Cressingham Magna						
1363	4.60	3.30	2.99	2.44	2.28	5.54
1376	4.47	4.50	2.88	1.57	3.50	3.00
1416	3.00	3.50	2.44		4.50	
Feltwell						
1345–6	2.50	1.40	3.20	7.60		1.40
1395–6	3.50	3.00	3.50	2.00		3.00
Fornham (A)						
1343	2.73	3.06	3.90	4.80	2.43	4.35
1347	3.22	2.78	4.05	3.14	1.67	6.43
1348	3.43	1.73	3.52	4.08	3.17	4.34
1366	1.45	3.03	3.70	3.30	1.92	2.51
1367	3.02	2.43	3.74	2.61	2.16	
1368	3.62	2.47	2.71	1.67	1.39	1.06
1400	2.10	3.44	3.52*	3.89*	2.00*	6.08*
1401	3.00	2.96	4.05*	3.68*	3.05*	4.00*
1402	3.64	2.58	4.07	3.06	4.43	3.83
1403	3.50	4.21	3.09*	3.10*	2.21*	3.75
1404	2.83	3.88	3.35*	3.36*	3.00*	
1405	2.44	4.70	3.38	3.00*	3.40*	
1409	3.00	2.33	2.53*	2.00*		2.64*
1410	2.21	4.91	2.89	1.54		
1411	3.22	2.31	3.01	4.36*		
1414	3.34	2.19	2.00		2.00*	
1420	3.08	5.34	3.41	3.65*	2.23*	
Fornham (C)						
1299	0.45	3.94	2.58	3.68		2.77
1300	2.99	3.79	3.31	4.19		3.88

Table 3.3a. (*cont.*)

Year	Wheat	Rye	Barley	Peas	Large oats	Small oats
1301	2.94	3.25	2.49	3.96		3.68
1302	3.36	3.00	2.69	2.16		4.40
1328	1.34	1.23	1.18	1.84		
1335	4.21	2.65	2.32			2.44
1336	2.01	3.18	2.42			3.32
1354	2.01	2.00	2.02	1.22	1.68	1.13
1355	1.29	2.54	3.00	2.63		1.28
Risby						
1352	6.31	2.47	2.24	0.85		1.35
1353	3.96	3.27*	3.01	0.73		1.24
1361	3.24	2.50	2.29			1.95
1377	2.01	4.48*	3.13			2.03*

Note:
* Includes an estimate for unthreshed corn.

Table 3.3b. *Grain yields on Breckland demesnes, net of tithes*
(bushels per acre)

Year	Wheat	Rye	Barley	Peas	Large oats	Small oats
Brandon						
1346		5.86	9.89	4.38		4.97
1347		4.76	10.54	4.75		6.65
1354					4.84	
1365		7.24	10.06*		4.00	6.60*
1367			17.57			10.39
1368		3.55	5.44			2.52
1369		5.48	8.77		5.29	3.56
1370		7.40	15.03		3.82	13.53
1371		4.45	12.34			5.20
1372		8.89	13.48			5.87
1386	10.00	11.63*	11.69			10.33
1389		6.98	15.19			8.00*
1390		7.31	12.79			9.05
1391		11.12*	15.24			9.54
1392		8.53	13.19			11.09
1393		4.69	11.39			5.39
1394		9.22	9.49			2.89
1395		8.89	10.36			10.22

Table 3.3b. (*cont.*)

Year	Wheat	Rye	Barley	Peas	Large oats	Small oats
Hilborough						
1412		4.09	11.06			
Icklingham						
1330			10.19	3.50		7.84
1331		3.48	4.08	3.53		5.22
1332		4.86	9.20	1.83		9.39
1333	12.43	8.33	11.08	1.33		4.85
1334	9.67	4.05	5.42			
1335	11.00	5.21	8.87	15.40		10.14
1340	4.00	2.91	8.80	4.00		4.82
1343	8.76	4.88	13.73	6.12		5.83
Lakenheath						
1356	5.50	4.68	9.24	4.17		5.66
1394	6.00	4.29	7.82	3.27		
1451	4.60	7.28	13.80			10.50
1459		8.43	12.27			
1460		5.68	17.79			
West Harling						
1328–36 (mean)		6.00	8.60	2.40		9.70
1367–77 (mean)	7.70	8.50	10.90	8.45		7.80
Barton Parva						
1289	8.05	2.82	14.83	13.70		2.31
1294	10.29	2.15	11.71	4.65		2.02
1297	15.38	4.30	8.42	2.58		3.25
1298	9.91	5.14	13.24	6.33		3.00
1299	10.30	2.54	14.51	7.69		
1300	10.14	3.48	11.42	9.00		
Cressingham Magna						
1363	9.20	6.60	11.98	4.89	9.10	22.18
1376	8.95	9.00	11.54	3.14	14.00	12.00
1416	6.00	6.32	9.13		13.09	
Wretham						
1302–39 (mean)	14.7	6.20	10.20	6.70		10.10
Feltwell						
1345–6	5.00	2.50	9.60	15.20		3.10
1395–6	14.00	7.80	14.40	5.60		10.50

Table 3.3b. (*cont.*)

Year	Wheat	Rye	Barley	Peas	Large oats	Small oats
Fornham (A)						
1343	6.93	6.36	13.62	9.60	6.96	10.14
1347	6.84	5.63*	15.88	6.18	5.60	13.49
1348	8.22	3.58	13.86	9.37	10.36	7.62
1366	3.72	6.10	12.00	6.51	6.03*	5.09
1367	7.93	4.72*	12.37	5.37	5.83	3.78
1368	9.76	4.85	8.75	3.39	4.31	2.12
1400	4.20	6.88*	11.14*	7.78*	4.00*	12.17*
1401	6.00	5.93*	11.88*	7.37*	6.11*	8.00*
1402	7.32	5.16*	12.11	6.11	8.86*	7.67*
1403	7.00	8.42	9.23*	6.19*	6.46*	5.00
1404	5.66	7.76	10.08*	6.73*	8.73*	
1405	4.92	9.40	10.41	6.00*	10.35*	
1409	6.00	4.47	8.22*	4.00*		5.28*
1410	6.20	9.81	8.57	3.07		
1411	6.44	4.61	9.03	9.08*		
1414	6.69	4.38	8.00		6.12*	
1420	7.60	9.76	13.64	6.62*	5.07*	
Fornham (C)						
1299	0.90	7.88	10.32	7.37		5.54
1300	5.97	6.50	9.27	8.37		9.00
1301	5.80	6.31	9.45	11.87		7.36
1302	6.73	6.00	10.78	4.32		8.80

Note:
* Includes an estimate for unthreshed corn.

Table 3.4. *Sowing thicknesses on Breckland demesnes, decennial means (bushels per acre)*

Decade	Wheat	Rye	Barley	Peas	Large oats	Small oats
Brandon						
1340–9		1.69	2.85	1.98		1.95
1350–9		1.81	2.81	2.25	2.13	1.93
1360–9		1.94	3.06		2.22	2.05
1370–9		2.18	3.07	2.00	2.70	2.22
1380–9	2.00	2.04	2.99	2.00		2.20
1390–9		1.88	2.96			2.19

Table 3.4. (*cont.*)

Decade	Wheat	Rye	Barley	Peas	Large oats	Small oats
Bridgham						
1290–9			3.51			4.00
Downham (I)						
1320–9		1.47	2.46			2.00
1330–9		1.62	2.05	1.33		2.00
1360–9		2.11	3.00			1.80
Downham (S)						
1340–9		2.50	2.72			
1350–9		1.96	2.95			2.00
Fakenham						
1330–9	2.00	1.95	3.02	1.64		3.15
Hilborough						
1370–9	2.00	3.00				
1410–19	2.05	3.08				
Hockham						
1380–9		1.82	2.58			1.95
Icklingham						
1320–9			2.75	2.00		1.50
1330–9	2.00	1.73	2.63	1.98		1.90
1340–9	2.21	1.75	2.88	1.98		1.90
Lakenheath						
1300–9		1.66	3.92	2.00		2.00
1320–9	2.46	2.03	3.50	1.98		2.16
1330–9	2.88	2.07	3.52	2.28		2.18
1340–9	2.83	2.04	4.01	3.33		2.02
1360–9	2.65	2.01	3.57	2.25		1.94
1370–9	2.83	2.01	4.00	1.97		2.00
1380–9	3.36	2.03	4.03	2.05		1.99
1390–9	3.51	2.06	4.00	2.07		2.00
1420–9	3.58	1.87	3.73			2.14
1430–9	3.18	1.75	3.84	2.14		3.00
1440–9	3.11	2.12	3.86	2.40		
1450–9	4.00	2.25	4.05	1.87		2.97
1460–9		2.63	4.05			
Langford						
1400–9	2.00	2.04	3.01	1.71	2.66	1.78
West Harling						
1320–9		2.20	3.80	1.50		2.90
1330–9		1.83	3.30	1.77		2.80

Table 3.4. (*cont.*)

Decade	Wheat	Rye	Barley	Peas	Large oats	Small oats
1350–9			2.90	2.00		2.90
1360–9	2.40	2.00	3.00			2.70
1370–9	2.40	1.95	3.00	2.00		3.00
West Tofts						
1310–19		1.51	2.00			2.00
Wretham						
1300–9		2.00	4.00	2.00		3.88
1330–9		2.00	4.00			4.00
1340–9	2.00	1.40		2.00		3.00
Barton Parva						
1270–9	2.98	1.15	3.56	1.31		1.17
1280–9	3.35	1.47	3.51	2.02		1.21
1290–9	3.59	1.26	3.57	2.08		1.25
1300–9	3.50	1.42	3.75	2.00		1.40
1310–19	3.09	1.31	3.47	1.51		1.22
Feltwell						
1340–9	2.00	1.70	2.90	2.00		2.20
1390–9	4.10	2.60	4.20	2.80		3.50
Fornham (A)						
1340–9	2.21	1.99	3.78	2.10		2.22
1350–9	2.08	2.05	3.92	2.10		2.01
1360–9	2.65	2.13	3.67	2.24	3.20	2.31
1370–9	2.69	2.26	3.20	2.30	2.77	2.24
1390–9		1.97	3.57	2.00	2.70	2.25
1400–9	2.00	2.00	3.08	2.00	2.44	1.87
1410–19	2.00	2.00	3.39	2.02	2.90	2.48
1420–9	2.46	1.95	4.00	1.94	2.26	
1430–9	3.10	2.53	4.00	2.35	3.03	
1440–9	3.08	3.00	4.07	2.50	3.00	
Fornham (C)						
1300–9	2.08	1.99	3.95	2.29		2.00
1310–19	2.00	2.61	4.00	2.00		3.00
1320–9	2.32	2.07	3.43	2.01		2.22
Gasthorpe						
1410–19		2.00	3.07	1.56	2.13	2.61
Kennett						
1270–9	3.85	2.48	3.91	2.35		3.00
1280–9	3.79	2.46	3.93	2.20		2.78
1290–9	3.80	1.94	4.41	2.24		2.38
1300–9	3.75	2.03	3.88	2.63		2.35

Table 3.4. (*cont.*)

Decade	Wheat	Rye	Barley	Peas	Large oats	Small oats
Methwold						
1440–9	2.00	2.00	2.50			2.00
Mildenhall						
1320–9	2.94	1.72	3.75	2.06		2.16
1380–9	2.76	1.99	4.02			
Northwold						
1290–9			2.97			

was its economy more sophisticated and efficient than we might have expected?

SETTLEMENT AND POPULATION, 1086–1300

In order to ascertain whether population and resources were balanced or if excessive pressure came to be exerted, it is necessary to describe Breckland's basic settlement pattern and consider any changes which might have occurred in the important period between 1086 and 1300. In fact its settlement history is more complex than the large empty spaces of medieval times would suggest. Anciently, the heavy, central claylands of East Anglia were covered by woodland and wet, clay moorland, which presented daunting obstacles to arable cultivation. On the other hand, the light soils of Breckland, west Norfolk and the Suffolk Sandlings were easily cleared and ploughed, and proved attractive to Neolithic settlers.[11] As a result, Neolithic Breckland was perhaps the most densely populated area of East Anglia, and archaeological evidence suggests that the region maintained its importance throughout the Bronze and Iron Ages.[12] In part the region's importance was derived from its excellent geographical position. It lay at the eastern end of the Lark/Gipping and Ouse/Waveney valleys which provided the main overland connecting routes with the coastal strip of light soils to the east, and it enjoyed ready access

[11] Clarke, *East Anglia*, pp. 24–5.
[12] P.H. Armstrong, *The changing landscape* (Lavenham, 1975), pp. 25–6; Clarke, *East Anglia*, pp. 69–109; A. Crosby, *A history of Thetford* (Chichester, 1986), pp. 3–10; West, 'West Stow', pp. 3–5.

to the sea via the fens. It was this continuous occupation, with the attendant tillage and grazing of the land, which prevented the regeneration of the original vegetation and ultimately caused the debilitation of the soil.

As the soil leached and heath plants became established, so other, wider changes contributed to Breckland's declining importance. The demographic and agrarian expansion of the Saxon age encouraged the development and more intensive settlement of the central claylands, a movement which could hardly have been sustained on Breckland's blowing sands.[13] Yet the region still acted as the gateway to a wealthy East Anglia, and as Norwich and Ipswich grew significantly, Thetford too maintained its status as a sizeable and prosperous town.[14] The basic distribution of modern Breckland villages originates from the Saxon period. Domesday Book, the earliest comprehensive survey, confirms the concentration of villages along the shallow valleys where the soils were slightly less porous. Only a few villages, such as Croxton and Elveden, defied the upland aridity. Elsewhere the main river valleys and their tributaries supported nucleated villages whose arable lands edged nervously upwards into the heaths, and whose parish boundaries and grazing rights were flung across a further three to four miles of heath. On the breck-fen edge, settlements were established on the Breckland sands literally where they met the fen waters, although manorial and parish jurisdiction included both heath and marsh. This strip of high land probably supported a large number of early Saxon farmsteads, which were then abandoned around the seventh century in favour of consolidated villages on their present sites.[15]

Breckland's long and varied settlement history exposes the simplicity of the 'Ricardian model of land colonisation', where it is assumed that the poorest soils were cultivated last. In Neolithic times Breckland was eminently attractive to farmers, whilst the heavy clays of central East Anglia were fertile but unworkable. It required technological changes in the durability and effectiveness of the plough before the clays could be properly exploited. Breckland's soil came to be regarded as poor only after technical

---

[13] Clarke, *East Anglia*, p. 163.   [14] Crosby, *Thetford*, pp. 11–24.

[15] T. Briscoe, 'Anglo-Saxon finds from Lakenheath and their place in the Lark valley context', *P.S.I.A.* 34 (1978), pp. 161–70; the 'heath' element in Lakenheath is, in fact, a late corruption of 'hithe', and Lakenheath means the 'landing place of Lacca's people', E. Ekwall, *English place names* (Oxford, 1960), p. 284. See also West, 'West Stow', p. 5.

changes rendered other areas more profitable to cultivate.[16] At Domesday, Breckland could scarcely have been designated marginal by location. In an economic context it stood on the periphery of East Anglia, but it was geographically well placed and as such enjoyed long established inter-regional links. The very thin settlement on upland heaths and the concentration of nucleated sites in river valleys by 1086 indicates that Breckland's soils had been extremely poor since before the early Saxon period. It was this infertility which prevented the region from matching the levels of aggregate growth experienced elsewhere in East Anglia during the late Saxon boom.

There were no new settlements created in Breckland after 1086, although a few had emerged late in the Saxon period. Most of these were small, secondary villages established mainly on the shallower sands of Norfolk Breckland.[17] The only probable example in Suffolk Breckland is Wordwell, a late Saxon village carved out of Culford and West Stow.[18] From Domesday Book it is apparent that the area south of the Little Ouse was less densely settled than the north, a direct function of the aridity of the Suffolk soils. Throughout central Breckland in 1086, villages were small and sometimes hardly larger than hamlets. However, the fen edge, with its wider resource base, was able to support a slightly higher density of population, and villages such as Feltwell and Mildenhall were reasonably large.[19] Not surprisingly, overall population density contrasted sharply with most other areas of East Anglia at Domesday. In many parts of Norfolk and Suffolk there were over thirty tenants per thousand acres, but in most parts of Breckland there was a maximum of fifteen: in Lackford hundred (Suffolk) there were under ten.[20]

The fact that there were no new villages established in Breckland in the two centuries after Domesday evidently contradicts Saltmarsh's claims, but the Breckland sites he visited were of late Saxon origin.[21] In fact, post-Domesday establishments are rare in

---

[16] A clear indication that 'marginality' cannot be applied to soils in some absolute and finite manner. That which constitutes marginal land can change over time according to technological change.

[17] Davison, 'Harling', p. 295, and 'The distribution of medieval settlement in West Harling', *Norfolk Archaeology* 38 (1983), pp. 329–35. See Hallam, *Rural England*, p. 35.

[18] West, 'West Stow', p. 12.

[19] Postgate, 'Historical geography of Breckland', pp. 60–1.

[20] Darby, *Domesday geography of eastern England*, pp. 113 and 117.

[21] Saltmarsh, 'Plague and economic decline', p. 24.

an old settled region such as East Anglia, and are more commonly found on the peripheries of Norman England. Thus, at Domesday, Breckland already harboured as many villages as its resource base could support, and any further expansion could only occur within the existing settlement and manorial structure. Put simply, there were few reserves of colonisable land left in Breckland in 1086. It could be argued, therefore, that this was a region of sub-marginal soils where opportunities for further arable expansion were strictly limited, rather than a region of marginal soils proper. Indeed, did not the confinement of settlement to the river valleys and fen edge create a more diverse economy than one wholly dependent upon the poorest soils and heath? How then can Breckland provide a valid test of the performance of the margin?

Such an argument is superficially attractive yet ultimately illusory. Although soils in the valleys and on the fen edge were better than on the upland heaths, they were still extremely poor and farming was still handicapped by the adverse climate. This feature accords well with historians' accepted definition of marginality – an inability to produce as much per acre as other lands – and the fact that much of Breckland was uncultivable (or 'sub-marginal') does not therefore invalidate it as a test of the margin in the population-resources model. On the contrary, it serves to demonstrate that accepted definitions of marginality are too simplistic and narrow. A model which equates marginality with poor location and infertile land would presumably regard wholly uncultivable areas as worthless and incapable of any development in the Middle Ages. But why should this be so? An area which is sub-marginal for cultivation might not be sub-marginal for pastoral farming or industry. Poor location and low arable potential certainly make for marginality, but true economic marginality is the function of wider factors. Whether Breckland was marginal in an economic sense depended on its success in overcoming the handicaps of its soil and climate. Unfortunately, settlement evidence is an imperfect measure of that success, because the failure to colonise vast tracts of heathland in the twelfth and thirteenth centuries does not imply that heaths were therefore a drag on the economy; indeed, the evidence presented in chapter 2 shows that the sub-marginal heaths were fully integrated into the region's agrarian system. Furthermore, if Breckland villages established mixed economies based on heathland activities and some grain farming, and also on ancillary employment from river and fen, or if they established a specialised role within a wider nexus, then they were merely countering natural limitations and inherent marginality. This argument does not fit easily into the population-resources model, where all poor soil and remote regions are, *ipso facto*, marginal regions. This widely accepted definition of the margin is patently too narrow, because it does not entertain the possibility that poor soil and remote regions may find ways to compensate for their disadvantages in arable farming.

As no new settlements emerged in Breckland in the crucial period 1086–1300, we might argue that a reasonably viable balance between population and resources was maintained, and that arable farming was not stretched to unacceptable limits. Conversely, this would make a really sudden retreat of settlement in the fourteenth century unlikely. Confirmation of this requires an examination of how far arable cultivation was extended within the pre-existing village framework after 1086. Although the period is poorly documented, it is doubtful whether much heathland was brought permanently under the plough. The total area of Breckland's arable had declined between 1066 and 1086, and so any subsequent expansion would first entail the removal of this slack capacity.[22] Thereafter, arable output was undoubtedly raised, although it is impossible to know exactly how far extensive methods contributed. The problem is that whilst some heathland became permanently integrated into the village arable, other areas were cultivated only temporarily and left no documentary evidence. There were certainly some twelfth-century assarts in Blackbourne hundred, which probably represented permanent intakes of heathland, but other decisive evidence is rare, as one would expect from a region of convertible husbandry.[23] Postgate is unequivocal: between the eleventh and thirteenth centuries 'there was little colonisation of the heathland'.[24] Field-name evidence shows that assarting did occur, but not in sufficient quantity to refute Postgate's dictum. On the Bishopric of Ely's demesnes at Brandon, Bridgham, Feltwell and Northwold, the only evidence of assarts in 1251 was the

---

[22] The fall in arable area is shown by a reduction in ploughteams between 1066 and 1086, which in Breckland fell by 74, Postgate, 'Historical geography of Breckland', pp. 62–5. For possible explanations of this fall, see R. Weldon Finn, *Domesday studies: the eastern counties* (London, 1967), pp. 181–5, and 201–4.

[23] For example, 40 acres at Ingham and 'eight acres on Maniebrakes' in Pakenham, Davis, *Kalendar of abbot Samson*, pp. 43 and 89; D.C. Douglas, ed., *Feudal documents from the abbey of Bury St Edmunds* (London, 1932), p. 128.

[24] Postgate, 'Historical geography of Breckland', p. 66.

addition of unspecified 'appendices' to the Estfeld in Feltwell.[25]
The best example is Brettenham, where fields bearing the 'breche'
suffix constituted 31 per cent of demesne area in the early fourteenth century, but in Suffolk the coarse sands presented formi-
dable obstacles to widespread brecking; at Culford the figure was
16 per cent, a mere 3 per cent at Fornham (A), and of all arable in
Coney Weston only 6 per cent.[26] Assarting was neither as widespread nor as extensive as in later periods, and in most medieval
parishes heath remained predominant.

Who was most active in breaking up heathland? Much of the
evidence emphasises seigneurial involvement. A 42-acre breck on
Bury abbey's manor at Culford was part of a larger intake which
included 50 acres of Easthall manor's demesne, and 4.5 acres
belonging to a notable freeman.[27] The same abbey seems to have
monopolised such intakes at Fornham. There appears to be a
parallel here with arrangements in Devon, where peasants were
allowed pasture rights on wastes, but where the right to cultivate
them was restricted to the lords.[28] Whether any compensation was
available to tenants for the loss of grazing and litter over a demesne
breck is uncertain.[29] Peasants were not forbidden to create
brecks themselves, either collectively or individually, but presumably a seigneurial licence was necessary. It was in later centuries
when evidence is more plentiful, for in 1719 John How of
Fakenham Magna was 'permitted to break up 20 acres of the great
heath (of Barnham) and put it in tilth'.[30] Unfortunately, surviving
medieval records do not contain any comparable examples, but
they do reveal small-scale peasant involvement in heathland intakes. At Mildenhall in 1323 bracken from Brademere was sold for
2s., whilst two tenants held 50 acres in the same place for an
unspecified term at the remarkably low rent of 1.54d. per acre –
strong indirect evidence of heathland being converted to arable
with low rents in deference to the initial conversion costs.[31]

25 CUL EDR G3/27 f.150.
26 NRO Ms 15170; BL Add.Ms 42055; BL Add.Ms 34689 f.6; Bodleian Ms Gough Suffolk
 3. At Fornham (C) in the early fourteenth century, brecks constituted only 4 per cent of
 the demesne, BL Harl. 3977 f.101.   27 BL Add.Ms 42055 f.45.
28 Fox, 'Outfield cultivation', p. 29.
29 The existence of common rights over heathland was undoubtedly an obstacle to its
 subsequent colonisation, see G.C. Homans, *English villagers of the thirteenth century*
 (Cambridge, Mass., 1941), pp. 361–3.   30 WSROB HA513/30/39.
31 Bodleian Suffolk Rolls 21. In the same year Robert de Pakenham held three acres of land
 'vocatur le breche', a project apparently initiated by one Thomas de Holmerseye.

Sokemen in Troston held 290 acres of arable and 20 acres of heath from the abbot of St Edmunds, and there are other such references in the *Pinchbeck register* which seem to represent assarts.[32] It is not always clear what tenurial status applied to the new lands. Barlibreche in Coney Weston was held as customary tenure and split between four tenants and contained seven *peciae* (average 1.57 roods), and was an older assart than those 4.5 acres at Culford, whose tenure remained unspecified.[33] The matter appears as varied as it was complex.

There were therefore two basic reasons why so little heathland was converted to arable land in this period. First, the scope for arable expansion was constrained by the sub-marginal nature of the heathlands, and by the structural and technological limitations of medieval agriculture. Secondly, Breckland lay in an old-settled part of England which had realised most of its arable potential prior to the Conquest, and so could not sustain the large reclamations from the waste recorded in other, less developed, regions.[34] Breckland villages certainly grew in the two centuries after 1086, although not as rapidly as in other parts of eastern England.[35] They did come to occupy a larger physical area: archaeological evidence indicates that Caldecote (in Cockley Cley) shifted and expanded in the twelfth century, causing the isolation of the Saxon church, and Chippenham was extended along the edge of the fen towards Snailwell.[36] Land plots became increasingly subdivided and buildings extended, so that tenants at Culford came to occupy one-third or one-quarter parts of messuages.[37] At Lakenheath in 1328 Thomas ad Ripam sold a plot of land to John Hottow for the construction of a new house, and an Ingham man was granted 'one acre of land . . . to build upon' by the cellarer of Bury abbey.[38]

As the pressure on the available arable land intensifed, so it

---

[32] *Pinchbeck register*, vol. II, p. 224; and also pp. 212 and 229 for Coney Weston and Knettishall.

[33] Bodleian Ms Gough Suffolk 3 ff.4–32; BL Add.Ms 42055 f.45. Cash rents would presumably have sufficed on temporary brecks, and only when the intake became permanently encompassed within the outfield was there any need to award it some fixed tenurial status. Robert de Pakenham's breck (above, n. 31) had been elevated to rents of assize by 1323 under 'increments'. His heirs still held the same land on the same basis nearly 60 years later, BL Add.Roll 53116.

[34] See, for instance, the rapid growth rates of villages in areas of northern England, Hallam, *Rural England*, pp. 179–92.   [35] *Ibid.*, pp. 32–40.

[36] Wade-Martins, 'Village sites in Launditch hundred', p. 80; Spufford, 'Chippenham', p. 15.   [37] BL Add.Ms 42055 ff.8–22.

[38] CUL EDC 7/15/II/Box 1/8 m.17; CUL Add.Ms 4220 f.81.

became subdivided between a greater number of tenants. Unfortunately, quantitative and comparative evidence of this process is not plentiful from Breckland, although the small size of many freeholdings in the late thirteenth century indicates that pressure on land resources was intense. At Livermere Parva in 1286 the average size freeholding from the lord was a paltry 3.37 acres.[39] Comparative evidence of subdivision is mainly limited to Hallam's work on the Bishopric of Ely's manors, where the growth of smallholdings is particularly noticeable at Brandon, Bridgham, Feltwell and Northwold between 1220 and 1251.[40] The growth of villages is also reflected in rent rolls. Many accounts contain sections entitled 'increments of rent', which represented amendments to the list of standard rents detailed in some earlier rental. At Lakenheath (Clare fee) these comprised nearly 4 per cent of total rents in 1334–5.[41] Increments of rent totalled 11s.11¾d. out of a rent roll of £6 2s.10¾d. in early fourteenth-century Lackford, and assize rents at Eriswell increased in value by 16 per cent between 1235 and 1308.[42] It is seldom clear whether these increases arose from the construction of new houses or merely a rise in rent charged for existing dwellings or land. Whatever their exact source, they do reflect concerted pressure of population on resources.

AGRARIAN SPECIALISATION AND THE DEVELOPMENT OF RESOURCES

Changes in the area under cultivation provide the most direct evidence of development in marginal regions, and so the failure or inability of Breckland farmers to extend arable cultivation very far after Domesday might indicate that its economy hardly developed in this important period. In fact such a statement says more about the limitations of using the extension of cultivated area as an indicator of regional development than it does about Breckland's economy. As the balance between population and cultivated area is regarded as the most potent influence on a peasant economy, historians have traditionally relied upon statistics of these, expressed as a function of total area, to demonstrate the varying levels of economic development throughout England. Hence Breckland

---

39 *Pinchbeck register*, vol. II, pp. 225; the figure refers to freeholdings held directly from the lord of the manor.
40 H.E.Hallam, 'The social structure of eastern England', in *The agrarian history of England and Wales*, vol. II (forthcoming).   41 CUL EDC 7/15/I/10.
42 WSROB E.3/15.12/3.7; Munday, 'Eriswell notebook'.

is regarded as under-developed at Domesday because its population and ploughteams per area were much lower than in other areas of East Anglia. But is this the best method of establishing levels of regional development? Certainly if the comparison is between regions blessed with similar resources, then this approach can realistically reflect levels of relative development. However, if a good soil region is compared with one of poor soil, then this statistical method will reveal the obvious differences in aggregate development, but reveal little about relative development. For instance, Breckland might have developed a reasonably sophisticated economy, highly adapted to its resource base, yet it would still be unable to support a larger population/arable density than an area of much better soils which was less well adapted to its resource base. Hence regional development should be considered in two ways; through computations of aggregate figures, but also by assessing whether a region was under-utilising or maximising its inherent potential.

Attempts to assess development according to relative potential inevitably encounter problems of quantification, yet a rough and ready analysis of this is possible from basic Domesday statistics. By dividing the figures for population densities in 1086 by those for ploughteam densities, an impression can be gained of the balance between population and arable resources in various areas:[43] so the problem is not whether Breckland as a whole supported as many people per square mile as other regions, but whether its cultivated area was able to sustain the same head of population as cultivated areas elsewhere. Hence population per square mile of ploughteams in 1086 ranged from under 2.1 persons in the North Riding, to 6 in Norfolk's Flegg district, to 4.7 in Colneis hundred near Ipswich, and to 4 in Babergh hundred (where the Suffolk textile industry was to flourish). In Suffolk Breckland the figure lay between 3.4 and 4, and nearer to 5 in Norfolk, a remarkable fact in view of the region's inferior soils (see table 3.2). If Breckland's arable was capable of sustaining as many people as most other parts of East Anglia, are we then to assume that its productivity matched that of areas of better soil? Such an achievement is hardly conceivable, and so to support such numbers arable farming in Breckland must have been supplemented by alternative sources of income.

The opportunities for earning income outside arable farming are

---

[43] See table 3.2.

considered below,[44] but of more immediate interest are Breckland's agrarian characteristics. Did the region's inability to increase its grain producing capacity significantly in the two centuries after Domesday preclude other forms of agricultural development? More specifically, were incomes raised by a movement towards specialised production? Indeed, an element of agrarian specialisation had been apparent at Domesday, when the region was distinguished by a large number of sheep. Norfolk Breckland had one of the highest sheep densities in the county, and Lackford hundred possessed the highest concentration in East Anglia. The availability of both heathland and marshland pastures enabled Mildenhall and Eriswell manors to keep a total of 2,680 sheep; of central parishes, Icklingham had flocks totalling 934, Downham 900 and Elveden 860.[45]

Was this feature still discernible in *c.* 1300, and had Breckland assumed any other specialised role? If so, what was the region's place in the East Anglian economy as a whole? A number of commentators have noticed the progressive and relatively commercialised nature of East Anglian agriculture in the Middle Ages. Norfolk in particular specialised in high productivity arable farming, producing large surpluses of barley for the market.[46] An analysis of Breckland's place within this framework is facilitated by the survival of a unique tax return for Blackbourne hundred in 1283. This material has already formed the basis of an important article by Postan on the amount and composition of peasant grain and livestock, and of an analysis of peasant wealth by Hallam.[47] However, historians are now considering the reliability of these taxes for this type of analysis more carefully. For example, it is unlikely that the whole community was assessed, for Langdon has estimated that one-third of Blackbourne's population either evaded or was exempt from payment in 1283. Postan preferred the much lower figure of 5 per cent, and also assumed that the details of grain and animals related to actual numbers of stock. Langdon, on

---

[44] See p. 158–91.

[45] Darby, *Domesday geography of eastern England*, pp. 150 and 201. These numbers represent demesne flocks only, and it is assumed that the amount of unrecorded sheep was considerable.

[46] On the development of regional specialisation in East Anglia, see Bruce Campbell, *The geography of seignorial agriculture in Norfolk 1230–1430* (Cambridge, forthcoming); Hallam, *Rural England*, pp. 46–7.

[47] M.M. Postan, 'Village livestock in the thirteenth century', reprinted as chapter 11 of *English agriculture*, pp. 214–48; Hallam, contribution to *Agrarian history*.

117

the other hand, believes that the grain totals referred only to saleable surpluses, although he concedes that livestock totals were recorded in a more comprehensive fashion.[48] Hence any statements about absolute levels of peasant wealth, grain and livestock are perilously difficult unless the reliability of the returns can be established. However, we can be less gloomy about comparative statements on these matters. The wealth and agrarian characteristics of the Breckland element of Blackbourne can be contrasted with those of its high Suffolk element, as it is reasonable to assume that evasion and exemption would be more or less equal throughout the hundred.

Pastoral specialisation

According to Postan, the number of sheep per capita represents the most striking difference between different Blackbourne villages in 1283. His methodology is simple enough: he calculates the average number of sheep per taxpayer in each vill, and compares this figure with the average for the hundred as a whole. Villages with a figure above the average are classified as 'pastoral'.[49] Table 3.5 does exactly the same, but is based on Powell's figures which include demesne flocks. It is instructive that the 14 pastoral villages correspond closely with the Breckland element of the hundred, the exceptions being Norton and Ashfield Magna.[50] A high concentration of sheep was obviously an important characteristic of Breckland villages in 1283.

If these villages were involved in a wide range of pastoral activities, then they would presumably have a higher than average number of cows and pigs and a lower than average number of plough beasts. Table 3.6 reveals that this was not the case, for there were as many plough beasts here as in the rest of the hundred.[51] The

---

[48] Langdon, *Horses, oxen and innovation*, pp. 179–80, and 184–5; Postan, *English agriculture*, p. 219. [49] Postan, *English agriculture*, pp. 215–21.

[50] The inclusion of Ashfield and Norton in the 'pastoral' villages is somewhat surprising. Both lie well to the east of Breckland, and are atypical of their neighbours. It is significant, however, that they qualify only marginally for the pastoral category. Norton is a sizeable parish of 2,454 acres, and it is probable that both had access to larger resources of waste and pasture than other high Suffolk villages, and were thus capable of supporting bigger flocks.

[51] If Ashfield and Norton are omitted from the calculations then the Breckland villages have an average of 1.3 plough beasts per head, which corresponds exactly with the hundred average. This reinforces Postan's observation that the distinction between 'pastoral' and 'arable' villages in medieval England was one of degree, Postan, *Medieval agriculture*, p. 239.

Table 3.5. *Total number of sheep assessed in Blackbourne hundred (Suffolk) in the subsidy of 1283*

Village	Number of sheep	Number of taxpayers	Mean sheep per taxpayer
*Ashfield Magna**	383	31	12.35
Badwell Ash	192	33	5.82
Bardwell	1,313	128	10.26
Barnham	2,525	47	53.72
Barningham	254	55	4.62
Culford	599	21	28.52
Elmswell	207	26	7.96
Euston	1,103	34	32.44
Fakenham	932	19	49.05
Hepworth	256	55	4.65
Hinderclay	232	41	5.66
Honington	197	38	5.18
Hopton	305	75	4.07
Hunston	99	19	5.21
Ingham	1,019	28	36.39
Ixworth	340	56	6.07
Knettishall	345	28	12.32
Langham	121	24	5.04
Livermere Parva	649	27	24.03
Market Weston	215	40	5.37
Norton	573	37	15.49
Rickinghall	446	59	7.56
Rushford	191	10	19.10
Sapiston	650	29	22.41
Stanton	395	99	3.99
Stowlangtoft	251	32	7.84
Thelnetham	213	53	4.02
Thorpe	372	40	9.30
Troston	612	33	18.54
Walsham	337	90	3.74
Wattisfield	239	45	5.32
West Stow	1,097	21	52.24
Wordwell	446	20	23.30
Total	17,128	1,393	12.29

Note:
* The 14 pastoral villages are italicised.
Source: Powell, *Suffolk hundred*, pp. xxx–xxxi.

Table 3.6. *Livestock totals in the pastoral villages of Blackbourne hundred in 1283*

Village	Number of taxpayers	Plough beasts	Cattle	Pigs
Ashfield Magna	31	66	143	102
Barnham	47	78	184	26
Culford	21	30	63	0
Euston	34	55	127	4
Fakenham	19	24	56	20
Ingham	28	43	126	0
Knettishall	28	35	151	40
Livermere Parva	27	17	51	17
Norton	37	68	177	122
Rushford	10	14	41	0
Sapiston	29	35	102	74
Troston	33	37	104	19
West Stow	21	25	74	0
Wordwell	20	27	51	0
Total	385	554	1,450	424
Per capita mean		1.4	3.8	1.1
Hundred per capita mean		1.3	3.4	1.5

Source: Powell, *Suffolk hundred*, pp. xxx–xxxi.

figures for dairy cattle are marginally above the hundred mean, but the differential is not large enough to argue that cattle rearing was a specialism of Breckland.[52] Nor do the statistics for pigs deviate drastically from the overall mean, although here the deviation is down rather than up. Significantly, five villages had no pigs at all, and Euston only had four. The Breckland average is patently bolstered by the returns for Ashfield and Norton, and without their contribution the average is a mere 0.6 pigs per capita. Breckland was evidently a specialised sheep-rearing area, rather than a general stock-raising district.

In other Breckland villages outside Blackbourne, sheep assumed an even greater prominence. In the late twelfth century there were 230 demesne sheep at Ingham, 1,154 at Elveden and nearly 3,000 at

[52] Excluding Ashfield and Norton the figure would be 3.6 dairy cattle per capita in Breckland villages.

Table 3.7. *Proportion of demesne sheep recorded in seven Breckland villages in 1283*

Village	Total no. of sheep	Demesne sheep	Percentage
Barnham	2,525	38	1.5
Culford	599	5	0.8
Euston	1,103	—	0
Fakenham	932	520	55.8
Ingham	1,019	111*	10.9
Rushford	191	15	7.9
West Stow	1,097	130	11.9

Note:
* Demesne flocks at Ingham actually totalled 311, but 200 of these are described as 'alien sheep in the fold of the Prior'.
Source: Powell, *Suffolk hundred*, pp. xxx–xxxi.

Lakenheath a century later.[53] In part this was due to the greater reserves of pasture in central and fen-edge villages, but also due to the tendency for demesnes in peripheral parishes to stock up their foldcourses with peasant sheep instead. This raises an important question: just how great was the peasantry's contribution to sheep rearing in Breckland, bearing in mind Bridbury's observation that peasant flocks were twice as large as demesne flocks in the country as a whole?[54] Unfortunately a representative figure is impossible to compute, because firm evidence is elusive and in any case manorial lords were gradually increasing their control over sheep farming as time progressed.[55] Despite these difficulties, the Blackbourne returns at least give some indication as to the balance between demesne and peasant flocks at the peak of peasant sheep farming. In nine villages in 1283, each taxpayer owned an average of over twenty sheep, and in many villages their combined operations far outweighed those of the demesne.

Table 3.7 shows that some lords, such as Tiltey abbey at Fakenham Magna, were active sheep farmers, but in many places they relied upon peasant sheep to stock foldcourses and provide

53 Davis, *Kalendar of abbot Samson*, pp. 119–20; CUL EDC 7/15/II/2.
54 A.R. Bridbury, *Medieval English clothmaking: an economic survey* (London, 1982), pp. 1–5. 55 See below, chapter 5, pp. 293–4.

badly needed tathe for the demesne soils. This was particularly true on Bury abbey manors in the thirteenth century, for apparently there was no large-scale sheep farming on the estate until the 1310s. Even at Lakenheath, where the Prior and Convent of Ely were energetic and prodigious rearers, peasant sheep constituted around 45 per cent of the village total in the 1340s.[56] The attraction of the sheep lay in its versatility, for it produced dung, meat, milk and wool. Manorial accounts categorise sheep according to age and gender, and all the indications are that rearing was a carefully managed and lucrative business.[57]

Much of the evidence for sheep management concerns demesne flocks, but as the demesne assumed responsibility for tending many of the peasantry's sheep, then we have a representative view of the manner in which most sheep were reared. Many landlords enjoyed the exclusive milking rights to ewes in their folds (lactage), which provided a useful source of income, although most manors farmed out the privilege rather than exploited it directly. Thus Lakenheath manor received a handsome £4. 1s. 8d. in 1326 and Icklingham averaged 16s. 6d. in extant accounts.[58] Most flocks were tended by one shepherd and his boy, although ewes were normally folded separately in Breckland and these flocks were the most labour intensive. Apart from the full-time shepherd, young boys were hired after Christmas to help with the lambing and then to tend the lambs during their first summer; others could also be employed to care for weaker lambs and younger sheep. The only other main demand for additional labour was at the shearing, washing and marking of sheep, tasks almost wholly performed by hired rather than customary labour. All other tasks were undertaken by the full-time shepherds, who were remunerated with a mixture of cash and corn livery, the latter comprising rye and barley. There were variations on this, and on the abbot of St Edmunds' manors the shepherds received little cash but were given two acres of demesne

---

[56] See below, tables 4.14 and 4.15.
[57] The generic name for sheep in manorial accounts is nearly always *bidentes*, and these were normally subdivided thus: *agni/agne* = lambs; *hoggastri* = castrated males in their second year; *gerce* = females in their second year; *multones* = castrated males in their third year and above; *oves matrices* = females in their third year and above; *hurtardes* = adult rams.
[58] CUL EDC 7/15/I/6; NRO Ms 13190–13200 and BL Add.Roll 25810. See Ryder, *Sheep and man*, pp. 688–90.

corn, a bellewether fleece each, and the right to eighteen nights folding by the flock over Christmas.[59]

Breeding the flocks was a simple process involving the introduction of a few rams to wander at random amongst the ewes, yet despite this rather haphazard arrangement fertility rates were good by medieval standards. Amongst Crowland abbey ewes between 1267 and 1314 mean fertility was around 84 per cent, and in sixteenth-century Norfolk it was between 50 and 80 per cent.[60] Where Breckland accounts provide specific information about the number of ewes aborting or sterile, it is possible to calculate overall fertility with some accuracy. Table 3.8 indicates a mean fertility of over 80 per cent, a performance comparable to Crowland and superior to sixteenth-century rates. The ratio of rams to ewes varied but tended to be high, ranging from 1:12 at Lakenheath in 1451 to 1:69 at Fornham (A) in 1409.[61] Peasant flocks were not served any better: in Rushford the heirs of Phillip de Shadwell had a fold for 100 sheep and a ram, and Richard le Breanse of Fornham had 200 sheep and 2 rams.[62] The average for demesne flocks was probably around 1:30/40, although the range of extant documentation is too narrow to decide if there was a strong correlation between the ram–ewe ratio and fertility. However, the lowest recorded ratio at Fornham (A) coincided with a high fertility rate, which suggests that factors such as disease and the debilitating practice of milking were more influential on overall ewe fertility than the number of rams serving them.

Approximate mortality rates are also calculable from manorial accounts. Annual deaths were lowest amongst the older wether and ewe sheep, although the complications associated with lambing pushed ewe rates a little higher, so that around 8 per cent of wethers died each year and 11 per cent of ewes. As younger and weaker sheep, yearlings had higher death rates, but because they were added to the total of ewes and wethers at an unspecified time of the agrarian year, exact mortality is difficult to calculate – it was probably around 15 per cent. The vulnerability of lambs meant that they frequently succumbed to disease, at a rate of at least 20 per cent

---

[59] BL Add.Ms 14849 f.20. The bellewether fleece was traditionally regarded as the second best fleece of the clip.
[60] K.J. Allison, 'Flock management in the sixteenth and seventeenth centuries', *Ec.H.R.* 11 (1958), pp. 104–7. [61] CUL EDC 7/15/I/41; WSROB E.3/15.6/2.44.
[62] NRO Ms 15170; BL Add.Ms 14849 f.25.

Table 3.8. *Lambing rates per ewe on Breckland demesnes, 1300–1500*

Demesne	Year	Ewes	Lambs of issue	Lambing rate
Lakenheath	1305	672	562	0.84
Lakenheath	1321	983	871	0.89
Lakenheath	1327	947	833	0.88
Lakenheath	1330	1,008	894	0.89
Icklingham	1333	22	14	0.64
Icklingham	1334	104	70	0.67
Icklingham	1336	37	35	0.94
Lakenheath	1337	531	505	0.95
Lakenheath	1338	128	115	0.90
Lakenheath	1345	824	644	0.78
Lakenheath	1348	799	612	0.76
Brandon	1354	288	268	0.93
Lakenheath	1356	402	372	0.92
Lakenheath	1357	462	348	0.75
Lakenheath	1362	612	428	0.70
Brandon	1363	61	46	0.75
Brandon	1365	265	235	0.87
Lakenheath	1365	706	518	0.73
Brandon	1366	313	275	0.88
Brandon	1367	317	250	0.79
Brandon	1368	239	224	0.94
Lakenheath	1368	705	486	0.69
Brandon	1369	178	165	0.93
Brandon	1370	147	135	0.92
Lakenheath	1373	711	618	0.87
Lakenheath	1377	766	606	0.79
Lakenheath	1379	757	535	0.71
Brandon	1380	340	253	0.69
Lakenheath	1381	516	280	0.54
Brandon	1383	361	325	0.90
Mildenhall	1385	328	269	0.82
Mildenhall	1386	334	257	0.77
Brandon	1386	358	297	0.83
Brandon	1387	370	309	0.83
Brandon	1389	473	320	0.68
Brandon	1390	386	340	0.88
Brandon	1391	395	342	0.86
Brandon	1392	388	352	0.91
Brandon	1393	365	308	0.84
Brandon	1394	378	302	0.80
Lakenheath	1394	485	360	0.74

Table 3.8. (*cont.*)

Demesne	Year	Ewes	Lambs of issue	Lambing rate
Lakenheath	1395	439	379	0.86
Brandon	1395	378	332	0.88
Fornham (A)	1409	207	200	0.97
Fornham (A)	1410	143	136	0.95
Lakenheath	1420	584	509	0.87
Lakenheath	1428	726	516	0.71
Lakenheath	1432	611	494	0.81
Lakenheath	1438	604	516	0.85
Totals		22,281	18,060	Mean 0.81
				Range: 0.54–0.97

between birth and Michaelmas, and such high losses presented a major obstacle to flock growth and profitability.[63] These mortality rates are slightly higher than on the Canterbury Cathedral Priory manors studied by Mate, although this is probably due to climatic factors rather than to poorer management.[64] High sheep mortality has been related to periods or places of prolonged frosts and heavy summer rainfall,[65] which are both features of Breckland's climate. The exact cause of death is never certain because scribes usually employed the generic phrase '*in morina*' to describe any epidemic, although occasionally they are more specific and attribute deaths to 'le pokkes' or 'le gastric'. This vagueness reflects the ignorance of medieval farmers about the diseases afflicting their flocks, but major scourges were probably scab and liverfluke; the incidence of

63 Total number of deaths was calculated from extant accounts and expressed as a percentage of (a) total sheep at the beginning of the account, and (b) total sheep 'received' during the year. Thus from all extant accounts of Brandon, Fornham (A), Icklingham, Lakenheath, Mildenhall and Risby (percentages in brackets):

Sheep	Deaths	Total sheep (a)	Total received (b)
Wethers	4,024	47,884 (8.4)	59,948 (6.7)
Ewes	3,988	33,847 (11.8)	42,878 (9.3)
Yearlings	3,651	19,792 (18.4)	24,744 (14.8)
Lambs	6,164	31,393 (19.6)	

64 M. Mate, 'Medieval agrarian practices: the determining factors?', *Ag.H.R.* 33 (1985), pp. 24–5.

65 J.A. Taylor, ed., *Weather and agriculture* (Oxford, 1967), pp. 129–35 and 193.

footrot in Breckland was likely to have been restricted by the porosity of the ground. That scab was a constant menace is reflected in regular purchases of butter, tar and pitch, which were mixed together and applied to the sheep's body in an attempt to restrict the spread of the scab mites.[66] In one early fourteenth-century account, the Wretham demesne purchased nearly 90 gallons of bitumen and over 200 lbs of grease and butter, and paid a greasor ('ungwentor') 2s. to carry out the work.[67] The Icklingham demesne was so concerned about the spread of scab in 1341 that it even paid for tenant sheep folded with the manorial flocks to be similarly treated.[68]

For all its subsidiary benefits, the primary objective of sheep farming was to produce as large a wool clip as possible. Medieval England was a prodigious wool producer, and a substantial proportion of its output was channelled into a highly profitable export trade. The mechanisms and financial complexities of this trade have been thoroughly researched,[69] but regional variations in the output and quality of wool have received less attention.[70] the principal concern of this trade was the fleece, *vellera*, shorn in June, and the sheep's hide, *pellis lanuta*, the skin of the adult which had died between Michaelmas and shearing.[71] Flock composition was important in wool production, for wethers carried the heaviest fleeces which often weighed around twice those of yearlings. Disease could affect fleece weight and quality, but more permanent regional differences were a function of local climate and soil. Breckland's poor pastures were not conducive to producing heavy, thick fleeces, and its sheep were of the shortwool variety whose fleeces were lightweight and low in quality.[72] This was true of East Anglia in general, but it would appear that Breckland fleeces were

[66] Ryder, *Sheep and man*, pp. 708–10.

[67] NRO Ms 18017.

[68] A 22-gallon cask of tarpitch was bought 'for the lord's sheep and those of other men with sheep in his custody', NRO Ms 13196. When an epidemic struck the Lakenheath flock in 1335, over 42s. was spent on bitumen, grease and butter in an attempt to curtail losses, CUL EDC 7/15/I/9.

[69] E. Power, *The wool trade in English medieval history* (Oxford, 1941); T.H. Lloyd, *The English wool trade in the Middle Ages* (Cambridge, 1977).

[70] Although see Ryder, *Sheep and man*, pp. 458–65.

[71] Accounts also refer to *pelleteria*, adult pelts after shearing, and *pellis agni*, lamb pelts, but these comprised little wool and were sold very cheaply, perhaps to peasants for subsistence purposes.

[72] M.L. Ryder, 'The history of sheep breeds in Britain', *Ag.H.R.* 12 (1964), p. 8; and 'Medieval sheep and wool types', *Ag.H.R.* 32 (1984), pp. 14–28.

Table 3.9. *Fleece weights in*
medieval Breckland

Demesne	Year	Weight (lbs)
Brandon	1342	1.41
	1348	1.04
	1350*	1.83
	1367	0.94
	1387	1.09
Cressingham	1309	1.75
	1363	1.36
	1364	1.41
	1374	1.94
	1377	1.61
	1381	0.93
Croxton+		1.05
Fornham (C)	1301	1.34
	1302	1.18
	1303	2.15
Freckenham	1350	2.35
Icklingham	1341	1.10
Methwold	1359	1.98
Mildenhall	1418	1.21
	1420	1.18

Note:
* Breckland flocks of the Bishopric of
  Ely shorn at Brandon.
+ Sibton abbey flocks.
Sources: PRO sc6.1304/23, 26, 27 and 30;
NRO DCN Supplement (R187A); A.H.
Denny, *The estates of Sibton abbey*, p. 25;
WSROB E.3/15.9/2.11–2.13; PRO
sc6.1110/25; NRO Ms 13196; PRO
DL29.288/4719; BL Add. Rolls 53133 and
53134.

poor even by these standards.[73] Few accounts record a weighted
value for Breckland's fleeces, but the limited evidence presented in
table 3.9 clearly indicates their levity.

Whilst commercial sheep rearing was clearly a regional

[73] East Anglian wool generally fetched a lower price per sack than most other areas of
England, especially Lincolnshire and the west midlands, Ryder, *Sheep and man*, p. 463;
N. Heard, *Wool: East Anglia's golden fleece* (Lavenham, 1970), p. 43.

specialism, evidence from most Breckland villages suggests a much stronger subsistence element to cattle and poultry farming. The shortage of quality meadowland and the local tendency to use sheep's milk for dairy purposes restricted the importance of cows to the economy. Dairy farming constituted only a small limb of demesne operations, and the biggest herds were confined to the fen edge and the eastern fringes of the region. Butter and cheese were produced for market at Barton Parva, Cressingham and Lakenheath in the 1300s, but most manors preferred to lease their cows to local peasants for a fixed annual sum.[74] Bury must have exerted some demand for dairy produce, and income from dairy leases at Fornham could constitute up to 10 per cent of gross manorial income. However, on central manors the figure was much lower, and the norm may have been closer to the 2 per cent recorded at Icklingham.[75] The same seems to have been true of the peasantry, for cows and calves feature less prominently in animal transgressions recorded in court rolls than other beasts. Yet a few men kept enough cows to be regarded as specialist producers for local markets. William Day of Eriswell had a herd of twenty cows in 1331, and John of Lakenheath saw fit to employ his own cowkeeper in 1347.[76]

Some manors fattened a few pigs and poultry for the seigneurial household, notably Mildenhall, and both Brandon and Fornham (C) raised a few shillings by selling poultry to the market. Only Kennett did this on any scale, selling 26 pigs in 1271 and 22 in 1274, probably at Bury or Cambridge.[77] Peasant geese – and increasingly pigs – appear in court rolls, but again not with enough prominence to indicate anything other than subsistence rearing. There were a few exceptions, especially on the fen edge: John Spink of Lakenheath was selling geese on behalf of another peasant in 1310, Geoffrey Mustard kept 18 geese in 1330, and Stephen Clerkson of Brandon illegally kept 40 in the lord's meadow.[78]

Another, increasingly valuable, facet of demesne pastoral farm-

---

[74] IESRO HD1538/88 m.11; NRO DCN Supplement (R187A); CUL EDC 7/15/I/2.
[75] Indeed, there were no cows at all recorded on the Downham manor of Ixworth priory, WSROB 651/35/7.
[76] CUL EDC 7/15/II/Box 1/9 m.11, court held November 1331, and Box 2/17 m.3, court held November 1347.   [77] PRO sc6.768/5 and 7.
[78] CUL EDC 7/15/II/Box 1/1, court held October 1310 and Box 1/8 m.9, court held July 1330; Bacon 289/6 July 1330.

ing was the commercial rearing of the rabbit.[79] Domesday Book makes no mention of rabbit warrens in Breckland, nor for that matter anywhere else in England. The rabbit, unlike the hare, is not indigenous to the British Isles, but was introduced by the Normans from either northern France or its native western Mediterranean.[80] Both the rabbit's meat and its fur were highly marketable, and one seventeenth-century observer wrote that 'no host could bee deemed a good housekeeper that hath not plenty of these at all times to furnish his table'.[81] Fur was commonly used for clothing, and although neither the most fashionable nor the most expensive, rabbit fur was increasingly popular in the Middle Ages.[82] There is some debate over the exact dating of the rabbit's introduction to England, but by the mid-thirteenth century it was established in many Breckland villages. However, its total population remained relatively small, and in many parts of East Anglia the animal was a rare beast until at least the eighteenth century. The concept of the prolific and ubiquitous rabbit is a modern one.

In the Middle Ages, the right to keep and kill rabbits – or coneys as the adults were known – was a fiercely guarded seigneurial privilege enshrined in the charter of free-warren.[83] This legally entitled the owner to hunt the beasts of free-warren (notably the pheasant, partridge, hare and rabbit) within a designated area, and strictly debarred others from doing so. The charter, available by purchase from the King, was a valuable commodity and owners rigorously pursued anyone who broke their monopoly. For instance, the manorial court at Fornham St Martin amerced Henry Stonham in 1367 for 'hunting in the lord's warren and taking a number of hares'.[84] The exact boundaries of free-warren were also a source of dispute between the various owners. In the 1270s the

---

[79] In medieval documents, *rabettus* refers to the young rabbit, probably those under three months old. The adult is referred to as *cuniculus*, or coney in its English form.

[80] For the introduction of the rabbit into England, see E.M. Veale, 'The rabbit in England', *Ag.H.R.* 5 (1957), pp. 85–90. Little work on commercial rabbit rearing in the Middle Ages has been done, but an excellent general study of the animal is J. Sheail, *Rabbits and their history* (Newton Abbot, 1971). For rabbiting in the early modern period, J. Sheail, 'Rabbits and agriculture in post-medieval England', *Journal of Historical Geography* 4 (1978) pp. 349–55.   [81] F. Hervey, ed., *Reyce's breviary of Suffolk* (1902), p. 35.

[82] E.M. Veale, *The English fur trade in the later Middle Ages* (Oxford, 1966), chapter 1 and p. 176.

[83] For the concept of free-warren, see Sheail, *Rabbits*, p. 35; M.D. Bailey, 'The rabbit and the medieval East Anglian economy', *Ag.H.R.* 36 (1988), p. 2.

[84] WSROB E.3/15.9/1.2 m.19.

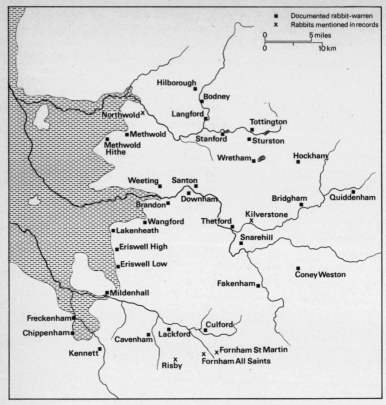

Map 3. Rabbit-warrens in medieval Breckland

bailiff of Gooderstone was illegally claiming the right to hunt in the fields of Cockley Cley, and in 1426 Sir Hugo Lottrell disputed the Duchy of Lancaster's right of free-warren on Feltwell heath.[85]

More than any other of the free-warren beasts, the rabbit could considerably enhance the charter's value. Not only were its meat and fur marketable commodities, but its preference for living and breeding in close communities facilitated its exploitation for commercial purposes, unlike the more solitary hare. The medium through which the rabbit was introduced and bred was the warren,

[85] Blomefield, vol. III, p. 403; PRO DL30.103/1423. In some Suffolk villages, although not in Breckland nor the Sandlings, the lands of free tenants were exempt from the free-warren charter, W. Illingworth and J. Caley, eds., *Rotuli hundredorum temp. Hen.III et Edw.I*, vol. II, (1818), pp. 144–5.

garrena, or coniger as it was variously known. There is obviously a distinction here between the warren in its legal and practical senses. In modern usage the rabbit-warren refers to any piece of ground on which wild rabbits burrow, but in the Middle Ages it specifically meant an area of land preserved for the domestic or commercial rearing of game. Indeed, these medieval warrens represented almost the sole source of supply for rabbits, and not until the eighteenth century did the animal successfully colonise a much wider habitat.[86] Nineteenth-century warrens were often delimited by ditches and banks topped with gorse to restrict the movement of prey and predators, but there is little to indicate this was normal in the Middle Ages. There was a ditch at Lakenheath warren, but it does not appear to have surrounded it completely.[87] Ditching was a long and costly business, and the absence of appropriate references in accounts suggests that most warrens lay open and without physical delimitation. Ditches were probably dug only where the warren abutted arable land or the village itself. In general, the presumption was that colonies of rabbits were not likely to wander as long as sufficient food was available within the warren area.

The concentration of warrens in Breckland and their comparative absence from other parts of East Anglia was not fortuitous, but a function of strict economic and topographic expediency. The modern rabbit has evolved a resilience to the damp British climate, but its medieval predecessor felt this aversion more keenly and was frail and uncomfortable in its new surroundings. The most successful medieval colonies were founded on dry, light soil, well drained and easily burrowed. The combination of Breckland's climate and soil provided an ideal habitat for the rabbit, and the first warrens were prominent on the deepest and poorest sands. In 1563, Brandon warren was described as 'very Wide and Large but of very Baren Soyle nevertthelesse very good for brede of Conyes'.[88] The economic significance of this was considerable, for rabbits

---

[86] Bailey, 'Rabbit and East Anglia', p. 2. Although the court at Walsham-le-Willows (only 8 miles east of Breckland) was jealously protective of the free-warren charter and therefore efficient at recording poaching cases, the rabbit was rarely mentioned in the fourteenth century, indicating its almost complete absence from the village. My thanks to Ray and Jean Lock for this information.

[87] CUL EDC 7/15/I/8 records a payment to 'make a ditch around the new warren at the head of the village', and in 1333 three men illegally grazed their animals '*in fossato de la coneger*', 7/15/II/Box 1/9 m.22. In 1347–8, 2s. 5d. was paid to make a hedge at the warren, 7/15/I/14.

[88] PRO E310.24/138. For the distribution of warrens in East Anglia, see Bailey, 'Rabbit and East Anglia', map 1.

represented an excellent medium through which to exploit land of otherwise limited utility and low value.

Ecclesiastical landlords possessed the necessary financial means and so were prominent in creating the early warrens of the thirteenth century. Henry Pie held land from the Bishopric of Ely at Brandon for the rent of six coney nets in 1251, which suggests an early foundation, and there was probably an episcopal warren in Bridgham as well.[89] The Prior and Convent of Ely were granted free-warren in Lakenheath in 1251 and in 1300 the specific right to a *cunicularium* was added to the charter; by 1304 a warrener was employed for 30s. 4d. a year, and 50 culled rabbits were returned to Ely.[90] The Bishop of Rochester secured free-warren over his demesne at Freckenham in 1248 as a preliminary to rabbit rearing, and Bury abbey had a productive warren at Mildenhall by 1323.[91] Lay landlords were also active in this process, notably the Warennes, earls of Surrey, at Methwold and Thetford and the Bigods, earls of Norfolk, at Kennett.[92] There were many smaller creations, such as the Eriswell warren valued at 30s. 4d. in 1308, and those at Cavenham and Fakenham, and as the rabbit population grew in the later fourteenth century, so other warrens continued to emerge.[93] Unfortunately, it is impossible to ascertain the exact size of these warrens, although clearly those at Brandon, Hilborough, Lakenheath, Methwold and Thetford had come to occupy large areas (perhaps of one thousand acres) by the late fifteenth century. The Norfolk family's warren at Kennett comprised around 400 acres in 1563, although some warrens were never larger than that at Coney Weston, which occupied two and a half acres in 1302.[94] The wide difference in warren size and capacity are illustrated by the variety of warren lease valuations: in the fifteenth century,

[89] CUL EDR G3/27 f.191; *CPR*, 1327–30, p. 208.
[90] Crompton, 'Lakenheath warren', p. 14; CUL EDC 7/15/I/2.
[91] E. Callard, *The manor of Freckenham* (London, 1924), pp. 59–60; Bodleian Suffolk Rolls 21.
[92] The Warennes were notable for their creation of rabbit-warrens throughout southern England, A.M. and R.M. Tittensor, *The rabbit warren at West Dean near Chichester* (published privately, 1986), section on 'Sussex rabbit warrens', no pagination. In 1347, many of their East Anglian estates were made over to the Duchy of Lancaster. It is often held that Thetford warren was created by the town's Cluniac priory, but the monks in fact held the warren on a long-term lease from the Duchy, PRO DL29.290/4765.
[93] J.T. Munday, 'Documents of Eriswell cum Coclesworth 1086–1340' (WSROB duplicated); Cavenham, *CPR*, 1313–17, p. 262; Fakenham, BL Add.Roll 9100 mentions a warrener, and in 1686 a rental refers to 'the coney ground' of 10 acres, WSROB HA513/30/21. See below, chapter 4, pp. 251–2.
[94] WSROB 339/5; BL Harl. 230 f.155. Coney Weston is a corruption of King's Weston.

Langford warren was valued at 15s., whilst one in Hilborough produced £15.[95]

The sites of the new warrens were mainly confined to heathland, although arable land was occasionally converted to pasture for the rabbit's benefit. At Chippenham the Hospitallers bought out common rights and exchanged land for inclusion in their warren in the 1280s.[96] Matthew Prall relinquished one acre of land into the lord's hands at Lakenheath in 1326 which was later described as lying 'opposite the rabbit warren'.[97] Its abandonment was related to the introduction of rabbits, perhaps through damage caused by their grazing or perhaps as a buffer zone between the west end of the warren and other arable land. In general, though, hardly any arable land was abandoned in Breckland prior to the Black Death, which indicates that, initially at least, warrens were largely confined to heathland; only after the late fourteenth century was arable land absorbed within the warren area on any scale.

Were all medieval warrens deliberate seigneurial creations, or did in fact some landlords just exploit an indigenous colony? Many of the earlier warrens were deliberate foundations, although no explicit evidence of the purchase and introduction of stock to Breckland has survived. However, the absence of the rabbit from most other parts of East Anglia and the distinctive geographical clustering of warrens proves that its migratory scope was very limited and that many warrens had to be created artificially. This might surprise a modern reader familiar with the animal's ubiquity and fecundity, but the medieval rabbit was under constant threat from predators and harsh winter conditions. Consequently, low fertility and high mortality rates restricted natural increase, even within the relative safety of the warren. This placed powerful restrictions on long-distance migration, although undoubtedly some fledgling colonies were spawned in the vicinity of the early warrens and these were then eagerly exploited by landlords. Rabbits spread gradually along the southern edge of Breckland, and are recorded in Saxham for the first time in the 1360s.[98] No warren is mentioned in late fourteenth-century Lackford accounts, although judging from poaching presentments in the court rolls a sizeable colony had established itself on the heath. Yet by 1525 its exploitation had been placed on a more formal footing by the lord, and was

---

[95] NRO NCC(Petre) Box 8/22; Blomefield, vol. III, p. 438.
[96] Spufford, 'Chippenham', pp. 22–3.   [97] CUL EDC 7/15/I/6 and 32.
[98] Bailey, 'Rabbit and East Anglia', p. 5.

leased to Thomas White of Cavenham for 140 rabbits and 20s. per annum.[99]

It is impossible to estimate the size of the rabbit population in Breckland warrens because of the obvious difficulties in counting rabbits, and documentation is consequently uninformative. The annual cullings recorded in manorial accounts (table 4.16) provide the best indirect indication of overall numbers, and these suggest a rapid expansion in the fourteenth century, a trend substantiated by the rising value of Hilborough warren from £2. 13s. 6d. in the 1250s to £30 in the late fifteenth century. Yet for all this growth, most warrens produced less than one-tenth the output they were to reach in the nineteenth century.[100] The most striking feature of medieval warrens was the inconsistency of cullings, reflecting wild fluctuations in the rabbit population from year to year. In the thirteenth and early fourteenth centuries cullings were small and variable, indicating the rabbit's scarcity and the difficulties involved in establishing a colony. Even in the fifteenth century in a large warren such as Methwold it was not always possible to cull any rabbits in some years because numbers were so low.[101] Warreners had to exercise considerable discretion over the number to be killed each year, and the primary concern was to maintain sufficient breeding stock.[102]

Successful warren management depended largely on the skill and dedication of the warrener, who guarded his fragile charges against hunger and predators, and even sought ways to encourage breeding. The early rabbits were often reluctant burrowers, particularly in water retentive soils, and so some warreners constructed artificial burrows or pillow-mounds.[103] There is no archaeological evidence that these were ever a feature of medieval Breckland warrens, although warreners were fiercely protective of the rabbits' own burrows. Hence Richard Hosteler of Brandon was amerced for keeping a dog which 'destroyed the burrows of rabbits in the lord's warren'.[104] Poachers were problem enough without their carelessness causing untold physical damage to the warren's

---

[99] For poaching in the 1390s, see WSROB E.3/15.12/1.13; for the lease of 1525, E.3/15.12/ 1.17.   [100] Bailey, 'Rabbit and East Anglia', pp. 5–6.

[101] See, for example, in the 1430s, NRO NRS 11336.

[102] Bailey, 'Rabbit and East Anglia', p. 6.

[103] Veale, 'Rabbit in England', pp. 88–9; Sheail, *Rabbits*, pp. 57–8; Rackham, *History of the countryside*, p. 47.

[104] Bacon 293/1, court held November 1399. For the protection of burrows on east-coast warrens, see Bailey, 'Rabbit and East Anglia', p. 8.

structure. Warreners also took steps to curtail the rabbit's high
mortality rates, particularly in the winter when food supplies ran
low: gorse, hay and sometimes oats were fed to the animals in the
leanest years. They also waged a constant war against the rabbit's
natural predators, and the growth of the warren population testifies
to their success. The fox, stoat, polecat, weasel and wildcat stalked
with ruthless efficiency, so that warrens were set with numerous
traps and snares, and the Kennett warrener was paid extra expenses
for killing foxes and polecats.[105]

Arable farming

Although pastoral farming was by far the main component of
Breckland's agriculture, grain production was not unimportant. In
part, this is reflected in the large number of corn mills established in
the region by the late thirteenth century. The windmill –
molendinum ad ventum – was a late invention and began to appear
regularly in England from the late twelfth century, after which it
was soon prominent in East Anglia.[106] Breckland villages took
advantage of the rivers by which they were settled, and contained a
large number of the more common watermill, *molendinum
aquaticum*. Mildenhall had at least two, whilst the river Lark below
Bury St Edmunds harboured a large concentration: five in the
Fornhams, two at Ingham, one at Culford, three at West Stow, and
one each at Wordwell, Flempton, Hengrave and Lackford.[107]
Most villages along the Little Ouse, Black Bourn and Wissey rivers
possessed watermills, and on higher ground windmills compensated for lack of water power at Risby, Elveden and Timworth.[108]
The cluster of mills around the lucrative Bury market cannot have
been coincidental, reflecting a high concentration of demand. The
construction and maintenance of watermills was an expensive
business, and the costs could only be justified by the presence of a
suitable market for milling. As early as Domesday there were 112
watermills in 67 villages in and around Breckland, and the even
greater number two centuries later testifies to the insistent demand

105 Sheail, *Rabbits*, pp. 9–10 and 31–2; D. Drew, *Man-environment processes* (London, 1983), p. 25; PRO sc6.768/14 and 22.
106 P.C.J. Dolman, 'Windmills in Suffolk: a contemporary survey' (duplicated, Ipswich, 1978).
107 *Pinchbeck register*, vol. II, pp. 128–9, 175, 191, 193–4, 220, 227, 243 and 255.
108 *Ibid.*, pp. 132, 180 and 259.

for corn and to the efficient mechanisms established for its processing.[109]

Unfree peasants were normally compelled to grind their corn at the lord's mill, for which the lord exacted a suitable toll. Milling was therefore regarded as an important seigneurial privilege, although recent research has shown that on many estates this monopoly had become alienated by the twelfth and early thirteenth centuries, only to be reasserted subsequently.[110] Fornham provides an excellent example of this: in 1280 its five mills were all held by freemen, but by 1357 all but one had been reacquired by Bury abbey and the seigneurial monopoly reimposed.[111] Rather than exploit their privileges directly, most landlords in Breckland preferred to lease the demesne mill to a local miller for a fixed annual sum. However, as landlords tried to reassert millsuit, so peasants strove to evade it and turned increasingly to grinding corn on private handmills. Nicholas Ger of Lakenheath was amerced for keeping a mill in his garden and allowing his neighbours to use it, three Fornham men 'held handmills without licence', and Freckenham peasants were ordered not to grind at the mills of other men.[112]

Did grain production in Breckland display any specialised traits? Once again, the Blackbourne returns provide an invaluable indication of arable preferences in west Suffolk in 1283 (see tables 3.10 and 3.11). The most striking feature of the hundred as a whole is the predominance of barley, which flourished on the light loamy soils. Barley was mainly used to make malt for the ubiquitous ale, although it was also occasionally employed in gruel and bread. The prominence of barley, coupled with its general unsuitability for subsistence purposes, indicates that this was the main cereal cash crop. However, grain production within the hundred was not homogeneous, and table 3.11 illustrates its regional variations.

The most surprising aspect of these figures is not just that barley was equally as important in Breckland as in high Suffolk, but that production of corn per capita was higher in Breckland (7.72 qu.

[109] Postgate, 'Historical geography of Breckland', pp. 96–7.
[110] R. Holt, 'Whose were the profits of corn milling? The abbots of Glastonbury and their tenants, 1086–1350', *Past and present* 116 (1987), pp. 3–23. [111] *Ibid.*, pp. 21–2.
[112] CUL EDC 7/15/II/Box 2/14 m.1, court held June 1315; WSROB E.3/15.9/1.1 m.11, court held December 1317; BL Harl.Charter 83 F 54, dated 1196. In Herringswell, Alice le Feuer paid a 6d. fine for the licence to use a handmill for one year, Livett, 'Documents relating to Herringswell', p. 332.

Table 3.10. *Crops assessed in all Blackbourne hundred villages in the 1283 Subsidy*

Crop	Total assessed (qu.)	Mean assessed per capita (qu.)	Percentage
Wheat	955	0.68	9.7
Rye	1,336	0.96	13.7
Barley	4,959	3.56	50.8
Oats	1,369	0.98	14.0
Legumes	1,153	0.83	11.8
Total	9,772	7.01	100

Table 3.11. *Crops assessed in the Breckland villages of Blackbourne hundred in the 1283 subsidy*

Crop	Total assessed (qu.)	Mean assessed per capita	Percentage
Wheat	48	0.1	1.3
Rye	692	2.2	28.5
Barley	1,139	3.6	46.8
Oats	494	1.6	20.8
Legumes	75	0.2	2.6
Total	2,448	7.7	100

Sources: Powell, *Suffolk hundred*, pp. xxx–xxxi.

against 6.81 qu.).[113] That each Breckland peasant should be rearing more sheep and producing a greater surplus of corn than his counterpart in an area of better soils is remarkable, and a function of the region's more extensive farming practices. High Suffolk's inferior output per capita reflects the intense pressure of population on resources there, in contrast to Breckland which appears to have maintained a more viable balance between the two, and perhaps was more market orientated. Breckland's low potential for

[113] In Blackbourne hundred as a whole, 1,393 taxpayers were assessed on 9,772 quarters of grain, or 7.01 qu. each. This breaks down into 317 taxpayers in Breckland assessed on 2,448 qu. and 1,076 in high Suffolk on 7,325 qu.

intensive agrarian operations was the very factor which restrained
its population growth since Domesday, and so ironically served to
maintain levels of per capita output above those of an adjacent
region of much better natural resources. This evidence also
supports Postan's point that even in the 'pastoral' regions of
medieval England, grain production was not unimportant.[114]

The main differences between Breckland and high Suffolk lay in
the relative importance of grains other than barley, for in
Breckland wheat and legumes were notably absent, and rye and
oats more abundant. The sandy soils thwarted most attempts at
growing wheat profitably, so the hardy rye was the most important winter crop.[115] Soil infertility also explains the greater prominence of oats and the relative absence of legumes.[116] The limited
geographical scope of these returns means that we have to rely
upon other sources to determine whether the same characteristics
appear in the rest of Breckland, especially in the barren central
areas. Table 3.12 offers a comprehensive overview of the relative
importance of crops sown on the region's demesnes. This evidence
illustrates the tendency for rye and oats to increase in importance as
soil quality deteriorated, and on the worst soils even barley production was difficult. However, the figures tend to understate the
importance of barley in terms of actual output because barley was
sown up to twice as thickly as other grains, and in reality it was
subordinate to rye only at Downham, Harling, Wretham and West
Tofts.

Peasant producers outside the Blackbourne area also concentrated on barley, perhaps even more so than the demesnes. At
Freckenham, an inventory of Walter de Merton's goods shows
there to be seven times as much barley as wheat or peas.[117] Where
tithe returns have survived from Mildenhall and Lakenheath,
barley again features with remarkable prominence (table 3.13).

---

114 Postan, *English agriculture*, p. 239.
115 This feature was still evident in the nineteenth century, when Breckland returned the
   lowest wheat yields in Suffolk – in some parishes, it was not grown at all, H.M.E. Holt
   and R.J.P. Kain, 'Land use and farming in Suffolk about 1840', *P.S.I.A.* 35 (1981),
   p. 130.
116 Hallam, *Rural England*, p. 49, believes that the soils were too infertile to benefit from the
   use of legumes. That these characteristics were exclusive to Breckland is confirmed by
   the returns for Ashfield and Norton, which correspond more closely to the hundredal
   averages with higher returns for both wheat and legumes, and less emphasis on rye and
   oats. The returns for wheat alone here were 162 qu.
117 Hallam, *Rural England*, p. 50.

Table 3.12. *Proportion of crops sown on Breckland demesnes (by area), 1250–1500 (%)*

Demesne	Wheat	Rye	Barley	Legumes	Oats	Others
Brandon	0.2	29.1	46.3	0.7	22.1	1.6
Downham (IP)		44.7	10.9	0.9	43.5	
Downham (S)		48.0	13.7		38.3	
Fakenham	9.3	30.7	23.1	8.5	28.4	
Hilborough		25.5	60.2	1.8	12.5	
Hockham		31.4	54.8		13.8	
Icklingham	1.2	42.6	31.6	2.6	20.6	1.4
Lackford		42.6	44.7	2.0	10.7	
Lakenheath	3.9	31.6	43.0	3.1	17.8	0.6
Langford	2.0	26.0	50.0	1.0	21.0	
West Harling	1.1	41.4	29.5	1.4	26.6	
West Tofts		55.1	17.3		27.6	
Wretham	0.4	51.7	22.9	3.0	23.0	
Barton Parva	7.2	30.9	29.8	8.5	20.7	2.9
Cressingham	10.8	18.4	48.2	7.3	15.3	
Feltwell (E)	14.3	4.7	57.6	4.5	14.7	4.2
Feltwell (EH)	20.6	4.0	46.8	11.3	14.4	2.9
Fornham (A)	14.8	19.5	40.6	10.7	14.1	0.3
Fornham (C)	16.9	23.9	30.8	4.2	24.1	0.1
Gasthorpe		28.6	42.9	6.4	22.1	
Kennett	9.3	18.0	33.3	7.1	32.3	
Methwold	7.5	18.7	59.8	2.0	12.0	
Mildenhall	13.4	10.1	53.6	6.9	5.7	10.3
Quiddenham	5.5	22.6	52.8	2.7	16.4	
Risby	24.4	21.3	29.1	7.1	18.1	
Wilton	6.9	20.9	55.1	8.1	9.0	

Table 3.13. *Composition of peasant grain tithes received at Lakenheath and Mildenhall, 1300–1500 (%)*

Village	Range	Accounts	Wheat	Maslin	Rye	Barley	Peas	Oats
Lakenheath	1336–1461	23	2	—	15	79	2	2
Mildenhall	1381–1420	20	19	10	3	68	—	—

Sources: CUL EDC 7/15/I/11–45; BL Add. Rolls 53116–53134 and WSROB
E. 18/455/1–2.

Court rolls occasionally describe the type and quantity of grain involved in peasant damage and debt disputes, and in this evidence barley features far more regularly than any other grain at Brandon, Fornham and Mildenhall; when barley was not involved, barley malt or rye were invariably mentioned instead. In Lakenheath courts between 1315 and 1348, barley and malt featured in 65 per cent of all cases where the grain was specified. In all extant Methwold courts, they constituted 35 out of 46 debt cases, or 76 per cent.

In the classic view of marginal regions, they are expected to produce inferior and subsistence crops and certainly not concentrate on the commercial production of barley.[118] In part, Breckland did not fulfil these expectations because its wide trading links broke down subsistence tendencies.[119] At a purely technical level, the peculiar farming practices of Breckland were particularly suited to growing spring-sown corn and these tempered the aridity of its soils to some extent. Once this had been achieved, there was one compelling reason to grow barley rather than any other grain. As every brewer knows, the best quality malt comes from barley with a low nitrogen content. Modern farmers can seek to reduce this with a variety of artificial aids, but in the Middle Ages the nitrogen content of barley was determined to a much greater extent by the nitrogen in the soil. Breckland's sands are notoriously low in this, and so, variable yields notwithstanding, produced a good malting barley.

Another feature of Breckland's agriculture is that peasant grain production was more specialised than on the demesnes. This is surprising, because one would have expected demesnes, with their greater capacity for output and investment, to have been more suited to specialised production. By distinguishing peasant from demesne taxpayers in Blackbourne hundred, this feature is well illustrated (table 3.14). Presumably demesnes grew more rye and oats than barley in order to feed the large numbers of livestock and full-time farm labourers (famuli) which they employed. Another illustration of barley's importance to the peasantry is the prevalence of barley and barley malt rents on some manors. This was particularly true of manors geared to producing food for the seigneurial household, and on the cellarer of Bury's Mildenhall manor in 1323 almost 100 acres of peasant land were leased for 38 qu. 5 b.; at Risby

---

[118] Postan, *Medieval economy*, pp. 137–8.   [119] See below, pp. 143–57.

Table 3.14. *Crop preferences of lords and peasants in the Breckland villages of Blackbourne hundred in the 1283 Subsidy (quarters)*

Village	Wheat qu.	b.	Rye qu.	b.	Barley qu.	b.	Oats qu.	b.	Legumes qu.	b.
Peasants										
Barnham			130		99	2	104	2	1	
Culford			31	4	46	4	5			
Euston			81		147		112		16	6
Fakenham		4	21		41	2	11		3	
Ingham		4	51		75	1	10	4	1	4
Knettishall	4	1	36		137	4	14	4	2	4
Livermere Pa.	5		39		65	4	12		2	
Rushford			8	5	24		15		1	3
Sapiston	10	2	43	4	99	4	27	7	21	2
Troston	7	6	53	2	134	6	22	2	15	3
West Stow			54		74		36		7	
Wordwell			41		48	5	15		1	5
Total	28	1	588	6	992	7	385	3	72	2
Percentage	1.4		28.5		48		18.6		3.5	
Lords										
Barnham			3		10		9	4		7
Culford	2		38		57		23		2	
Euston										
Fakenham			3		4		3			
Ingham	20		38		50		48			4
Knettishall										
Livermere Pa.										
Rushford			8		9		10			
Sapiston										
Troston										
West Stow			15		18		18		2	
Wordwell										
Total	22		105		148		111	4	5	3
Percentage	5.6		26.8		37.8		28.4		1.4	

and Fornham (C) tenants rendered barley malt instead.[120] The use of barley as rent payment reflects its importance in Breckland, but how exactly did this come about and when? What came first, landlords demanding barley rents and so imposing their will upon peasant grain preferences, or vice versa? Dating their introduction is difficult, but it was probably around the mid-thirteenth century. The Risby account for 1286–7 notes that rent totalling 48 qu. 4 b. of oats malt had been substituted by 30 qu. 2 b. of barley malt at an unspecified date, and Bury abbey rentals from the early thirteenth century record a prevalence of oats malt rents not evident a century later.[121] Was this move a function of changes in demesne or peasant grain preferences? In part it may reflect higher seigneurial living standards based on the rising value of land, but more realistically it must reflect changes in peasant crop preference, and perhaps the later stages of a shift from oats subsistence to barley specialisation.

In addition to food crops, flax and hemp were grown in medieval Breckland, although not in the same quantities as in the woodpasture region of East Anglia. Neither plant was sown in the open fields, but was confined to courtyards and gardens. In 1342 the Icklingham demesne sold flax (*linum*) grown in the courtyard, and the manorial garden at Quiddenham was sown with hemp (*cannabus*) in 1399.[122] The peasants were active growers, and hemp and flax tithes from Troston and Livermere Magna were valued at 72 shillings in 1341.[123] Manorial courts occasionally referred to illegal retting of the plants in private waters. William Grey of Fornham All Saints was amerced 4d. in 1347 for 'putting his hemp in the lord's fishery', and in 1536 two Kilverstone men illegally put flax and hemp in the river Thet.[124] Most cultivation was on a modest scale and in the main for domestic use. It was used to make linen cloth, nets for rabbiting and fishing, and rope.

[120] Bodleian Suffolk Rolls 21; for Risby and Fornham, see, for instance, WSROB E.3/15.3/ 2.8 and E.3/15.6/2.25.

[121] WSROB E.3/15.13/2.4. Fourteenth-century accounts of Risby and Fornham (C) concern barley and barley malt rents alone; yet compare these with the large oats rents paid in the early thirteenth century, BL Harl. 638 ff.13–14 (Risby) and BL Harl. 3977 f.103 (Fornham).

[122] BL Add.Roll 25810; NRO Phi/493. The Brandon demesne also regularly grew hemp, Bacon 644.

[123] W.R. Gowers, 'The cultivation of flax and hemp in Suffolk in the fourteenth century', *The East Anglian: notes and queries* 5 (1893–4), pp. 180–3 and 200–2.

[124] WSROB E.3/15.7/1.6; NRO Ms 15167, court held October 1536. Retting the hemp in this way polluted the river, often killing the fish.

East Anglian Breckland: a marginal economy?

Regional trade and integration

Specialised agricultural production and the corresponding development of regional exchange and integration is an under-researched aspect of the general growth in trade which occurred in the two centuries after Domesday. New towns were established and older ones grew apace, for urban markets were important media in the exchange of a wide range of goods, from local, primary produce to urban consumer and fine imported goods. As their economic strength developed, so townsmen sought greater freedom from the trappings of manorialism and secured new privileges and status.[125] The hostility of feudal lords towards further freedom in towns was to become a source of friction and violence,[126] but it will suffice to record here that the establishment of these franchises distinguished towns like Bury, Cambridge and Thetford from the surrounding countryside.

The growth of a more commercialised economy is further reflected in the creation of new markets, particularly in the thirteenth century. Between 1227 and 1350 the Crown granted some 1,200 new market rights in England and Wales, and, as Britnell comments, 'the growth in trade most relevant to the founding of [these] new markets was an increase in local purchases by small households'.[127] Many of these foundations did not signify the creation of a new town, but related to communities hardly larger than villages. Unlike the towns, these market villages remained firmly under feudal control and seldom developed any large industrial capacity, and the few resident artisans often maintained a direct interest in husbandry.[128] East Anglia harboured a high concentration of markets, particularly when compared to northern and western England, reflecting a greater intensity of local and regional trade. Nine markets are mentioned in Suffolk Domesday, a further 65 were granted between 1227 and 1327, and

---

[125] For this process, see M.W. Beresford, *The new towns of the Middle Ages: town plantation in England, Wales and Gascony* (London, 1967); Miller and Hatcher, *Rural Society and economic change*, pp. 64–83; Bolton, *Medieval English economy*, pp. 119–49; S. Reynolds, *English medieval towns* (Oxford, 1977).

[126] Violence flared recurrently in the struggle for power between the burgesses of Bury St Edmunds and the abbey, R.S. Gottfried, *Bury St Edmunds and the urban crisis 1290–1539* (Princeton, 1982), pp. 215–36.

[127] Miller and Hatcher, *Rural Society and economic change*, p. 77; R.H. Britnell, 'The proliferation of markets in England 1200–1349', *Ec.H.R.* 34 (1981), p. 218.

[128] J. Cornwall, 'English country towns in the 1520s', *Ec.H.R.* 15 (1962–3), pp. 54–7.

143

most of the 138 markets in medieval Norfolk were of thirteenth-century origin.[129]

In regions which are marginal for grain production we might reasonably expect to find a low concentration of markets. In medieval Derbyshire, for instance, there were palpably few markets established on land above 800 feet, but in Breckland there was no shortage of markets for local produce.[130] Nearly all the foundations date from the thirteenth century and show a bias towards the fen edge: Brandon (1271), East Harling (?), Feltwell (1283), Gooderstone (1286), Hilborough (1347), Hockham (1267), Ickburgh (1257), Lakenheath (1201), Merton (1227), Methwold (?), Mildenhall (?), Oxborough (1249), Snetterton (1315), Stanford (1283) and Worlington (1258).[131] Hence most Breckland peasants were a short distance from half-a-dozen markets, which must have encouraged commercialisation and streamlined local trade. In general, though, these village markets merely complemented the dominant regional centres of Bury, Thetford, Lynn and Cambridge.[132] Bury and Thetford were important Anglo-Saxon markets, but thereafter Bury's influence increased at Thetford's expense. Indeed, Thetford's relative decline after Domesday can be largely explained by the remarkable successes of Lynn and Bury in the same period.[133] The power of the abbot of St Edmunds is also reflected by the conspicuous absence of market villages within a ten-mile radius of the town. Even the licence obtained for Lakenheath by the Prior and Convent of Ely in 1201 was vigorously disputed and then squashed by the abbot for fear of undermining the importance of his Bury market, and the Honor of Clare employed 200 armed men in an attempt to break Bury abbey's market monopoly in Mildenhall.[134]

---

[129] N. Scarfe, 'Markets and fairs in medieval Suffolk', *Suffolk Review* 3 (1965), pp. 4–11; D.P. Dymond, *The Norfolk landscape* (London, 1985), pp. 152–5. Compare these figures with those for Oxfordshire, where there were only 26 recorded medieval markets, D. Postles, 'Markets for rural produce in Oxfordshire, 1086–1350', *Midland History* 12 (1987), p. 16.   [130] Donkin, 'Changes in the early Middle Ages', p. 117.

[131] Information from sources cited in n. 129 above.

[132] For the regional importance of Cambridge, see M. Rubin, *Charity and community in medieval Cambridge* (Cambridge, 1987), pp. 33–7.

[133] Crosby, *Thetford*, pp. 27–9.

[134] The distribution of markets in Suffolk and their conspicuous absence around Bury is apparent from the map in Scarfe, *Suffolk landscape*, p. 166. The Lakenheath licence was reaffirmed and the market operational by 1309, Copinger, *Manors of Suffolk*, vol. IV, p. 173. The Clare/cellarer of Bury abbey clash occurred in the late thirteenth century, CUL Add.Ms 4220 f.126.

This fierce protectionism reflects the economic and social value of markets in the thirteenth century and was not an attitude unique to the Abbot, for the Hundred Rolls reveal that one Robert de Scalis had appropriated 'the market and fair in Worlington' without warrant.[135]

There can be no doubt that Breckland's economy underwent significant transformation in the thirteenth century, but not in the manner which historians have predicted. Rising population may not have resulted in the widespread conversion of heathland for arable cultivation, but it did encourage changes within the existing economic framework. As an old settled region, Breckland had reached the broad limits of agrarian expansion before the thirteenth century, and any subsequent changes were most likely to occur at the intensive margin. Not only did more complicated cropping and pasturing arrangements emerge, but the structure of trade became more clearly defined. The growth in marketing facilities and the movement towards specialisation in agricultural production were continuous and mutual developments which accelerated in the thirteenth century, and which resulted in a distinct commercialisation of the economy.[136] Campbell's work on de-mesne farming illustrates that this process was in no way unique to Breckland, but affected East Anglian agriculture as a whole.[137] By the early fourteenth century, Breckland had developed within the East Anglian economy as a sheep and rabbit rearing region which also exported some grain, and stood alongside other specialist areas such as the dairy region of south Suffolk and the prodigious arable region of north-east Norfolk.

For all the general expansion of trade, it is important to emphasise the point that most exchanges involved small transactions on a purely local scale. This was the century when the pressure of population on resources was greatest, and when the capacity of most peasants to meet even subsistence needs was limited. The poverty of Blackbourne taxpayers confirms this, for poor peasants

---

[135] *Rotuli hundredorum*, vol. II, p. 196.
[136] Indeed, geographers employ changing market densities as useful indicators of developing regional structures, P.O'Flanagan, 'Markets and fairs in Ireland 1600–1800: an index of economic development and regional growth', *Journal of Historical Geography* 11 (1985), pp. 364–78.
[137] B.M.S. Campbell, 'Towards an agricultural geography of medieval England', *Ag.H.R.* 36 (1988), pp. 91–8.

constituted 79 per cent of all those assessed in 1283.[138] Furthermore, they possessed a saleable average of only 3.38 qu. of grain
each, which was hardly sufficient to make a substantial contribution to inter-regional trade. Yet, as Postan has forcibly argued, all
peasants had to obtain cash to meet fiscal and feudal dues, and so
were compelled to sell some produce to the market.[139] This must
explain why the distinctive traits of specialisation are evident even
amongst the grain preferences of poor peasants: in 1283, 57.6 per
cent was barley, 27.5 per cent was rye and only 10.6 per cent was
oats.[140] It would appear that market influences affected all strata of
Breckland society.

What were the main markets for Breckland surpluses and what is
the evidence for regional inter-dependence? Without doubt, the
scope of Breckland's markets was broadened by its excellent geographical siting and communications. First, the region lay in the
hinterland of a clutch of sizeable and prosperous towns, notably
Bury but also Thetford, Cambridge, Ely and Lynn, all of which
exerted consistent demand for primary produce.[141] Secondly, it
lay in close proximity to the textile manufacturing area of south
Suffolk and north Essex where rural division of labour was high by
medieval standards and artisans were dependent on others for their
subsistence requirements. Thirdly, the adjacent fenland developed
rapidly in the twelfth and thirteenth centuries, but was heavily
dependent on grain imports – particularly barley – and had to
balance its trade by exporting salt and dairy produce to its grain
suppliers.[142] Lastly, the Great Ouse provided good communi-

---

[138] Poor peasants are taken to be those assessed at under £3 in 1283. For a fuller discussion of
this methodology, see below, pp. 192–3.

[139] Postan, *Medieval economy*, pp. 224–6; indeed, these dues and burdens were heaviest at the
end of the thirteenth century when land was in short supply, Rubin, *Charity and
community*, pp. 17–19.

[140] A further 0.9 per cent was wheat, and 3.4 per cent legumes. See also table 3.17 and n. 370.

[141] For towns and their hinterlands, see Reynolds, *English Medieval towns*, p. 145. The court
rolls of Breckland manors abound with references to Bury men trading in the region.
The Fornhams were obviously geared to the Bury market, a fact clearly illustrated by
the contract production of barley by Thomas Curteys of Fornham St Martin for one
Pagan, merchant of Bury in 1304, WSROB E.3/15.9/1.1 m.17. The influence of the
Suffolk markets spread well into Norfolk Breckland, for in 1358 a Newmarket
merchant was trading in Hockham, NRO Ms 13848, court held February 1358. In the
main, though, the Norfolk villages looked towards the north and east, so that Norwich
and Lynn merchants could be found in Methwold, PRO DL30.104/1472 m.4, court held
March 1371, and DL29.289/4754.

[142] H.E. Hallam, 'Population density in the medieval fenland', *Ec.H.R.* 14 (1961–2), p. 79;
H.E. Hallam, *Settlement and society: a study of the early agrarian history of south Lincolnshire*
(Cambridge, 1965), p. 196.

cations with the thriving port of Bishop's Lynn, whence much East Anglian produce was shipped either northwards, or to London, or further afield to the Baltic and the Low Countries. Some Breckland wool, barley, rye and rabbits certainly found their way to Lynn. As Gras writes, 'the proximity of western Suffolk [and Norfolk] to the Ouse would seem to justify our adding [it] as contributor to Lynn's corn supply'.[143]

These particular trading links are suggested by substantial evidence rather than mere supposition. When recording debt and damage disputes, court rolls will occasionally distinguish outsiders from local residents by explicitly stating their place of origin. Some scribes were more meticulous than others about including this information, but by plotting the home villages of those 'aliens' mentioned in the Brandon, Lakenheath and Methwold courts we can learn much about patterns of trade in Breckland (map 4 and appendix).[144] The most basic aspect of this trade was regular contact with other Breckland villages, particularly between the fen edge and central areas, yet superimposed upon this was a much wider range of trading links. From this, the overall pattern seems clear: peasants in central Breckland enjoyed easy access to a number of markets where their produce entered a regional network extending as far afield as Lynn and the East Anglian textile manufacturing regions. Fenland links appear to have been especially strong, suggesting that it might have been the main recipient of Breckland's grain surpluses.

The inter-development between Breckland and the fens was obviously important, but so was its trade with other areas of East Anglia. Breckland was everywhere surrounded by the low-price

---

143 N.S.B. Gras, *The evolution of the English corn market* (Harvard, 1915), pp. 61–3. By the seventeenth century Lynn's trade was dominated by barley and malt, J.A. Chartres, *Internal trade in England 1500–1700* (London, 1977), p. 19. Medieval Lynn was an important centre for the distribution of goods produced on the Ely estates, Miller, *Bishopric of Ely*, pp. 85–6. For an excellent general survey of Lynn and its trade see D.M. Owen, ed., *The making of King's Lynn: a documentary survey* (London, 1984), especially pp. 41–51. Owen explicitly states that trading links between Lynn and Lakenheath were particularly strong, p. 51.

144 The map is not based on surname evidence, although this can be a fair indication of place of origin up until the fourteenth century. Hence we might suspect that the Henry de Lincoln who appears just once in the Methwold courts was in fact from Lincoln, PRO DL30.104/1477 m.1. Instead the map is based upon specific references to individual villages, such as Henry Smith de Lincoln. This, and the tendency for some scribes not to distinguish aliens at all, means that the map understates the extent of Breckland's trading links.

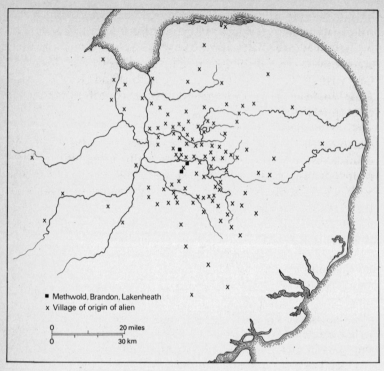

Map 4. Village of origin of aliens recorded in three Breckland villages
(see appendix)

wheat areas of Norwich, Cambridge and east Suffolk, which are
deemed to have been producing a surplus of wheat for export to
higher-price areas.[145] Presumably a reciprocal trade in barley and
wool also existed, so that Breckland farmers were absolved from
the need to produce wheat for their own purposes and were able to
concentrate on producing and exporting those products best suited
to their peculiar environment. Much of this trade was conducted
through the larger market centres, which explains why Bury
merchants feature so prominently in the court rolls of Suffolk

[145] Gras, *English corn market*, p. 41; R.A. Pelham, 'Fourteenth-century England', in *An
historical geography of England before 1800*, ed. H.C. Darby, (Cambridge, 1936), p. 236,
comments that 'the low priced areas were approximately the principal wheat growing
regions'.

Breckland villages.[146] Manorial accounts often record the sale of
large quantities of grain in bulk ('*in grosso*') to anonymous merchants, but unfortunately the exact destination is seldom given. On
the rare occasions that the markets are stated, the large regional
centres feature prominently. Kennett manor sold some corn in
Freckenham and Newmarket, but much of its barley was taken
over ten miles away to sell in the Bury market, and that from the
Langford demesne was sent for sale at Santon fair near Thetford.[147]
Evidence that Breckland wool found its way into central areas of
East Anglia is more plentiful, for demesne clips were variously sold
to merchants of Beccles, Bury, Cambridge, Lincoln and
Norwich.[148] Local peasants, too, are noted as trading with mer-
chants of Clare and Norwich, and in one case Henry Jacob,
'woolman' of Sculton (Norfolk), allegedly owed £3 3s. 4d. to
Andrew Bernereve of Coney Weston.[149]

Firm evidence for wider trading links, particularly with London
and the continent, is necessary if we are to prove that Breckland
assumed an important position in the wider economic nexus. In this
respect the frequent disputes involving Lynn merchants in court
rolls are highly suggestive, because Lynn is known to have exported grain and wool to various parts of England and the continent. Given this information, it would be unlikely if some
Breckland produce did not find its way into international trade,
although it would only constitute a very small proportion of the
region's overall production. Some produce was sent into northern
England, for merchants from Thetford and Worlington are

---

[146] The few surviving Thetford court rolls indicate that the town served as a market for
villages in northern Breckland, thus substantiating the hinterland suggested by Crosby,
Thetford, p. 28.

[147] PRO sc6.768/5 and 6; NRO NCC(Petre) Box 8/22. In the late fifteenth century, the
vicar of Hockham sold large quantities of malt to Thetford priory, CUL Add.Ms 6969
f.46.

[148] Wool from Risby was sometimes sent to Beccles, WSROB E.3/15.13/2.17. In 1320–3,
much of the Lakenheath clip was sold to Robert de Aula of Norwich, and in 1345 to
Roger Hardegrey of Norwich. Some fleeces were also sent to Cambridge, CUL EDC 7/
15/I/4 and 13. The 1326–8 clips were sold to the powerful Bury merchant Robert de
Eriswell, a leading burgess and subsequently alderman, CUL EDC 7/15/I/6 and 7, and
Gottfried, *Bury and the urban crisis*, p. 98. Bury merchants also bought most of the
Fornham (A) clip in the fifteenth century, see also p. 271. Bury merchants could then be
found selling wool in the north Essex textile manufacturing region, R.H. Britnell,
Growth and decline in Colchester, 1300–1525 (Cambridge, 1986), p. 142.

[149] *CPR*, 1422–9, pp. 437 and 517; *CPR*, 1436–41, p. 332 and 1452–61, p. 320.

recorded as taking cargoes to York and Newcastle, and York merchants were known to be trading in Mildenhall.[150]

Trade with London was certainly more regular. The capital's merchants occasionally appeared in Thetford market, and in the fifteenth century Cavenham manor sold 362 fleeces to one 'John Copemylle of London, Draper'.[151] London poulters and skinners looked to East Anglia for rabbits, and both Methwold and Brandon warrens sold on contract to London merchants. One such man was William Staunton, buyer to Richard II's household in the late 1370s and a notable merchant in his own right.[152] Breckland's trade with London was not just restricted to demesne produce, and Brandon, Hengrave and Fakenham peasants were named in debt disputes with London drapers in the fifteenth century. Similarly, Edmund Cote and Robert Dobson of Mildenhall, respectively a skinner and dyer, were trading with London merchants, and John Glatton, parson of Northwold, ran up substantial debts with London cloth-iers.[153] In general, it seems that Breckland's grain surpluses were absorbed by local urban markets, or filtered into the Great Ouse river system. Grain was bulky relative to its value, and therefore unable to sustain long-distance transportation overland. On the other hand, the more highly valued wool and rabbits could sustain larger transport costs, and were more likely to be sent to distant markets.

Breckland's trade was not just in one direction, and the region was dependent on surrounding areas for the provision of certain basic goods and materials. Wheat and dairy products are the most obvious food imports, and manorial accounts often record sending carts to collect fenland salt from the markets at Brandon and Santon.[154] Freshwater fish were readily available along the fen

---

[150] *CPR*, 1321–5, p. 134; John Payn of York (*de Eboraco*) owed a 6d. amercement to the Mildenhall court in 1390–1, WSROB E.18/455/1.

[151] PRO DL30.105/1489, court held October 1455; PRO SC6.1117/12.

[152] John Edmund, 'pulter' of London, bought up Methwold warren's stock of culled rabbits in 1453–4, PRO DL29.293/4829. For William Staunton, see Bacon 653, 655–7. His trading operations were extensive, *CPR*, 1377–81, pp. 3, 274, 368 and 540; *CPR*, 1381–5, p. 302. He owned property in Wimpole (Cambs.), which might explain his interest in East Anglian warrens, S. Thrupp, *The merchant class of medieval London 1300–1500* (Chicago, 1948), p. 367.

[153] *CPR*, 1396–9, p. 586; *CPR*, 1408–13, p. 255; *CPR*, 1416–22, p. 338; *CPR*, 1441–6, pp. 308–9; *CPR*, 1494–1509, p. 212; *CPR*, 1381–5, p. 172.

[154] See, for example, WSROB E.3/15.6/2.30b when Fornham carts were sent to collect salt, originally from Tilney in the Norfolk fens, from Brandon, and E.3/15.7/2.2b for Santon. In Brandon itself, John Edward of Walpole, another fenland village, was involved in a debt plea over sales of salt in October 1462, Bacon 296/3.

edge, and their provision and distribution was an important function of the Lakenheath and Mildenhall markets. Salted fish was a
speciality of Thetford market, but otherwise was fetched from
Lynn and Yarmouth.[155] The main type of salted fish was herring,
the standard produce of the east-coast fishing ports. Herrings were
regularly provided for demesne harvest workers in Breckland,
suggesting that they comprised a common component of the
peasant's diet.

The bulkiest of Breckland's imports were building materials, for
the region was poorly endowed with timber and high-quality
building stone. At Domesday Breckland was distinguished by a
lack of woodland. The Norfolk entries contain few references,
whilst Lackford hundred was almost devoid of woods.[156] Later
surveys and accounts reveal small clumps in peripheral villages, but
central areas were very open and almost bereft of even the smallest
copse.[157] Some of Breckland's timber came from supplies in
central Norfolk and Suffolk, so that Bury and Ely abbeys often
turned to manors such as Chevington, Bradfield, Elmswell and
Rattlesden to supply their Breckland manors, or else looked to the
markets at Bury and Ixworth.[158] Estonian boards and wainscot
were purchased either directly at Lynn or shipped into Brandon or
Thetford and sold there.[159] This appears to have been another
specialisation of Thetford, for an area of the town was designated
'le tymbermarket'.[160] Thus any substantial wooden building in the
region was largely constructed with imported materials, although
the plastering often comprised a mortar based on local deposits of
clay. Clay was regularly dug from glacial deposits in the subsoil,

[155] PRO DL30.105/1491; for the distribution of Yarmouth herrings throughout East
Anglia, see A. Saul, 'The herring industry at Yarmouth *c*.1280–*c*.1400', *Norfolk
Archaeology* 38 (1981), p. 37. Carts from Breckland villages often made the overland trip
to Yarmouth; Risby, WSROB E.3/15.13/2.17; Fornham (A) E.3/15.6/2.39a; Lakenheath
CUL EDC 7/15/I/4.

[156] Darby, *Domesday geography of eastern England*, pp. 127–8 and 182.

[157] For instance, Sykelond woods lay between Timworth and Fornham St Martin, and le
Hyde copse at Risby, Hengrave and Fornham All Saints. The Fakenham Magna
account includes receipts from wood herbage and sales of *subboscus*, BL Add.Roll 9100.
This was presumably from Fakenham wood, which supplied some timber to Thetford
priory in the late fifteenth century, CUL Add.Ms 6969 f.46. The Coney Weston
demesne included ten acres of woodland, Bodleian Ms Gough Suffolk 3 f.1.

[158] Fornham (A) often received timber from Chevington and Elmswell, WSROB E.3/15.7/
2.6, and in 1368–9 wooden clats for the foldcourse were made in Badmondsfield
(Suffolk), E.3/15.6/2.33. For Ixworth, see CUL EDC 7/15/I/13 and 14. Thetford priory
secured some of its supplies from nearby Bardwell in 1513, CUL Add.Ms 6969 f.111.

[159] See WSROB E.3/15.6/2.39b; CUL EDC 7/15/I/20.   [160] PRO DL29.288/4719.

and the marks of numerous medieval pits are apparent at Rymer Point.[161]

Sedges and reeds were used in roofing and were obtainable from fens or river valleys, even in central Breckland. At Langford in 1378, eleven people were amerced for illegally removing reeds from the lord's marsh.[162] Far greater quantities were available on the fen edge, and Mildenhall supplied other Bury abbey manors with most of their requirements.[163] Tiles were occasionally used for roofing, but they had to be imported: in 1413, 4,200 tiles were shipped from Lynn to Hockwold and then carted to Methwold warren lodge.[164] Many of the region's larger buildings were made from local flints and 'clunches', but foundation and corner stones had to be imported. When a stone bridge was built across the Little Ouse at Brandonferry in the early 1330s, larger stones had to be brought by water from Peterborough, whereas 444 cartloads of small flints and stones were collected from the surface of local fields and permission was obtained to dig chalk from the fields of nearby Bromehill priory.[165] A kiln was used to burn some of the chalk, and this was then mixed with local sand to make a mortar into which the rubble was set, a task performed by hired specialists from Thetford. The magnificent abbey at Bury comprised a flint core faced with best ashlar imported from the east Midlands via the Nene and the Ouse. Other stones to be imported were millstones, sometimes fetched from Ipswich or Lynn, but often shipped into Brandon, Lakenheath or Thetford.[166] In 1288 a millstone was purchased in Lynn, shipped in a hired boat to Worlington and then carted the short distance to Kennett.[167] Tin, iron and iron goods, wine and sea coal are amongst other goods mentioned in Breckland documents, and must also have formed a significant part of its

---

[161] This information was kindly provided by the owner of Rymer farm, Mr Nigel Rush, who has conducted a private survey.

[162] NRO NCC(Petre) Box 8/21, court held July 1378.

[163] See, for instance, WSROB E.3/15.13/2.16.   [164] PRO DL29.290/4765.

[165] PRO E101.543/4. When the warren lodge was constructed at Brandon in 1386–7, corner stones were imported from Northamptonshire, Rackham, *History of the countryside*, p. 293. Thetford priory regularly purchased cartloads of stones for repairs, presumably from local fields, J.H. Harvey, 'The last years of Thetford cluniac priory' *Norfolk Archaeology* 27 (1938), p. 9.

[166] The collection of millstones from Lynn or even Ipswich was common enough, CUL EDC 7/15/I/8 and 26; WSROB E.3/15.6/2.44. Occasionally they would be shipped down the Little Ouse as far as Downham or Thetford, WSROB E.3/15.13/2.20; BL Harl. 3977 f.85.   [167] PRO SC6.768/13.

import trade.[168] There are also regular references in Bury abbey and Thetford priory accounts to men visiting the great medieval fair at Stourbridge in Cambridge, and returning with tar, pitch and 'other victuals'.[169]

Just as agrarian specialisation is a function of regional integration, so this integration cannot possibly be achieved without the development of appropriate transport facilities. Communications in medieval England were generally slow and inefficient due to constraints imposed by technology and lack of capital, and consequently the transport system was rather primitive.[170] The most fortunate regions were those on the coast or those with access to a navigable river system, for water was by far the cheapest method of transporting bulky goods. Breckland was one such region, for all its rivers flowed into the Great Ouse and then into the sea at Lynn.[171] The river Wissey was navigable to Northwold at least, and the Lark to Mildenhall and Worlington. Manorial accounts note that wool merchants had free passage by boat on the Little Ouse as far as Thetford, and in 1555 a petition reported that vessels of 'twelve or sixteen loads burden' could reach the town.[172]

These natural advantages had been exploited to the full by Breckland communities. Most of the villages along the fen edge had any number of small staithes and hithes to facilitate the loading and unloading of boats, and in some places narrow waterways or 'lodes' were cut in order to improve access to the fenland rivers. Lodes had been systematically constructed since Roman times, and place-name evidence in Feltwell reveals just how extensive they had become by 1251; there was a 'bruneslode', 'hereslode',

---

[168] It is impossible to quantify the extent to which 'luxury' goods were imported into Breckland, but Lynn merchants would have tried to balance their trade with the region's wealthy elite by introducing them. The variety of imports to Lynn is certainly impressive: dried fruits, nuts, peppers, ginger, salmon, porpoise, dye-stuffs, furs, brass, hawks and wax, Miller, *Bishopric of Ely*, p. 86; Owen, *Making of King's Lynn*, pp. 42–3.

[169] WSROB E.3/15.6/2.44 and 2.46; Harvey, 'Thetford priory', p. 11. See also Rubin, *Charity and community*, p. 35.

[170] See R.E. Glasscock, 'England circa 1334', in *New historical geography of England*, ed., Darby, pp. 174–6. It is impossible to quantify the cost differences in transport by land and by water, because no exact information is available and because it varied according to the type of goods carried. Yet, whenever the region's rivers were afflicted by drought and bulky goods had to be diverted by land, transport costs rose sharply. For instance in 1331–2, 44s. 3d. was spent on transporting stones to Brandon *'plusque solebat ob defectum aque'*, PRO E101.542/4.   [171] J. Willard, 'Inland transportation', pp. 371–2.

[172] PRO DL29.291/4791; Crosby, *Thetford*, p. 79.

'witecredelode' and a 'glomeslode'.[173] Near Methwold, where a cutting from the river Wissey met the Breckland edge, the small settlement of Oteringhithe had emerged, presumably to act as a small outlying port.[174] As integral components of Breckland's communications network, it was important for these lodes to be maintained in a navigable condition, and hence a cutting at Mildenhall was occasionally dredged to ensure that laden craft could reach the annual fair from the river Lark.[175] There can be little doubt that villages on the fen edge provided important debarkation posts for the passage of goods to and from many villages in western Norfolk and Suffolk, and particularly for the successful wool and cloth market of Bury St Edmunds. Gottfried has emphasised the international flavour of Bury's trade and its role as a market for Suffolk cloth, and believes that half its exports went through Lynn, and by implication the breck-fen villages.[176]

Goods travelling by water were carried in shallow draught boats, often described in documents as *batelli*. The exact size and structure of these are unknown, but the name covered a variety of types, from small rafts used to shift reeds from the fens, to larger craft capable of carrying animals and heavier loads. Documents occasionally distinguish *batellus* from *navicula*, although it is impossible to know whether this implied a different form of boat.[177] Larger vessels were certainly used in the deeper waters and could get at least as far as Brandon, for in 1471 a 'kele' valued at £5 12s. was docked at the village.[178] This particular boat seems to have belonged to a consortium of Brandon men, and there are indications that water transport was mainly in the hands of specialist carriers, rather than left to the merchants themselves.[179] Officials

---

[173] CUL EDR G3/27 f.150. See also Rackham, *History of the countryside*, p. 384; J.R. Ravensdale, *Liable to floods: village landscape on the edge of the fens, 450–1850* (Cambridge, 1974), pp. 21–8. The Lark was not navigable to Bury until the late seventeenth century, CUL Hengrave Hall Ms 1 (1), p. 4.

[174] PRO DL29.298/4754 records that 'le lode' extended from Methwold hithe to the common river.

[175] In 1411–12 30s. was spent on dredging for 'boats laden with meat, fish and corn', BL Add.Roll 53129.

[176] Gottfried, *Bury and the urban crisis*, pp. 91–2. It was also common for woollen cloths from Hadleigh to pass through Lynn, G.A. Thornton, *A history of Clare, Suffolk* (Cambridge, 1928), p. 148.

[177] Although Ravensdale, *Liable to floods*, p. 32, equates the *navicula* with the long fen barge.

[178] Bacon 296/17, court held July 1471. 'Keels' were large enough to be employed in the east-coast coal trade, A. Luders *et al.*, *Statutes of the realm* (1810–28), vol. I, p. 516.

[179] A view supported by other research on the medieval fenland, Ravensdale, *Liable to floods*, p. 33.

of the Bishopric of Ely regularly hired boatmen to move episcopal victuals to various destinations, sometimes at considerable expense. In 1367 these goods were shipped by a boatman from Wells on the Norfolk coast, and the bailiff also employed one Roger Paas, 'boatman of Brandon . . . with his own boat'.[180] On the fen edge, boat ownership was reasonably common. Lakenheath accounts regularly mention payments for '*botesgangs*' or wharf fees, and in 1330 Robert Gopayn claimed that another peasant had illegally removed his boat from its mooring at Gopaynesshythe.[181] At Methwold too, illegal sedge and reed cutting was undertaken by men operating from their own boats.[182] Boatmen's services were in regular demand from the Prior and Convent of Ely to carry vast quantities of produce across the fens. This could be a lucrative business, for they paid over 62s. to move barley from Lakenheath to Ely in 1365, whilst twenty years later a boat was hired on fourteen occasions to carry rabbits at 6d. a trip.[183] In some places landlords were required to provide ferrying services, and in 1406 it was reported that the lord of Oxborough was failing to provide a boat for the use of travellers between Oxborough and Northwold.[184]

It was not just demesnes who demanded the services of boatmen, and, if the Bury–Lynn link was as strong as Gottfried suggests, then there must have been a regular movement of goods and commercial travellers along the Great Ouse. As Breckland lay directly between west Suffolk and the waterway to Lynn and the sea, it was ideally placed to exploit that trade, and the Lakenheath court rolls provide a glimpse of peasants so employed. There is evidence of an agreement to take 30 quarters of rye to a shop in Lynn and of another to deliver goods at a Bury residence. Henry Knopping was contracted to take a passenger to Lincoln, and Reginald le Bule was in the village carrying goods en route from Yaxley (Suffolk) to Boston.[185]

Whilst water transport to and from Breckland was obviously an

[180] PRO sc6.1304/30. In 1393 a specialist was hired on thirteen separate occasions to carry timber from Brandon across the fens to Somersham (Hunts.) at 8s. a load, Bacon 657. In the same period, the bishop's victuals were transported by boatmen of Hockwold and Lynn, Bacon 660, 661 and 663. Boat transportation was crucial to the economy of the Ely estates, Miller, *Bishopric of Ely*, p. 125.   [181] PRO sc2.203/95.
[182] PRO dl30.104/1469.   [183] CUL EDC 7/15/I/20 and 28.
[184] PRO dl30.104/1480, court held May 1406.
[185] CUL EDC 7/15/II/Box 1/1, court held September 1310, and Box 1/6 m.45, court held May 1326. Brandon men were also carrying goods to Bury, Bacon 296/16 June 1470.

efficient and specialised business, there is less evidence to suggest that overland carriage was as well organised. The cart was the main form of heavy-duty haulage, and although manorial demesnes employed specialist carters, there is no indication that this provided a full-time occupation amongst the peasantry at large.[186] This did not mean that carting could not provide a useful source of supplementary income, nor that long-distance hauls were seldom attempted. Whilst most peasants carted their produce to market either individually or collectively, some merchants and landlords were prepared to pay for the service. Why else was the Lakenheath demesne accustomed to leasing out its unemployed carts to peasants who used them to visit Bury regularly?[187] By the thirteenth century, much of Breckland's haulage was performed by horses rather than oxen, and this was far more relevant to the greater efficiency of overland transport than any elaborate division of labour. As Langdon has forcibly argued, the dominance of horse-hauling increased access to markets, particularly for the peasantry, and encouraged regional specialisation.[188] Evidence that Breckland peasants used the horse rather than the slower ox is overwhelming from damage presentments in court rolls. At Lackford between 1354 and 1467, around 45 per cent of all damage presentments where the animal was identified concerned horses, and oxen were hardly mentioned: at Brandon in Richard II's reign, 45 per cent were horses, 3 per cent oxen and 7 per cent unspecified 'beasts'.[189]

Road travel within the region was quick by medieval standards for the terrain was not arduous nor were the soils prone to flooding, and the need to create efficient overland links is reflected in the ambitious construction of Brandon bridge in 1332 at a cost of over two hundred pounds.[190] The ancient Icknield Way and Peddar's Way traversed the region, and in the Middle Ages this section of the Icknield Way comprised the main overland route from London to Norwich. The volume of traffic passing along this road is indicated by the level of tolls collected from travellers crossing the Ouse at

---

[186] J.F. Willard, 'The use of carts in the fourteenth century', *History* 17 (1932), pp. 246–50. See also Willan, *The inland trade*, pp. 1–13.

[187] In 1361–2 the demesne leased its carts to an unspecified peasant who used them to travel *'usque St Edmunds per vices'*, CUL EDC 7/15/I/21.

[188] Langdon, 'Horse hauling', pp. 65–6; Langdon, *Horses, oxen and innovation*, p. 273.

[189] WSROB E.3/15.12/1.1–1.8, and 1.12–1.16; Bacon 292.

[190] PRO E101.542/4.

Thetford: in Henry III's reign they were valued at £15.[191] Tollage over Brandon bridge also earned the Duchy of Lancaster £3 each year, and the road south out of Brandon towards Mildenhall was known locally as 'Londonweye', reflecting a wide perspective: that travelling east from Kilverstone was dubbed 'Norwichwaye'.[192]

A detailed study of overland transport in medieval England is still awaited, but, in East Anglia at least, we should not underestimate its importance. Demesne carts from Breckland regularly travelled to Yarmouth, Ipswich and Norwich to collect herrings, whilst Matthew Outlawe of Lakenheath borrowed another peasant's horse to draw a cart on a private visit to Ipswich.[193] Estate records also indicate that water and land transport were fully integrated and carefully administered. Bury abbey was accustomed to shipping millstones from Lynn as far as the breck-fen edge, and then moving them by carts to their inland destination. Thus customary tenants at Barton Magna (Suffolk) were compelled to collect the cellarer's millstone whenever required from the staithes at either Lakenheath or Thetford.[194] Unfree tenants on the Bishopric of Ely's estates were also expected to perform a variety of carriage services for the lord. At Bridgham, they were required to cart demesne produce from other bishopric manors in central Norfolk and Suffolk.[195] This produce was invariably destined for the breck-fen edge, whence it was shipped to Ely, Wisbech and Littleport by tenants of Feltwell, Northwold and Brandon.[196] We might conclude therefore that the communications network serving Breckland was very efficient by contemporary standards.

Whilst many Breckland peasants concerned themselves with the

191 PRO DL29.290/4720 and 4765. Thetford priory accounts of the late fifteenth century indicate that the road was still busy with travellers. I am grateful to David Dymond for this information.
192 Bacon 295/62, court held April 1457; NRO Ms 15166 m.3, court held June 1467.
193 For Yarmouth and Ipswich, see the Risby accounts WSROB E.3/15.13/2.16 and 2.17. For Norwich, see the Lakenheath account CUL EDC 7/15/I/4. Lakenheath is a full 45 miles from Ipswich, and Outlawe's case is recorded in the September court of 1314, CUL EDC 7/15/II/Box 1/6 m.14. In the 1340s, famuli from Culford and Fornham were sent on an errand to Brancaster, which was not a Bury manor, WSROB E.3/15.7/2.2b.
194 BL Harl. Ms 3977 f.85.
195 Customary tenants of Roudham and Bridgham had to perform carriage services to and from the Bishopric's manors of Brandon, Feltwell, Northwold, Shipdham, Pulham, Dereham, Wetheringsett, Barking, Rattlesden and Hetham, and also to Thetford, Attleborough and Buckenham, CUL EDR G3/27 ff.146 and 148.
196 *Ibid.*, f.151.

production of primary agrarian goods for domestic or local consumption, there can be no doubt that some produced surpluses of grain and wool specifically for export from the region. The ability to achieve this depended upon both the existence of suitable markets and the capacity to reach those markets cheaply and efficiently. It would seem that the Middle Ages marked the growth of some degree of rural specialisation and interdependence in East Anglia, developments presumably encouraged by a dense, prosperous and relatively free population. The Breckland economy evolved a specialist role within this economic nexus, a process dependent upon the coterminous development of an efficient transport system. The system connecting Breckland with its markets was fast and cheap by medieval standards, and was based upon a readily accessible and improved waterway network where haulage was conducted by specialist boatmen. Overland transport was inevitably more expensive for bulky goods, but the terrain was relatively propitious and the roads were frequently used by a steady volume of traffic. Increased specialisation of production in Breckland and its environs, and some specialisation of labour in the transport system, combined to increase economic efficiency and so enable Breckland to counter its inherent marginality in arable production.

TRADES AND OCCUPATIONS

In comparison to agriculture, medieval industry was extremely limited in scope and output. England in the thirteenth century was an important source of much of western Europe's tin and lead, but these deposits were mainly restricted to a few upland areas.[197] Large concentrations of woodland could foster a variety of related 'forest industries',[198] but, apart from these, most specialist crafts tended to be concentrated in urban areas. Yet even these 'industrial' crafts were mainly dependent upon the agrarian resource base, and involved little more than the treating, processing and dressing of its raw materials, notably wool and hides. Nor was there any certainty as to the availability or regularity of this type of employment, particularly in the countryside. Not surprisingly, this proved an effective constraint to specialisation outside agriculture, and it is

---

[197] See Donkin, 'Changes in the early Middle Ages', pp. 106–14; Glasscock, 'England circa 1334', pp. 169–73.   [198] Birrell, 'Peasant craftsmen', pp. 91–107.

doubtful whether as much as one-tenth of England's population was involved primarily in industry.

On the other hand, it would be too simplistic to regard all of rural England as geared exclusively to agriculture. Although the scope of industrial occupations was limited, it is apparent that some trades, most notably the manufacture of woollen textiles, spread from the towns to the countryside in the later Middle Ages.[199] In addition there were always some workmen providing a variety of non-agrarian services and products for the village community, such as blacksmiths, bakers and brewers. These occupations were not always full-time, but were important because they provided smallholders with an alternative source of income. Similarly, in villages blessed with large tracts of pasture, woodland or fen, a greater variety of employment opportunities was available. In a region where arable farming was notoriously difficult, we might reasonably expect to find a correspondingly stronger dependence upon non-agrarian or industrial occupations. Such diversity would broaden the economy's base and increase its resilience in periods of agricultural difficulty.

Evidence for non-agrarian employment – be it full-time or part-time – is plentiful from Breckland, and is best documented in court rolls. If industrial activity is practised regularly enough, then it will almost certainly come under the gaze of manorial officials sooner or later. However, such references tend to be rather irregular, unlike those relating to land transactions, for instance, and it is often difficult to establish just how widespread was a given activity. Hence one Mildenhall court might explicitly describe a particular peasant as, say, a weaver, but there is seldom evidence of the same man practising his craft in the records of other courts. Another source of evidence for industrial activity is surnames, although these should be used with care.[200] Surnames had largely become hereditary by the early fifteenth century, but before that date were often flexible and so can be a reasonable guide to employment. Yet the most reliable documentation is the Poll Tax returns of 1381, for these normally name those involved in non-agrarian crafts, or 'artifices' as they are called. Where the 1381 returns have not survived, those from the 1379 tax can yield unexpected results. In

---

[199] E. Miller, 'The fortunes of the English textile industry in the thirteenth century', *Ec.H.R.* 18 (1965), pp. 64–82.

[200] R.H. Hilton, 'Small town society in England before the Black Death', *Past and Present* 105 (1984), p. 64.

Breckland neither the 1379 nor the 1381 returns were recorded in a standardised format, but two basic differences between them are evident. First, the 1381 tax was levied at a fixed rate of 12d. per head, but in 1379 the sum varied. Secondly, it was uncommon for occupations to be designated in the 1379 returns,[201] although it is still possible to detect those involved in industrial occupations. By far the most common tax levied per head in 1379 was 4d., although a few paid 6d. and others rather more. At Methwold the returns are exceptional, and nine artificers were specifically named, eight of whom paid at the higher rate of 6d.[202] Significantly, in the other returns where artificers are not nominated, there is a striking coincidence between those taxpayers with occupational surnames and those paying at the higher rate. In Stanford, Weeting and Methwold Hithe there was a total of twelve taxpayers with occupational surnames, of whom eight paid 6d.[203] McKinley concluded that surnames were still a reasonable guide to employment in the Poll Tax returns, and from this evidence we might assume that roughly 75 per cent of higher-rate taxpayers with occupational surnames in 1379 were actually involved in industrial employment:[204] the correlation is too strong to be coincidental. These assumptions were employed in constructing Tables 3.15 and 3.16.

Provision and processing of natural resources

Occupational diversity was potentially greatest along the breck-fen edge, reflecting a wider range of available resources. The southern fens bordering Breckland were largely waterlogged, comprising a hybrid of streams, marshes, pools and small islets, although in summer the water level receded sufficiently to permit grazing on certain pastures. The fen economy fostered a variety of pursuits, depending on the degree of local wetness and saturation.[205] Stock raising, fishing, fowling, reed gathering, turf cutting and hay production were all possible, but were subject to strict manorial control. The enormous value of these products resulted in many boundary disputes and much litigation. The Hundred Rolls record

---

[201] Although the 1379 returns from Methwold and Thetford are an exception and do record those involved in non-agrarian employment.

[202] PRO E179.149/51 m.2.   [203] PRO E179.149/51 mm. 1–2.

[204] R.A. McKinley, *Norfolk and Suffolk surnames in the Middle Ages* (London, 1975), p. 19–20.

[205] The best introduction to the fenland economy is still H.C. Darby, *The medieval fenland* (Cambridge, 1940).

that 'the vill of Lakenheath makes a purpesture on the vill of Wangford in the marsh and turbary', although in later documents Lakenheath men themselves were constantly protesting against intrusions by men from other villages.[206]

Fishing

Fishing was sufficiently important to merit both occupational specialism amongst the peasantry and careful regulation by manorial edict. Breckland's waters were subject to seigneurial jurisdiction no less than its heaths and arable land. Most villagers possessed some fishing rights in their local river or fen, but the exploitation of large tracts of water remained the exclusive preserve of the manorial lord. Residents of Bridgham possessed some fishing rights in the river Thet, but not in the carefully delimited 'separate fishery of the lord'.[207] Likewise the exact bounds of the Bishopric of Ely's fishery in the Little Ouse at Brandon were carefully described in accounts and any unlicensed fishing there was strictly prohibited.[208] Yet few landlords directly exploited these fisheries themselves, and preferred to lease them instead for cash rents to local fishermen. The size of these rents varied according to the extent and quality of the fishery, and to prevailing economic conditions. But even as rentiers landlords retained full responsibility for protecting the lessees' monopoly, and court rolls reveal their constant struggle to prevent illegal fishing. It was in their interests to do so, because uncontrolled and gratuitous plundering of stocks would reduce both the fisheries' value and their attractiveness to potential lessees. Nevertheless, landlords were to find poachers determined opponents. Gangs in boats from Wilton and Hockwold repeatedly anchored in the Bishopric of Ely's Brandon fishery, while armed monks from Bromehill priory (in the south-east of Weeting parish) did likewise in four *navicula*.[209] Lessees were also required to help keep their fisheries in good condition by maintaining dams, weirs and boundary markers.[210]

The most prominent lessees were probably full-time fishermen, and the large rents charged for some fisheries indicate it must have been a lucrative occupation. John Knight paid between three and

---

[206] *Rotuli hundredorum*, vol. II, pp. 153–4.   [207] CUL EDR G3/27 f.146.
[208] See, for example, the terms of the lease in Bacon 650.
[209] Bacon 296/8, court held July 1465.
[210] See, for instance, Bacon 291/19, court held September 1350.

four pounds each year for the Brandon lease for 40 years after the Black Death, although on occasions he was obviously in partnership with other men.[211] His participation in the land market during the same period was limited, implying that fishing was his major, if not only, source of income. This seems to have been the case with other Brandon men, such as Thomas Taylor and Stephen Nobbys, who were both designated 'fyshermen' in court rolls.[212] The Lyricock family of Lakenheath also appear to have been specialists in this line. John Lyricock obtained a special licence to take eels from the marsh in 1326, Richard was amerced for illegal fishing in 1324 and leased three fisheries in 1356, and Walter had two '*botesgangs*' in the fens that same year.[213] Other villagers had rights of access to certain common fisheries from which they could obtain supplies of freshwater fish for domestic consumption at the very least. These rights must have been important to the peasantry for they clashed frequently in attempts to protect them. In 1394 a gang of Hockwold men attacked another group of fishermen in the fens near Wilton, and allegedly stole boats and nets valued at ten pounds, and murdered John Cob of Lakenheath.[214]

The greatest concentration of fisheries was obviously along the breck-fen edge, and it was here that fishing assumed a prominent role in diversifying the village economy.[215] In 1086 there had been 3½ fisheries in Mildenhall and 7 on the Methwold demesne.[216] Income from fishery leases constituted around 14 per cent of gross manorial revenue in early fourteenth-century Lakenheath, where some rent was still valued in eels.[217] The eel was common in fenland pools and rivers, but other freshwater fish also abounded. Turbot, pike, roach and dace are amongst those specifically mentioned.[218] Fishing was not just confined to the fen edge, but was common enough in the river valleys of central Breckland. On the

---

[211] In 1361–2 the fishery was leased to Knight *et alii*, PRO SC6.1304/29.

[212] Bacon 296/12 and 296/25, court held March 1475.

[213] CUL EDC 7/15/II/Box 1/6 m.54, court held October 1326, and m.37, November 1324; 7/15/I/16.   [214] CUL EDC 7/15/II/Box 2/22 m.19.

[215] See also Ravensdale, *Liable to floods*, pp. 48–50.

[216] *V.C.H. Suffolk*, vol. I, p. 428; *V.C.H. Norfolk*, vol. II, pp. 135–6.

[217] Income from fisheries was higher at Lakenheath than on any other manor. By the early fourteenth century, most eel rents had been commuted for cash, as on the Clare fee where 172.5 sticks of eels rent had been replaced with 43s. 1½d. by 1290, PRO SC6.1001/5.

[218] Eels were to be found as far down the river Lark as Icklingham, BL Add.Roll 25810. Dace and roach are common in shallow freshwaters and tend to shoal together, and would have abounded in Breckland rivers. In the late eighteenth century, the Lark was noted to have harboured pike, perch, eel and otter, CUL Hengrave Hall Ms 1 (1), p. 4.

Lark there are recorded fisheries at Tuddenham and Hengrave, and specialist fishermen in Bury St Edmunds itself.[219] At Icklingham in 1342 the reeve hired two fishermen 'with their own nets' for three days' work on the mill pond.[220] On the Little Ouse above Thetford there was a fishery and liberty of a boat at Rushford, and others at Euston, Gasthorpe and Harling.[221] On the Thet and Wissey, fisheries are documented at Breckles, Brettenham, Cressingham Magna, Colveston, Hockham, Kilverstone, Langford, Quiddenham and Threxton, and the prior of Thetford even had a fish house next to Hockham mere.[222]

Peat and sedge

Local shortages of woodland meant that peat turves were an important source of fuel, and they were extracted in great quantities from fenland turbaries. The processing and sale of turves were carefully controlled by manorial courts, and the claims of commoners took precedence over commercial demands. Exact regulations varied over time and place according to the size and state of the turbary and to the prevailing economic climate. Residents in some villages were entitled to a strict annual allowance, for example 4,000 at Eriswell and 500 at Barton Parva.[223] Elsewhere the only restrictions concerned illegal diggings by neighbouring villages: in one Feltwell marsh it was ordained that 'the lord Bishop and the other lords of this village with all of the villagers ought to have common of pasture, mowing and digging', but that men of Wilton and Hockwold were 'neither to mow nor dig'.[224] The most common demand was that the turves should not be sold outside the home village, but it is obvious that peasants frequently ignored the ban. Court rolls abound with amercements levied for illegal extraction and distribution of turves, so that in practice the payments amounted to little more than temporary licences to do so.[225] In November 1328, fourteen Lakenheath men sold 17,500

219 Darby, *Domesday geography of eastern England*, p. 185; WSROB 449/2/338; Gottfried, *Bury and the urban crisis*, pp. 111–20.   220 BL Add.Roll 25810.
221 Blomefield, vol. I, p. 193; John Rylands Lib. Phillipps Charter 19; Powell, *Suffolk hundred*, p. 83; Darby, *Domesday geography of eastern England*, pp. 133–4.
222 Darby, *Domesday geography of eastern England*, pp. 133–4; Blomefield, vol. I, pp. 301, 314, 525, 561 and 622; vol. III, p. 373. The demesne fisheries at Hockham and Quiddenham were leased for 51s. 8d. and £2 respectively in the 1380s, NRO Ms 13853 and Phi/493.
223 Munday, 'Eriswell notebook'; Bodleian Ms Suffolk Rolls 1 m.4.
224 CUL EDR G3/27 f.150.
225 This was common in fenland villages proper, Ravensdale, *Liable to floods*, pp. 52–3.

turves against the statute and were amerced a total of 55d.[226]
Brandon men were variously noted as selling them in Thetford,
Bromehill and Wangford, and on other occasions men were contracted to carry the turves to other villages.[227] The scale of these
operations should not be underestimated. In one transaction, John
Tunte purchased 10,000 turves for 13s., and John Sadde of Brandon
was contracted to dig 20,000 turves.[228] This was certainly enough
to make turve production a useful if not important supplementary
occupation on the fen edge, so that two Brandon men were
described as 'habitual diggers of turves'.[229] Court presentments of
illegal diggings were most frequent during the period before the
Black Death, and the coincidence of names in brewing and turve-
cutting amercements suggests that these were particularly valuable
sources of extra income in times of land hunger and economic
hardship.

Reeds and sedge, which made excellent thatch, also abounded in
river valleys and the fens, but once again their exploitation was
carefully regulated. Residents were allowed to mow an allotted
quantity of sedge each summer, after which it was left to dry and
eventually removed. Any mown sedge remaining in the marshes
after a specified date (usually 1 November) could then be claimed
and taken by anyone. The dried sedge, or *lesch* as it appears in the
documents, was tied into sheaves and used primarily for thatching,
but sometimes as fuel and fodder.[230] The regulations varied in
detail, but again the main restriction was on sales outside the
village. However this did not apply to manorial lords, as evidenced
by the vast quantities of sedge and reeds sent by Bury abbey from
Mildenhall to other manors in west Suffolk. In 1348 Lakenheath
manor raised £5 16s. 9d. through such sales.[231] Yet, as in turve
production, peasants frequently transgressed the formal regulations and sold large quantities to other villages. Lakenheath peasants were known to have illegally sold sedge in Eriswell,
Mildenhall, Thetford and Wangford, and in May 1348 thirty-two

---

[226] CUL EDC 7/15/II/Box 1/8 m.16. In May 1326, nine men sold 3,000 turves and 26
cartloads of turves, Box 1/6 m.45.

[227] Bacon 295/31 (Wangford), 295/35 (Bromehill) and 296/3 (Thetford).

[228] CUL EDC 7/15/II/Box 1/9 m.32, court held August 1334; Bacon 296/1, court held
March 1461.

[229] Bacon 296/17, court held July 1471. Turves were also to be found in some central
villages, and sales at Hockham raised nearly 55s. in 1383–4, NRO Ms 13854.

[230] T.A. Rowell, 'Sedge in Cambridgeshire: its use, production and value', *Ag.H.R.* 34
(1986), p. 142. [231] CUL EDC 7/15/I/14.

men were amerced for unspecified sales.[232] The Methwold court ordered its marsh custodians to ascertain the names of those selling sedge in other villages in 1273, and in 1369 John Stayard of Feltwell was amerced twenty shillings for mowing 6,000 sedges and selling them externally.[233]

Although this was basically an ancillary occupation, it could still be lucrative. Sedge requires no management other than harvesting, and as an evergreen can be taken at any time during the year.[234] Communal restricions on the harvest were imposed, but the sheer weight of transgressions in court rolls suggests that these were often ignored. The value of sedge was considerable. At the Star Chamber in 1543 John Grant of Lakenheath claimed that twenty 'riotouse et evill disposed' people burnt sedge and reeds valued at £10 growing in marsh under his lease.[235] An inquisition taken on the death of John de Warenne at Methwold in July 1347 valued his sedge at the same sum.[236] Nor was growth confined to the fen edge. In 1459 there was a 'leschemere' in West Wretham, and in 1378 eleven men illegally mowed reeds from the lord's marsh at Langford.[237] Sedge was more flexible and durable than reed, but the latter could still be used as lower-quality thatch.[238] Lackford manor sold 360 bundles of reed to a local man in 1444, and 1,212 sheaves were sold for 20s. 3d. at Icklingham in 1343, along with 9s. of '*magnis cirpis*'.[239]

Minerals

Although there were no natural deposits of coal or metallic ores in Breckland, there was still some employment in extractive processes. Flints had been mined by Neolithic man at Grimes Graves but were equally abundant on the surface of local fields. Brandon has always been famous as a source of flints and in medieval times they were used mainly in the construction of buildings and for skinning furs. Unfortunately manorial records seldom mention flints, but most peasants must have collected and sold them by the

232 CUL EDC 7/15/II/Box 2/16 m.1, court held May 1347, and Box 2/17 m.5a.
233 PRO DL30.104/1469.   234 Rowell, 'Sedge in Cambridgeshire', p. 145.
235 PRO STAC2.11/26.   236 PRO DL30.104/1469.
237 NRO Ms 18018; NRO NCC(Petre) Box 8/21, court held July 1378.
238 Rowell, 'Sedge in Cambridgeshire', p. 142; Ravensdale, *Liable to floods*, p. 54.
239 WSROB E.3/15.12/5.3; BL Add.Roll 25810. The price of turves and sedge in medieval Cambridge was high, indicating both their importance and their commercial value, J.E.T. Rogers, *A history of agriculture and prices in England 1259–1793*, vol. 1 (Oxford, 1866), p. 423.

cartload. Flint mining was still practised in the nineteenth century, and the extent of flint flushwork on East Anglian churches suggests that it must also have been widely undertaken in the medieval period.[240] Another specialism was the mining of high-quality building chalk from shafts sunk up to twenty feet into the ground.[241] On the coarsest soils between Brandon, Downham, Thetford and Elveden peasants dug, extracted and sold both chalk and sand for industrial purposes. In 1447 two Brandon men illegally dug gravel (*gabolo*) pits, as did two Thetford men at Kilverstone in 1536.[242] Between Downham and Brandon in 1532 six men were digging 'lyme et sonde', and 18 loads of sand were dug from local pits during repairs to Methwold warren lodge in 1414.[243] At Thetford in 1514 there was a place known as 'calk pit yeerde', and one Ivan Skarlet dug chalk near Downham and took it by the cartload 'to his limekiln and made lime [*calcium*] . . . and he sold the said lime'.[244] The limekilns were probably fired by local turves, and were certainly common enough for one area of fourteenth-century Thetford to be known as 'lymburners street'.[245] The lime itself probably entered inter-regional trade, to be used in agriculture or in the preparation of building mortar.

Provision of services

Nearly every medieval village created a demand for the provision of certain basic services, and Breckland was no exception. Whilst many tasks were performed within the household itself, most villages possessed commercial brewers and bakers to meet local demand, and perhaps also blacksmiths, millers, tailors and shoemakers. Another regular source of employment was in repair work on local houses and barns. Some wealthy peasants were prepared to hire part-time labourers to tend their needs, whilst work on manorial buildings was regularly available. Local people were hired by

---

[240] A.J. Forrest, *Masters of flint* (Lavenham, 1983), pp. 42–4.

[241] R.L.S. Bruce-Mitford, 'A late medieval chalk-mine at Thetford', *Norfolk Archaeology* 30 (1947–52), pp. 220–2; H.D. Hewitt, 'Chalk mines at Thetford', *Norfolk Archaeology* 31 (1955–7), pp. 231–2. Such activity was common in chalk regions, see R.F. LeGear, 'Three agricultural chalk mines in north-west Kent', *Archaeologia Cantiana* 99 (1983), pp. 67–72.

[242] Bacon 295/43; NRO Ms 15167, court held October 1536. In the seventeenth century, gravel digging was an important source of ancillary employent in the heathland areas of England, J. Thirsk, *England's agricultural regions and agrarian history, 1500–1750* (London, 1987), p. 48.   [243] Bacon 297/25; PRO DL29.290/4765.

[244] Crosby, *Thetford*, p. 51; Bacon 295/43.   [245] Crosby, *Thetford*, p. 51.

the day at the reeve's discretion to dig chalk and clay, to fetch materials and to provide general labour, whilst the more specific tasks were performed by teams of local thatchers and carpenters. Ambitious projects, notably the construction of large timber or stone buildings, were undertaken by skilled specialists from nearby towns. For instance, during the construction of Brandon bridge in 1332, 'cementars' were brought from Thetford to prepare the mortar, and fifty years later there were still four master masons living in the town.[246]

So it would appear that the more specialised goods and services could only be found in the towns, or the larger market villages of the breck-fen edge. Brandon and Mildenhall certainly offered a wide range of services, for butchers, poulters, spicers, chandlers, wheelwrights and coopers, ropemakers, basketmakers, glovers, saddlers and locksmiths are recorded as operating there. These centres were important focal points in local and to a certain extent inter-regional trade, allowing Breckland peasants both to dispose of their agrarian surpluses and to utilise the available specialised services.

The existence of numerous local markets also gave peasants the opportunity to turn a quick penny by forestalling. Here, market-bound goods were intercepted in order to create a temporary shortage and so to raise prices; the astute operator then chose his moment to sell at a profit. This illegal practice was particularly common in the fish trade, although court rolls sometimes refer to 'common forestallers in the market', which implies their involvement in other trades too.[247] Baking was a regular occupation in these market villages, but of greater importance was the brewing and provision of ale. Manorial edict demanded that ale was brewed to certain standards of measure and quality and sold at a fixed price, and courts amerced any transgression of these regulations. However, the frequency of transgressions by the same body of brewers suggests that these amercements were in fact merely licences to brew. Brewing has long been recognised as an important source of income for the poor and landless, especially young women.[248] This is certainly a feature of Breckland, for in nearly every assize of ale

---

[246] PRO E101.542/4; E179.242/27 m.1.
[247] For the fish trade, see Bacon 291/27. In October 1429 William Bryd was described as an 'habitual handler and forestaller of corn, meat, fish and other victuals in Brandon market', 295/15. For a general discussion of forestalling practices, see Britnell, *Colchester*, pp. 39–41 and 131–4.   [248] Smith, 'Families and their land', pp. 27–30.

one or more brewers are pardoned payment 'because they are paupers'. In Fornham St Martin, where May le Gammok was a known brewer and pauper, a court entry notes that she brewed 'in the house of Robert Tillot'.[249] Yet whilst many brewers eked an existence on the edge of subsistence, there were patently those who enjoyed greater well-being. Nor is it entirely accurate to write only of ale-wives, for married couples appear regularly as brewers, although admittedly they are most often represented in the assize by the female partner.[250] In all, the techniques and methods of brewing were probably known to all Breckland peasants, and indeed it was a compulsory labour service on some manors.[251]

A natural complement to the region's concentration upon barley production was the frequent processing of malt by the peasantry. Malting was a simple process and easily performed in the household. The barley was immersed in tubs of water for several days and then spread over the floor to germinate, after which the seeds were oven-fired to dry and to terminate germination. Most peasants would have utilised the various ovens normally used for baking bread, although output on the Risby demesne was sufficiently high for the cellarer of Bury abbey to construct his own malt-kiln.[252] The peasants' familiarity with the malting of barley is illustrated by many examples. Land rents on some manors were paid in malt, so that many peasants had to acquire the skill as part of their feudal due. It also provided a source of supplementary income, for many manors often hired local people to malt their demesne barley; at Lakenheath in 1378, 50 quarters were malted at a cost of 6d. per quarter.[253] Peasants also malted their own barley for sale to the market and in the Lakenheath court between 1315 and 1348 malt constituted 18 per cent of all debt disputes where the grain was named. Simon Bachecroft, a substantial tenant farmer living at Methwold in the late fifteenth century, malted much of his surplus barley.[254] Unfortunately the subsequent destination of all this malted barley is rarely specified. The great Benedictine households of Ely and Bury were apparently voracious consumers, but some

---

[249] WSROB E.3/15.9/2.2 m.15, court held June 1326.
[250] For a full discussion of brewing in an East Anglian village in the thirteenth century, see Smith, 'English peasant life-cycles', pp. 150–71.
[251] See, for instance, Quiddenham, NRO Phi/493; see also BL Harl. 743 f.101.
[252] This is mentioned in most of the Risby accounts. There were certainly demesne malt-kilns at Mildenhall, Fornham, and Methwold too.
[253] CUL EDC 7/15/I/25. In 1410 John Maltster of Fornham and his wife were paid 36s. for 17 weeks brewing, WSROB E.3/15.6/2.46.   [254] NRO Ms 19591.

malt undoubtedly entered inter-regional trade. In the fifteenth century the Cavenham demesne sold 60 quarters to John Horsehede of Saffron Walden, and malt from the Earl of Norfolk's estate at Kennett was almost certainly sent to the Bury market.[255] Local brewers, too, undoubtedly exerted some demand. In 1332 Christiana de Livermere of Brandon, a regular brewer, owed Philip Porter 8 shillings for malt she had purchased, and Alice Marshall stole 3 bushels of malt from Gilbert Driver and passed it on to Alice Hegon, another known brewer.[256]

The large number of commercial travellers and pilgrims (en route to Thetford and Walsingham) passing through the breck-fen edge, and the swollen, market-day populations must have stimulated a thriving trade in victualling; in fact this must partly explain the large number of brewers in Mildenhall, Lakenheath and Brandon (see table 4.17). Brewers were most prolific in the early fourteenth century, when many probably operated either in the market square or outside their own houses. As the numbers dropped with demographic decline in the later Middle Ages, and as the introduction of beer necessitated more concentrated production, the indications are that a higher proportion of brewers now operated from proper ale-houses.[257] At Brandon in 1471 a regular brewer called Joanna Skeppere 'maintained a servant known as a Tapster', and her house apparently attracted 'lecherous and suspicious' men.[258] For its size Brandon seems to have possessed an unusually large number of inns, none of which enjoyed a particularly salubrious reputation. Robert Sykes 'kept a house of bad and suspicious repute' where the clientele played 'at card tables and other illegal games'.[259] Nor was it just the hostellers themselves who incurred the courts' wrath, for Thomas Sadler was amerced for being an habitual gambler (*lusor*) who 'often played at cards and dice and other illicit games'.[260]

Specific references to the activities of ale-house keepers and gamesters are rare in medieval court rolls, and these Brandon examples are unique amongst the Breckland material. Their appearance reflects a zealous attempt by the court to control the

[255] PRO sc6.1117/12. Kennett's contact with the Bury market has already been established, and in this light the sale of large quantities of malt in 1289 is significant, PRO sc6.768/13.
[256] Bacon 291/3, court held November 1332; Bacon 291/6, court held November 1333.
[257] P. Clark, *The English alehouse 1200–1800* (London, 1983), chapter 1.
[258] Bacon 296/18, court held April 1471.
[259] Bacon 297/14, court held October 1530; Bacon 297/10, court held August 1516.
[260] Bacon 297/14, court held October 1520.

taverns' excesses and to regulate social behaviour, a movement paralleled in the Essex village of Havering during the same period (1450–1500).[261] We might even suspect that Brandon and perhaps Thetford had emerged as centres of illicit gambling and prostitution. Such a suggestion is not quite as far-fetched as it may appear, for both communities proved popular haunts for criminals and fugitives from justice. The Brandon court rolls contain frequent references to the capture of criminals and their subsequent incarceration at East Dereham gaol.[262] Andrew Henke of West Tofts scandalised the 'honest men' of Thetford in 1467 by proclaiming the town full of thieves and condemning its lawlessness.[263] His bitter outburst was confirmed in the very next court when Nicholas Lysse was amerced a trifling eight pence for keeping a whore-house.[264] The attraction of Brandon and Thetford to the criminal fraternity seems obvious. When medieval criminals were outlawed, they were so by and in the county of their offence only. Both these vills straddled the Norfolk/Suffolk border (Brandon also lies only seven miles from Cambridgeshire), and both were well served by water and land communications. In other words they were ideal lairs for outlaw refuge and escape. Furthermore, the surrounding heaths were alive with rabbits and sheep, and acted as magnets to cattle rustlers and poachers. The local ale-houses must have provided regular meeting places for these men, and it seems hardly surprising to find hostelers amongst the leaders of poaching gangs.[265]

Specialised crafts and industries

Without any doubt, the most widespread specialised crafts in medieval East Anglia were those connected with the manufacture of woollen textiles. In the twelfth and thirteenth centuries textile production was concentrated in the towns, especially Bury St Edmunds, Colchester, Norwich and Thetford, but thereafter it

[261] M.K. McIntosh, *Autonomy and community: the royal manor of Havering, 1200–1500* (Cambridge, 1986), pp. 255–9; M.K. McIntosh, 'Local change and community control in England, 1465–1500', *Huntington Library Quarterly* 49 (1986), pp. 219–42. See also Owen, *Making of King's Lynn*, p. 268.

[262] See, for example, Bacon 292/5, court held March 1383; 293/5, court held April 1402; 294/7, court held December 1416; 295/56, court held December 1452.

[263] PRO DL30.105/1490, court held January 1467.

[264] *Ibid.*, court held June 1467.   [265] See below, chapter 5.

developed in rural areas.[266] This process of dissemination accelerated in the fourteenth and fifteenth centuries and produced a belt of prosperous, semi-industrial villages famous for their woollen cloth. Around Norwich a clutch of villages concentrated on light worsteds, whilst the rural areas of north Essex and south Suffolk were internationally famous for their production of coloured broadcloths (mainly blue) and the heavier textured kerseys. These cloths were produced in quantities well beyond the requirements of local demand and figured prominently in exports from all the leading East Anglian ports. The success of these villages and the wealth of individual clothiers have been documented in a growing volume of literature, yet their most lasting testimonies are the magnificent perpendicular churches of the Stour, Brett and Colne valleys.[267]

The mechanisms of the medieval cloth industry, both technical and entrepreneurial, have been described at length elsewhere but merit brief elucidation. The industry was essentially organised on an outwork system, whereby a large number of independent craftsmen worked from home using their own tools and equipment. There was a clear division of labour in production, from specialist spinners of wool to dyers, weavers, fullers and dressers of cloth. These independent and geographically dispersed activities were coordinated by middlemen or substantial clothiers who provided the craftsmen with nearly all their wool and cloth, and contracted work on a piece-rate basis. Some clothiers had control over all stages of manufacture, from the purchasing of raw wool direct from the primary producers to the distribution of finished cloths, whilst others concentrated on the intermediary stages and depended on middlemen to supply their wool and on other merchants to distribute their cloths.

The techniques of woollen cloth manufacture are well enough documented. Raw wool was rubbed, combed and then spun by a distaff and spindle, or on a fly-wheel which speeded up the process after its widespread introduction in the thirteenth century. After weaving, the cloth was traditionally cleansed and shrunk prior to

[266] *V.C.H. Suffolk*, vol. II, pp. 253–5; E. Miller, 'The fortunes of the English textile industry in the thirteenth century', *Ec.H.R.* 18 (1965), pp. 64–82.

[267] J.E. Pilgrim, 'The cloth industry in East Anglia', in *The wool textile industry in Great Britain*, ed. J.G. Jenkins (London, 1972), chapter 15; D.P. Dymond and A. Betterton, *Lavenham: 700 years of textile making* (Woodbridge, 1982); Thornton, *History of Clare*, p. 143; Britnell, *Colchester*, pp. 53–71.

dyeing and finishing by the process of fulling, wherein the cloth was immersed in troughs of water and urine and trodden with fuller's earth. By the late twelfth century this arduous and unpleasant task had undergone mechanisation with the harnessing of water power to drive large wooden hammers to beat the cloth in the trough. Whilst it is certain that the presence of fulling mills indicates that production was geared beyond just local consumption, the absence of mills does not necessarily mean that cloth production was therefore limited in scope. The light worsteds of Norfolk required little or no fulling, which explains the relative scarcity of fulling mills there, and although Clare court rolls provide abundant evidence of fulling throughout the fourteenth century, the town had no recorded fulling mill until 1388–9.[268] This was true for much of the region, and evidence for fulling mills before the fourteenth century is rare in East Anglia, although they were certainly established at Sudbury by 1290 and at Hadleigh by 1305.[269]

The fulling process was traditionally followed by the dyeing of cloths, although Lavenham's famous blue cloth was often dyed before it was fulled. The basic medieval dyes offered only a limited range of colours and fell into two classes, the vat and the mordant dyes. Indigo and especially woad, imported from abroad, were the vat dyes and were used to produce the distinctive blue shading of many Suffolk cloths. The mordant dyes, notably madder which was grown locally and was certainly available on the Norwich market, needed the cloth to be treated with alum or bark for the colour to fix onto the wool permanently.[270] Madder itself produced a red finish, but by using it in conjunction with woad and in various concentrations it was possible to create different shades of blue, grey, black and red. This process obviously required specialised equipment, including vats, cisterns, hearths and watercourses, most of which were kept in the dyer's own yard. The need for copious supplies of water often dictated that these dyehouses were situated close to rivers or streams. The cloths were then transferred to shearmen and cloth cutters, who prepared them for distribution. Suffolk cloths were cut to a standard size of approximately thirteen

---

[268] Bridbury, *Medieval English clothmaking*, pp. 17–21; Thornton, *History of Clare*, p. 175.

[269] V.B. Redstone, 'Early Sudbury clothiers', *P.S.I.A.* 14 (1910), p. 101; J. Hervey, 'Extent of Hadleigh manor, 1305', *P.S.I.A.* 11 (1903), p. 152.

[270] C.O. Clark, 'The dyeing of wool and woollen goods', in *The wool textile industry in Great Britain*, chapter 9; Dymond and Betterton, *Lavenham*, pp. 16–18.

yards long known as a 'duodena'. Their width varied and is difficult to estimate exactly, although the broad-cloths probably measured two yards.[271] However, more than half the Suffolk cloths were either straits (half cloths of around one yard), or narrow cloths (*panni stricti*, probably a quarter the width of the broad-cloths).

As one would expect from a sheep rearing district, there is ample evidence of the collection and distribution of raw wool in Breckland. Although the region's aggregate demesne output of wool was certainly less than the corresponding aggregate peasant output during much of the Middle Ages, the more centralised nature of demesne production facilitated sales in bulk and on contract to prominent merchants. In contrast, peasant wool was derived from a far greater number of producers and so tended to be collected, stocked and graded by part-time middlemen before its sale and distribution in the regional network. As we have seen, it is impossible to be certain of the exact destination of much of Breckland's wool, although these middlemen would generally sell it to clothmakers, larger English merchants or directly abroad. Such a system involved the granting of some credit facilities and defaults of payment were sometimes recorded in the court rolls, thus affording a glimpse at the range of activity. At the lower end of the scale were men like John Joye of Lakenheath, whose main concern was a small yet persistent trade in wool and sheep, so that in June 1324 he owed money for wool fells to two different local men.[272] Wool occurs elsewhere amongst Lakenheath court business, and one William Pratt was described as an habitual thief of fleeces.[273] In 1551 a partially illegible ordinance was directed at 'wool collectors' in the village, implying them to be regular features.[274] At Methwold, most disputes over wool sales involved small operators, and such men were common throughout East Anglia.[275] This is not to deny the existence of more substantial merchants. Robert le Chapman was in dispute with William Chadacre over six stones of wool at Brandon in 1333, and around the same time Peter Wolchapman was involved in debt pleas with two other men, one concerning 30 fleeces valued at 12s. and the

---

271 Britnell, *Colchester*, pp. 58–60.
272 CUL EDC 7/15/II/Box 1/6 m.33.
273 CUL EDC 7/15/II/Box 1/8 m.19, court held May 1328; see also Box 1/8 m.11, court held March 1330; Box 1/9 m.23, court held January 1334.
274 CUL EDC 7/15/II/Box 4/Ed.VI m.5.
275 Britnell, *Colchester*, p. 74; for Methwold, see PRO DL29.104/1472, court held September 1371, and DL29.104/1479 m.1, court held December 1393.

other over 14 stones of wool at 42s.[276] A century later, court rolls
mention one Richard Taylor 'alias Woolman', and one Clement le
Woollemonger resided in Hengrave in the 1340s.[277] Matthew
Clericus operated on an altogether grander scale, purchasing 500
fleeces from two Brandon peasants for £20 in 1318, whilst John
Davy of Thetford owned wool in the cargo of a ship stranded on
the sands at Wells (Norfolk) in 1363.[278]

Although trade in raw wool was commonplace, there are few
direct indications that it was spun in Breckland on any great scale.
As spinning was often associated with impoverished and landless
young women, we might reasonably expect them to leave little
trace in medieval documents, yet fiscal records from central and
southern Suffolk are full of references to spinners.[279] It might be
that local opportunities in malting and brewing proved more
attractive to Breckland women than did spinning, or that
Breckland itself looked to the wood–pasture region for its spun
wool. There again, there may have been little division of labour at
this stage and perhaps Breckland weavers did most of their own
spinning. For example, Robert Woolpit of Fornham St Genevieve
was described as 'an habitual spinner [*filarius*] and weaver of
woollen and linen cloth', who employed both an apprentice and a
female servant, probably to help with the spinning.[280] This might
well have been the case in Thetford where William Archard and
William Wevegreene, both 'websters', employed five servants
between them.[281]

It is difficult to find more substantial evidence, but the obvious
presence of weavers in the region makes the corresponding lack of
spinners something of a paradox. The 1327 Lay Subsidy provides
surname evidence of weavers in Barnham, Brandon and
Herringswell, and from later evidence they were also working in
Didlington, Lackford, Knettishall, Mildenhall, Northwold,

---

[276] Bacon 291/3, court held June 1333; 291/41, court held November 1363. One Peter de
Rysby forfeited 20 fleeces at Clare fair in 1362, Thornton, *History of Clare*, p. 177 and
PRO SC6.1111/9 m.4. This was almost certainly Peter le Verdonn of Risby, a prodigious
sheep farmer in southern Breckland after the Black Death. In 1365 he was involved in an
interesting dispute with the lord of Lackford over the provision of hurdles for his
foldcourse, WSROB E.3/15.12/1.3a.

[277] Bacon 296/36, court held March 1480. CUL Hengrave Hall Ms 1 (1), p. 27.

[278] Bacon 289/23, court held March 1324; *CPR*, 1361–4, p. 364.

[279] E. Powell, *The rising in East Anglia in 1381* (Cambridge, 1896), appendices, being a
transcription of the 1381 Poll Tax.

[280] WSROB E.3/15.9/1.5 mm.1 and 7 (1384 and 1391).

[281] PRO E179.242/27 m.2.

Thetford and Tuddenham.[282] At Lakenheath in 1327 John
Bretham was accused of stealing trestles, while John Stone 'wevere'
stole a number of cloths from the houses of other villagers, themselves probably weavers.[283] There were certainly a number in
Brandon in the early fourteenth century who escaped mention in
the 1327 assessment, and the occupation is mentioned repeatedly in
later court rolls. One man, John Lestere, was amerced for damaging 6 lbs of raw wool (presumably on credit from Alex Archer, the
defendant), yet significantly was also owed for 'one ell of cloth' by
Nicholas de Hecham.[284] Nor was weaving confined solely to the
river valleys, for amongst the Elveden community in the 1440s,
'Webber' was by far the commonest surname.[285]

Evidence relating to the dyeing of wool and cloth in Breckland is
unfortunately much more limited, and appropriate references appear hardly at all before the fifteenth century. Both madder and
woad could be found locally throughout the Middle Ages, but not
on the scale that one would associate with a large regional involvement with the dyeing process. The Mildenhall demesne raised over
8s. in 1323 from the sale of 19½ stones of madder (*warantia*) grown in
the garden of the manor house.[286] In 1406 it received 3s. 4d.
'from tithes of madder', and it was certainly grown in fifteenth-
century Harling.[287] There is also a suggestive debt plea from 1461
concerning John Ellyngham of Brandon's failure to deliver 'unam
bale de Woode' to John Toly of Bury.[288] Surname evidence of
dyers is rare in Breckland, as it is for the rest of East Anglia before
the mid-fourteenth century. Indeed, the limited extant evidence
indicates that dyers only became a discernible group in Breckland
in the fifteenth century, and even then were largely confined to
Mildenhall and Thetford. In the 1460s and the 1470s there were at
least four full-time dyers working in Mildenhall, including Robert
Dobson who held a pightle appropriately named 'le Dyeres-
yerd'.[289] In 1482 one was amerced after being found guilty of

[282] Hervey, *Suffolk in 1327*, pp. 189 and 201; NRO Ms 18630 m.15; PRO E179.242/27 m.2;
PRO E179.149/53 m.10; Powell, *Rising in East Anglia*, appendices.
[283] CUL EDC 7/15/II/Box 1/8 m.24, court held November 1327; Box 4/R.III m.2, court
held June 1485.
[284] Bacon 291/48, court held December 1367 and 291/50, court held February 1370.
[285] WSROB 651/31/4.   [286] Bodleian Suffolk Rolls 21.
[287] BL Add.Roll 53123; Davison, 'West Harling', p. 297. At Mildenhall in 1412, 6s. was
raised from the sale of demesne madder, BL Add.Roll 53129.
[288] Bacon 296/16, court held June 1469.
[289] WSROB E.18/451/5 and 6, and E.18/400/1.3 f.36.

industrial pollution: 'John Bury, dyer, floods the King's highway with the water of his trade known as madderwater.'[290]

In common with much of East Anglia, fulling was a specialised craft in Breckland long before fulling mills appeared in the records. This we know from early fourteenth-century surname evidence which reveals that 'le Fullere' was one of the most ubiquitous occupational surnames. In the 1327 Lay Subsidy fullers constituted a third of all textile related surnames in Suffolk Breckland, including tailors and drapers, and were recorded in Cavenham, Icklingham, Timworth and Troston; they were also known in Ingham and in Knettishall.[291] Although 'fuller' appeared as a surname but once in Lakenheath court rolls before the Black Death, it was altogether more common in Brandon.[292] In 1324 the Brandon court ordered Roger le Fuller to respond to Henry le Fuller of Roudham in a plea of debt, probably over sub-contracting of work.[293] Surname evidence of higher-rate taxpayers in the 1379 Poll Tax indicates their presence in Lynford, Rushford and Stanford.[294] Other, more explicit, evidence confirms the existence of fullers in Fornham St Martin, Mildenhall, Thetford and Tuddenham, and a deed of 1466 mentions a locality called 'Fulleryshedlond' in Flempton.[295] Most of these examples are taken from villages situated next to the river Lark, and this – together with the large number of fulling mills built along its banks in the late fourteenth century – indicates that fulling was an important specialism of the valley, with productive capacity in excess of purely local requirements.

The main technical problem in establishing watermills on Breckland rivers was their slow-moving waters, but this difficulty was overcome by constructing mill-races to dam the river and force water to drop quickly over a short distance in order to drive

[290] WSROB E.18/451/6, court held July 1482.
[291] Hervey, *Suffolk in 1327*, pp. 172, 193 and 202–3; CUL Add.Ms 4220 f.85; Powell, *Rising in East Anglia*, appendices.
[292] Simon le Fullere was involved in a debt dispute in Lakenheath in June 1348, but other court records indicate that he did not hold any land in the village, CUL EDC 7/15/II/Box 2/17 m.4. Yet this surname abounds in Brandon, see Bacon 289/4 John and Roger Fuller, 289/14 Thomas le Fuller, and 289/7 Adam le Fuller.
[293] Bacon 289/23, court held March 1324.
[294] PRO E179.149/51 m.2; E179.149/55 mm.3–4.
[295] For the Fornhams, see WSROB 449/2/284; HA528 Hengrave Hall Deposit 114 f.32; E.3/15.6/2.59. Mildenhall and Tuddenham, WSROB E.18/451/69 f.82, and Bodleian Suffolk Rolls 1 m.4, court held September 1498. Flempton, WSROB 449/2/99.

an overshot wheel. Although requiring considerable capital investment, this simple technical solution was employed to drive the corn
and latterly the fulling mills; indeed, it seems likely that some of the
early grain mills were converted for fulling after the mid-
fourteenth century.[296] Hence there were two 'watermills' in
Cavenham in 1347, yet fifty years later one was described as a
fulling mill.[297] Barton Parva housed one of the earliest
documented in East Anglia, for a *molendinum fullonum* was recorded
in 1284, and later documents refer to a locality known as
'fullersdych'.[298] There was certainly one at Lackford by 1400, one
at West Stow in 1540 and probably much earlier, and a man was
granted lands in Fornham St Martin near the 'fullyngmelle' in
1385.[299] Indeed, were wider evidence available, we might expect
to find a high concentration of such mills on the Lark between Bury
and Mildenhall. The same might be true of the Little Ouse and the
Wissey, although conclusive documentation of fulling mills is
restricted to Thetford, Kilverstone and Langford.[300]

Many of the Breckland communities could boast a tailor
amongst their ranks, although it is not certain whether these were
involved with the retailing or the finishing of cloths. Evidence of
workers employed specifically in cloth cutting, sometimes known
as 'cissores' and 'pannermakers', is rarer but suggestive nonetheless.
Apart from late thirteenth-century surname evidence from
Fakenham Magna, Icklingham and Knettishall, we hear of one
John Denyel, cissor, living in Risby and of others at Cressingham
Magna, Methwold, West Harling and West Wretham in 1379.[301]
At Methwold in 1369 Stephen de Bedleem was accused of taking
'unum par de Shermannes shers' valued at forty pence from an-
other villager.[302] There is, however, ample evidence of the trade in
cloths, occasionally involving peasants with significant surnames.
Ralph Listere, a Lakenheath man, was twice involved in debt cases

296 Miller, 'Fortunes of the textile industry', p. 72.
297 Compare PRO c135.87/27 with c136.47/27.
298 IESRO T.4373/88 m.7, and WSROB E.7/24/1.3.
299 WSROB E.3/15.12/2.2; Hervey, *West Stow and Wordwell parish registers*, p. 177;
     WSROB E.3/15.9/1.5 m.14.
300 Crosby, *Thetford*, p. 59; NRO Ms 15167, court held October 1546; NRO NCC(Petre)
     Box 8/22. There was another fulling mill in Thetford, held by the town's priory, CUL
     Add.Ms 6969 f.110.
301 Hervey, *Suffolk in 1327*, p. 202; Powell, *Rising in East Anglia*, appendices; WSROB 449/
     2/491; PRO E179.242/27 mm.1–2; E179.149/51 m.2; E179.149/53 m.11.
302 PRO DL30.104/1471 m.7, court held November 1369.

in 1320–1, initially over 20 ells of 'bluet' cloth and then over 17 ells valued at 6s. 11d.[303] Elsewhere red cloths are mentioned, and in Fornham St Martin the court jurors presented that William Taillor abandoned a bundle of various cloths at the home of Robert Baxter.[304]

Some of the cloth trade was patently catering for local demand, as when John and Joanna Attames of Methwold allegedly owed four shillings to Thomas Taillor of the same village for four ells of cloth.[305] On other occasions, the cloth was merely passing through the region in transit from the south Suffolk manufacturing zone to Lynn, which explains why seizure of all cloths belonging to the insolvent Payne le Soutere of Bury St Edmunds was ordered at Lakenheath in 1347.[306] One of his creditors was Robert de Eriswell, the powerful Bury merchant whose activities were noted earlier (p. 149). Yet a proportion of Breckland's own cloth was destined for distant markets, for merchants from outside Breckland were certainly trading in the region. Not all did so in a manner becoming their status, for in October 1368 Thomas de Swaffham of London raped Alice Bonde of Thetford and stole a number of cloths from her master, Andrew Frere.[307]

Who controlled the trade in Breckland cloth? References to Londoners are rare, but unfortunately so are those relating to local clothiers. They certainly existed, because at least three were resident in Thetford in 1379.[308] Yet the general documentary silence surrounding their activities suggests that they controlled only a small proportion of the region's overall trade. If this was so, then a man like Robert de Eriswell's close connection with the Breckland economy gains significance, because it indicates that the Bury burgesses largely controlled and dominated the region's wool and cloth trade. The ulnage accounts present the best opportunity to confirm this hypothesis, because they contain details of all cloths brought for sale in English markets. These potentially valuable records have been used only sparingly by historians, because many

---

[303] CUL EDC 7/15/II/Box 1/6 m. 28, court held October 1320, and m.27, court held June 1321.
[304] WSROB E.3/15.6/1.3 m.30, court held August 1370. See also the activities of Stephen Dunwich in Mildenhall in the early sixteenth century, WSROB E.18/451/69 ff.17 and 37.   [305] PRO DL30.104/1474 m.1, court held March 1378.
[306] CUL EDC 7/15/II/Box 2/16 m.2, court held May 1347.
[307] *CPR*, 1370–4, p. 219.
[308] PRO E179.242/27 m.2 lists Radulphus Braben, John Steyk, and Robert Jade. Braben and Steyk had 4 servants between them and both paid tax at the high rate of 12d.

of the later accounts merely repeat information contained in earlier ones. However, a careful study by Gladys Thornton has shown that many of the East Anglian accounts provide accurate information until as late as the 1470s.[309] Although their exact format varies from year to year (reflecting the lack of any standardised system of recording the subsidy), the accounts occasionally distinguish the major Suffolk cloth markets and list the individual clothiers selling cloth there.

The ulnage accounts clearly emphasise Bury's dominance of north-west Suffolk and Thetford's prominence in south-west Norfolk. In 1466–7 Bury was Suffolk's fourth largest marketing centre behind Hadleigh, Lavenham and Nayland, yet it was the only vill titled with the suffix '*cum membris*', reflecting its role as the administrative centre of a number of smaller, rural cloth communities.[310] Amongst the merchants enrolled that year were Robert and Stephen Gardner and Richard Bagot, both surnames of prominent Mildenhall families; indeed, a Richard Bachot held land in Mildenhall around that time, and the family were substantial benefactors to the rebuilding of the church in the fifteenth century.[311] Much of the present building dates from the 1420s and incorporates outstanding Perpendicular features comparable to the churches of south Suffolk, almost certainly reflecting the current prosperity of the cloth trade. It would appear that drapers from the Breckland cloth villages moved to the towns once they had become successful, whilst still maintaining their links with the region. Hence when William Smith of Thetford died in the summer of 1480, his heir, William, was described as a citizen and draper of Norwich.[312] Despite this dominance by the major urban centres, there were still a few drapers operating more locally. The largest single tax payment made at Bury in the 1466–7 ulnage account was by 'diverse aliens coming to the town', which refers to sales by merchants from the smaller rural centres.[313] The suspicion that this included Breckland is confirmed by the 1467–8 account, which specifically mentions drapers from Mildenhall and Brandon selling their wares in Bury.[314] The Bury market concentrated mainly on narrow cloths and straits, although Breckland produced some broadcloths.

[309] Thornton, *History of Clare*, p. 148.   [310] PRO E101.343/2.
[311] For instance, in 1464–5 he held 12 acres and two granges on leasehold for 25s. 4d., BL Add.Ms 53138.   [312] PRO DL30.105/1491.   [313] PRO E101.343/2.
[314] PRO E101.343/4. A different account notes that one Robert Cake of West Stow was selling cloths in Bury, E101.342/25.

It is one thing to prove that woollen textiles were manufactured in Breckland and another to establish the scale of production there. In relative terms, the region compares unfavourably with the major centres of East Anglian production. It neither dominated the west Suffolk market nor did it possess the high degree of labour specialisation prevalent in the leading 'industrial' villages of south Suffolk and north Essex, or north Norfolk. Yet this should not surprise us, for, as Britnell writes, 'most villages within the cloth-making region of Essex and Suffolk had no cloth industry worth mentioning', and large-scale production was concentrated in the towns and a few villages.[315] In many Breckland villages there were never more than a few (if any) workers involved in textile-related trades. Yet there were some concentrated pockets of production which manufactured cloth for a wider market, such as Mildenhall, whose dyers featured in debt disputes with London drapers (see above, p. 150). Some Breckland textile workers were highly regarded by other East Anglian clothiers, an indication of their repute and excellence. In the spring of 1380 a Brandon court recorded the attachment of Robert Skaldar and Roger Darr 'drapers and bailiffs of Sudbury' for enticing five Brandon men away from the manor to work in Sudbury, and there is also a suggestion that a Bury draper was doing likewise.[316] So, whilst Breckland was hardly at the centre of East Anglian textile production, it had certainly created a distinct niche for itself on the periphery.

Whilst other villages increased their contribution to Breckland's overall output from the fourteenth century, Thetford appears to have done little more than hold its own, if that. A notable textile industry had been established there since Saxon times, and was still evident in the early fourteenth century, although a lack of documentation makes it impossible to decide whether the industry had declined along with the town in this period.[317] However, late fourteenth-century documents provide evidence of post-Black Death contraction in Thetford's economy, and hardly any signs of industrial growth.[318] Norfolk cloth production came to be dominated by the markets of Norwich and Lynn and, by 1467–8,

---

[315] Britnell, *Colchester*, p. 85.   [316] Bacon 292/3.
[317] Crosby, *Thetford*, pp. 21 and 50.
[318] In 1414, William Stryker paid 1d. new rent to have a pair of 'tentes' on the common of Thetford, these being frames on which cloth was stretched, but this solitary reference hardly constitutes a burgeoning textile industry, PRO DL29.290/4765. Crosby seems to have been unaware of the Duchy of Lancaster material when preparing his study of the town, but see *Thetford*, p. 51 for other evidence.

Table 3.15. *Occupations recorded in the 1379 Thetford Poll Tax returns*

Trade	Number nominated	Extras in household	Surname evidence	Total
Spinner	0	0	1	1
Weaver	6	6	1	13
Fuller	3	3	2	8
Dyer	1	2	0	3
Cissor	2	0	0	2
Tailor	2	0	0	2
Draper	3	6	0	9
Lister	1	0	1	2
Glover	0	0	1	1
Skinner	1	0	2	3
Mason	4	0	0	4
Thatcher	2	0	0	2
Cobbler	1	0	0	1
Brewer	13	20	0	33
Cooper	1	0	0	1
Smith	3	2	0	5
Carpenter	1	0	0	1
Total				91

Source: PRO E179.242/27 mm. 1–2.

Thetford clothiers handled only 7 per cent of the county's total rural output.[319] Despite the decline in Thetford's relative importance in Norfolk, it still remained an integral part of cloth production in Breckland, meriting a separate entry in the ulnage accounts, and output of both broad and narrow cloths, mainly red, continued. The town's Poll Tax returns are unfortunately incomplete and contain much under-recording of residents, particularly women, but still provide a clear indication of its occupational structure (table 3.15).

Although little is known about the medieval linen industry, there is certainly evidence for the manufacture of linen cloths in Breckland. Hemp was grown locally, as occasional references to peasants depositing it illegally in rivers and streams indicate. At Freckenham in 1550 the manorial court ordained that 'no-one shall

[319] Rural output is taken to be all Norfolk production outside Norwich, PRO E101.343/4.

put hemp in the common river', which refers to the washing or retting of the hemp.[320] Robert Woolpit of Fornham was described as a weaver of woollen and linen cloths, Thomas Wymark had 25 green linen cloths amongst his chattels in Brandon, and at Lakenheath John Crowe was unable to deny that he detained 46 ells of linen cloth from Nicholas Schayss.[321] Yet there was not a large market for linen cloths in the Middle Ages, and a market-orientated industry did not emerge properly until the early modern period.[322] When it did emerge, central areas of East Anglia were prominent but not Breckland. Indeed, the region appears to have been burdened by certain inherent disadvantages in linen production, although there were a few linen weavers recorded at Brandon, Coney Weston, Honington, Mildenhall and Sapiston.[323]

The preparation of animal skins and the making up of whole garments – notably from sheep pelts and rabbit skins – were separate processes, each requiring considerable skills, and the local proliferation of both sheep and rabbits stimulated its development as a specialist craft. The skins were separated from the carcasses, scraped to remove any remaining fat, and then soaked so that water could penetrate the fibres of fur or wool. When clean, the skins would be stretched out to dry on stakes and the remaining membrane of flesh removed with a sharp flint to allow absorption of the tanning agent. They were then trodden in a tub of oil, butter, grease or alum and hung to dry. The skins were now supple and easily stretched, and any remaining grease was removed by beating chalk into the wool or fur, a process which also helped to bring up its lustre. The practitioners of this art were referred to as *pelliparii* or skinners in medieval documents and, apart from preparing the skins, these men would also make up complete furs and stitch furs onto clothing. However, there appears to have been some division of labour at these various stages, with some workers concentrating specifically on tanning. Sometimes prepared skins were passed on to tailors, glovers and cordwainers for the finishing process.

Evidence for skinners and barkers in Breckland is less widespread than for textile craftsmen, but is suggestive nonetheless. Surnames

---

[320] WSROB 613/686/1, court held October 1550. Eight men were amerced in Brandon in 1419 for doing likewise, Bacon 294/13. Of course, hemp was used to make rope and not just cloth.

[321] Bacon 295/56, court held December 1452; CUL EDC 7/15/II/Box 1/8 m.13, court held November 1329.

[322] N. Evans, *The East Anglian linen industry: rural industry and local economy, 1500–1800* (Aldershot, 1985), p. 41.   [323] *Ibid.*, pp. 44–5.

point to the existence of skinners in Brandon, Bridgham, Eriswell, Feltwell, Hilborough, Lakenheath, Northwold and Stanford, and there was a 'skinnerslane' in Flempton and a skinner in Hockham, but only at Mildenhall and Thetford do they appear with any regularity.[324] John Skinnere of Mildenhall, labelled an 'artifex' in the 1381 Poll Tax, was notable for his wholesale purchase of sheep and lamb pelts from the manor in 1386 and John Cope, *pelliparius*, could afford 8s. rent for a newly constructed tenement in 1384.[325] Overall, the dearth of specific references to skinners in other villages probably belies the local importance of the craft. In 1403 the bailiff of Langford had 57 lamb pelts tawed locally for the lord.[326] In 1323 Lakenheath manor sent 331 lamb pelts to a local skinner for bleaching and to have twelve skins, each of 22 pelts, made up; in 1327 66 pelts were dispatched to a pelterer in Thetford and returned directly to Ely after bleaching.[327] Many rabbit carcasses from the largest warrens were transported directly to London, thus denying local skinners important trade, yet the preparation and dressing of rabbit skins was still common enough in Breckland, particularly in Brandon. In 1406 Thomas Estmor of Methwold sold 50 rabbits to a Brandon man, and in 1477 the lessee of the local warren, Robert George, was owed 26s. 8d. by Simon Glover of Brandon for 253 skins.[328] If Simon was – as his name suggests – a glover, then the implication is that warreners and tailors/glovers/listers often performed their own skinning rather than employ a specialist middleman. It is also possible that rabbit fur was shorn from the skin and then felted, again for use in clothing. Felting in fact was known in Roman Britain and was an important industry at Brandon in the nineteenth century, but unfortunately there is no direct evidence of the practice in medieval Breckland.[329] However, if felting was undertaken by the group collectively known as 'skinners', then it is unlikely that the craft would leave any more precise record in medieval documents.

References to barkers are more widespread than references to

324 Brandon, Bacon 289/9 and 30; Bridgham, CUL EDR G3/27 f.149 (Daike le Parmenter); Feltwell, PRO E179.149/51 m.1; Hilborough, PRO E179.149/53 m.11; Lakenheath, CUL EDC 7/15/II/Box 2/17 m.14; Northwold and Stanford, PRO E179.149/51 m.2; Flempton, WSROB 449/2/115; Hockham, NRO Ms 13848, court held February 1358; there was also a skinner at Fornham, WSROB E.3/15.9/1.8, court held October 1494.
325 John Skinnere purchased 36 pelts for 3s., BL Add.Roll 53118. Cope had taken up his lease in 1382, although in 1386 he had fled the manor, BL Add.Rolls 53117 and 53118.
326 NRO NCC(Petre) Box 8/22.   327 CUL EDC 7/15/I/4 and 6.
328 PRO DL30.104/1480; Bacon 296/29, court held June 1477.
329 M.E. Burkett, *The art of the feltmaker* (Kendal, 1979), pp. 100–4.

skinners in Breckland, perhaps because barkers could also be associated with the preparation of wool for dyeing. Documents designate such men as either 'tannatores' or 'barkers', although Barker was certainly the more common surname in Suffolk.[330] In the early fourteenth century there was a 'tannator' living in Timworth, and surname evidence of barkers in Brandon, Feltwell, Lakenheath, Mildenhall, Mundford and Weeting.[331] The 1381 Poll Tax identifies barkers in Cressingham Parva and Fornham All Saints, and there is suggestive evidence for their presence in Barton Parva and Tuddenham.[332] Once again, the greatest concentration was to be found in Mildenhall, where there was a locality called 'barkershove', and Thetford.[333] Both Robert and John Sygo were known barkers in the 1420s and held stalls on Mildenhall market; in 1429 one was amerced by the manorial court for the poor quality of his tanning.[334] By the sixteenth century there was an extensive leather working and tanning industry in Thetford centred on the north bank of the river Thet.[335]

The growing importance of commercialised rabbit rearing undoubtedly stimulated other occupational opportunities in the region. The position of warrener was financially lucrative, either as a manorial employee or as a self-employed lessee, and such men were obviously substantial and important figures within the village community. They lived with their families in the isolated but well-protected warren lodges and assumed responsibility for all aspects of rabbiting. Skilled warreners were much sought after and they were amongst the highest paid manorial officials. In 1358–9 two warreners at Methwold shared 75s. 10d. each year, whilst Ely abbey paid its Lakenheath warrener over £5 per annum in 1411.[336] In part the high wages were designed to reward the warrener's loyalty, for the ruthlessness of poachers could make this a dangerous occupation. Isolated from the village and without a protective

---

[330] McKinley, *Norfolk and Suffolk surnames*, p. 45.
[331] Timworth, CUL Add.Ms 4220 f.84; Brandon, Bacon 289/6, court held July 1330; Feltwell, CUL EDR G3/27 f.352; CUL EDC 7/15/II/Box 1/6 m.31, court held May 1321; Mildenhall, WSROB E.18/451/1 and 2; Mundford and Weeting, PRO E179.149/51 m.1–2.
[332] Cressingham, PRO E179.149/53 m.11; Fornham, Powell, *Rising in East Anglia*, appendix; Barton and Tuddenham, WSROB E.7/24/1.3.
[333] 'Barkershove' is mentioned in the description of land leases in BL Add.Roll 53116.
[334] BL Add.Rolls 53134 and 53135; WSROB E.18/451/4, court held November 1429.
[335] Crosby, *Thetford*, pp. 58–9. [336] PRO DL29.288/4719; CUL EDR G/2/3.

lodge, the custodian of Lackford warren was attacked by two poachers from Ingham in 1459.[337]

Rabbit rearing also created a variety of seasonal employment opportunities for local peasants. Skilled labour was required in the autumn and winter to help trap and cull the rabbits, as at Lakenheath in 1384 when an extra seven men were hired for twenty weeks.[338] The most common method of trapping was with the aid of ferrets and nets, although occasionally polecats were used. Most warreners and trappers would presumably have reared and used their own ferrets, although demesnes were known to hire them from unspecified breeders for the trapping season. In some cases professional ferreters were brought in at considerable expense, notably at Kennett in 1291–2.[339] Ferret breeding must have been a successful money-spinner, because Thomas Wymere and Thomas Benyng of Brandon were amerced 6s. 8d. in 1449 for doing just that, an extraordinary reference which suggests they were suppliers to poachers.[340] The ferrets – the most easily trained member of the polecat family – were released into specific burrows in order to drive the rabbits above ground and into nets tended by trappers. These nets, locally known as 'hayes', could be anything up to 180 feet long and could cost over 30s. to purchase.[341] As the King's ferreters were accustomed to making their own nets,[342] it seems likely that many warreners and trappers did the same for themselves from locally grown hemp, and presumably made a few extra for sale to a wider market. Other men were able to earn money by constructing and tending traps to snare predators.[343]

Knowledge of trapping techniques must have been widespread in medieval Breckland, and poaching was consequently a common pursuit. It was conducted on all scales, from one-off offenders to habitual poachers (*communes venatores*) such as Thomas Church of Risby who was amerced £10 'as an example to other malefactors' for his activities in Lackford warren in 1516.[344] These men often

[337] WSROB E.3/15.12/1.5.   [338] CUL EDC 7/15/I/28.
[339] PRO sc6.768/16. See also CUL EDC 7/15/I/31.
[340] Bacon 295/46, court held August 1449. See also Bailey, 'Rabbit and East Anglia', p. 17.
[341] Bacon 650.   [342] *CPR*, 1413–17, p. 338.
[343] At Methwold in 1482 a man was hired to make traps for vermin '*in saluacion* *cuniculorum*', PRO DL29.291/4782.
[344] WSROB E.3/15.12/1.17. Poaching was regarded as a full-time occupation around Cannock chase in Staffordshire in the eighteenth century, D. Hay *et al.*, *Albion's fatal tree: crime and society in eighteenth century England* (London, 1975), pp. 203–5. I am grateful to Ian Archer for this reference.

reared lurchers and greyhounds which were released into the warren area to pick off rabbits one by one. Raising and training these dogs was a skilled business, and profitable too, because experienced dogs were then used to train younger ones.[345] John Gardener of Langford was amerced for keeping a dog which, in the jurors' opinion, was used for 'hunting rabbits in the lord's warren', and William Ram of Brandon kept greyhounds for the same purpose.[346] Poaching proved so lucrative that highly organised and ruthless gangs were formed to operate on a large scale in the bigger warrens (see chapter 5). A black market for rabbits inevitably evolved, and a profitable, efficient one too. John Kellying of Brandon was one dubious character who received six stolen rabbits from John Sherman, and was also known to have dealt in stolen sheep.[347]

The large number of poaching cases in the court rolls reflects its importance as a source of income to the peasantry, and even honest villagers could earn some money through it. The Methwold demesne paid 3s. 4d. to those men who had helped the warrener apprehend a number of malefactors in the warren in 1421.[348] More importantly, the rabbit industry stimulated growth in a number of skilled trades involved with the preparation of the fur and skin. The common grey rabbit abounded in Breckland and its fur had potential in the mass clothing market. Being rather undistinctive it was used for warmth rather than show, although the Norfolk warrens of Black Rabbit and Methwold bred the rarer black and silver-grey rabbits whose furs were more popular as adornments on garments; Veale reveals that Henry VII possessed night attire lined with black furs.[349] An important but little-known characteristic of rabbit fur is its similarity to the more valuable ermine, and so it was much in demand among the lower classes, especially in the fifteenth century, as a very passable imitation fur. Breckland documents occasionally allow a glimpse at the popularity of rabbit skins: amongst the chattels of an unnamed thief arrested at Brandon was '*j gouna furred cum cuniculis*'.[350]

[345] L.R. Haggard, ed., *I walked by night: being the life and history of the king of the Norfolk poachers* (Woodbridge, 1974), pp. 157–8.
[346] NRO NCC(Petre) Box 8/21, court held March 1376; Bacon 295/12, court held October 1428. See also Bailey, 'Rabbit and East Anglia', p. 17.
[347] Bacon 293/16, court held December 1410; 294/10, court held July 1417.
[348] PRO DL29.290/4773.
[349] Veale, *English fur trade*, pp. 15, 141 and 176.
[350] Bacon 293/5, court held April 1402.

Non-agrarian occupations and economic development

Whilst involvement in any of these various trades and occupations was undeniably important, few peasants regarded them as their sole source of income. On the contrary, some indulged in a wide variety of occupational activities, such as John Gylboun of Barton Parva who was amerced for offences associated with sheep rearing, fishing, arable farming and perhaps labouring.[351] John Starlyng lived in early fifteenth-century Lakenheath, farmed at least 15 acres of arable, sold both meat and sedge illegally, and leased a fishery from the demesne.[352] Even those in the textile trades rarely abandoned arable farming entirely. Walter Webbe, a Lackford weaver, held two cottages, an orchard and over thirteen acres of land in the late 1390s, and also kept a small flock of sheep; Radulph Baldewyn, a tailor in the same village, held a tenement, 24 acres and a meadow.[353] Although a Fornham tailor called Lawrence Brynse held only a tenement and a croft of three roods, John Fote, a fuller of the same village, held a messuage and miscellaneous pieces of arable.[354] John Sygo the Mildenhall barker held at least ten acres of arable, and John Sly (a butcher) held fourteen acres.[355] The warrener of Brandon in 1373, John Philip, also held a toft and sixty acres of arable.[356] This feature was not exclusive to Breckland, but was also common amongst textile workers in Lavenham.[357]

Maintaining an arable holding could provide a safeguard against the irregularity of specialist work, and was eminently sensible in the fifteenth century when land was available cheaply and free of onerous labour services. In the thirteenth century, however, when the tension between population and resources was much greater, we might expect to find a closer correlation between smallholders and non-agrarian employment. After all, it was those with only a few acres of land who were most dependent on alternative sources of income to make ends meet. This association is particularly evident in the Coucher Book, the survey of the Bishopric of Ely's estates made in 1251. Occupational surnames were rare amongst

---

[351] WSROB E.7/24/1.3. He was amerced for illegally ploughing common land, for digging a clay pit, for illegal pasturing of sheep and for fishing 'cum rete et fishlepys'.
[352] CUL EDC 7/15/II/Box 3/H.V. mm. 2 and 3.
[353] Powell, *Rising in East Anglia*, p. 79; WSROB E.3/15.12/3.1 and 3.3; in October 1409 and December 1410, Webbe was amerced for illegal grazing with his sheep, E.3/15.12/1.14.
[354] BL Add.Ms 34689 f.33; WSROB E.3/15.6/2.51a and 2.59.
[355] BL Add.Rolls 53126 and 53134.   [356] Bacon 643.
[357] Dymond and Betterton, *Lavenham*, p. 5.

peasants holding full and half lands (40 and 20 acres), but were much more common among the smallholders. At Bridgham there were two smiths, two shepherds, a carter, a chapman and a skinner ('le Parmenter') amongst the toftholders.[358] At Feltwell there were two cobblers, two smiths, a basketmaker and a tanner.[359]

The existence of a sizeable non-agrarian sector is a useful index of economic development. A reduction in the proportion of people involved in primary production releases a larger section of the labour force for secondary and tertiary employment. This increased division of labour results in a higher volume of exchange of goods, greater economic efficiency, and hence regional development.[360] From the Poll Tax returns it is possible to calculate approximately what proportion of the population was involved in non-primary employment, and so to compare economic development in Breckland with other regions. Unfortunately, a lack of evidence prevents us from computing the overall production levels achieved by the non-agrarian sector, and it is impossible to quantify the relative importance of demand from local or wider markets. Yet the Poll Tax evidence may also present a rough and ready answer to this problem. As it is reasonable to assume that a rural subsistence economy would have only a small proportion of its population industrially occupied, then evidence of a large proportion would obviously imply production beyond local requirements.

Unfortunately not all the Poll Tax returns for Breckland are extant. Those which have survived are invariably in a poor condition, and unfortunately are not entirely reliable for use in either demographic or occupational analyses. The extant Norfolk returns are a mixture of the 1379 and 1381 taxes and record both occupational status and female residents somewhat imperfectly. For instance, there are no occupational designations for any of the 392 recorded names in fifteen villages in Grimshoe hundred in 1379, and only 26 (7 per cent) are women.[361] Most of the Suffolk returns date from 1381 when there were clearly many evasions, and little consistency in the recording of occupations.[362]

[358] CUL EDR G3/27 f.149.   [359] *Ibid.*, f.152.
[360] Paterson, *Economic geography*, p. 39.
[361] PRO E179.149/51. The villages are Mundford, Ickburgh, Colveston, Stanford, Feltwell, Cranwich, Wilton, Hockwold, Weeting, Methwold Hithe, Santon, Croxton, Lynford, Sturston and Tofts.
[362] R.H. Hilton, *Bondmen made free: medieval peasant movements and the English rising of 1381* (London, 1977), p. 170.

The basic format in the 1381 returns is to list residents according to one of four categories, namely farmers, artisans, labourers and servants (*agricole, artifices, laboratores* and *servientes*, but these are not applied to every village and there are considerable variations.[363] Returns from some villages are more specific, distinguishing cultivators from shepherds (*cultivatores, pastores* and *bercarii*), so that men performing essentially similar tasks may be categorised differently from one village to another.[364] Similarly, other returns are far more detailed as to the exact occupation of each artisan. At Thetford each one is carefully described as, for example, *cissor* or *fullere*, while at Mildenhall 104 persons are merely labelled *artificers*.[365] This variation in detail between places must reflect differing standards of efficiency and thoroughness by the diverse tax assessors and scribes from one village to another, and one suspects that at times their work degenerated into either carelessness or indolence. This might well have been the case at Flempton, Risby and Hengrave, where there were no registered artificers in 1381, yet evidence already presented demonstrates clearly that tailors, smiths and even skinners and fullers worked and were resident there. As it seems unlikely that such specialists were temporarily absent in the 1380s, one might reasonably assume that these returns merely failed to nominate those involved in specialist trades. There were also discrepancies in the nomination of bakers and brewers, which were given separate groupings in the Mildenhall and Norfolk returns but nowhere else.

Table 3.16 reveals the proportion of residents employed in service and industrial occupations in Breckland villages in 1381. The wide range (0–39 per cent) reflects the inadequacies of the data as much as any real division between agrarian and industrial villages in the region. Primarily, the figures serve to emphasise the agrarian nature of employment in the medieval village. Yet the high proportion of artificers at Euston, Fornham and Mildenhall undoubtedly reflect specialised, proto-industrial villages whose manufacturing interests concentrated mainly on textiles. Furthermore, by not including the ancillary occupations of fishing, turve cutting, rabbiting and the like, the returns understate the full range

363 *Ibid.*, pp. 170–4.
364 See also McKinley, *Norfolk and Suffolk surnames*, pp. 19–20, 'there are a few cases of persons listed as *servientes* or *laborates* who have names hardly consistent with such descriptions'.
365 PRO E179.242/27 mm.1–2; Powell, *Rising in East Anglia*, appendices.

Table 3.16. *Proportion of population occupied in secondary and tertiary employment in selected Breckland villages in 1379 and 1381*

Village	Artificers	Recorded population	Percentage
Cressingham Magna	11	51	22
East Wretham	5	41	12
Euston	12	53	23
Fakenham Magna	2	29	7
Flempton	0	33	0
Fornham All Saints	10	32	31
Hengrave	0	36	0
Lackford	8	49	16
Methwold	16*	158	10
Mildenhall	124*	399	31
Risby	0	57	0
Thetford	91*	234	39
West Harling	7*	50	14
West Wretham	4*	31	13
Wordwell	2	19	11

Note:
* Includes brewers and bakers.
Sources: PRO E179.242/27; E179.149/51; E179.149/53; E179.149/55; Powell, *Rising in East Anglia*, appendix. Column 1 includes all members of household.

and potential of non-agrarian pursuits in the region. Indeed, even without allowing for under-representation in the Risby, Flempton and Hengrave returns, it appears that nearly one-quarter of Breckland's population was employed predominantly in non-agrarian occupations, suggesting that its industrial capacity exceeded purely local demands.

The discrepancies between the various Poll Tax returns render any attempts to compare the proportion of industrially occupied population in Breckland with the rest of East Anglia somewhat tenuous. However, the extant returns from the Suffolk wood-pasture area do show a distinct tendency for greater specialisation of employment there, especially in textile preparation and production. Spinners are almost absent from the Breckland returns, but are much more prevalent in the high Suffolk villages of Ixworth Thorpe, Hinderclay and Langham.[366] Between Stowmarket and

[366] All of these are transcribed as appendices to Powell, *Rising in East Anglia*.

Hadleigh, signs of cloth manufacture are even more evident with numerous textores (weavers), cissores (shearmen), pannermakers, fullers, dyers, and so on. Hadlcigh was, by medieval standards, a highly specialised industrial centre, and its smaller neighbours also possessed a large proportion of artisans; 30 per cent of the population of Finborough, 32 per cent of Old Newton and 45 per cent of Combes. So occupational stratification in Breckland was not as pronounced as some areas of Suffolk, although south Suffolk did represent perhaps the most industrialised rural area in medieval England. Given this, it is hardly surprising that its occupational specialism was more pronounced than in Breckland. What is surprising is that the Breckland economy offered such a variety of occupations. Many of these were responding to demand generated in and around Breckland, but there were certainly pockets of specialised production supplying a wider market.

THE WEALTH OF A MARGINAL ECONOMY

Given the strong elements of specialisation and diversification in Breckland, the low level of taxable wealth noted above (p. 100) appears somewhat incongruous. By presenting wealth solely as a function of total area, historians have sometimes failed to grasp just how wealthy were individual peasants, and how well they had adapted to their environment. The best method of demonstrating this is by expressing taxable wealth in per capita terms, although medieval tax assessments rarely lend themselves to this type of analysis. Furthermore, as pointed out earlier, evasion and exemption were rife and rendered tax returns unrepresentative of the total wealth and population in each community.[367] Yet until it is proven that exemption and evasion were far worse in some areas than others, tax records will continue to be used for comparative assessments of wealth. Hence in Blackbourne hundred in 1283, 1,389 taxpayers were assessed on grain and livestock valued at £3,636 14s. 6d., or £2 12s. 2½d. each. However, within the hundred, peasants in the Breckland segment were individually much wealthier: 317 taxpayers paid £1,152 3s. 8d. at an average of

---

367 For example, Poos believes that only a minority of householders in the Essex villages of Waltham and High Easter were assessed in the 1327 Lay Subsidy, and at Broughton (Hunts.) only 40 per cent of resident families appear in the 1327 and 1332 returns: L.R. Poos, 'The rural population of Essex in the later Middle Ages', *Ec.H.R.* 38 (1985), p. 529; E. Britton, *The community of the vill: a study in the history of the family and village life in fourteenth century England* (Toronto, 1977), pp. 70–6.

£3 12s. 8d., whilst high Suffolk comprised 1,072 taxpayers at
£2 6s. 2d. each.[368]

The Blackbourne returns also present a unique opportunity to
compare the extent and the sources of relative wealth in the two
regions. Hallam has already undertaken an assessment along these
lines, although his regional delimitation within the hundred is at
considerable variance to the one employed in this study.[369] In
order to measure the distribution of wealth amongst the peasantry,
Hallam employed a cut-off line of £3 to distingish between rich
and poor peasants, and this is used in table 3.17. The returns are
biased towards wealthy peasants producing for the market, but are
instructive nonetheless. The main feature to emerge is the existence
of a more distinct peasant elite in Breckland than in high Suffolk.
The rich constituted 35 per cent of the taxable peasant population in
Breckland, and produced 62 per cent of all peasant barley, 70 per
cent of its rye, and 82 per cent of its oats; in high Suffolk the rich
comprised only 17 per cent of the peasant population and produced
45 per cent of the barley, 53 per cent of the rye, and 59 per cent of
the wheat.[370] The distinction was even more pronounced in sheep
farming, to the extent that Breckland's rich peasants owned 73 per
cent of all peasant sheep compared with the 49 per cent controlled
by the comparable group in high Suffolk. Not only did the rich
peasants of high Suffolk own fewer sheep than those in Breckland,
but they also controlled a much smaller proportion of what peasant
sheep there were. Peasant sheep farming was concentrated into
fewer hands in Breckland, so that the rich peasants of Euston and
Troston owned 93 per cent of peasant sheep, and in Fakenham
Magna 11 per cent of the peasantry controlled 72 per cent of the
sheep. Sheep ownership was concentrated into the hands of a
peasant elite in Breckland, whilst the wider distribution in high

[368] Figures taken from Powell, *Suffolk hundred*, pp. xxx–xxxi.
[369] Hallam, contribution to *Agrarian history of England and Wales*, vol. II, forthcoming,
includes Stowlangtoft, Hunston and Honington among the Breckland villages.
Honington is certainly on the periphery of the region, but Stowlangtoft is at least five
miles further east and Hunston even farther. Hallam also categorises Hopton in a
separate 'fenland' section, and does not include the Hepworth returns because of damage
to the original manuscript. However, both are included in the high Suffolk section of
this analysis. Hopton lies on a marshy bend of the Little Ouse, but is some distance from
the fens proper, and those entries from Hepworth which are legible are included because
it is per capita, and not aggregate village, wealth that is of concern to this study.
[370] Breckland's rich peasants were assessed on 13.26 bushels of grain each, of which 44 per
cent was barley, 29 per cent rye, and 22 per cent oats.

Table 3.17. *Assessed wealth in the Breckland villages of Blackbourne hundred in the 1283 Subsidy*

Village	Lords				Rich peasants				Poor peasants			
	£	s.	d.	No.	£	s.	d.	No.	£	s.	d.	No.
Barnham	7	13	11	1	164	6	1	20	39	10	6	26
Culford	27	9	11	2	30	18	5	6	22	3	11	13
Euston	1	12	4	1	107	4	3	17	21	18	7	17
Fakenham	23	14	0	1	20	12	4	2	20	2	0	16
Ingham	54	2	10	1	49	4	5	8	31	17	11	19
Knettishall				0	48	9	2	10	22	14	11	18
Livermere Pva.				0	46	11	8	6	30	13	6	21
Rushford	6	17	6	1	6	17	6	1	13	7	6	8
Sapiston				0	59	16	5	9	27	18	11	20
Troston				0	72	11	6	11	31	2	7	22
West Stow	16	19	6	1	76	4	11	12	12	19	9	8
Wordwell				0	31	16	2	5	25	0	8	15
Total	138	10	0	8	714	12	10	107	299	10	9	202

High Suffolk Villages

Total	426	13	5	25	913	13	7	183	1160	19	10	864

Source: Powell, *Suffolk hundred*, appendices.

Suffolk would indicate a stronger subsistence element to its sheep farming.

Having established that individual taxpayers were wealthier in Breckland, it would be instructive to compare the fortunes of each class of taxpayer by region. Breckland lords were assessed (to the nearest shilling) at £17 6s. each, rich peasants at £6 14s. and poor peasants at £1 8s. each, compared with £17 12s., £5 and £1 6s. in high Suffolk. It is hardly surprising that the poor should fare equally badly regardless of region, although they were a proportionally larger group in high Suffolk (82 per cent of all taxpayers) than in Breckland (65 per cent). The most striking aspect of these figures is the superior wealth of rich peasants in Breckland, who were each about 34 per cent more wealthy than their high Suffolk counterparts. From prior knowledge of agriculture in the hundred, it would seem reasonable to attribute that wealth to higher levels of output per capita in both grain and sheep farming. However, closer analysis of the wealth of the peasant aristocracy reveals that wealth through corn alone was greater in high Suffolk villages (58s. 3d. per capita) than in Breckland (47s. 9d.). The explanation for this paradox is straightforward enough; although Breckland as a whole produced more grain per capita than high Suffolk, after barley it produced more of the less valuable crops (rye and oats, assessed at 5s. and 2s. per quarter), and less of the more valuable crops (wheat and peas, at 6s. and 3s.). Wealth derived from sheep was greater in Breckland, amounting to an average of 59s. 11d. for each rich peasant compared with a mere 13s. 4d. each in high Suffolk. Sheep were obviously the source of the wealth differential between the two regions of Blackbourne, but it must be reiterated that 'pastoral' Breckland still produced a reasonable grain surplus.

Yet before the superior wealth of Breckland's peasantry is regarded as proven conclusively, the cautious historian may be wary of the rather limited geographical scope of the Blackbourne evidence: its Breckland component is not necessarily representative of the region as a whole (particularly as it does not contain the coarsest soils), just as the high Suffolk component is not necessarily representative of all areas of good soil. Such reservations cannot be dispelled by further reference to the 1283 returns because of their narrow geographical scope, but the survival of the 1327 Lay Subsidy provides an opportunity for wider comparative analysis and hence the chance to test the validity of the Blackbourne evidence. Within Blackbourne in 1327 there were 282 Breckland taxpayers paying a total of 563s. for an average of 24d. each, together with 521 high Suffolk taxpayers who rendered 952s. 10d. at 21.9d. each.[371] In Suffolk as a whole (including towns), 11,717 taxpayers paid the Crown £1,082 17s. 1d. for an average of 22.2d. each. In Lackford hundred, wherein lay the bulk of Suffolk Breckland, each taxpayer paid an average of 34.9d. each, a remarkable figure comparing favourably with 23.5d. per capita in Babergh hundred and 33.6d. in the town of Ipswich.[372] The Norfolk returns are incomplete and in poor condition, and probably date from the 1332 assessment.[373] The differences in per capita wealth between Norfolk Breckland and the rest of this prosperous county are less marked than in Suffolk, but the region

---

[371] The 1327 Blackbourne returns are in Hervey, *Suffolk in 1327*, pp. 180–95.
[372] *Ibid.*, p. xi.
[373] PRO E179.149/7. There is no dating on the roll, and the returns for Grimshoe and South Greenhoe hundreds are missing.

still features favourably. Central Breckland parishes in Shropham and Guiltcross hundreds were assessed at an average of 19.8d. per taxpayer, which appears poverty stricken beside the 68d. paid by the residents of South Lynn.[374] However, the 7 non-Breckland villages of Shropham hundred were assessed at only 16.7d. each, and the 5 non-Breckland villages of Guiltcross at 17.3d. each; furthermore, the residents of 16 villages in Taverham hundred on the loams near Norwich paid an average of 13.3d. each.[375]

These statistics demonstrate beyond doubt that Breckland peasants were amongst the wealthiest in Suffolk, and reasonably prosperous in Norfolk. But was the region itself entirely homogeneous? It might be argued that the Suffolk figures were bolstered by the returns from breck-fen villages such as Mildenhall and Eriswell (assessed at the large sums of 175s. 8d. and 97s. 6d.), which consequently obscured poverty in the central parishes. Table 3.18 presents the Suffolk and Norfolk returns, and splits the region into the three categories established in chapter 1, namely central, peripheral and breck-fen villages. The results clearly illustrate the superior wealth and size of those villages enjoying all the resource and trading advantages of the fen edge, but significantly the central parishes were far from destitute. Peasants living on the coarsest soils were wealthier than those both on the periphery and on better soils elsewhere. This proves conclusively that heathland was not a drag on the economy, and that peasant incomes were not determined primarily by soil type.

Unfortunately, our knowledge of regional changes in per capita wealth in the century or so after 1330 is limited, because in 1334 the system of taxation changed from an assessment of individuals to a fixed quota for communities. This 1334 subsidy forms the basis of Glasscock's analysis of regional wealth in East Anglia, which was cited above.[376] His analysis measures wealth as a function of area, but it has been argued that such an approach provides little indication of how far individuals were overcoming the limitations of their environment. In fact, the relative prosperity of Breckland is discernible from the 1334 subsidy if the average wealth of its villages is compared to the rest of East Anglia. Hence, Lackford

---

[374] *Ibid.*, mm.4–6 Shropham, m.56 Guiltcross, and m.57 South Lynn.
[375] *Ibid.*, mm.4–6 and 56; m.62 for Taverham hundred. The 12 non-Breckland villages in Shropham and Guiltcross are New and Old Buckenham, Ellingham Magna, Attleborough, Besthorp, Rockland, Eccles, Banham, Garboldisham, Blonorton, Kenninghall and Lopham.   [376] See above, p. 100.

Table 3.18. *The Lay Subsidies of 1327 and 1332 in Breckland*

Village	Assessment		No. of taxpayers
	s.	d.	
SUFFOLK (1327)			
Central parishes			
Ampton	Assessed with Timworth		
Barnham	84	10	28
Cavenham	43	6	22
Culford	28	0	15
Downham	37	9	11
Elveden	64	7	16
Euston	34	1	21
Fakenham Magna	40	4	12
Herringswell	49	8	22
Icklingham	90	11	23
Ingham	34	10	21
Knettishall	38	9	21
Lackford	64	4	24
Livermere Parva	36	7	25
Rushford	11	10	8
Troston	54	2	27
Tuddenham	61	5	24
West Stow	45	7	18
Wordwell	34	0	20
Total	855	2	358
	= 28.7d. per capita		
Peripheral villages			
Barton Parva	56	11	24
Coney Weston	50	0	35
Fakenham Parva	36	0	9
Flempton	31	9	19
Fornham All Saints	31	8	20
Fornham St Martin and St Genevieve	35	6	14
Hengrave	20	9	15
Higham	33	1	17
Honington	42	3	20
Hopton	58	0	35
Livermere Magna	68	9	31
Risby	62	0	21

Table 3.18. (*cont.*)

Village	Assessment s.	Assessment d.	No. of taxpayers
Sapiston	34	0	22
Timworth	72	10	50
Total	633	6	332
		= 22.9d. per capita	

Breck-fen villages

Village	Assessment s.	Assessment d.	No. of taxpayers
Brandon	93	10	39
Eriswell	97	6	21
Freckenham	64	6	27
Lakenheath	116	7	30
Mildenhall	175	8	73
Wangford	52	4	17
Worlington	86	2	20
Total	686	7	227
		= 36.3d. per capita	

NORFOLK (1332), Shropham and Guiltcross hundreds

Central villages

Village	Assessment s.	Assessment d.	No. of taxpayers
Brettenham	29	0	16
Bridgham	49	4	29
East Wretham	30	3	22
Illington	32	9	23
Kilverstone	33	8	27
Riddlesworth	55	2	29
Roudham	50	0	42
Rushford	51	3	33
Snarehill	33	1	20
Thetford	191	9	87
West/Mid Harling	70	0	48
West Wretham	37	4	26
Total	663	7	402
		= 19.81d per capita	

Peripheral villages

Village	Assessment s.	Assessment d.	No. of taxpayers
Gasthorpe	34	3	16
Hargham	29	9	18

Table 3.18. (*cont.*)

| Village | Assessment | | No. of |
	s.	d.	taxpayers
Hockham	65	8	38
Larling	57	3	40
Shropham	102	11	75
Snetterton	86	7	63
Wilby	49	1	35
Total	425	6	285
		= 17.92d. per capita	

Sources: Hervey, *Suffolk in 1327*; PRO EI79.149/7.

Table 3.19. *Mean tax per village in the 1334 Lay Subsidy, selected areas*

| Area | Total tax | | | No. of | Mean tax | | |
	£	s.	d.	villages	per village		
Breckland	253	1	8	52	4	17	4
Babergh hundred	119	19	11	32	3	15	0
Diss hundred	39	6	0	15	2	12	5
Happing hundred	95	6	4	17	5	12	2
Taverham hundred	45	15	2	18	2	10	10

Sources: R.E. Glasscock, ed., *Lay Subsidy of 1334* (1975), pp. 192–208, 284–96.

hundred, assessed at £73 16s. 7½d., has a very low tax per area rating, yet the mean tax per village in the hundred is £4 18s. 5d., making it by far the wealthiest village grouping in the county – the average tax per village in the whole of Suffolk was a mere £2 16s. 7d.

Medieval tax records have some potential for illustrating differentials in peasant wealth between regions of different resources. Wealth per capita in Breckland was higher than many other areas of better soil, a fact confirmed by two separate tax assessments and suggested by another one. Even more significant, perhaps, was the high stratification of peasant wealth in Breckland, for its elite was twice as numerous and thrice as wealthy as its high Suffolk counterpart. It has been a common theme in this book that increased economic specialisation and diversification resulted in more trade, greater economic efficiency and hence higher incomes in the twelfth and thirteenth centuries. Recent work on medieval Bed-fordshire has also emphasised the correlation between extensive marketing facilities and increased peasant wealth. Biddick con-cluded that peasants with proximity to more than one weekly market enjoyed higher incomes, because good positioning near a second market increased their marketing choices, enhanced their knowledge of local prices and kept down transport costs.[377] Soil quality was not the only influence governing peasant income in Breckland: the diversity of employment opportunities, the special-ised nature of agrarian production, and the breadth and efficiency of trading links, were of greater importance.

[377] K. Biddick, 'Medieval English peasants and market involvement', *Journal of Economic History* 45 (1985), pp. 826–8.

Chapter 4

GROWTH, CRISIS AND CHANGE: ECONOMIC PERFORMANCE 1300–1399

The economic history of the fourteenth century is hotly contested. While historians acknowledge it as a century of disease and demographic upheaval, there is little agreement on the causes and consequences of these traumas. However, the view that marginal regions were the most sensitive barometer of economic change stands unchallenged and thus we would expect Breckland to have responded quickly and decisively. Demographic decline in England as a whole ought to have resulted in swift and sharp falls in demand for land in the region, particularly in the aftermath of the agrarian crisis of 1315–22 and with the arrival of plague in 1349. Similarly, these disturbances ought to have resulted in permanent disruption to farming in Breckland, as peasants gradually abandoned their holdings in search of more responsive soils elsewhere. Yet how far did Breckland's experience fit these predictions?

THE AGRARIAN CRISIS OF 1315–22 AND ITS AFTERMATH

A traumatic combination of successive harvest failures and epidemic cattle disease between 1315 and 1322 had profound effects on agriculture throughout Europe.[1] In upland areas of northern England this 'agrarian crisis' marked an economic turning point, and ushered in over a century of decline.[2] The extent of its impact on the marginal soils of Breckland is difficult to evaluate exactly,

---

[1] For general descriptions of the agrarian crisis in Europe, see H.S. Lucas, 'The great European famine of 1315, 1316 and 1317', *Speculum* 5 (1930), pp. 343–77, and I. Kershaw, 'The great famine and agrarian crisis in England, 1315–1322', *Past and Present* 59 (1973), pp. 3–50.

[2] The problems in the north were also compounded by the destructive raids of the Scottish army. On the estates of Bolton priory in the 1320s, centred in the Yorkshire Dales, two manors lay uncultivated and six were leased out at greatly reduced rents, I. Kershaw, *Bolton priory: the economy of a northern monastery 1286–1325* (Oxford, 1973), p. 37. See also McDonnell, 'Medieval assarting hamlets', p. 276.

because thorough documentation is lacking, but it would appear to have been serious rather than critical. In this respect, Breckland's experience mirrors that of East Anglia in general, which appears to have avoided the worst of the elements in 1315–22.[3]

Recorded deaths at Lakenheath were above average in 1314, 1316 and 1322, and there was an unusually large number of land transactions in 1316–17, a sure sign of some economic disturbance.[4] Grain production was severely disrupted at Fornham (C) in 1317 and 1318, and the profitability of the manor turned into large deficits.[5] Between 1300 and 1314 (5 years) the reeve had disposed on average 156 quarters of wheat, rye and barley each year, whilst in 1317–18 the mean was 124 quarters, a drop of more than 20 per cent. Nevertheless, sale prices of Breckland grain were not appreciably above pre-crisis prices: wheat was selling at 6s. 8d. a quarter in 1317 and a modest 4s. 3d. in 1318, emphasising the relatively bountiful harvests in those years. Yet 1318 saw the onset of cattle murrain, for the number of cattle at Fornham (C) fell from 35 in 1317 to 24 in 1322, and at Lakenheath there were 11 cows in 1320 compared with 21 in 1305.[6] Similar losses took over twenty years to replace on the Ramsey abbey estates, but at Fornham, Lakenheath and Risby stocks had been restored by purchase to pre-crisis levels by the mid-1320s.[7] At Wretham there were 26 adult cattle on the demesne in 1308 and 27 in 1336, and 25 cattle at Cressingham in 1309 yet 36 in 1322.[8] Sheep farming was temporarily disrupted, if the totals detailed in table 4.14 are representative. In successive winters 1321–2 and 1322–3 the Lakenheath demesne lost a quarter of its flock, and the number of sheep at Cressingham was halved between 1309 and 1322.[9] There was further disruption to arable farming in 1321–2, caused this time by a shortage of rainfall, for the region was especially vulnerable to

[3] H.E. Hallam, 'The climate of eastern England 1250–1350', *Ag.H.R.* 32 (1984), pp. 124–32.

[4] From extant estreat and court rolls, Helena Graham has calculated that there were 1.6 deaths per annum in Lakenheath between 1308 and 1348. In 1314 there were six deaths, one in 1315, four in 1316 and six in 1322.

[5] WSROB E.3/15.6/2.3 and 2.4, the losses were £7 4s. 11d. and £7 11s. 8d.

[6] *Ibid.*, and WSROB E.3/15.6/2.5; CUL EDC 7/15/I/2 and 4.

[7] J.A. Raftis, *The estates of Ramsey abbey* (Toronto, 1957), p. 137. In 1324 there were 33 cattle on the Fornham (C) demesne, WSROB E.3/15.6/2.6. In 1304–5 there had been *c.* 65 cattle at Lakenheath and the same number in 1326–7, CUL EDC 7/15/I/2 and 6. At Michaelmas 1313 there were 21 cattle on the Risby demesne and 27 in 1329, WSROB E.3/15.13/2.6 and 2.8.

[8] Eton College Records, vol. 30, nos. 44–5; NRO DCN Supplement (R187A).

[9] CUL EDC 7/15/I/4. NRO DCN Supplement (R187A).

drought. Production of wheat and rye at Fornham (C) was down further on the trough of 1317–18, and peas and barley – sown later in the growing season – were afflicted more severely.[10] Drought was not the only problem, for the Lakenheath reeve was allowed a bushel of rye by the auditors in 1321, 'due to the great cold lasting for one month'. The combined effect was to reduce the famuli's livery from 95 qu. 5 b. to 76 qu. 5 b., with the barley component suspended.[11] The dislocation affected peasant farming too, and in the same village Peter Swyft was pardoned the entry fine on an acre of land because of its impoverishment in 1321, and the lease of Cranescroft fell in value from 24s. 6d. in 1291 to 15s. 8d. in 1321.[12]

While limited in scope, the evidence nonetheless suggests that Breckland did not suffer from the crisis as badly as many areas of England. The reason for this is not entirely clear. It may simply have been that climatic conditions were more propitious than elsewhere, so that its agriculture was not severely disrupted in the long term.[13] This conclusion is confirmed by the performance of arable farming in Breckland, which entered a period of consolidation and perhaps stagnation in the 1320s and early 1330s, but recovered strongly thereafter. This trend is particularly evident among the region's demesne farmers. On many English estates, the heyday of direct demesne exploitation was reached well before the end of the thirteenth century, and was followed by a gradual running down of activity.[14] By the close of the fourteenth century, many estates no longer practised direct exploitation but depended upon cash rents for the bulk of their income. The exact pace and extent of this transformation naturally varied according to a host of factors, but by the Black Death most landlords had reduced the area under cultivation and experimented with partial or complete leasing of demesnes.[15] The explanation for this general movement

---

[10] WSROB E.3/15.6/2.3–2.5. In 1322 the reeve handled only 36 qu. 6 b. of barley (the lowest pre-plague total), compared with 58 qu. 7 b. in 1318, a drop of nearly 40 per cent.

[11] CUL EDC 7/15/I/4.

[12] CUL EDC 7/15/II/Box 1/6 m.31, court held May 1321; PRO sc6.1001/5 and CUL EDC 7/15/I/4.

[13] Hallam, *Rural England*, p. 53, and Hallam, 'Climate of eastern England', pp. 126–7. In any case, the light sandy soils of Breckland would not have been as badly affected by torrential rains as, for instance, regions of heavy clay.

[14] For general surveys of this process, see Miller and Hatcher, *Rural society and economic change*, pp. 59–61 and Bolton, *Medieval English economy*, pp. 185–90.

[15] See, for instance, R.H. Hilton, *The economic development of some Leicestershire estates in the fourteenth and fifteenth centuries* (Oxford, 1947), pp. 88–9; Raftis, *Ramsey abbey*, p. 217; Miller, *Bishopric of Ely*, p. 100; Harvey, *Westminster abbey*, p. 149; and Dyer, *Lords and peasants*, p. 82.

towards rentier farming is complicated, although it was rooted in the declining profitability of grain farming. In the course of the fourteenth century, and especially after *c*. 1375, prices fell relative to costs, a problem which was exacerbated by the large overheads and inherent inefficiencies of estate farming.

The contraction in demesne activities should, presumably, have been most evident at the margin of cultivation, but in fact many Breckland demesnes continued in direct cultivation until at least mid-century, and often for a good deal longer. This is not to argue that the post-crisis years were easy ones. Grain prices were generally low in the quarter-century after 1323, and offered landlords little incentive to reinvest in their manors and make good the capital losses incurred in 1315–22, which undoubtedly delayed recovery. Calculations of manorial profitability on the cellarer of Bury abbey's manors reflect the difficulties involved with demesne farming in this period. Risby enjoyed a profit of £22 7s. 5½d. in 1309 but could manage only 35s. 3¼d. in 1329, and Fornham only managed to secure consistent profits after the mid-1330s.[16] Thereafter, arable farming expanded at a rapid rate, so much so that on many demesnes the area under cultivation was often higher in the 1340s than in any other documented decade (see table 4.2). Only at Wretham was the demesne acreage appreciably lower in the 1340s than it had been prior to the agrarian crisis, where the decline was borne largely by oats and barley. The sown area at Cressingham was 40 per cent higher in the 1320s than it had been in the 1300s, although the increase necessitated the more widespread sowing of oats, perhaps on heathland intakes. Hardly any landlords were tempted to convert even small areas of their demesnes to tenant leaseholds in this period. Odd acres of demesne were leased to tenants at Brandon and Lakenheath, but not inconsistently, and the lay manors at Downham, Fakenham, Icklingham and West Tofts display no such tendency.[17] Not only was piecemeal leasing entirely absent at Fornham (A) in the 1340s, but Bury abbey was seeking to expand its own operations by cultivating peasant

16 Calculations of manorial profitability were made annually on the cellarer's estates and entered at the base of the cash account by the central authorities. Risby, WSROB E.3/ 15.13/2.6 and 2.8. Fornham, 1326 profit £3 16s. 11d.; 1327 loss £22 16s. 2d.; 1334 profit £2 19s. 4d.; 1341 profit £6 14s. od.; WSROB E.3/15.6/2.8, 2.9, 2.13 and 2.17. Similar calculations were introduced on the Ramsey abbey estates in the 1380s, Raftis, *Ramsey abbey*, p. 262.

17 For instance, 6.75 acres of Lakenheath demesne were leased at Coupetwong in 1304–5, CUL EDC 7/15/I/2, and one acre of demesne was seized from Margaret Marchall in Brandon in November 1333, Bacon 291/5.

land, and by ploughing up 2.5 acres of permanent pasture at Heynesmerewong.[18]

The expansion of demesne area under cultivation in Breckland was accomplished without any notable deterioration in yields or sowing thicknesses, and so represented a genuine increase in output. That this should occur in a period of low grain prices is surprising, and is difficult to explain convincingly. It might reflect a recovery in population and hence in demand; such a movement would not necessarily cause a rise in grain prices if harvests were consistently good and if monetary deflation occurred.[19] A more plausible explanation is that landlords responded to depressed grain prices simply by producing more and trying to reduce costs per acre, which was certainly the response of Breckland's farmers to the late seventeenth-century depression. Whatever the reason, the continuation of direct demesne farming on such a scale reflects a quiet confidence in grain production in this period. On the Bury abbey estates this confidence was strong enough to overcome further dislocation and losses of stock in 1327. In the autumn of that year, rioting flared in Bury and the abbey was sacked before order could be restored.[20] During the disturbances, four Breckland manors were looted and at Fornham (C) the auditors wrote off corn valued at 51s. 4d. that had been stolen 'at the time of the burning of the manor', and livestock also disappeared.[21] The manor's profitability slumped to a record deficit of £22 16s. 2d., but the cellarer was not prepared to allow the manor to be run down permanently and immediately invested over £21 to make good the losses in stock. Subsequent accounts of this, and the other manors, reveal no long-term disruption of arable farming. Similar acts of insurrection disrupted arable farming for an indeterminable length of time in Derbyshire, but their failure to do so in Breckland is significant.[22]

18 WSROB E.3/15.7/2.2b.
19 On the question of monetary factors in this period, see N.J. Mayhew, 'Numismatic evidence and falling prices in the fourteenth century', *Ec.H.R.* 27 (1974), pp. 1–15.
20 M. Lobel, 'A detailed account of the 1327 rising at Bury St Edmunds and the subsequent trial', *P.S.I.A.* 21 (1933), pp. 215–31; Gottfried, *Bury and the urban crisis*, pp. 220–31.
21 The four manors sacked were the two Fornhams, Ingham and Risby. WSROB E.3/15.6/ 2.8 reveals that Fornham (C) was attacked in October 1327 when feeling against the abbey was at its height, and when the manorial granges were full. The unusually small amount of grain handled this year is explained 'because the residue was burnt at the time of the burning of the manor'. The livestock which disappeared amounted to 3 stotts, a bull, 5 oxen and 9 cows. The manors most at risk in this revolt were those nearest to Bury, and there is no evidence that the more distant manors of the Bury estate were affected.
22 I.S.W. Blanchard, 'Derbyshire in the late Middle Ages', (Ph.D., London University 1967), p. 25.

There is much indirect evidence of the high pressure on land resources immediately prior to the Black Death. The average size of peasant holding was small in East Anglia, but particularly so in this period. At Fornham All Saints in 1283, 37 per cent of the peasantry held under five acres of land, whilst at Culford in 1348 54 per cent held under five acres and only 14 per cent held over twenty acres.[23] The demands placed on these holdings were inevitably high. At Mildenhall in 1346, landholders were required to render 3.4 bushels of barley per acre as rent, which meant that each acre had to yield at least 8 bushels just to break even on the season's sowing.[24] The proportion of each holding sown each year was also high, so that 5.5 acres of a 7-acre holding in Brandon were under corn in 1332.[25] Demand for land at Hockham remained buoyant, and resulted in further colonisation of the wasteland in the 1330s. An area of 'the common' was broken up into small parcels and granted to various peasants as nineteen 'new rents' in March 1338.[26] Most of these represented extensions onto existing crofts, presumably for building. Elsewhere, the shortage of arable land forced the Fornham (A) demesne to cultivate peasant land for its own purposes, and at Lakenheath part of the warren was ploughed up and sown with oats.[27]

The insistent demand for all types of land inevitably made the average peasant's existence more precarious. At Coney Weston in 1302, 82 *nativi* paid an average of 18d. *recogniciones* to the new abbot of Bury. However, 65 per cent of these paid less than 18d., and 34 per cent were noted as possessing no livestock at all.[28] At Culford in the same year, two out of twenty peasants were labelled 'beggars', and Robert Miller of Fornham had no possessions and his land lay uncultivated.[29] In 1313, Henry le Man of Risby was pardoned rent worth 4 bushels of malt 'because he did not have this crop'.[30] Such examples substantiate Miller and Hatcher's belief that many

---

[23] BL Add.Mss 34689 ff.8–9 and 42055 ff.8–22.
[24] CUL Add.Ms 4220 f.152. The calculation assumes that peasants sowed barley at the demesne rate of 4 bushels per acre. There is hardly any other rent evidence of this kind which accurately reflects the market value of land before the Black Death.
[25] Bacon 289/9.   [26] NRO Ms 13848 m.1, courts held 7 and 26 March 1338.
[27] In the 1340s the Fornham demesne was cultivating land 'once John Underhill's' and 'once Marshall's', WSROB E.3/15.7/2.1–2.4. At Lakenheath in October 1330, Adam Outlaw was amerced for damaging 4 bushels of demesne oats 'apud le Coneger', CUL EDC 7/15/II/Box 1/8 m.5.
[28] BL Harl. 230 ff.62–3. In total they paid 121s., of whom 53 paid under 18d., and 28 possessed no recorded livestock.   [29] BL Harl. 230 f.62.
[30] WSROB E.3/15.13/2.5.

English villagers stood on or below the poverty line in the early fourteenth century, although certainly the problem was no worse in Breckland than elsewhere.[31] Indeed, 'poor' peasants were equally poor throughout Blackbourne hundred in 1283, but in high Suffolk they comprised 82 per cent of the taxpaying population as against 65 per cent in Breckland.

Nor is there any evidence that the pressure of population on the land had been decisively reduced before the Black Death, for the land market remained buoyant and there is no evidence that holdings were being abandoned.[32] The majority of completed land transactions in early fourteenth-century Breckland were *inter vivos* and involved peasants with no known familial relationship, which are both characteristics of a fluid and active land market. Of 178 cases of land transacted *inter vivos* in Lakenheath between 1325 and 1335, only 11 per cent were between members of the same family and 94 per cent involved cottages and land parcels under 5.5 acres; in the period 1308–34, 68 per cent of all transactions were *inter vivos* and involved non-kin. But perhaps the best indicator of buoyancy is the number of sub-leases amongst peasants. Peasants were permitted to sub-let their land – free or unfree – as long as the lessee paid a small sum to the manorial court and notified officials as to the length of the lease. Sub-letting dominated the land market in early fourteenth-century Brandon. Between 1300 and 1349 such leases constituted 40 per cent of all land transactions there, and many concerned very small pieces of land, often of just one rood. Sub-letting was an important safety-valve in periods of land shortage because it enabled peasants to accumulate a little more land or cash as personal circumstances changed.[33] Its importance is probably understated in court rolls because many sub-leases went undetected by manorial officials as peasants attempted to evade payment of fines. Hockham courts record a certain amount of legitimate activity, but were hard pressed to keep track of all such transactions.[34] The Brandon court was occasionally informed about illegal sub-leases, such as the five acres recorded in 1331, but was not always as successful.[35] In July 1317 the scribe noted that John

[31] Miller and Hatcher, *Rural society and economic change*, pp. 61–2.
[32] This was also the case at Coltishall in eastern Norfolk, B.M.S. Campbell, 'Population pressure, inheritance and the land market in a fourteenth-century peasant community', in *Land, kinship and life-cycle*, ed. Smith, pp. 110–20.
[33] *Ibid.*, pp. 120 and 129.
[34] See, for example, NRO Ms 13848 m.1, court held December 1338.
[35] Bacon 289/20, court held February 1331.

Table 4.1. *Analysis of completed land transactions at Brandon*
1300–1540 (% in brackets)

Period	Post mortem	Inter vivos	Sub-leases	Grants from the lord	Death-bed	Total
1300–49	39 (19)	78 (37)	83 (40)	4 (2)	5 (2)	209 (100%)
1350–99	19 (7)	47 (17)	5 (2)	208 (73)	4 (1)	283
1400–49	7 (5)	65 (46)	1 (1)	51 (37)	16 (11)	140
1450–99	10 (8)	71 (55)	1 (1)	16 (13)	30 (23)	128
1500–40	23 (13)	131 (75)	— —	5 (3)	16 (9)	175

Source: Bacon 289–97.

Godwyne leased an unknown area of land to various sub-tenants, but no subsequent action was taken.[36] The problem of tracing sub-tenants was sometimes compounded by the fact that they were not resident on the manor. In 1338 Simon le Whyte of Roudham and John Dilwode of Somersham (Hunts.) were named as sub-tenants of land in Fornham.[37]

That much of Breckland's arable land did remain in full employment in the early fourteenth century is also suggested by evidence presented in the *Inquisitiones nonarum* of 1341. The previous assessment of ecclesiastical tithes had been in 1291 and at this new inquiry jurors were required to explain any interim fall in the value of tithe in each village, and any decline in the corn tithe was often blamed on abandoned arable land. Sizeable areas of lowland England, including parts of East Anglia, had suffered contraction since 1291, and in Dorset it was the coarse, acidic soils south of Yetminster which bore the brunt of decline, suggesting early retreat from marginal soils.[38] Twenty-six per cent of all Cambridgeshire villages contained evidence of contraction, although significantly the eastern tip of Staploe hundred, which equates with the Breckland element of the county, was absent from the general tale of woe.[39] Most instances of abandonment in Suffolk occurred on the fertile but heavy boulder clays around Chedburgh, Ousden and

[36] Bacon 289/16.   [37] WSROB E.3/15.9/1.2 mm.7 and 8.
[38] A.R.H. Baker, 'Evidence in the *Nonarum inquisitiones* of contracting arable lands in England during the early fourteenth century', *Ec.H.R.* 19 (1966), p. 522. There was also contraction in upland areas of Oxfordshire, Postles, 'Markets for rural produce', p. 21.
[39] Baker, 'Evidence of contracting arable', pp. 525–6.

Hawkedon, but nowhere was this a feature of Breckland.[40] Indeed, our evidence confirms Baker's general conclusion that any contraction which did occur was more due to tenant than to soil poverty.

How did Breckland's farming system cope with the large area under cultivation in the 1330s and 1340s? Tables 4.2 to 4.5 reveal that output was raised by reducing the lengths of recuperative fallows on existing arable land rather than by the ploughing up of large areas of heathland, and this increased pressure on the arable resulted in refinements to the shift system. This development is clearest at Fornham, where Buryweywong seems to have been cropped according to a shift operating on a three- or four-course rotation in 1342–4, but the same symmetry was not evident in 1346–9: either the *pecia* was now divided betwen two shifts of uneven sizes, which seems unlikely, or the bailiff was now sowing the demesne as he saw fit and without reference to a pre-set pattern. This is suggested by the sowing of 4.5 acres of barley in 1347–8, in what might otherwise have been a completely fallow year.

The demanding cropping sequences imposed on Breckland's open-fields relied heavily on the provision of tathe to maintain soil fertility. In 1302 an acre of tathe was valued at 12d. by the Coney Weston demesne, yet in the 1340s the Fornham (A) bailiff was prepared to pay peasants up to 3s. 8d.[41] By the 1330s and 1340s some landlords were employing more labour services and hiring extra labour for the express purpose of carrying and spreading manure, and in some cases were purchasing additional supplies. In 1336–7 the Lakenheath reeve bought manure valued at 15s. and paid 2s. 3d. to have it spread on 18 acres of land, and in 1344–5 he purchased tathe from the village fold for 7s. 1½d.[42] The mucking out of sheepcotes became an important feature of Icklingham accounts after the late 1330s, and over twenty men were employed to this end in the summer of 1340.[43] The adoption of such measures reflects the acute shortage of manure which inevitably accompanied the movement to shorter fallows and the increase in area under cultivation. Yet the most effective solution to this problem was to refine pasturing arrangements so that sheep could reach a

---

[40] *Inquisitiones nonarum* (London, 1807), reveals that there were 400 acres lying *frisce* at Gazeley, 184 acres at Chedburgh, 240 acres at Moulton, 700 acres at Lidgate, pp. 99ff. W.A. Wickham, 'Nonarum Inquisitiones for Suffolk', *P.S.I.A.* 17 (1921), p. 104.

[41] Powell, *Suffolk hundred*, p. 68; WSROB E.3/15.7/2.2b.

[42] CUL EDC 7/15/I/11 and 13.   [43] NRO Ms 13195.

Table 4.2. *Average area sown on manorial demesnes, decennial means 1250–1500 (acres)*

Decade	Accounts	Wheat	Maslin	Rye	Barley	Drage	Legumes	Large oats	Small oats	Total
Brandon										
1340–9	5			120	102	18	9		81	330
1350–9	4			71	64	8	1	5	49	198
1360–9	6			45	65			5	29	144
1370–9	5			40	78		1	5	31	155
1380–9	5	2		36	88		1		31	158
1390–9	6			32	92				21	145
Downham (IP)										
1320–9	1			36	7				36	79
1330–9	1			34	11		1		32	78
1360–9	1			17	5				18	40
Downham (S)										
1340–9	1			61	14				46	121
1350–9	2			35	12				30	77
Hilborough										
1370–9	1			49	140		8	8	22	227
1410–19	3			35	69			1	13	118
Icklingham										
1320–9	1			51	41		2		19	113
1330–9	7	2		62	52	1	5		33	155
1340–9	5	4		81	48	8	5		45	191

Table 4.2. (cont.)

Decade	Accounts	Wheat	Maslin	Rye	Barley	Drage	Legumes	Large oats	Small oats	Total
Lakenheath										
1300–9	1			156	80		12		105	353
1320–9	5	3	7	114	111	12	14		92	353
1330–9	3	2		116	124	8	13		102	365
1340–9	2	3		142	121		6		137	409
1350–9	2	4		112	111		14		50	291
1360–9	3	18		101	140		7		79	345
1370–9	3	9		88	121		10		70	298
1380–9	2	14		83	104		18		34	253
1390–9	2	10		59	124		9		33	235
1420–9	2	14		38	71				15	138
1430–9	2	17		37	77		3		10	144
1440–9	1	9		32	88		3			132
1450–9	4	1		46	76		3		7	133
West Harling										
1320–9	1			51	30		2		31	114
1330–9	3			50	31		2		35	118
1350–9	1			40	32		2		30	104
1360–9	1	5		47	31				30	113
1370–9	2	1		43	40		2		24	110
Wretham										
1300–9	5			136	72		7		75	290

1330–9	3	1		123	64		7		44	239
1340–9	1	3		139	c. 41		9		53	244
Barton Parva										
1270–9	2	16	2	75	72		20	1	52	238
1280–9	4	18	8	70	65		21		45	227
1290–9	7	18	6	71	66	1	18		48	228
1300–9	2	17	9	65	63		20		42	219
1310–19	2	15	6	78	81	3	20		54	254
Cressingham										
1290–9	5									205
1300–9	7									211
1320–9	2	29		74	123		17		53	296
1360–9	3	31		46	98		17		38	230
1370–9	3	21		27	109		15		38	210
1380–9	1	25		28	121		18		31	223
1410–19	3	22		29	104		20		24	199
Feltwell (E)										
1340–9	1	50	27	12	126		23		82	320
1390–9	1	28		13	163		4		7	215
Fornham (A)										
1330–9	1	55		85	122		36	17	51	366
1340–9	5	53	1	80	118		34	17	53	357
1350–9	2	41	8	83	102	1	32	1	35	302
1360–9	6	44		73	111		17	32	33	310
1370–9	2	37		62	120		12	42	33	304
1390–9	1	40		62	117		26	27	24	296
1400–9	8	41		39	110		37	19	9	255

Table 4.2. (cont.)

Decade	Accounts	Wheat	Maslin	Rye	Barley	Drage	Legumes	Large oats	Small oats	Total
1410–19	5	51		35	117		36	20	10	269
1420–9	3	34		43	81		39	15		212
1430–9	2	32		31	90		20	21		194
1440–9	1	26		34	111		24	14		209
Fornham (C)										
1290–9	1	44		54	66		8	30	28	230
1300–9	5	40		53	70		13	38	23	237
1310–19	2	22		43	66		8		37	176
1320–9	3	37		48	53		7	21	25	191
Kennett										
1270–9	2	29		74	122		16		146	387
1280–9	2	35		62	139		22		130	388
1290–9	6	40		84	131		33		124	412
1300–9	1	40		60	125		40		100	365
Methwold										
1360–9	1	39		83	144		14		72	352
1440–9	1	12		40	230				10	292

Mildenhall

1320–9	1	32	57	41	397		31	46	604
1380–9	3	110	43	69	212		44	19	509
1420–9	1	62	9	14	140	12		c. 40	c. 265

Risby

1290–9	2	28		46	51		8	50	183
1310–19	1	48		43	54		13	37	195
1320–9	1	45		53	51		6	51	206
1340–9	1	60		45	48		19	45	217
1350–9	1	57		37	72		8	14	188
1380–9	1	78	8	34	97		46	26	289

Table 4.3. *Proportion of demesne acreage devoted to crops, decennial means (%)*

Decade	A/cs	Winter corn	Spring corn	Legumes	Leased	Fallow	Sown
Brandon							
1340–9	5	21.2	35.6	1.5		41.7	58.3
1350–9	4	12.6	22.3	0.2	5.0	59.9	40.1
1360–9	6	8.0	17.5		6.3	68.2	31.8
1370–9	5	7.1	20.2	0.1	12.5	60.1	39.9
1380–9	5	6.8	20.9	0.2	13.1	59.0	41.0
1390–9	1	5.6	20.1		11.0	63.3	36.7
Hilborough							
1370–9	1	10.2	35.4	1.7		52.7	47.3
1410–19	3	7.2	17.4		3.0	72.4	27.6
Icklingham							
1320–9	1	14.4	17.0	0.6		68.0	32.0
1330–9	7	18.3	24.0	1.4		56.3	43.7
1340–9	5	23.9	28.5	1.5		46.1	53.9
Lakenheath							
1300–9	1	24.0	28.5	1.8		45.7	54.3
1320–9	6	19.0	33.1	2.2		45.7	54.3
1330–9	3	18.1	36.1	2.0		43.8	56.2
1340–9	2	22.3	40.0	0.9		36.8	63.2
1350–9	2	17.8	24.8	2.1		55.3	44.7
1360–9	3	18.3	33.7	1.1		46.9	53.1
1370–9	3	14.9	29.4	1.5		54.2	45.8
1380–9	2	14.9	21.1	2.8		61.2	38.8
1390–9	2	10.5	24.2	1.4		63.9	36.1
1420–9	2	8.0	13.2		6.3	72.5	27.5
1430–9	2	8.2	13.5	0.5	6.6	71.2	28.8
1440–9	1	6.3	13.5	0.4	6.6	73.2	26.8
1450–9	4	7.3	12.7	0.5	6.6	72.9	27.1
Barton Parva							
1270–9	2	31.0	42.0	7.0		20.0	80.0
1280–9	4	32.0	37.0	7.0		24.0	76.0
1290–9	7	32.0	38.0	6.0		24.0	76.0
1300–9	2	30.0	36.0	7.0		27.0	73.0
1310–19	2	33.0	45.0	6.0		16.0	84.0
Fornham (A)							
1330–9	1	32.0	43.3	8.3		16.4	83.6
1340–9	5	30.7	43.2	7.7		18.4	81.6
1350–9	2	29.9	31.8	7.4		30.9	69.1
1360–9	6	26.5	40.4	3.9		29.2	70.8

Growth, crisis and change

Table 4.3. (cont.)

Decade	A/cs	Winter corn	Spring corn	Legumes	Leased	Fallow	Sown
1370–9	2	22.5	44.1	2.9		30.5	69.5
1390–9	1	23.4	38.4	6.0		32.2	67.8
1400–9	8	18.2	31.4	8.6		41.8	58.2
1410–19	5	19.7	33.5	8.2		38.6	61.4
1420–9	3	17.6	22.0	8.8		51.6	48.4
1430–9	2	14.4	25.2	4.7		55.7	44.3
1440–9	1	13.7	28.6	5.5		52.2	47.8
Fornham (C)							
1290–9	1	33.8	42.7	2.8		20.7	79.3
1300–9	5	32.0	45.3	4.3		18.4	81.6
1310–19	2	22.3	35.3	2.7		39.7	60.3
1320–9	3	29.0	34.2	2.3		34.5	65.5
Mildenhall							
1320–9	1	10.8	37.0	2.6		49.6	50.4
1380–9	3	18.4	20.3	3.7	*c.* 10	47.6	52.4
Risby							
1290–9	2	29.4	40.1	3.2		27.3	72.7
1310–19	1	36.2	36.2	5.1		22.5	77.5
1320–9	1	38.9	40.6	2.4		18.1	81.9
1340–9	1	41.7	36.9	7.6		13.8	86.2
1350–9	1	37.3	34.3	3.2		25.3	74.7

Sources: (for demesne extents): Brandon, 564.25 acres, 1251, CUL EDR
G3/27; Hilborough, 480 acres, 1458, NRO Hilborough Deposit Box T
(Daleth), vii m. 8; Icklingham, 353.25 acres, 1459, WSROB E. 3/10/9.9;
Lakenheath, *c.* 650 acres, estimate by J. Williamson in M. Barber, P.
McNulty and P. Noble, eds., *East Anglian and other studies: essays presented to
Barbara Dodwell*, Reading medieval studies monograph 3, p. 135; Barton
Parva, 300 acres, early fourteenth century, CUL Gg.iv.4 f.108; Fornham (A),
437.25 acres, early fourteenth century, BL Add. Ms 34689 f.6; Fornham (C),
291 acres, early fourteenth century, BL Harl 3977 f.101; Mildenhall, 1,200
acres, early fourteenth century, BL Harl 3977 f.80; Risby, 251.75 acres, early
fourteenth century, BL Harl 638 f.13.

Table 4.4. *Cropping intensity on demesne 'peciae'* in Fornham All Saints, 1340–9 and 1360–9

Pecia	Value per acre (d.)	Area (acres)	Total area sown (acres)		% Area fallow	
			1340–9 (5 yrs)	1360–9 (6 yrs)	1340–9 (5 yrs)	1360–9 (6 yrs)
Nethercroft	14	20	88	88	12	17
Overcroft	14	24.75	106.5	112.75	14	24
Risbrede	12	18	81.5	97	9	10
Clipshowe	6	21	96	82.5	9	35
Cavenaswong	6	18	64	79	29	27
Merkeswong	6	14	67	46.5	4	45
Marchelcroft	6	8	35.5	38.75	11	19
Buryweywong	4	23	88.5	98.25	23	29
Byndych	3	9	27	46.25	40	14
Howong	3	20	81	75	19	38
Bradewong	2	32.5	116	134	29	32
Neplond	2	15.75	51.5	53.75	35	43
Heysmerewong	2	47.5	155.25	189.25	35	34
Aldersmere	2	9.25	25.25	46.25	44	17
Berneslade	2	13	39	50	40	36
Breche	2	14	27.5	40.5	61	52

Note:

* There appears to have been some slight reorganisation of these *peciae* after the Black Death. For example, Karldon was rated at 106 acres in the 1340s, but in the 1360s was split into north and south Karldon and measured 133.5 acres and so is excluded from this comparative assessment. The acreages given correspond with the 1340s ratings.

greater area of the arable each year, and this is exactly what happened.

Erecting temporary foldcourses and allowing some peasants to tathe their own lands was the most effective method of extending the overall area manured. It disrupted communal sowing patterns, but rationalised the tathing of arable by allowing farmers to concentrate folding on more areas of land.[44] At Downham (S) the

---

[44] The incidence of foldcourse abuse increased markedly on many manors in the 1330s and 1340s. At Mildenhall, Richard de Walsham raised an illegal fold in June 1332, and in 1336 four men were granted folds of 100 sheep for one year, WSROB E.18/451/2. At Lakenheath in 1336–7 John Wangford paid 6s. 8d. for an annual fold and 3s. 4d. for shackage rights over a specified piece of ground, CUL EDC 7/15/I/11. By the mid-1340s, an unprecedented number of peasants were amerced for not keeping their sheep

Table 4.5 *Cropping sequence at Buryweywong 'pecia'* * *in Fornham All Saints, 1340–71 (acres)*

Year	Rye	Barley	Oats
1342–3		21	
1343–4	20		
1346–7	4	7.5	8.5
1347–8		4.5	
1348–9	10.5	12.5	
1360–1		21.25	
1363–4	15.25		
1365–6			
1366–7		21.25	
1367–8	15.25	6	
1368–9	6		13.25
1370–1	4	18	

Note:

* This *pecia* lay to the south-east of the village, around map reference TL844672.

lord created an extra demesne fold between Pentecost and Michael-mas 1346, and so did the Icklingham demesne in exactly the same period.[45] Demand for manure was also high among the peasantry as they too expanded their arable operations, and consequently grants for short-term folds reached unprecedented heights. At Brandon in the 1340s temporary fold leases were explicitly

in the allotted fold, presumably because they were tathing their own lands instead. In May 1345, 9 men kept at least 29 sheep out of their designated fold, 16 men did the same in May 1347, 5 men kept their sheep out of the village fold in June 1348, as did 10 others in August; CUL EDC 7/15/II/Box 2/15 m.1, 16 m.1, 17 m.4, 16 m.3. A similar situation prevailed at Fornham (A) in the 1340s. In April 1345, the abbot's shepherd, Humphrey Dole, was amerced for not keeping sheep in the demesne fold and for alienating them 'in the folds of other men'. In June he was ordered to explain why 'he drew sheep from the lord's fold to lie in the fold of Hugo Edrich'. In May 1347, 20 men were amerced for not pasturing their sheep in the lord's fold, WSROB E.3/15.6/1.5 and 1.6. These offences reflect a concern with *where* sheep were being pastured, rather than a desire to increase the scale of sheep farming *per se*, and so indicate an increased pressure on the cultivated arable land.

45 At Downham a fold of wethers belonging to one William Payn was kept '*super terram domini*' between Pentecost and Michaelmas, WSROB 651/35/2; NRO Ms 13200.

designed to enable peasants to tathe their own land.[46] The exigencies of the 1340s are best illustrated by a Brandon court entry in March 1348:

the jurors say that in the same village is a certain *tenementum* called Edithsfee, that is now in the hands of diverse tenants due to alienation during the last hundred years, and that before this alienation the tenant enjoyed liberty of fold, that is to say it no longer applies. And now John Butenhagh, with the assent of all the tenants of the *tenementum*, raises the fold.[47]

Evidently the pressing need for tathe outweighed any practical difficulties of establishing a foldcourse over greatly subdivided land. All of these short-term grants were annulled with the onset of plague, but they still testify to the flexibility of the foldcourse system when the occasion demanded.

The adoption of more complex pasturing arrangements obviously required greater expenditure, either in the purchase of manure or in the employment of more labour. Yet why was this a feature of a marginal region such as Breckland and not of other, more fertile, regions in central England? The most plausible answer is that Breckland's rye and its excellent malting barley were sent in large quantities to a number of urban markets where they could fetch higher prices, and that transport costs were low enough for Breckland to supply those markets profitably. It is impossible to quantify Breckland's transport costs relative to those in many Midland areas, but price data from the region suggests that its barley fetched a significantly higher price than the national average (table 4.6).[48] This price differential encouraged Breckland farmers to adopt progressive, albeit selective, agrarian techniques. The area under legumes remained small, sowing rates were low and static, and there is little indication that increases in ploughing, harrowing

---

[46] In October 1335, four men were amerced for illegally abducting their own sheep from the lord's fold, Bacon 291/7. In January 1348 four men paid 4s. or 5s. each for the right of a fold *'super terras suas proprias'*, Bacon 291/15.   [47] Bacon 291/15.

[48] Any comparison of regional price data with a national series is fraught with difficulties, not least because the regional data will invariably be culled from a narrower range of documentation. In Breckland a further difficulty is the use of both heaped and level measures of grain, although the latter was more common and is the measure used in these price computations. Farmer's figures concern sale prices although the Breckland material includes some purchase prices. The comparisons are patently very crude, but the consistently higher prices in Breckland are suggestive. In fact, the 1300–13 figures tend to understate the real difference in prices between the national average and Breckland, because both Farmer's and Roger's statistics include material from the scarcity years of 1307–10, whilst the Breckland figure does not.

Table 4.6. *Comparison of barley prices in Breckland with national prices (d. per quarter)*

Place	Period	Number of years	Mean price
England*	1300–13	14	45.6
England+	1300–13	14	44.1
Breckland	1300–13	6	51.8
England+	1335–48	14	38.6
Breckland	1335–48	13	43.8

Sources: D.L. Farmer, 'Some grain price movements in thirteenth-century England', *Ec. H. R.* 10 (1957–8), table III (*); Rogers, *History of agriculture and prices*, vol. 1 (+); M.D. Bailey, 'At the margin: Suffolk Breckland in the later Middle Ages' (Ph.D., Cambridge University 1986), table 4.20.

and weeding in the 1330s and 1340s were any greater than the rise in area cultivated. Yet were the increments in manure sufficient to ward off soil deterioration in this period? Unfortunately, the yield data is too scanty to allow any exact answer, although yields at Brandon certainly improved with less demanding rotations in the later fourteenth century.[49] Calculations of animal ratios must be used with caution, but their progressive decline on most manors by the 1340s is significant (see table 4.7). In part, this evidence is substantiated by miscellaneous references to poor corn and land, notably at Fornham (A). In 1343, a year of reasonable harvest, the bailiff disposed of 'one measure of poor quality barley', whilst eight acres in Carledon were described as 'badly laid' in 1347–8.[50] None of this evidence is as conclusive as one would like, but we must suspect that soil quality began to deteriorate as the fields became more frequently cropped, and that the release of population pressure by the Black Death was a welcome relief to Breckland's soils.[51]

[49] See table 3.3. In fact, this yield evidence might be ambiguous. The rise in yields after the Black Death certainly suggests that the soil was exhausted in the 1340s, but there again the figures might merely reflect the concentration of cropping onto the infield after the Black Death and the abandonment of the poorer outfields. In other words, yields on the infield may have been as high in the 1340s as in the 1390s, but the *overall* level of yields in the 1340s was lower because it included calculations of crops sown on the poorest lands.

[50] WSROB E.3/15.7/2.2a and b.

[51] Whilst there were some signs of soil deterioration in the 1340s, it might have been possible to protect the valuable barley crop from the general malaise. In chapter 2 it was shown that barley was sown late in the agrarian year and enjoyed a longer preparatory period, and so was most likely to benefit from the changes in the foldcourse system in the 1330s and 1340s. Indeed, barley yields per acre were much higher than those of other crops, which testifies to its importance and its special place in the region's farming. Unfortunately, the lack of yield data makes it impossible to verify this hypothesis.

A marginal economy?

Table 4.7. Animal ratios on Breckland demesnes, decennial means 1300–1500

Decade	Beasts*	Sheep*	Animal units*	Mean area sown (acres)	Animal ratio
Brandon					
1350–9	45.6	699.6	220.5	197.9	111.4
1360–9	15.6	266.5	82.2	143.9	57.1
1380–9	5.0	514.1	133.5	157.5	84.8
1390–9	5.0	739.1	189.8	145.1	130.8
Downham (IP)					
1320–9	3.0	154.0	41.5	78.5	52.9
1330–9	4.0	161.5	44.4	78.0	56.9
1360–9	2.0	150.0	41.5	40.3	103.0
Downham (S)					
1340–9	20.5	733.0	203.8	120.5	169.1
1350–9	9.8	1,159.5	299.7	77.6	386.2
Hilborough					
1370–9	5.0	5.0	6.3	227.0	2.8
1410–19	4.2	1,163.0	294.9	118.0	249.9
Icklingham					
1330–9	5.6	248.3	67.7	154.5	43.8
1340–9	8.0	334.6	91.6	190.5	48.1
Lakenheath					
1300–9	64.0	1,707.0	490.8	353.0	139.0
1320–9	54.4	2,419.3	659.3	352.6	187.0
1330–9	64.8	2,082.8	585.5	365.0	160.4
1340–9	47.5	2,280.3	617.6	408.6	151.1
1350–9	73.0	1,370.0	415.5	290.5	143.0
1360–9	59.7	1,907.2	536.5	345.3	155.4
1370–9	66.0	2,085.8	587.4	298.0	197.1
1380–9	67.8	1,583.8	463.8	252.5	183.7
1390–9	70.7	1,528.5	452.8	234.8	192.8
1420–9	20.8	1,645.0	432.0	138.0	313.1
1430–9	14.5	1,403.5	365.4	144.3	253.2
1440–9	7.5	1,422.0	363.0	131.5	276.0
1450–9	6.0	1,150.8	293.7	133.2	220.4
West Harling					
1320–9	22.0	125.0	53.3	114.0	46.7
1330–9	18.8	70.8	36.5	117.7	31.0
1350–9	17.5	391.0	115.3	104.1	110.7
1360–9	5.0	253.5	68.4	112.5	60.8
1370–9	7.8	246.5	69.4	110.3	62.9

Table 4.7. (*cont.*)

Decade	Beasts*	Sheep*	Animal units*	Mean area sown (acres)	Animal ratio
Wretham					
1300–9	56.2	1,001.0	306.5	289.9	105.7
1330–9	49.3	1,139.0	334.1	239.1	139.7
1340–9	54.0	1,221.0	359.3	244.3	147.1
Barton Parva					
1280–9	25.0	28.0	32.0	227.3	14.1
1290–9	20.9	10.9	23.6	227.9	10.4
1300–9	21.5	7.5	23.4	219.4	10.6
Cressingham					
1300–9	29.0	102.0	54.5	211.3	25.8
1320–9	44.8	78.8	64.5	295.8	21.8
1360–9	33.2	60.0	48.2	230.1	20.9
1370–9	41.8	180.0	86.8	210.3	41.3
1380–9	30.5	113.5	58.9	223.0	26.4
1410–19	14.3	0	14.3	199.2	7.2
Feltwell					
1340–9	20.5	0	20.5	319.6	6.4
1390–9	27.5	380.0	122.5	215.0	57.0
Fornham (A)					
1340–9	71.4	428.0	178.4	357.0	50.0
1350–9	59.7	318.5	139.3	302.2	46.1
1360–9	62.1	194.3	110.7	309.8	35.7
1370–9	76.5	405.0	177.8	303.9	58.5
1390–9	35.3	338.5	119.9	296.3	40.5
1400–9	25.8	255.8	89.8	254.7	35.2
1410–19	17.1	543.8	153.1	268.6	56.9
1420–9	10.4	345.1	96.7	211.7	45.7
1440–9	10.0	1,538.0	394.5	209.0	188.7
Fornham (C)					
1300–9	35.3	54.6	48.9	237.4	20.6
1310–19	24.8	53.3	38.1	175.6	21.7
1320–9	28.6	27.0	35.3	190.7	18.5
Mildenhall					
1320–9	118.0	882.5	338.6	604.2	56.0
1380–9	97.8	805.9	299.3	509.4	58.7
1420–9	36.0	352.3	124.1	265.0	46.8
Risby					
1290–9	25.2	154.5	63.8	183.0	34.9
1310–19	24.0	250.5	86.6	195.0	44.4

Table 4.7. (*cont.*)

Decade	Beasts*	Sheep*	Animal units*	Mean area sown (acres)	Animal ratio
1320–9	26.0	95.0	49.8	206.3	24.1
1340–9	11.5	152.5	49.6	217.0	22.9
1350–9	36.5	209.6	88.9	188.1	47.3
1380–9	21.0	204.0	72.0	289.0	24.9

Note:
* These figures represent Michaelmas means.

THE BLACK DEATH AND ITS AFTERMATH

Direct demographic evidence is extremely poor from the extant Breckland material, but indirect evidence from the land market and the area under cultivation suggests that its population had recovered from the effects of famine and disease in 1315–22. Certainly, recovery was slow, but then population continued to press hard upon available resources and there are no signs that Breckland's economic turning point occurred in the first half of the fourteenth century.[52] Yet any recovery was savagely curtailed by the arrival of plague in the spring of 1349. Whilst scholars debate the level of national mortality, few doubt that East Anglia was severely afflicted or that it lost at least a third of its population in the first epidemic.[53] Recorded deaths in the Lakenheath courts between 1308 and 1348 averaged 1.6 per annum, but rocketed to 67 in 1349. In Timworth and Fornham (A) mortality rates amongst tenants of Bury abbey were 50 per cent and around 47 per cent, and

---

[52] This substantiates other evidence from East Anglia, Hallam, *Rural England*, p. 55; Campbell, 'Population pressure and the land market', p. 120. Gottfried, *Bury and the urban crisis*, p. 55, argues that the population of Bury continued to rise through the 1330s and 1340s.

[53] For a review of the evidence, see Hatcher, *Plague, population*, pp. 21–6. Even Shrewsbury, who otherwise prefers a conservative estimate of plague mortality, writes 'mortality . . . was both absolutely and relatively greater in East Anglia than in the rest of England', J.F.D. Shrewsbury, *The history of bubonic plague in England* (Cambridge, 1970), p. 31. For specific East Anglian studies, see A. Jessopp, 'The Black Death in East Anglia', in his *The coming of the friars and other historical essays* (London, 1889); C. Ritchie, 'The Black Death at St Edmunds abbey', *P.S.I.A.* 37 (1955), pp. 40–50; and R.S. Gottfried, *The Black Death: natural and human disaster in medieval Europe* (London, 1983), pp. 65–6.

amongst the beneficed clergy of Thetford and Blackbourne, 50 and 36 per cent.[54]

The immediate impact of plague on the land market was catastrophic. On the death of a tenant, the land reverted to the lord before it was passed on to the heirs, but in 1349 few heirs appeared at the manorial court to claim their inheritance. Hence around 40 per cent of customary lands at Timworth lay abandoned, and in December 1349 an inquiry was ordered at Brandon to establish the extent of lands 'rendered in the lord's hands after the death of diverse tenants at the time of the pestilence'.[55] The explanations for the non-appearance of heirs were varied. In some cases they had fled the village, in others they refused to take up their holdings, but in most cases the immediate heirs had died and their successors were as yet unknown. Some landlords responded promptly to the crisis, and the first post-plague court at Hilborough (held 12 June 1349) ordered all heirs to come and perform fealty, and also a check on all villein lands.[56] By September 1349 it was established that of 34 tenant deaths, heirs had come in 15 cases and were known in 5 others. The Black Death affected Brandon more severely, and no courts were held in the latter part of 1349. By January 1350, of 30 land parcels in the lord's hands, the heirs had appeared in only eight cases.[57] This was obviously a difficult period for landlords, but the most immediate and serious problem was the loss of rent income. Income from leaseholds at Fornham (A) fell from by more than half to 19s. 4d. between 1348 and 1349, and although assize rents were still valued at 54s. 2d. at Risby in 1351–2, decays had risen from 12s. 3d. to 37s. 4d.[58] At Brandon in 1349–50 decays of assize rents rose from 6d. to 8s. 4d., and the reeve was allowed a further £5 4s. 6d. for other uncollectable rents and perquisites.[59]

Expediency and flexibility dominated the seigneurial response to this unprecedented collapse. Whilst heirs of the abandoned holdings were sought, landlords raised some money by allowing other tenants to occupy the empty cottages or to cultivate small parcels

[54] A Timworth rental of 1348 was amended by a different scribe after the Black Death, and 18 out of 36 tenants seem to have perished, CUL Add.Ms 4220 f.84. In 1349–50, the Fornham courts record the deaths of 27 tenants, whereas in the previous rental (1283) there had been 57 tenants, WSROB e.3/15.6/1.7 and 1.8, and BL Add.Ms 34689 ff.8–11. Clergy mortalities from Shrewsbury, *Bubonic plague*, p. 99.
[55] CUL Add.Ms 4220 f.84; Bacon 291/17.
[56] NRO Hilborough Deposit Box T (Daleth), iv.   [57] Bacon 291/17.
[58] WSROB e.3/15.7/2.4 and e.3/15.13/2.10.   [59] PRO sc6.1304/27.

of arable on a temporary basis; in exchange, the tenants made a small payment to the manorial court, and by this method 49s. was recovered at Fornham (A) in 1349.[60] At Brandon in September 1350, 21s. 3d. was received for the temporary occupation of 15.5 tofts.[61] Another expedient was to sow parcels of redundant peasant land alongside that of the demesne, as at Risby where the cellarer of Bury abbey cultivated land once belonging to Dulae of Risby in 1351–2.[62] On another occasion, the manor leased 41 acres of arable land as pasture on an *ad hoc* basis for 27s. 4d.[63] These methods enabled landlords partially to offset losses in rent income, but their cumulative importance should not be overstated. At Brandon in 1350, out of 480 acres of customary land in the lord's hands, 14.5 acres were sown by the lord, 19 acres were sown by unnamed peasants, and the rest was described as *frisca* 'and not possible to lease'.[64] The arrival of plague also caused temporary disruption to demesne farming. Yields were low in 1348–9, mainly due to the shortage of labour with which to harvest the crops. At Brandon, Fornham (A) and Risby additional labour had to be hired 'for want of famuli', and many labour services were not performed because tenant land had been abandoned: in 1352–3, 770 out of 890 *operari* owed at Fornham (A) were not rendered 'because of the pestilence'.[65]

With the disruption to economic activity, the government granted some villages tax relief in the 1350s. These details have survived for Norfolk, and indicate, somewhat surprisingly, that Breckland was no more disrupted by plague than the rest of the county. Indeed, a belt of villages in central Norfolk and the Goodsands were granted substantial relief (over one-third the tax assessed in 1334), whereas much of Breckland received less than this.[66] After the plague's initial impact, recovery of the land market on many English estates was remarkably rapid and complete. At first glance, such a recovery is difficult to reconcile with such a drastic fall in population, and this paradox has led some commentators to conclude that any estimates of high mortality are therefore

[60] WSROB E.3/15.7/2.4.
[61] Bacon 291/19.
[62] The stock account refers to crops issued from the lands of Dulae of Risby, WSROB E.3/15.13/2.10.   [63] This was in 1355–6, WSROB E.3/15.13/2.13.
[64] Bacon 291/19, court held September 1350.
[65] WSROB E.3/15.6/2.23b.
[66] Allison, 'Lost villages of Norfolk', map 1.

inaccurate.[67] Such conclusions reveal a poor understanding of prevailing economic forces in the mid-fourteenth century. Certainly the demand for land was lower in the 1350s than in the 1340s, but it does not follow that the fall in demand was commensurate with the drop in population. Immediately prior to the Black Death, the demand for land exceeded its supply, and the result was a proliferation of smallholdings and much under-employment in agriculture. Yet, in the 1350s, the release of intense pressure on resources presented peasants with the opportunity to increase the size of their holdings and to secure fuller employment on the land, which explains the relatively complete uptake of land in the 1350s.

In general, Breckland's land market had recovered by the end of the 1350s, although the exact pace of recovery depended upon local mortality rates and the nature of seigneurial response. Lakenheath was one of the worst affected villages, for substantial *de exitis* payments were still being received for redundant arable as late as 1355–6, and arrears climbed steadily throughout the decade.[68] Rents from the Clare manor fetched £12 14s. 4d. in 1347–8 and only £8 19s. 11d. in 1355–6, of which £2 9s. 9½d. was not paid by the collector; effectively a fall in income of 49 per cent.[69] At Downham (S), on the other hand, there were no decays of rent and hardly any arrears in the 1350s.[70] The land market was sluggish at Fornham (A) for more than a year after plague had struck, but began to pick up in the summer of 1352.[71] The same was true at Fornham (C), and here it continued to rise briskly in the late 1350s when a tenant was even found for 2 roods of land which 'lie at the heathland'.[72] The conversion of some customary lands to leaseholds was a powerful inducement to prospective tenants, and represented a major concession by landlords because it stripped

---

[67] Shrewsbury, *Bubonic plague*, p. 123; A.E. Levett and A. Ballard, *The Black Death on the estates of the See of Winchester* (Oxford, 1916), pp. 75–88; A.R. Bridbury, 'The Black Death', *Ec.H.R.* 26 (1973), pp. 590–1.

[68] CUL EDC 7/15/I/14–17. There were no arrears on the 1347–8 account, but in 1355–6 there were £14 17s. 5d. arrears, and £16 4s. 7d. in 1356–7.   [69] *Ibid.*

[70] WSROB 651/35/3–6.

[71] Few lands were taken up in the 1351 courts, WSROB E.3/15.7/1.9, but by Michaelmas 1352 five 8-*acreware* tenements had been converted to leaseholds, E.3/15.6/2.23b. Peasants were unwilling to hold customary virgates on the Ramsey abbey manors of Slepe and Wistow (Hunts.), and 12 remained untenanted in the lord's hands in 1351. However, when the abbey eventually offered them in a new format and free of most labour services in the 1360s, they were rapidly taken up, Raftis, *Ramsey abbey*, p. 252.

[72] WSROB E.3/15.6/1.3 mm.7 and 26–9. In 1358 alone, 42.5 acres were granted to tenants from the lord's hands.

them of important labour services. At Risby the Black Death heralded the demise of the old malt rents, and although the amount of land let out for cash leaseholds remained static for much of the 1350s, there was a rapid growth in the number of barley leaseholds. Nine leases were initiated in 1349–50 (including a demesne parcel of 6 acres 'at the heath') and another fourteen in 1350–1, so that by 1351–2 there were 90.25 acres leased at an average of 1.96 bushels per acre.[73] The rising cost of labour after 1349 contributed to the demise of the malt rents, and the shift to barley leases helped to ensure that the monastic community at Bury was fed in an uncertain period.

The willingness of ecclesiastical landlords to convert customary tenures to leaseholds helps to explain the land market's recovery at Fornham (A). Leaseholds resembled contractual rents, where the lessee rendered a fixed cash or grain payment for a nominated period of years, and they had been known on a few manors before the Black Death. The peasant's improved position in the labour market after 1349 resulted in an increased demand for leaseholds, particularly on ecclesiastical estates, because few leaseholds carried liability for the onerous labour services. Consequently, an extension of the area at leasehold represented a major concession by landlords, although it was still uncommon for the area under leaseholds to exceed the area of land on customary tenures.[74] A further concession in the early 1350s was the granting of leaseholds at very low rents per acre. Such concessions were necessary in years of crisis, and landlords who refused to grant them were faced with a sluggish demand for land on their manors. At Brandon the land market began to pick up in 1351 with the granting of small parcels of arable on leases of two to three years.[75] Tofts and houses were in greater demand, but peasants were reluctant to hold composite full- or half-lands on the old terms, not least because large areas of these holdings would lie uncultivated in the outfield each year. The stalemate was finally broken in the early 1360s when the Bishopric

[73] WSROB E.3/15.13/2.10–11.
[74] Dyer, 'Background to the revolt', p. 26. Leaseholds were most common on the large ecclesiastical estates, and were not evident everywhere. For instance, no peasant land was converted to leasehold on the lay manors of Hockham and Quiddenham.
[75] The first post-plague leases here were in December 1350 and January 1351, when about six tofts, two cottages and twelve acres in small parcels were granted (manuscript faded), Bacon 291/20. For the gradual recovery of the land market, see also the January courts of 1352 and 1353, and September 1353, Bacon 291/24 and 30. In the latter court, 32.5 acres were granted in 23 separate leases.

of Ely abandoned attempts to reassert the old form of tenure, and granted them as leaseholds and without labour services.[76] The overall disruption to the land market is illustrated by the drastic change in the nature of land transactions at Brandon after the Black Death. Between 1350 and 1399 transfers *inter vivos* and sub-leases were greatly curtailed, and transfers from the lord rose to 73 per cent of all completed transactions as the bishop was forced to break hereditary tenures and redistribute abandoned holdings or convert them to leaseholds.

As the immediate plague crisis passed and as economic conditions improved in the 1360s and 1370s, so landlords were able to claw back at some of their earlier concessions. At Lakenheath the area at leasehold was reduced from an average of 129 acres each year in the 1360s back down to its pre-plague level by the 1370s. The level of rents per acre was also increased, so that barley leaseholds at Risby rose from under 2 bushels per acre in 1352 to 2.6 bushels per acre in 1369–70 and 3.04 bushels in 1376–7.[77] On many manors overall rent income recovered to at least pre-plague levels, although this did not necessarily imply that demand for land also returned to the same heights. In fact direct comparisons of rent levels before and after the Black Death demand some caution, for the value of the new leaseholds was determined largely by market forces whilst customary influences had been important in artificially depressing rent levels before 1349. Hence the growth in total rent income in the 1360s and 1370s reflects a change in the predominant form of land tenure rather than a return to former levels of demand for land.[78] Any gains in rent income after the plague should be weighed against the attendant losses of labour services which were often commuted on the conversion of customary lands to leasehold. The most reliable indicator of the demand for land is therefore not total rent income but the changing value of leasehold rents per acre shown in table 4.8. The differences in values between manors are largely explained by reference to soil factors, and hence the peripheral manors have appreciably higher rents than central manors, although population density and marketing opportunities inflated rents at Fornham and Mildenhall even further. In general, rent levels per acre in Breckland were high, especially in

76 See table 4.9. The old composite full-lands were converted to leasehold by 1363, Bacon 291/42.   77 WSROB E.3/15.13/2.17–18. .
78 See Davenport, *Development of a Norfolk manor*, p. 78; Britnell, contribution to *Agrarian history of England*, vol. III (forthcoming).

Table 4.8. *Leasehold arable rents per acre, decennial means*
1300–1399

Decade	A/cs	Total rent (d.)	Total area (acres)	Mean rent per acre	Indices
Brandon					
1350–9	2	723.0	181.0	3.99	61
1360–9	7	2,710.8	416.0	6.52	99
1370–9	5	2,250.0	336.0	6.70	102
1380–9	5	2,734.5	369.5	7.40	112
1390–9	6	2,591.0	370.5	6.99	106
Lackford					
1390–9	2	3,978.0	485.3	8.20	100
1400–99	2	3,668.0	543.0	6.76	82
Lakenheath					
1340–9	1	708.0	105.0	6.74	97
1350–9	3	2,454.0	363.0	6.76	98
1360–9	3	2,836.0	388.0	7.31	106
1370–9	3	2,396.0	330.0	7.26	105
1380–9	2	1,798.0	286.3	6.28	91
1390–9	2	1,640.0	240.5	6.82	99
1400–99	12	29,658.0	5,270.8	5.63	81
Hilborough					
1370–9	2	442.0	101.0	4.41	100
1400–99	4	7,484.0	1,865.3	4.01	92
Fornham (A)					
1350–9	1	1,109.0	88.3	12.57	97
1360–9	6	9,926.0	727.5	13.64	104
1370–9	2	3,459.0	255.0	13.56	104
1390–9	1	1,943.0	193.5	10.04	77
1400–99	25	46,750.0	4,777.8	9.78	75
Methwold					
1390–9	1	8.0	1.0	8.00	100
1400–99	10	7,925.0	1,257.5	6.30	79
Mildenhall					
1320–9	1	5,518.0	295.5	18.67	86
1380–9	4	61,918.0	2,891.5	21.41	100
1390–9	1	15,641.0	720.3	21.72	101
1400–99	20	342,182.0	19,420.3	17.62	82
Risby					
1350–9	5	1,695.0	198.8	8.53	91
1360–9	2	750.0	78.0	9.61	103
1370–9	3	1,935.0	180.3	10.73	115

Table 4.8. (*cont.*)

Decade	A/cs	Total rent (d.)	Total area (acres)	Mean rent per acre	Indices
1380–9	1	1,178.0	136.3	8.63	92
1390–9	1	752.0	83.0	9.06	97
1400–99	6	6,187.0	789.8	7.83	84
				1350–1399 = 100	

comparison to the 6d. per acre in Sherington (Bucks.) in the 1360s, the 11d. per acre in Forncett (Norfolk) in the 1370s, and the 6d. per acre at Lawshall (Suffolk) in the 1390s, all villages on more fertile soils.[79] They were certainly much higher than the 4d. per acre universal rent demanded by the Mile End rebels in 1381, which might suggest that rents in Breckland were kept high by seigneurial pressure.[80] But tenant refusals to pay rents are very rare in Breckland prior to the 1380s, which indicates that landlords were charging no more than that which the market could sustain. Again, our conclusion must be that, despite its poor soils, the region was enjoying a period of relative economic prosperity.

Whilst many marginal areas of England were suffering from agricultural recession by the early 1370s, Breckland's experience was more favourable.[81] The land market continued to recover until at least the 1380s, after which it stabilised and then declined gently in the 1390s; only at Fornham was there an appreciable drop in land values. At Brandon, an expanding textile industry helped to stimulate a rapid rise in rents between 1360 and 1399 (table 4.9). To some extent this recovery was aided by financial inducements offered in 1374 by the new bishop of Ely, Thomas de Arundel. In this year, new land leases were drawn up for a standard term of ten years, in which the tenants were granted substantial reductions on the first year's rent. Hence, on 31 separate leases valued at 187s. 4d.

---

[79] A.C. Chibnall, *Sherington: fiefs and fields of a Buckinghamshire village* (Cambridge, 1965), p. 125; Davenport, *Development of a Norfolk manor*, p. 78; H.W. Saunders, 'A bailiff's roll for the manor of Lawshall, 1393–4' *P.S.I.A.* 14 (1910), pp. 122–4.

[80] See Dyer, 'Background to the revolt', p. 26.

[81] Or could it be that those marginal areas too have been misunderstood? Upland Derbyshire was experiencing some distress by the 1370s, Blanchard, 'Derbyshire in the Middle Ages', pp. 67–8. Hamlets on the north Yorkshire moors had become deserted by the late fourteenth century, McDonnell, 'Medieval assarting hamlets', p. 278.

Table 4.9. *Rents for full-lands and tofts in Brandon, decennial means*
1350–99

Decade	A/cs	Total rent (d.)	Number of full-lands*	Mean rent	Indices
1360–9	5	3,635	66.5	54.7	77
1370–9	5	4,368	72.0	60.7	85
1380–9	4	4,938	62.0	79.6	112
1390–9	8	10,224	124.0	82.5	115
			Number of tofts		
1350–9	1	372	12.0	31.0	53
1360–9	2	1,652	34.5	47.9	82
1370–9	5	4,390	82.0	53.5	91
1380–9	4	4,444	68.0	65.4	111
1390–9	8	8,592	135.0	63.6	108

1350–1399 = 100

Note:

* A full-land contained 40 acres; originally they had a toft, or large messuage, attached. On conversion to leaseholds, both elements were let separately.

per annum, the tenants were only required to pay 136s. 7d., or 73 per cent, in 1374–5.[82]

Not every landlord was sensitive to the peasantry's stronger bargaining position in the land market after the Black Death, and in some cases their incomes suffered accordingly. In particular, the Duchy of Lancaster at Methwold and the Prior and Convent of Ely at Lakenheath encountered problems. Few holdings at Methwold were converted to leaseholds, and those that were still had boonworks attached to them.[83] The antipathy towards leaseholders went even further, and their animals were excluded from basic commoning rights.[84] At Lakenheath there had been 105 acres at leasehold in 1348, *c.* 150 acres in 1356 and 120 acres in the 1390s, in direct contrast to most other manors on ecclesiastical estates where

[82] Bacon 291/58, court held May 1374.
[83] See, for instance, leaseholds granted in PRO DL30.104/1473 m.3, court held July 1375.
[84] This is evident from a case in August 1381: '*Robertus Whyte communicat cum averis suis in communa de Methwold ubi non debet communicare eo quod dimisit terras suas ad firmam*', PRO DL30.104/1476 m.2.

the area under leasehold was increasing in the same period. Here the peasant response *was* to withhold rents, so that in the period 1360–89 around 28 per cent of all rents and court dues owed by them were written off by manorial officials as uncollectable, and a number of peasant houses were burnt in protest.[85] It is hardly surprising to find that social unrest was endemic on both manors in the 1370s, and that both featured prominently in the Peasant's Revolt of 1381.[86]

The recovery of land rents in the quarter-century or so after 1349 reflects a recovery in economic activity, and in some villages perhaps a gradual increase in population. However, overall demographic recovery was hampered by further outbreaks of plague in 1361–2 and 1369. Although it is impossible to calculate the exact mortality of these later epidemics, the disruption is reflected in the land market at Brandon, where the value of an average acre at leasehold fell from 7.96d. to 4.68d. between 1361 and 1363. Such values also fell at Fornham (A) and Risby.[87] Breckland, along with most areas of late fourteenth-century England, patently suffered from recurrently high mortality, and this proved a cogent depopulating force. However, the population-resources model contends that depopulation was exacerbated in poor soil regions by the emigration of large numbers of peasants to areas of better soil and to towns. Indeed, historical research has indicated that the mobility of peasants became of great concern to manorial courts everywhere as landlords strove to arrest the declining number of tenants on their rent-rolls. But was the problem any greater in Breckland?[88]

85 CUL EDC 7/15/I/16–28. The burning of houses occurred a good three years before the celebrated revolt of 1381. In 1378–9 the messuages of John atte Chamber, John Maihew, John Horold, John Scot and Reginald Fisher had been burnt, and many others lay vacant. John Fairchild's reaping works were not performed '*propter combustionem tenementi sui*', 7/15/I/25. By 1384–5 five other tenements had been burnt, along with two cottages on the Clare manor, 7/15/I/27 and 28.

86 Powell, *Rising in East Anglia*, p. 13. At Methwold, 25 and then 22 tenants failed to perform court suit in the October courts of 1379 and 1380, PRO DL29.104/1475 m.3 and 104/1476 m.1. In October 1370, 38 tenants had paid to opt out of court suit, 104/1472 m.3.

87 The 1361–2 Brandon works account notes that eleven full-lands had been in the lord's hands since the first pestilence, and that 14.5 acres had fallen into the lord's hands thereafter. The distinction of a first pestilence indicates the visitation of a second, PRO sc6.1304/29 and Bacon 647. At Risby, the mean rent of an acre at leasehold was 10.74d. in 1361–2 and 8d. in 1369–70, WSROB E.3/15.13/2.16 and 2.17. At Fornham (A) it was 15.61d. in 1360–1 and 13.89d. in 1363–4, WSROB E.3/15.6/2.28 and 2.30b. At no other time do rent values fall so quickly in so short a period.

88 Raftis, *Tenure and mobility*, pp. 130–53.

Many late fourteenth-century court rolls record the flight of unfree peasants from their home manor, partly through a genuine concern about continued depopulation, but also to exact an annual sum – or chevage payment – from the peasant as recompense. In comparison, most Breckland courts record this information only occasionally, and even then they merely demanded that the offenders be presented before the next court and it was uncommon for them to exact any chevage. Yet these references still provide a clear indication of the destination of most emigrants. Four men are recorded as having fled the manor of Langford between 1376–8, of whom two had settled in Lynford and Hilborough, and two had gone further afield.[89] In August and October 1396 three Lakenheath men are recorded as having fled to Chippenham, Cavenham and Ely, and one other was an itinerant.[90] The flight of tenants from Fornham in the 1390s was a more serious problem: four had settled in Lopham (Norfolk), but six others had all moved to villages elsewhere in Breckland.[91] By 1380, four tenants had left Methwold to live in various fenland villages, one had gone to Lynn, two to Swaffham and six more to other Breckland villages, including two men who had become a weaver and a cooper in Feltwell.[92] So, despite the obvious fact that falling grain prices were a powerful push factor to migration from areas of poor soil, much of the recorded movement in Breckland was either to urban areas or was contained within the region itself; there was certainly no evidence that its residents were lured by the prospect of more responsive soils in central East Anglia. Evidently the argument for rapid abandonment of poor soils after the Black Death is only tenable if arable farming constituted the main source of peasant income, which was patently not the case here.

Table 4.2 reveals the disruption to demesne arable farming after the Black Death. The buoyancy of the 1340s was no longer evident, although nowhere did farming collapse.[93] Indeed, despite the

[89] NRO NCC(Petre) Box 8/21, courts held March 1376 and March 1378.
[90] CUL EDC 7/15/II/Box 2/25.
[91] WSROB E.3/15.7/1.12, courts held June 1392, October 1396 and October 1398.
[92] PRO DL30.104/1475 m.6; DL30.104/1477 m.2, court held May 1381.
[93] Demesne farming in Breckland compared reasonably well with other parts of the country. The fall in area under cultivation was greater than in eastern Norfolk, as one would expect; at Martham, for instance, the fall was only 7 per cent between 1300–24 and 1400–24, Campbell, 'Agricultural progress', p. 38. Yet it was comparable to the decline on other East Anglian demesnes. At Hevingham (Norfolk) the area under crops fell by 24 per cent between 1327–8 and 1417–18, and by 34 per cent at Langenhoe (Essex) between 1325–48 and 1388–97; Campbell, 'Field systems in eastern Norfolk during the

difficulties of poor soil farming, most manors display signs of recovery or at least stability between 1355 and 1380. Grain production at Cressingham was still affected as late as 1362–3, when hardly any corn was sold to the market and net manorial income was correspondingly low. Yet by the 1370s grain sales had been revived and constituted 49 per cent of gross manorial income (excluding arrears).[94] At Risby, where the cellarer of Bury abbey was concentrating production as part of a wider estate reorganisation, there was a startling expansion in output, and at Harling the area under cultivation held steady throughout the century. This temporary recovery was largely inspired by the buoyancy of grain prices until the mid-1370s, which served to counteract the rising value of labour. *Why* grain prices were higher in the period 1355–75 than in 1325–45, especially when population had fallen by at least one-third, requires some explanation. If population is known to have fallen and yet prices rose, then there must have been a contraction of supply, although high prices could have been accentuated by monetary factors.[95] A manuscript attributed to Babwell priory in Fornham All Saints contains information suggesting that local weather conditions were particularly inclement in the 1360s and early 1370s, which would obviously have disrupted farming.[96] Furthermore, peasant knowledge of the market was imperfect even in the most propitious years, and in the wake of the Black Death there was bound to be some dislocation as they rebuilt trading links and re-evaluated the extent and nature of commercial opportunities; and in a period of poor harvests, this process was likely to have been delayed further, thus exacerbating the problems of undersupply.

Whatever the reasons for the buoyant grain prices, they inspired

Middle Ages' (Ph.D., Cambridge, 1975), table 4.1; R.H. Britnell, 'Production for the market on a small fourteenth-century estate', *Ec.H.R.* 19 (1966), p. 386. At Marley, on the Battle abbey estate, the fall was much more drastic, from 404.5 acres in the 1310s to 76 acres in the 1380s, E. Searle, *Lordship and community: Battle abbey and its banlieu* (Toronto, 1974), p. 460. On a number of Kent manors belonging to Canterbury Cathedral Priory there was a notable fall in the area under cultivation. On eleven chalkland manors it fell by 40 per cent between 1291 and 1371, by 34 per cent on four clayland manors, and by 15 per cent on six marshland manors, A. Smith, 'Regional differences in crop production in medieval Kent', *Archaeologia Cantiana* 78 (1963), p. 159.

94 NRO DCN Supplement (R187A) (3 years). Compare this figure with that for 1322–3, when 75 per cent of manorial income was raised through such sales.

95 For the movement of prices and wages, see Hatcher, *Plague, population*, p. 50, and tables II and III. See also Bridbury, 'The Black Death', pp. 577–92.

96 Raftis, *Ramsey abbey*, pp. 258–9.

a well-documented 'Indian summer' of demesne farming in the
third quarter of the fourteenth century, although its presence in a
marginal region might otherwise be considered surprising.[97] Some
Breckland landlords further strove to maintain the profitability of
large-scale arable farming by controlling costs in a number of ways.
At Risby, Bury abbey rationalised its operations by concentrating
production on a more consolidated area: far-flung pieces of demesne were leased whilst other land parcels were exchanged with
local landowners for more conveniently sited land.[98] Eventually
the cellarer himself became the lessee of a lay manor in the village,
and cultivated it alongside his own.[99] Elsewhere, attempts were
made to cut costs by invoking government statutes to depress
wages artificially. In 1363 the reaping of barley by hired labour was
charged in the Brandon account at 12d. per acre, but this was
deleted by the auditors and replaced instead with 9d.; in 1368 12d.
was charged once more, although this time the auditors settled for
10d.[100]

Despite attempts to cut costs, the fall in grain prices in the last
quarter of the fourteenth century brought an effective end to the
recovery in demesne farming. Concerted population decline had
caused wages to rise, thus finally undermining the profitability of
direct exploitation. The drastic reduction in the labour services
owed by unfree tenures after the Black Death deprived landlords of
a vital source of cheap labour at a time when it was most needed.
Landlords often demanded labour services, but this was met with
increasing resistance amongst the peasantry, and they were forced
to enter the open labour market in order to work demesnes.[101]
Even at Quiddenham, where labour services survived for a longer
period, two-thirds of the demesne crop was reaped by customary

[97] For the 'Indian summer', see the discussion and references in Dyer, *Lords and peasants*,
p. 113. See also M. Mate, 'Agrarian economy after the Black Death: the manors of
Canterbury Cathedral Priory 1348–91', *Ec.H.R.* 37 (1984), pp. 341–54.
[98] See, for example, the number of land exchanges with Richard Charman, WSROB 449/
2/542 and 545.　　　[99] WSROB E.3/15.13/2.25.
[100] Bacon 647; PRO SC6.1304/31. This was a common practice elsewhere in East Anglia,
G.A. Holmes, *The estates of the higher nobility in fourteenth-century England* (Cambridge,
1957), p. 91.
[101] Dyer, 'Background to the revolt', pp. 27–9. At Barton Parva there were regular refusals
to perform services, WSROB E.7/24/1.3. In one court at Hockham, there were 17
separate presentments for the non-performance of labour services, NRO Ms 13848,
court held June 1367. See also the court held in March 1376 at Langford, NRO
NCC(Petre) Box 8/21.

services and boonworks, and the remainder by hired labour in 1389.[102] Without a ready-made, cheap labour force, the costs of demesne farming rose rapidly. The cost of harvesting in Downham (IP) was roughly the same in 1362 as it had been in 1335, despite almost a halving of the area sown.[103] The Brandon famuli each received an average of 63d. in 1362–3, which rose to 106d. in 1388–9.[104] Faced with mounting costs, landlords scaled down their own operations and also began to lease small parcels of demesne to the peasantry, although it is doubtful whether these leases ever constituted more than 15 per cent of the total demesne area (see table 4.3). Nor was leasing a feature of every estate, but it was largely confined to manors belonging to the cellarer of Bury abbey and the Bishopric of Ely.

By the 1380s and 1390s, many English estates had resorted to leasing demesnes for a fixed annual sum, although a sizeable minority of Breckland manors remained in direct exploitation until the early fifteenth century at least. Direct demesne farming was certainly difficult in this period but not impossible. Where Breckland manors were leased, it was for reasons of estate re-organisation and not because of the difficulties of farming in the region specifically. The cellarer of Bury abbey, for instance, leased his Fornham manor to a Lakenheath man in 1374, and the Bishopric of Ely abandoned arable farming at Brandon in the late 1390s; there is no evidence of a shortage of willing lessees.[105] Only on the Duchy of Lancaster's estate at Methwold was there any serious disruption to arable farming, for the manor was leased at £80 prior to 1381 but could only fetch £28 12s. 2d. in 1388. By way of explanation, the auditors commented that arable farming was 'a graunde meschief', that murrain had decimated sheep flocks, and that the 1381 revolt had resulted in considerable devastation to the manor.[106] In fact it was the two latter events which largely explain

---

[102] NRO Phi/493.

[103] BL Add.Roll 9168 (1335–6), and WSROB 651/35/7.

[104] Bacon 647 and 653 (1388–9). At Fornham (A) the famuli each received 66d. per annum in 1360–1 and 84d. in 1395–6, WSROB E.3/15.6/2.28 and 2.35.

[105] WSROB 449/2/285, and see 286–7 for subsequent leases of Fornham (C) in 1433 and 1444. Bacon 660 (1395–6). Compare this state of affairs with the Battle abbey manor of Marley, where there were difficulties in finding tenants in the 1380s, Searle, *Battle abbey*, p. 329. See also Bolton, *Medieval English economy*, p. 214.

[106] PRO DL29.289/4737 and 728/11975. The decision to lease the Methwold and Thetford demesnes was certainly part of a wider estate policy: nearly all of the Duchy of Lancaster's demesnes were at farm by the 1370s, Holmes, *Estates of the higher nobility*, p. 116.

Methwold's poor performance in the 1380s, and by 1394 gross income from the manor had recovered to £83 7s. od.[107]

The falling price of bread grains after the mid-1370s led to the introduction of less intensive cropping sequences on much of Breckland's arable land, which removed the need for the labour-intensive expedients adopted in the 1340s. Marling was probably performed less assiduously, and the temporary, short-term foldcourses disappeared, mainly because the returns on the labour required for these activities were no longer economical.[108] Longer fallows were imposed on the poorer and exhausted soils, and in some instances this land reverted permanently to heathland. It is impossible to calculate this area of abandoned and untenanted arable, but it was generally the least accessible and least fertile land. In the 1350s, temporary leases of arable in Brandon had been confined mainly to the infields, and tenants would only take outfield land in small parcels and at much lower rents; outfield in Oxwickfeld was not leased at all.[109] In Risby, too, poorer land situated at some distance from the village in Westfeld and Stokhill could only be leased at under half the rent per acre of other arable and was widely abandoned as grain prices tumbled in the 1390s and early 1400s.[110] Land lying in *quarentenae* adjacent to Mildenhall heath at 'le Donne' was abandoned by tenants and subsequently employed as permanent pasture for sheep and rabbits.[111] The shedding of land at the physical margin of cultivation demonstrates

[107] The Duchy of Lancaster's estates at this time were held by John of Gaunt, a prominent target during the Peasant's Revolt. His estates in East Anglia were attacked during June 1381 by the East Anglian rebels, *CPR*, 1382–5, p. 144. PRO DL29.289/4737.

[108] For instance, the Mildenhall demesne hired a fold from John Swage to manure 5 acres of demesne wheat land at Thremhowe in 1399, at a cost of 2s. an acre, WSROB E.18/455/2. The same operation had cost a similar amount at Fornham in the 1340s, although then the price of wheat had been appreciably higher, WSROB E.3/15.7/2.2a.

[109] In January 1353, 22 new leases of arable land were instigated, of which 17.5 acres were on infield and valued at around 5d. per acre. Only 7.5 acres were on outfield and valued nearer 2d. per acre, Bacon 291/28. Oxwickfield was obviously outfield in the 1251 extent of Brandon, and contained 54 acres of demesne land. It appears to have lain derelict after the Black Death and absorbed into the rabbit-warren, see below, n.139.

[110] For instance, 19.5 acres of leasehold land in 1384–5 had fallen out of cultivation by 1397–8, of which 12.25 acres were in Westfeld and valued at 3¾d. per acre (mean rent in 1384–5 was 8.63d.), WSROB E.3/15.13/2.20 and 2.21.

[111] In 1389 the collector of rents was allowed 8d. for a parcel of land at the heath abandoned by Thomas Gange, BL Add.Roll 53119. In 1391 he was allowed 4s. rent for a piece of arable at le Donne, now occupied by the lord's rabbits, WSROB E.18/455/1. By 1402–3 more arable land had been abandoned at le Donne, along with a piece near the warren on the Barton road, BL Add.Roll 53121. Compare this with a century before, when John de Camera of Eriswell had held 18 acres of *arable* land at le Dune with a liberty of fold, WSROB E.18/451/1, court held March 1299.

that the recovery of Breckland's land market after 1349 was based on selective demand for arable, notably the infield and better outfield land.

The exact balance of crops sown varied according to the specific demands of each manor, but there were distinct changes in this balance as the overall level of output was reduced. At the peak of demesne farming before the Black Death, rye and oats were widely sown to feed both the demesne livestock and the famuli. Both were inferior grains which fared better in periods of land hunger, but which bore the brunt of falling demand for grain in the later fourteenth century. In the same period wheat, although never an important crop, became relatively more common on some manors, although barley did even better (see table 4.10). On many manors after the Black Death the growth in area under barley was absolute as well as relative. The Bishopric of Ely's demesne at Feltwell had 126 acres sown with barley in 1347 compared with 163 acres in 1397, and at Harling the proportion of land sown with barley rose by 10 per cent between 1320–9 and 1370–9. At Lakenheath in the 1360s, barley had come to occupy a greater area than at any time in the Middle Ages, in contrast with eastern Norfolk where barley had declined in importance.[112] A reason for this growth is suggested by table 4.13. In the early fourteenth century, many lay manors such as Icklingham, Fakenham, Downham (S) and Kennett sent a remarkably high proportion of their barley to market, whilst the monastic estates geared their production more towards domestic needs.[113] Yet, in the later fourteenth century, demand for Breckland barley fell less than demand for other grains, presumably because consumption of ale increased with the general improvement in living standards.[114] Even monastic landlords shed their traditional conservatism and

---

[112] At Martham before 1350, a mean of 110 acres of barley was sown each year (57.5 per cent of sown area), but only 88 acres after that (52.2 per cent), Campbell, 'Field systems' pp. 108–9. On numerous Kent demesnes, there are no real indications that barley was becoming either relatively more or less important, Smith, 'Regional differences', p. 159. In contrast, barley was also increasing in importance on several north Essex demesnes in this period, Britnell, *Colchester*, p. 144.

[113] The proportion of produce sold to market on some of these Breckland demesnes – 70 per cent at Icklingham and 48 per cent at Fakenham – was remarkably high. At Langenhoe in the same period, 29 per cent of demesne wheat (the principal cash crop) was sold to market, a figure which Britnell regards as 'substantial', Britnell, 'Production for the market', p. 381.

[114] Britnell, *Colchester*, p. 144. C.C. Dyer, 'Changes in diet in the late middle ages: the case of harvest workers', *Ag.H.R.* 36 (1988), pp. 24–9.

Table 4.10. *Proportion of crops sown by acreage on Breckland demesnes, decennial means 1270–1500 (%)*

Decade	A/cs	Wheat	Maslin	Rye	Barley	Drage	Legumes	Large oats	Small oats
Brandon									
1340–9	5			36.4	30.8	5.6	2.5		24.7
1350–9	4			36.0	32.4	3.7	0.5	2.6	24.8
1360–9	6			31.3	44.8			3.8	20.1
1370–9	5			26.0	50.3		0.4	3.1	20.2
1380–9	5	1.5		23.0	55.5		0.6		19.4
1390–9	6			21.8	63.7				14.5
Downham (IP)									
1320–9	1			45.9	8.2				45.9
1330–9	1			43.6	13.5		1.9		41.0
Downham (S)									
1340–9	1			50.6	11.6				37.8
1350–9	2			45.5	15.8				38.7
Fakenham Magna									
1320–9	1	9.3		30.7	23.1		8.5		28.4
Hilborough									
1370–9	1			21.6	61.5		3.5		13.4
1410–19	3			29.4	58.9				11.7
Hockham									
1380–9	2			31.4	54.8				13.8
Icklingham									
1320–9	1			45.1	36.3		1.8		16.8
1330–9	7	1.4		40.4	33.5	0.2	3.2		21.3
1340–9	5	2.1		42.3	25.0	4.1	2.8		23.7
Lackford									
1390–9	1			42.6	44.7		2.0		10.7
Lakenheath									
1300–9	1			44.2	22.7		3.4		29.7
1320–9	5	0.7	2.0	32.3	31.5	3.3	4.0		26.2
1330–9	3	0.4		31.8	33.9	2.2	3.7		28.0
1340–9	2	0.7		34.8	29.5		1.5		33.5
1350–9	2	1.4		38.6	38.2		4.6		17.2
1360–9	3	5.1		29.3	40.6		2.0		23.0
1370–9	3	3.0		29.5	40.7		3.3		23.5
1380–9	2	5.3		33.1	41.0		7.3		13.3
1390–9	2	4.3		24.9	52.9		3.8		14.1
1420–9	2	10.1		27.6	51.1				11.2
1430–9	2	11.6		25.3	53.6		2.4		7.1

Table 4.10. (*cont.*)

Decade	A/cs	Wheat	Maslin	Rye	Barley	Drage	Legumes	Large oats	Small oats
1440–9	I	6.9		24.3	66.9		1.9		
1450–9	4	0.9		34.7	57.0		2.5		4.9
Langford									
1400–9	I	1.0		26.0	50.0		2.0	0.8	20.2
West Harling									
1320–9	I			44.7	26.6		1.8		26.9
1330–9	3			42.7	26.2		2.0		29.1
1350–9	I			38.4	31.1		1.5		29.0
1360–9	I	4.4		41.8	27.1				26.7
1370–9	2	1.1		39.2	36.4		1.8		21.5
West Tofts									
1310–19	I			55.1	17.3				27.6
Wretham									
1300–9	5			47.0	24.8		2.5		25.7
1330–9	3	0.2		51.2	27.1		3.1		18.4
1340–9	I	1.0		56.9	16.8		3.5		21.8
Barton Parva									
1270–9	2	6.5	0.8	31.7	30.3		8.5	21.6	0.6
1280–9	4	7.9	3.4	30.9	28.8		9.3	19.7	
1290–9	7	8.0	2.6	31.2	29.3	0.2	7.8	20.9	
1300–9	2	7.8	3.9	29.9	28.7	1.4	9.2	19.1	
1310–19	2	6.0	2.4	30.7	31.7		7.8	21.4	
Cressingham Magna									
1310–19	I	9.5		25.4	46.9		4.8		13.4
1320–9	2	9.7		25.0	41.8		5.6		17.9
1360–9	3	13.6		20.1	42.5		7.5		16.3
1370–9	3	9.8		13.0	51.7		7.5		18.0
1380–9	I	11.2		12.6	54.0		8.1		14.1
1410–19	3	11.2		14.7	52.0		10.0		12.1
Feltwell (E)									
1340–9	I	15.6	8.4	3.7	39.4		7.2		25.7
1390–9	I	13.0		5.8	75.8		1.9		3.5
Feltwell (EH)									
1340–9	I	20.6	2.9	4.0	46.8		11.3		14.4
Fornham (A)									
1330–9	I	15.0		23.3	33.2		10.0	4.5	14.0
1340–9	5	14.9	0.4	22.3	33.2	0.2	9.5	4.7	14.8
1350–9	2	13.4	2.5	27.4	33.9		10.7	0.4	11.7
1360–9	6	14.0		23.5	35.8		5.5	10.4	10.8

Table 4.10. (cont.)

Decade	A/cs	Wheat	Maslin	Rye	Barley	Drage	Legumes	Large oats	Small oats
1370–9	2	12.0		20.4	39.5		4.1	13.8	10.2
1390–9	1	13.5		21.1	39.4		8.8	9.1	8.1
1400–9	8	16.1		15.2	43.0		14.8	7.4	3.5
1410–19	5	19.1		12.9	43.4		13.4	7.6	3.6
1420–9	3	16.1		20.3	38.3		18.2	7.1	
1430–9	2	16.5		16.0	46.1		10.6	10.8	
1440–9	1	12.4		16.3	53.1		11.5	6.7	
Fornham (C)									
1290–9	1	19.3		23.3	28.7		3.5	13.0	12.2
1300–9	5	16.7		22.5	29.5		5.3	16.2	9.8
1310–19	2	12.4		24.5	37.5		4.5		21.1
1320–9	3	19.1		25.2	27.6		3.6	11.4	13.1
Gasthorpe									
1410–19	1	28.6	42.9		6.4		22.1		
Kennett									
1270–9	2	7.5		19.0	31.5		4.1		37.9
1280–9	2	9.0		15.8	35.8		5.8		33.6
1290–9	6	9.7		20.5	31.8		7.9		30.1
1300–9	1	11.0		16.4	34.2		11.0		27.4
Methwold									
1360–9	1	10.9		23.7	40.9		4.0		20.5
1440–9	1	4.1		13.7	78.8				3.4
Mildenhall									
1320–9	1	5.4	9.4	6.7	65.7		5.1		7.7
1380–9	3	21.5	8.4	13.5	41.6	2.5	8.8		3.7
1420–9	1	23.4	3.4	5.3	52.8				15.1
Quiddenham									
1380–9	1	5.5		22.6	52.8		2.7	4.6	11.8
Risby									
1290–9	2	15.3		25.1	27.9		4.4		27.3
1310–19	1	24.6		22.1	27.7		6.6		19.0
1320–9	1	21.8		25.7	24.7		2.9		24.9
1340–9	1	27.7		20.7	22.1		8.8		20.7
1350–9	1	30.3		19.7	38.4		4.1		7.5
1380–9	1	27.0	2.8	11.8	33.6		15.8		9.0
Wilton									
1350–9	1	6.9		20.9	55.1		8.1		9.0

Table 4.11. *Disposal of demesne crops, 1300–1500 – wheat (%)*

Period	A/cs	Net total disposed (qu.)	Seed	Lord	Expenses /harvest	Sold	Famuli	Misc.
Brandon								
1300–49	5	41					99	1
1350–99	27		19			81		
Fakenham								
1300–49	1	4	75			25		
Icklingham								
1300–49	12	55	15			34	51	
Lakenheath								
1300–49	11	46	17	54	6	18		5
1350–99	13	244	23	56	10	3		8
1400–99	11	163	18	66	6	8		2
Barton Parva								
1280–1349	17	415	31	3	5	61		
Cressingham								
1300–49	2	70	21		4	72		
1350–99	7	201	23	5	11	61		
1400–99	2	46	23		3	74		
Fornham (A)								
1300–49	5	247	30	56		9		5
1350–99	11	361	36	22	4	24	12	3
1400–99	21	668	32	42	5	11	1	9
Fornham (C)								
1300–99	19	633	30	31		35	2	2
1350–99	9	177	45	24		23	7	1
Kennett								
1250–99	13	81	23	4	4	68	1	1
Methwold								
1400–99	1	19	16			13		71
Mildenhall								
1300–49	1	35	56			16	24	4
1350–99	6	799	30	49	12	4	1	4
1400–99	15	2,233	34	62		2	1	1
Quiddenham								
1350–99	1	6	25			75		
Risby								
1300–49	5	284	23	38		30	7	2
1350–99	12	746	32	53	3	5	3	4
1400–99	5	443	33	52	2	4		10

Table 4.12. *Disposal of demesne crops, 1300–1500 – rye (%)*

Period	A/cs	Net total disposed (qu.)	Seed	Lord	Animals	Sold	Famuli	Misc.
Brandon								
1300–49	5	391	32	5	2	31	27	3
1350–99	27	978	28		2	26	39	5
Downham (IP)								
1300–49	2	45	30	13		16	40	1
Downham (S)								
1300–49	2	72	33	2	1	14	45	5
Fakenham								
1300–49	1	72	37		2	31	23	7
Hilborough								
1350–99	2	24	50				36	14
1400–99	2	67	26	7		19	38	10
Icklingham								
1300–49	12	518	32	4	2	37	19	6
Lackford								
1350–99	1	35	39	29	1	3	28	
Lakenheath								
1300–49	11	1,431	24	6		12	50	8
1350–99	13	1,091	25	15	3	2	40	15
1400–99	11	562	23	1	1	23	38	14
Langford								
1400–99	1	44	27		2	14	56	1
Barton Parva								
1280–1349	17	524	40	1	1	24	33	1
Cressingham								
1300–49	2	84	42		1	37	11	1
1350–99	7	189	33		12	4	38	13
1400–99	2	51	27			17	47	9
Fornham (A)								
1300–49	5	362	29	5	7	17	38	4
1350–99	11	690	30	2	12	5	48	3
1400–99	21	709	26	7	5	14	46	1
Fornham (C)								
1300–99	19	687	37		12	19	28	4
1350–99	9	357	33	2	9	13	42	1
Hockham								
1350–99	2	64	35		2	4	33	26

Table 4.12. (cont.)

Period	A/cs	Net total disposed (qu.)	Seed	Lord	Animals	Sold	Famuli	Misc.
Kennett								
1250–99	13	64	32	2	8	10	39	9
Methwold								
1400–99	1	70	14			7	24	55
Mildenhall								
1300–49	1	42	52		40		8	
1350–99	6	256	37		42	8		13
1400–99	15	226	48		21	4	6	21
Quiddenham								
1350–99	1	21	29			10	46	15
Risby								
1300–49	5	186	29	7	6	19	32	7
1350–99	12	384	32	5	12	10	29	12
1400–99	5	177	28	7	7	9	48	1

Table 4.13. *Disposal of demesne crops, 1300–1500 – barley (%)*

Period	A/cs	Net total disposed (qu.)	Seed	Lord	Malt	Sold	Famuli	Misc.
Brandon								
1300–49	5	449	40		26	26	4	4
1350–99	27	2,875	26	3		55	14	2
Downham (IP)								
1300–49	2	17	27				73	
Downham (S)								
1300–49	2	30	28			29	33	10
Fakenham								
1300–49	1	39	29	2		48	8	13
Hilborough								
1350–99	1	110	48		11	21	16	4
1400–99	2	210	38	10		30	17	5
Icklingham								
1300–49	12	735	28			70	1	1
Lackford								
1350–99	1	82	32	25	12	17	12	2

Table 4.13. (*cont.*)

Period	A/cs	Net total disposed (qu.)	Seed	Lord	Malt	Sold	Famuli	Misc.
Lakenheath								
1300–49	11	2,878	19	64	2	4	6	5
1350–99	13	3,073	23	52	3	3	8	11
1400–99	11	1,856	22	61	3	1	12	1
Langford								
1400–99	1	156	22			61	13	4
Barton Parva								
1280–1349	17	1,613	29	8	16	38	7	2
Cressingham								
1300–49	2	371	33		4	56	4	3
1350–99	7	1,245	29		21	24	17	9
1400–99	2	362	28		2	60	8	2
Fornham (A)								
1300–49	5	959	23	2	47	8	12	8
1350–99	11	1,856	30		48	2	14	6
1400–99	21	2,982	28	7	40	10	11	4
Fornham (C)								
1300–99	19	1,306	42		11	29	12	6
1350–99	9	540	39	1		43	16	1
Hockham								
1350–99	2	182	31			53	12	4
Kennett								
1250–99	13	231	29	3	5	43	15	5
Methwold								
1400–99	1	459	16		61		4	19
Mildenhall								
1300–49	1	879	21		11	56	4	8
1350–99	6	2,873	22	4	40	20	7	7
1400–99	15	6,103	24	2	54	8	6	6
Quiddenham								
1350–99	1	147	17		2	74	7	
Risby								
1300–49	5	431	29	37	4	17	9	4
1350–99	12	1,603	29	2	26	30	12	1
1400–99	5	743	30	7	18	27	13	5

responded to these new opportunities by increasing their barley sales, a trend particularly apparent at Brandon, Fornham (C) and Risby.[115]

PASTORAL FARMING

Sheep farming was continually disrupted by outbreaks of disease. After the agrarian crisis of 1315–22, an even more virulent epidemic struck throughout Breckland in the winter of 1334–5, reducing flock size by 56 per cent at Lakenheath, 64 per cent at Icklingham and 49 per cent at Fornham (C).[116] The demesne flock at West Harling fell from 110 at Michaelmas 1333 to 2 on the corresponding date in 1335.[117] There is little evidence that lords replaced decimated flocks by large-scale purchases, although Lady Elizabeth Berners did aid recovery at Icklingham by transferring 124 lambs from her manor at Horsley in 1336 and 111 hoggs from Isledon in 1337.[118] Thus, if flocks were to recover, many had to do so gradually by the processes of natural increase. The general disruption caused by the Black Death was exacerbated in sheep farming by murrain in 1351–2, and the 1360s saw a spate of particularly virulent epidemics.[119] In 1381 murrain killed 231 out of 293 lambs at Lakenheath and struck again in 1384–5, confirming the observations of the Methwold auditors.[120] Without doubt, disease was the single most influential factor in medieval sheep farming.

The market price of a Breckland fleece was remarkably high before the Black Death, rarely falling below 3½d. and peaking at over 10d. during the murrain of 1318.[121] Prices were reasonably buoyant in the third quarter of the century, but dropped in the 1380s and 1390s. The number of sheep on each demesne varied according to estate policy, but there was a general tendency to increase flock sizes in the 1330s and 1340s. In part this was stimulated by rising demand for manure, but also by a genuine rise in the

[115] At Langenhoe after 1370, sales to the market slumped drastically, so that only 7.3 per cent of all wheat was thus disposed, Britnell, 'Production for the market', p. 386.
[116] CUL EDC 7/15/I/9; NRO Ms 13191; WSROB E.3/15.6/2.12.
[117] J. Ryland Library, Phillipps Charters 11 and 13.
[118] NRO Ms 13192 and 13193.   [119] Notably in 1361–2, 1367–8 and 1369–70.
[120] CUL EDC 7/15/I/26 and 28.
[121] Bailey, 'At the margin', table 4.21. The trend of Breckland fleece prices corresponds closely with those tabulated for East Anglia in general by T.H. Lloyd, 'The movement of wool prices in medieval England', Ec.H.R. supplement 6 (1973).

Table 4.14. *Numbers of
demesne sheep, decennial
Michaelmas means, 1290–1500*

Decade	A/cs	Mean no. of sheep
Brandon		
1340–9	5	0
1350–9	4	699.6
1360–9	6	266.5
1380–9	5	514.1
1390–9	6	739.1
Wretham		
1300–9	5	1,001.0
1330–9	2	1,139.0
1340–9	1	1,221.0
1440–9	1	252.5
Downham (IP)		
1320–9	1	154.0
1330–9	1	162.0
1360–9	1	150.0
Downham (S)		
1340–9	1	733.0
1350–9	2	1,159.5
Hilborough		
1370–9	1	5.0
1400–9	1	441.0
1410–19	3	1,163.0
Icklingham		
1330–9	7	248.3
1340–9	5	334.6
Lakenheath		
1300–9	1	1,707.0
1320–9	5	2,419.3
1330–9	3	2,082.8
1340–9	2	2,280.3
1350–9	2	1,370.0
1360–9	3	1,907.2
1370–9	3	2,085.8
1380–9	2	1,583.8
1390–9	2	1,528.5
1420–9	2	1,645.0
1430–9	2	1,403.2
1440–9	1	1,422.0

Table 4.14. (*cont.*)

Decade	A/cs	Mean no. of sheep
1450–9	4	1,150.8
1460–9	2	1,222.5
1480–9	2	1,007.0
West Harling		
1320–9	1	125.0
1330–9	3	70.8
1350–9	1	391.0
1360–9	1	253.5
1370–9	2	246.5
Barton Parva		
1270–9	2	18.3
1280–9	3	28.0
1290–9	9	10.9
1300–9	2	7.5
Cressingham		
1300–9	1	102.0
1320–9	1	78.8
1360–9	3	60.0
1370–9	3	180.0
1380–9	1	113.5
Fornham (A)		
1340–9	5	428.0
1350–9	2	318.5
1360–9	6	194.3
1370–9	2	405.0
1390–9	1	338.5
1400–9	8	255.8
1410–19	5	543.8
1420–9	3	345.1
1440–9	2	1,538.0
Fornham (C)		
1300–9	3	54.6
1310–19	2	53.3
1320–9	2	27.0
1330–9	6	86.5
1350–9	4	180.5
1360–9	6	138.5
Feltwell		
1340–9	1	0
1390–9	1	138.0

Table 4.14. (cont.)

Decade	A/cs	Mean no. of sheep
Kennett		
1270–9	3	343.5
1280–9	2	551.3
1290–9	5	522.3
1300–9	2	687.0
Methwold		
1360–9	1	800.0
1440–9	1	593.0
Mildenhall		
1320–9	1	882.5
1380–9	4	805.9
1390–9	1	772.0
1400–9	7	270.7
1410–19	8	330.6
1420–9	2	352.3
Risby		
1290–9	1	154.5
1310–19	1	250.5
1320–9	1	95.0
1340–9	1	152.5
1350–9	5	209.6
1360–9	2	162.3
1370–9	3	280.8
1380–9	1	204.0
1390–9	1	865.5
1400–9	2	591.0
1410–19	3	838.0

demand for wool; few sheep were sold for their meat. This increased demand might have been generated by textile manufacturers in south Suffolk, who were known to be raising output in this period.[122] Hence the number of demesne sheep at Lakenheath and Wretham reached its recorded medieval peak in the 1340s. After losses to murrain in the 1350s and 1360s, there was renewed

---

[122] Preliminary research indicates that the Suffolk towns of Clare and Sudbury were experiencing an economic revival in the 1330s and 1340s, Britnell, *Colchester*, p. 21. Flock sizes were also being increased on the East Anglian manors of the Honor of Clare, Holmes, *Estates of the higher nobility*, pp. 89–90.

interest in sheep farming amongst demesnes and peasants alike. In per capita terms, the number of peasant sheep was at its height in the 1380s and 1390s, as evidenced by the constant disputes over foldsoke throughout the region. Villagers in Fornham St Martin were in dispute with the cellarer of Bury abbey over pasture rights, and the townsmen of Bury were illegally exploiting other pastures in the village in an attempt to sustain their own activities.[123] A procession of men were amerced for overstocking foldcourses whilst others attempted to raise new folds without permission.[124] Access to the Bury market undoubtedly heightened interest in the Fornham pastures, but activities also expanded in other villages. Three men illegally raised folds in Methwold in 1381, and Robert Cok of Langford 'occupied a fold without licence'.[125] Margaret Hethe of Lackford leased two large heathland pastures for £7 in 1397, and the jury at Barton Parva was to inquire 'who occupies newly erected folds and who have more sheep in their folds than they ought to have'.[126] Although it was much rarer, a few landlords even resorted to granting temporary folds: at Hockham in 1384 Adam Hele paid 30s. for herbage and the licence to erect a new fold, and at Lackford one mark was received 'from the lord of Hengrave for a fold in Flempton'.[127] John Flempton secured the lease of a temporary fold for 200 sheep in Lackford in the 1390s, and appears to have become a specialist sheep farmer. Described as a labourer in the 1381 Poll Tax, he held little arable land and was repeatedly amerced for overstocking pastures with his flock.[128] On many demesnes there was a resurgence in sheep farming

---

[123] WSROB E.3/15.6/1.5 m.14, court held August 1385, and 1.3 mm.24 and 30, courts held August and September 1371.

[124] Stephen Gamyn and Roger Palyser both raised folds in Fornham without permission, WSROB E.3/15.7/1.13 and 1.14, courts held March 1398 and November 1399. In 1382, Richard Batesford and John Stubbard were guilty of placing more sheep in their folds than allotted, E.3/15.7/1.9a, court held November 1382; see also John Bole and John Toller, E.3/15.6/1.18, court held November 1386. These foldcourse transgressions were on a similar scale to those of the 1340s, but were basically concerned with different matters. In the 1340s, peasants were clearly trying to fold sheep on their own arable land, whereas in the 1380s the concern was simply to keep as many sheep as possible.

[125] PRO DL30.104/1476 m.1, court held November 1381. NRO NCC(Petre) Box 8/21, court held October 1393.

[126] WSROB E.3/15.12/2.2; WSROB E.7/24/3.1, court held February 1385.

[127] NRO Ms 13854; WSROB E.3/15.12/1.13.

[128] Powell, *Rising in East Anglia*, appendix. Between 1396 and 1400, the rent for Flempton's foldcourse rose fivefold, WSROB E.3/15.12/2.2 and 2.3. He held no arable land on leasehold in the 1390s and 1400s, merely a tenement, a cottage and a messuage for 23¼d. rent, WSROB E.3/15.12/3.2. For his overstocking amercements, see E.3/15.12/1.13, courts held May 1402, August and December 1403.

A marginal economy?

Table 4.15. *Peasant sheep in Lakenheath, decennial means 1300–99*

Decade	A/cs	Fleeces	Lambs	Total tithes	Mean flock size
1300–9	1	128	25	153	1,377
1320–9	5	786	184	970	1,746
1330–9	3	317	68	385	1,155
1340–9	2	419	101	520	2,340
1350–9	2	356	99	455	2,048
1360–9	3	479	116	595	1,785
1370–9	3	502	141	643	1,929
1380–9	2	227	46	273	1,229
1390–9	2	281	92	373	1,679
1400–99	13	1,027	458	1,485	1,028

Note: At Lakenheath, village tithes were presented direct to the manor, and consequently the number of fleeces and lambs received are recorded in each demesne sheep account. These figures are totalled above. To produce the total number of peasant sheep (the last column), each figure in the penultimate column was divided by one-ninth, and then divided again by the number of accounts to obtain a decennial mean flock size.

towards the end of the fourteenth century, and on some estates flocks returned to their pre-Black Death size or even surpassed them.[129] The cellarer of Bury abbey's manors of Fornham, Mildenhall and Risby expanded their activities, and then, after Fornham and Ingham were leased in the 1370s, concentrated operations on the buoyant Risby demesne (see table 4.14). The Bishopric of Ely rebuilt flocks decimated by murrain in the 1360s at Brandon and probably Feltwell, as did Norwich Cathedral Priory at Cressingham.[130] At Hilborough large-scale sheep rearing was adopted at a rapid and impressive rate after the 1370s. On most manors the flocks were predominantly wethers, emphasising that wool remained the prime objective of sheep farming. There was also a slight but discernible increase in the number of sheep sold to market on some manors. At Lakenheath in the 1360s around 10 per cent were thus sold, and 16 per cent in the 1390s. However, many of these sheep were either old or weak, and so the sales really represented a clearance of poor stock rather than an attempt to supply the

[129] See, for instance, Raftis, *Ramsey abbey*, pp. 147–51.
[130] For instance, there were 48 ewes bought at Cressingham in 1363–4, NRO DCN Supplement (R187A).

market with high-quality mutton.[131] The importance of sheep farming to landlords is reflected by continued capital investment, most notably in the construction of new sheep-cotes at Lakenheath in 1394–5 at a cost of £8 5s. 9d., and at Fornham St Genevieve in the 1370s.[132]

In many ways, landlords were looking to sheep farming to counteract the declining profitability of large-scale grain production after the Black Death.[133] Sheep farming possessed distinct advantages in this respect, because the price of wool declined less than that of bread grains, especially with the expansion of the East Anglian textile industry, and sheep farming was less labour intensive, an important consideration in a period of sharply rising wages. So, even when Bury abbey leased the manor of Fornham (C) in 1374, it retained the right to graze 300 sheep there.[134] Furthermore, their privileged position in the foldcourse system gave landlords an opportunity to increase their own operations at the expense of the peasantry, albeit gradually. By absorbing peasant folds, landlords could rationalise sheep farming and thus minimise the rise of unit costs whilst still maintaining their income. Hence the rapid expansion of flock size at Risby should be explained within the context of the deliberate accumulation of peasant folds by both the cellarer of Bury and Richard Charman in the 1350s.[135]

Quite the most remarkable aspect of Breckland's economy in the fourteenth century was the rapid growth of commercialised rabbiting. As table 4.16 indicates, warren output was low before the Black Death, with annual cullings rarely exceeding 200. The rabbits were seldom sent to market, but were dispatched instead to the kitchens of the seigneurial household and consumed as a delicacy. Yet, on the few occasions when a good crop was taken in this period, it was obvious that the animal was capable of raising seigneurial income significantly. In such a year at Kennett (1270–1), rabbit sales amounted to 22 per cent of net manorial income.[136] In the 1350s and 1360s warren output did not rise significantly,

---

[131] At Fornham (A) in 1370–1, sheep were sold '*quia putred*', and in 1395–6 the manor sold '*multones defices*', WSROB E.3/15.6/2.34a and 2.35.

[132] CUL EDC 7/15/I/32; WSROB 449/2/285.

[133] See Mate, 'Agrarian economy after the Black Death', p. 344 for a similar trend on the Canterbury estates, and also Davenport, *Development of a Norfolk manor*, p. 80.

[134] WSROB 449/2/285.

[135] See chapter 2, n.152. Richard Charman absorbed a tenant fold on his manor in the 1350s, WSROB 449/2/529.   [136] PRO sc6.768/5.

Table 4.16. *Culled rabbits and their disposal, decennial means* 1250–1500

Decade	A/cs	Mean culled	Sold (%)	Lord (%)	Misc. (%)
Brandon					
1340–9	4	158	11	89	—
1350–9	3	160	81	11	—
1360–9	6	301	46	48	6
1370–9	4	622	29	62	9
1380–9	4	2,811	85	5	10
1390–9	7	2,267	86	4	10
Hilborough					
1370–9	1	348	60	26	14
Kennett					
1270–9	4	414	75	25	—
1280–9	4	195	78	22	—
1290–9	6	750	91	9	—
1300–9	4	213	96	4	—
Lakenheath					
1300–9	1	50	—	100	—
1320–9	3	34	—	100	—
1330–9	3	327	14	86	—
1340–9	2	265	17	83	—
1350–9	2	788	70	29	1
1360–9	3	382	73	27	—
1370–9	3	850	73	27	—
1380–9	2	3,639	80	19	1
1390–9	2	3,056	80	20	—
1420–9	1	758	99	1	—
Methwold					
1350–9	1	320	75	25	—
1390–9	1	9,450	100	—	—
1420–9	3	3,933	100	—	—
1430–9	6	1,972	100	—	—
1440–9	4	2,055	100	—	—
1450–9	4	1,031	100	—	—
1460–9	3	1,897	100	—	—

Sources: Brandon, PRO SC6.1304/23–36, Bacon 644–63; Hilborough, NRO Hilborough Deposit Box T (Daleth), vii; Kennett, PRO SC6.768/5–24; Lakenheath, CUL.EDC. 7/15/I/1–31; Methwold, various accounts in series PRO DL29.288/4719 to DL29.310/5007.

although the proportion sold to the market did. This change was a presager for the last two decades of the fourteenth century when annual cullings in the successful warrens rose tenfold and domestic consumption by landlords became far less important. The rewards were equally spectacular. Between 1300 and 1349 the Brandon demesne received a negligible income from rabbit sales, yet between 1350 and 1399 they constituted 21 per cent of gross manorial income and in 1386–7 fetched a record £40 4s. or 40 per cent of gross income.[137] Methwold was Breckland's biggest warren, culling a record 9,450 rabbits in 1390 and realising over £80 per annum from sales during that decade.[138]

The rapid increase in output can only have been the product of an expanding rabbit population, and this was reflected in the growth of warren area. The older warrens undoubtedly expanded in size, often absorbing redundant arable land lying close to their original borders. In 1388–9 the bailiff of Brandon was acquitted rent owed on 60 acres of free land which had now been colonised by the lord's rabbits, and it seems likely that the whole of Oxwickfeld became enclosed in the warren at this time.[139] The value of Mildenhall warren increased almost threefold in the quarter-century after 1381, corresponding with a spate of rent allowances on an unspecified area of arable which had been absorbed within the warren.[140] There were also a number of villages where references to rabbits and warrens appear for the first time after the Black Death, implying either the gradual spread of wild colonies from the larger warrens, or the foundation of new ones. At Risby, where no medieval warren existed as such, twelve rabbits were culled and dispatched to Bury in 1370, and the 1368–9 stock account of Fornham (A) contained the heading '*cuniculi*', although none were actually taken.[141] This was also true for the Hockham account of 1383–4, and the court rolls mention rabbits for the first time in

137 IESRO HD 1538 (formerly Iveagh Suffolk Ms 148). At Lakenheath in 1384–5 some 4,500 rabbits were culled, of which 78 per cent were sold direct to the market for nearly £37, or 30 per cent of gross manorial income (including arrears). Compare this to the wool clip that year which fetched a paltry £17, CUL EDC 7/15/I/28.

138 PRO DL29.310/4980 and NRO NRS 11336.

139 Bacon 653. For Oxwickfield, see above, n.109. In the 1566 field book of Brandon, Dedhedlondfeld is delimited and lay adjacent to 'the warren called Oxwicks'. There were also 3 acres of arable called Oxwicks, IESRO V.11/2/1.1.

140 See above, n.112.

141 WSROB E.3/15.13/1.17; WSROB E.3/15.6/2.33. At Culford in 1435, the abbot of Bury held 4 acres called 'le conyngger', BL Add.Ms 42055 f.38.

1375.[142] At Quiddenham, too, a rabbit warren is mentioned in 1389, but it was not yet productive.[143]

The rabbit population grew rapidly for several reasons, most notable of which was a distinct improvement in the climate of the late fourteenth century. Falling grain prices at this time probably reflected a sustained period of fine, warm weather, during which the rabbit population flourished. Not only was the climate conducive to a demographic expansion, but landlords were also making greater efforts to reduce its high mortality rates. Arable farming had been important prior to the Black Death, probably to the direct detriment of rabbit rearing. But with the contraction of the area under crops, rabbit farming assumed greater importance. More care and expense went into feeding the rabbits during the lean winter months, often on hay but sometimes on rye and oats grown in the warrens for that express purpose. At Hilborough in 1376 and again in 1377, 6 acres of oats were planted 'in the warren to sustain the rabbits there', and furze was sown for the same purpose.[144] Another priority was to reduce the great losses at the hands of natural predators, and warreners set numerous snares and traps to catch preying 'vermyn' and 'wild nocturnal beasts':[145] in part, the growth in rabbit population testifies to the success of these measures.

Yet poachers remained the biggest threat to the landlords' new-found wealth. Not only did they damage the rabbits' precious burrows, but their wanton plundering could reduce the warren stock to dangerously low levels. As warrens were often sited on heathland up to seven miles from the nearest village, they were particularly vulnerable to theft and attack. In response to this, a wooden watchtower was erected in the middle of Lakenheath warren in 1365, and a wooden lodge was built at Brandon three years later at a cost of £7.[146] Even this was considered inadequate and was replaced fourteen years later by a flint lodge costing over

[142] NRO Ms 13854. In the January court of 1375, John Aleyn was amerced for taking rabbits in the warren, the first extant reference of its kind, NRO Ms 13848. This evidence is similar to that found in various east Suffolk villages around the same time, Bailey, 'Rabbit and East Anglia', p. 5.   [143] NRO Phi/493.
[144] NRO Hilborough Deposit Box T (Daleth), vii mm.2 and 3.
[145] In 1368–9, 2s. 1d. was spent amending three snares '*pro feris nocivis*' in Brandon warren, PRO sc6.1304/32. More snares were made in 1389–90 and 1390–1, Bacon 654 and 655. At Lakenheath, 6 boards were purchased to make a trap for 'vermyne' in the warren, CUL EDC 7/15/I/13.
[146] CUL EDC 7/15/I/20 records the purchase of 200 estrich boards for 'le garrett'; PRO sc6.1304/32.

£20 to build.[147] These lodges were a feature of medieval Breckland, and provided a home for the warrener and his family, and a cool storage area for culled rabbits. Yet they were expensive buildings to maintain, let alone build, and repairs cost £9 9s. 9d. at Methwold in 1413–14.[148] They were large, defensive structures built of stone, whose main role was to provide a safe and effective base for operations against poachers. Thetford lodge is Breckland's only remaining example, and stands two storeys high, with flint walls three feet thick.

The protection offered by the lodges was certainly justified, for not only did poaching become more common in the later fourteenth century but it also became more violent. As the incidence of poaching increased, so the Brandon court was hard pressed to keep track of all the offenders, and ordered the jurors to establish the names of '*malefactores in warrena*' in 1383.[149] The dangers involved in tending warrens were revealed at Methwold in 1426 when the warrener was attacked by a poacher wielding a cudgel.[150] The amount of investment in lodges serves as a powerful illustration of the threat posed by poachers and the determination of landlords to protect their assets. That poaching was becoming a national problem in the 1380s is reflected in the introduction of the poaching statute of 1389. This made it an offence, punishable by imprisonment, for poorer laymen and clerics to keep ferrets, dogs and nets for the purpose of hunting, and after this date manorial courts were prone to search peasant houses for such incriminating evidence.[151]

The success of commercial rabbiting was as much a function of changes in demand for the animal as changes in supply. In the thirteenth and early fourteenth centuries, rabbit was a luxury enjoyed almost exclusively by feudal lords in an era of depressed real wages for the mass of Englishmen. At this time, an East Anglian rabbit could fetch almost 5d., which was equivalent to double the daily wage of an unskilled labourer, and this inevitably restricted its marketing potential.[152] Yet the demographic upheaval of the later

---

[147] Bacon 651 (1382–3).   [148] PRO DL29.290/4765.

[149] Bacon 292/5, court held December 1383. In November 1385, the court demanded a list of all those breeding dogs for poaching, Bacon 292/11.

[150] PRO DL30.103/1423, court held April 1426. In 1379–80, the Brandon warrener hired three men to help him guard against 'malfactors of the night', Bacon 650.

[151] *Statutes*, vol. I, p. 388; see below, chapter 5. Laymen 'which hath not lands or tenements to the value of 40s. by year, nor any priest nor other clerk if he be not advanced to the value of £10 by year' were thus prohibited.

[152] Bailey, 'Rabbit and East Anglia', p. 12.

fourteenth century resulted in rapid gains in real wages, especially after the 1370s, inducing a change in diet from grain to meat consumption.[153] There are no grounds for supposing that the rabbit suddenly became the meat of the masses because it was still relatively expensive, but it did descend the social scale. Indeed, the consumption of a product previously regarded as an exclusive preserve of feudal lords may have been a tangible – if somewhat ostentatious – symbol of rising social expectations. The rise in real wages also stimulated demand for better clothing, including lower-quality furs like rabbit. Fur-lined tunics were particularly popular, and late medieval chroniclers noted that dress standards were rising amongst the masses;[154] indeed, rabbit fur's similarity to other, more expensive furs would have enhanced its popularity with an increasingly clothes-conscious society.

In all, it would seem reasonable to attribute the fortunes of commercial rabbit production to a ready combination of rising market demand for better food and clothing, and a strong seigneurial desire to offset flagging income from rents and cereal production. Not only did the market expand at the very time that demand for the demesne staples was declining, but landlords also recognised the rabbit's potential and transferred investment accordingly. Yet how can rising demand for the rabbit after 1370 be reconciled with the fact that its price fell in the same period? It would appear that the rapid expansion of the rabbit population resulted in a rise in supply that exceeded the rise in demand, thus deflating its price. In fact, rabbit prices fell less than the price of other products which also suffered from over-supply during the same period, notably bread grains.[155] Furthermore, rabbit rearing was less labour intensive than either arable or even sheep farming, an enormous asset when wage rates were rising. Indeed, as the huge increases in cullings were achieved without any significant rise in the warren's labour force, the cost of producing one rabbit fell sharply after the 1370s.[156] The construction and maintenance of lodges absorbed much of the expenditure on rabbit rearing, and it was otherwise a relatively inexpensive business.

Dairy farming was conducted on a modest scale overall, but

---

[153] C.C. Dyer, 'English diet in the later Middle Ages', in *Social relations and ideas: essays in honour of R.H. Hilton*, eds. T.H. Aston, P.R. Coss, C.C. Dyer and J. Thirsk (Cambridge, 1983), pp. 209 and 214.   [154] Hatcher, *Plague, population*, p. 34.

[155] Bailey, 'Rabbit and East Anglia', table 2 and pp. 12–13.

[156] Bailey, 'At the margin', table 4.18.

again its fortunes were more stable than arable production after the
Black Death. Both disease and the insurrection of 1327 disrupted
demesne and peasant herds in the 1310s and 1320s, but, on demesnes
at least, the losses were quickly replaced by purchase. The annual
value of a cow at full lease varied from 2s. 10d. at Mildenhall in 1381
to 6s. 8d. at Lackford in 1400, but the modal rent was 4s. 6d., and
there is no evidence for a general decline in value after the Black
Death.[157] On the contrary, the second half of the fourteenth
century represented a period of consolidation in dairy farming, and
on some manors herds were expanded. At Downham the stock of
demesne cows was a third larger in the 1350s than it had been in the
1340s, and at Mildenhall there were 24 cows in 1323 and around 35
in the 1380s.[158] The agrarian crisis of 1315–22 probably halved the
Lakenheath herd, but by 1327 there were 26 cows on the demesne, a
number which remained more or less constant for the rest of the
century.[159] At Risby prior to the Black Death the demesne herd
had seldom exceeded half a dozen cows, but this was rapidly
expanded to 12 and then 15 cows in 1354 and 1361, and at Fornham
the crises of 1315–22 and 1327–8 proved to be only temporary
interruptions and the herd was increased from 10 to 16 cows in the
1360s.[160]

Access to urban markets, the availability of quality meadowland,
and estate policy all influenced dairy farming in the second half of
the century. On some manors it became an early casualty of the
running down of demesne farming. The Brandon herd disappeared
with the accession of John Barnet to the episcopate of Ely in 1367,
the Risby stock was eventually sold in 1385, and there were no
cattle at West Harling after 1368.[161] However, proximity to Bury
and Norwich encouraged dairy farming on the lusher pastures of

[157] BL Add.Roll 53116; WSROB E.3/15.12/2.3. These levels were low compared with
leases in the stock-rearing regions of central East Anglia. The lease of one cow at
Worlingworth commonly fetched 7s. per annum in the fourteenth century, J.M.
Ridgard, 'The local history of Worlingworth Suffolk, to AD 1400' (Ph.D., Leicester,
1984), p. 151.
[158] There were no cows on the Ixworth priory manor at Downham, but on Shardelowe's
manor there were six in 1345 and eight in 1351, WSROB 651/35/2 and 5. Bodleian
Suffolk Rolls 21 and BL Add.Rolls 53117 and 53118.
[159] CUL EDC 7/15/I/6.
[160] WSROB E.3/15.13/2.12 and 2.15; WSROB E.3/15.6/2.26 and 2.31. Dairy farming was
likely to benefit from the rise in real wages and the changes in diet after the Black Death.
See Raftis, *Ramsey abbey*, p. 281 and Mate, 'Agrarian economy after the Black Death',
p. 345.
[161] Bacon 649 and PRO SC6.1304/30; WSROB E.3/15.13/2.20; J. Rylands Library, Phillipps
Charters, 15–16.

Breckland's eastern fringe, and dairy income at Fornham (A) averaged around 101s. per annum in the 1340s (5 years), and 102s. between 1350 and 1396 (11 years).[162] Dairy farming accounted for 10 per cent of gross income (including arrears) at Quiddenham in 1388–9, and a 19-strong herd contributed 13 per cent at Hockham in 1383–4.[163] At Cressingham too, income from the dairy rose after the Black Death.[164] Peasants were obviously prepared to continue leasing the demesne herds without pressing for a reduction in the rent of a cow and its lactage, an indication of its profitability. They also expanded their own operations, for the number of illegal commoning amercements featuring cows grew rapidly at Hockham in the 1370s. In the October court of 1377, 58 cows were thus recorded, and in December Ogbourne priory had 40 cows in local pastures and ten other men had a further 43 cows.[165] Yet it is important to stress that this interest in dairy farming was restricted to the peripheral manors, even among the peasantry. At both Lakenheath and Brandon cows constituted only 7 per cent of all animal trespass/damage amercements in courts in Richard II's reign, whilst at Fornham (C) and Barton Parva they comprised 40 per cent and 15 per cent.[166]

Our knowledge of the fishing industry is largely limited to the breck-fen edge, but that evidence confirms the general buoyancy of the early fourteenth century. Income from the Lakenheath fisheries was at its highest – around £16 per annum – in 1320–2 despite the prevailing drought, perhaps suggesting that fish were important as an alternative source of food in years of grain shortage.[167] Indeed, drought was the greatest scourge of the fisherman, and in 1327 it reduced net income (including allowances) at Lakenheath to just over £9.[168] Otherwise fishing remained a popular and prosperous business for much of the fourteenth century. Buoyant demand obviously motivated John Thury of Lakenheath, for in 1311 he was amerced for having two boats when

---

[162] At Lackford, a few miles down the river Lark from Bury, the 19-strong herd fetched over £6 in 1400–1, despite a general running down of demesne activity, WSROB E.3/ 15.12/2.3.   [163] NRO Phi/493; NRO Ms 13854.

[164] Prior to the Black Death, it was rare for dairy income to exceed 20s. per annum. Yet in 1363–4 alone it fetched £6 7s. 0d., NRO DCN 40/13 f.40 and DCN Supplement (R187A).   [165] NRO Ms 2522 m.3; see also m.3, court held May 1378.

[166] At Lakenheath between 1324 and 1342, and at Brandon in 1330–4, cows constituted 8 per cent and 4 per cent of all such amercements, emphasising the fact that – despite the changing conditions after the Black Death – there was no real movement towards dairy farming in central areas of Breckland in the late fourteenth century.

[167] CUL EDC 7/15/I/4.   [168] CUL EDC 7/15/I/6.

he was only allowed one, and in 1330 two men illegally created a second *botesgang*.[169] In the 1340s, the value of the Brandon fishery was raised from 66s. 8d. per annum to 73s. 4d.[170] The number of forestallers of fish in Lakenheath market was at its height around this time, and in one court case Thomas Donne allegedly detained 8,000 eels valued at £7 from Laurence Critman.[171] The Black Death brought only temporary disruption, and by 1367 the Brandon lease had been increased to £4.[172] The number of forestallers at Lakenheath disappeared with the pressing land hunger, but fishery leases soon increased in value. Between 1355 and 1361 'middlebusk' rose from 20s. per annum to 30s., and 'millemarch' from 24s. to 30s.[173] The recovery at Lakenheath was sustained until the mid-1370s, so that between 1304 and 1348 gross mean annual income from fisheries was 249s., and in 1355–76 it was 323s. However, as with grain production, it then experienced a rapid slump in the last quarter of the century. The Brandon lease of £4 was rarely paid in full in the 1380s, and by the next decade its annual value had been reduced by 33 per cent.[174] The Lakenheath fisheries produced only 138s. per annum in this period, and some fisheries could not be let for want of a tenant: 'roveneystamp' was untenanted between 1378 and 1394, whilst one *botesgang* (valued at 4s. in 1355) fell into disuse after 1384.[175]

TRADE

The large number of people involved in ancillary occupations testifies to the hive of economic activity and to the pressure on resources before the Black Death; the numbers forestalling in Breckland markets, selling turves and sedges in this period were unsurpassed. This was also the only period when gammokers of ale were prominent, and they all but disappeared from the records after the Black Death. Baking and brewing also provided a livelihood for a greater number of people than at any other time in the Middle Ages. The number of brewers, which has been used to provide a rough and ready indicator of population levels,[176] declined on most manors during the troubled decade 1310–19,

[169] CUL EDC 7/15/II/Box 1/4 m.2, court held June 1311, and Box 1/8 m.9, court held May 1330. [170] PRO sc6.1304/23 and 26.
[171] CUL EDC 7/15/II/Box 1/9 m.21, court held June 1333.
[172] PRO sc6.1304/30. [173] CUL EDC 7/15/I/16 and 21.
[174] In 1388–9 the lessee paid only £2, Bacon 653.
[175] CUL EDC 7/15/I/28, 29 and 32. [176] Britnell, *Colchester*, pp. 89–91.

especially at Mildenhall, but recovered with the general economic climate to unprecedented heights in the 1340s (see table 4.17). After 1349 there was a drastic fall in all types of ancillary activities, and the number of brewers was cut by half on the larger manors, and in smaller villages brewing became restricted to just one or two ale-wives.

On the breck-fen edge the most striking feature is the accordance between numbers brewing and the behaviour of the land market. The drastic fall at Lakenheath corresponds with the disruption of the land market there, and might suggest that the village was grievously and permanently afflicted by plague. Mildenhall displays signs of a sluggish but nevertheless distinct recovery, and at Brandon numbers recovered almost to pre-plague levels by the 1380s, reflecting the resurgence of economic activity there. In contrast, the number of brewers at Hockham was higher after the Black Death than before. The size of amercements levied there was also high, and resembles the 'urban' pattern of retailing identified by Dyer.[177] Ale was traditionally sold and consumed outside the producer's house, but in Hockham after the Black Death it appears to have been increasingly brewed and consumed in proper ale-houses. Indeed, in 1367 four brewers refused to sell ale outside their houses and were amerced for selling it inside their establishments. Hockham would appear to be an early rural example of the development of the public house.[178]

There can be little doubt that in terms of sheer volume, the level of Breckland's trade declined after mid-century. However, the drop in volume was not exactly commensurate with the drop in population, because the general rise in living standards presented a new range of commercial opportunities. The fourteenth century represented a watershed in the development of the woollen textile industry, and this proved to be an important factor in compensating for the fall in cereal production. The output of cloths in Suffolk, Essex and Hertfordshire rose at least eightfold between 1358 and 1398, and the expansion of some villages was startling.[179] Yet, as Britnell argues, this was not a universal phenomenon amongst the textile villages, and some of the old-established cloth-producing centres – such as Clare and Sudbury – experienced little industrial

---

[177] Dyer, *Lords and peasants*, p. 347.
[178] NRO Ms 13848, court held March 1367.
[179] The ulnage accounts indicate a rise from 700 cloths per annum in 1356–8, to 5,600 cloths in 1394–8, Thornton, *History of Clare*, p. 146. See also Britnell, *Colchester*, p. 79.

Table 4.17. *Number of brewers amerced per court, decennial means*
1290–1550

Decade	Total brewers	Total courts*	Brewers per court
Brandon			
1310–19	46	4	11.5
1320–9	180	13	13.8
1330–9	223	13	17.2
1340–9	83	4	20.7
1350–9	142	11	12.9
1360–9	169	11	15.4
1370–9	135	8	16.9
1380–9	182	10	18.2
1390–9	215	14	15.4
1400–9	244	18	13.6
1410–19	274	19	14.4
1420–9	272	18	15.1
1430–9	210	15	14.0
1440–9	178	16	11.1
1450–9	186	16	11.6
1460–9	215	17	12.6
1470–9	206	19	10.8
1480–9	51	6	8.5
1510–19	53	8	6.6
1520–9	59	9	6.5
1530–9	41	6	6.8
Hilborough			
1290–0	29	2	14.5
1300–9	23	2	11.5
1310–19	38	3	12.7
1340–9	7	1	7.0
1430–9	6	2	3.0
1440–9	3	1	3.0
Hockham			
1330–9	22	2	11.0
1340–9	11	1	11.0
1370–9	73	5	14.6
1380–9	26	2	13.0
1390–1	12	1	12.0
1440–9	19	4	4.8
1450–9	8	2	4.0
1460–9	4	1	4.0
Lakenheath			
1310–19	229	8	28.6
1320–9	270	10	27.0

Table 4.17. (*cont.*)

Decade	Total brewers	Total courts*	Brewers per court
1330–9	417	14	29.8
1340–9	120	4	30.0
1370–9	19	2	9.5
1380–9	97	9	10.8
1390–9	112	18	6.2
1410–19	57	13	4.4
1420–9	33	7	4.7
1480–9	13	3	4.3
1540–9	11	2	5.5
Mildenhall			
1290–9	90	2	45.0
1310–19	38	1	38.0
1330–9	49	1	49.0
1350–9	48	2	24.0
1370–9	17	1	17.0
1400–9	104	4	26.0
1420–9	617	28	22.0
1430–9	206	10	20.6
1460–9	575	33	17.4
1470–9	283	22	12.9
1480–9	102	12	8.5

Note:
* Courts in which brewers are recorded, rather than all courts.

growth after the 1350s.[180] Breckland was hardly at the centre of these general developments, but it did participate at the periphery, and its experience serves to illustrate Britnell's point.[181] Thetford was the centre of Breckland's cloth manufacturing industry before the Black Death, but failed to maintain its relative importance thereafter. On the other hand, the rapid spread of fulling mills in rural sites, and the development of a manufacturing sector in villages such as Mildenhall and Brandon, suggest that the emerging

[180] Britnell, *Colchester*, pp. 82–5.
[181] It is impossible to measure Breckland's contribution to this general expansion, although the establishment of fulling mills in this period is indicative that output did increase. Yet nowhere is there evidence of growth similar to that experienced in Hadleigh or Colchester, Mate, 'Agrarian economy after the Black Death', p. 351; Britnell, *Colchester*, part II.

areas of production provided the main impetus for the industry's growth.

Whatever the extent of cloth manufacture in Breckland itself, it was the growth of the East Anglian industry in general which helped to sustain the region's sheep farmers, carrying trades and even barley producers.[182] A petition of 1394 commented that East Anglian cloth tended to be fairly coarse and of 'inferior' quality, which would not exclude Breckland as a source of supply, and there is strong indirect evidence that Breckland wool was supplied to the Colchester market.[183] Furthermore, Bury's success as a cloth market in this period and its contacts with Lynn would have compensated – to some extent – the region's carriers for the drop in grain trade.[184] That Ipswich and Colchester were not the only outlets for cloth produced in south Suffolk and north Essex was emphasised in 1403, when cloths belonging to a Hadleigh man were seized at Lynn.[185] The expansion of commercial rabbiting also provided a large fillip to the carrying trades, particularly on the overland route to London: a culled rabbit could easily survive this journey without rotting, and its high value justified the transport costs.

Basic foodstuffs had formed the main component of Breckland's trade before the Black Death, and inevitably bore the brunt of the general contraction thereafter. The reduction in overall trade affected the smaller markets in particular, and some of them must have gradually declined to the point of redundancy. This was a commonplace throughout East Anglia, and the depression also affected larger markets; at Sudbury, for instance, the number of stalls leased fell from 107 in 1340 to 62 in 1361.[186] Lack of documentation makes it impossible to be sure of the exact fortunes of Breckland's markets, although some did show signs of temporary recovery after the Black Death. At Hockham, for example, John Sayene was granted a small piece of land in the market on which to build a stall in 1358, and three new stalls were constructed and one other repaired at Lakenheath in 1378.[187] At Hilborough in

---

[182] The importance of industrial occupations in stimulating local agriculture is stressed in I.S.W. Blanchard, 'The miner and the agricultural community in later medieval England', *Ag.H.R.* 20 (1972), pp. 100–4.

[183] Thornton, *History of Clare*, p. 147. Merchants from Bury St Edmunds supplied wool to the Colchester market, Britnell, *Colchester*, p. 142.

[184] Gottfried, *Bury and the urban crisis*, p. 92.   [185] PRO E101.342/18.

[186] C.G. Grimwood and S.A. Kay, *A history of Sudbury, Suffolk*, (Sudbury, 1952), p. 86.

[187] NRO Ms 13848, court held February 1358; CUL EDC 7/15/I/25.

1377, a carpenter and his boy spent over five days making new market stalls.[188] In many places, though, signs of decay were only too evident. On the Clare manor of Lakenheath in 1364–5, rents totalling 16s. 4d. on at least nine 'schoppas' in the market were written off as uncollectable.[189] The farm of bridge tolls at Thetford was valued at £13 6s. 8d. in Henry III's reign, but fetched only £8 3s. 4d. in 1360.[190]

CONCLUSION

Breckland's economic performance was surprising for a marginal region so severely afflicted by plague. Despite the effects of famine and civil disturbance, its economy showed no signs of long-term depression before the Black Death, a fitting testimony to the region's wide and efficient trading links. Population certainly pressed hard on resources during this period, although its rate of growth had definitely slowed. The availability of ancillary employment, flexible access to the land market, highly adapted agrarian techniques, and specialised production all raised peasant incomes and helped to avert the classic Malthusian trap. Perhaps the economy would have creaked under further demographic strain, but after 1349 it was suddenly faced with a very different set of problems. Heavy losses of population in East Anglia seriously undermined the profitability of commercial grain production, a problem exacerbated in Breckland by its inherent disadvantages in arable farming. Consequently, the acreage under cultivation declined, although not as drastically as we might have expected and not appreciably more than in areas of better soils. Nor did people migrate from the region on any exceptional scale. Demand for the staple Breckland products of wool and barley fell less rapidly than for other basic goods, and landlords were quick to develop new projects with greater potential, notably commercial rabbit rearing: indeed, the later fourteenth century saw the strengthening of the region's specialisation in primary production for the market rather than its disintegration. None of these post-plague developments could restore the previous levels of overall trade and aggregate wealth in Breckland, but they did enable it to weather a difficult and potentially destructive storm with assurance.

[188] NRO Hilborough Deposit Box T (Daleth), vii m.3.
[189] CUL EDC 7/15/I/20.   [190] PRO DL29.288/4720.

Chapter 5

DECLINE AND RECOVERY: ECONOMIC
PERFORMANCE 1400–1540

Many historians regard the fifteenth century as a period of continued demographic decline and agrarian recession. While there is some debate over the fortunes of urban areas in this century, evidence from the countryside is unequivocal. Seigneurial income from rural estates fell sharply, reflecting a drop in land values, a contraction in the area under cultivation, the abandonment of holdings, and the dereliction of buildings. This severe depression probably reached its nadir around mid-century, after which there were some stirrings of recovery before 1500. There was regional variation in the extent and chronology of decline, but historians believe that the brunt of contraction was borne 'at the margin'. Marginal regions had to contend with their inherent disadvantages in grain production in an over-supplied market. Under such difficult conditions, it is assumed that tenants migrated in search of more responsive soils elsewhere, leaving abandoned fields and villages behind them. Was this the case in Breckland? Some evidence of decline was apparent in the latter decades of the fourteenth century, but this was hardly an unusual occurrence: indeed, our task in this chapter is to establish whether the fall in Breckland's economic activity was more pronounced than in areas of better soils.

THE LAND MARKET

Many authorities regard falling demand for land as one of the most distinctive features of the fifteenth-century economy.[1] Unfortunately, evidence of this from the various estate and sectoral studies is seldom presented in a consistent format, which renders exact quantitative comparisons of the decline almost impossible.[2] Yet on

---

[1] Hatcher, *Plague, population*, p. 36–44.   [2] *Ibid.*, p. 37.

many estates the most marked contraction in the land market occurred in the early fifteenth century, and in the long run rents declined by around one-third between *c.* 1400 and *c.* 1470.[3]

Evidence from Breckland reveals a similar pattern. Demand continued to fall below fourteenth-century levels until a nadir was reached around the 1460s, but this fall was neither precipitous nor continuous (see table 5.1). On many manors the most rapid decline occurred between 1390 and 1410 as land values readjusted to falling grain prices and perhaps as landlords temporised and lowered rents in the wake of the Peasants' Revolt.[4] This was certainly a critical period at Lackford where the value of an average acre fell by 20 per cent in the space of eight years. The rapid decline was then arrested and replaced by perhaps a quarter-century of stability or, in the case of Fornham, even slight recovery. At Hilborough tenants could be found for twenty-seven 15-acre *tenementa* (with messuages) in 1412–13, paying an average rent of 62.5d. each, and exactly the same number was still leased in 1469–70 at 65.9d. each.[5] Yet the slump in grain prices in the 1440s coincided with another fall in rents at Mildenhall and Fornham. The indices suggest that, at their worst, fifteenth-century land values fell *c.* 33 per cent from their fourteenth-century peaks.[6] This certainly constitutes a depressed land market, but it is important to stress that the fall does not appear to have been any worse than in most other areas of England. Many other areas of East Anglia fared no better than Breckland, and in certain parts of southern England rents per acre halved between 1360 and 1450.[7]

[3] *Ibid.*, pp. 38–9; Dyer, *Lords and peasants*, p. 283.
[4] These years have been identified as a period of severe agricultural depression in north Essex: Britnell, *Colchester*, p. 157.
[5] NRO Hilborough Deposit Box T (Daleth), vii mm.5 and 8.
[6] In comparison, rents at Brandon might have performed slightly better. The average value of a full-land at lease in Brandon had been 82.4d. per annum in the 1390s, see table 4.9. From a rental of 1525, it is possible to identify 12.5 full-lands at leasehold which were valued at an average of 68.5d., a fall of around 17 per cent, NRO Ms 3992.
[7] In many southern counties, rents per acre fell by up to two-thirds of their former level after the 1420s, M. Mate, 'Fifteenth-century population trends in south-east England', paper presented to Cambridge medieval economic history seminar, 1985. See also D. Keene, 'A new study of London before the Great Fire', *Urban History Yearbook* (1984), p. 18, and Searle, *Battle abbey*, pp. 329 and 369. At Sherington (Bucks.) the value of some arable lands fell by 50 per cent between 1408 and 1439, Chibnall, *Sherington*, p. 153. At Forncett, situated on strong loams in central Norfolk, the value of an acre of arable fell by almost 50 per cent between the 1370s and 1450s, Davenport, *Development of a Norfolk manor*, appendix VII: in 1376–8, mean rent per acre was 10¾d. and only 6¼d. in 1451–60. Even in Newmarket, which had enjoyed some prosperity after the Black Death, rents fell by at least 20 per cent in the course of the fifteenth century, P. May, 'Newmarket 500

Whilst rents per acre provide an invaluable barometer of shifts in the demand for land, they do not reveal whether landlords were actually receiving all of the rent income due to them. Throughout fifteenth-century England it was not uncommon for tenants to run up substantial arrears of rent, because of either their inability or outright refusal to pay. Landlords had little chance of recovering these rents, and again we would expect the problem to have been particularly severe in Breckland.[8] Unfortunately, because of the nature of the documents, it is impossible to calculate exactly the amount of 'rent refusals' each year, but it is possible to gain an impression of their extent.[9] At the end of the financial year manorial officials were held responsible for any non-payment of rent and other dues, and so many Breckland rent collectors compiled a list of the debtors and their debts and presented it at the next audit. The auditors would then consider each case and decide whether to cancel or pursue the debt. If they accepted that it was uncollectable, the debt was 'allowed' to the collector, although sometimes it was postponed or 'respited' where payment had not been received, but might be levied at some future date. Claims that were rejected would then be added to an unspecified lump sum of unpaid income, and these arrears were then charged to the manorial officials and carried over to the next year's account.

Why exactly did manorial officials have more difficulty collecting rents and amercements in the fifteenth century? The main problem was the prevailing agricultural depression and increased personal mobility, both of which served to weaken the peasants' ties to the land.[10] In consequence arable land could often be

years ago', *P.S.I.A.*, 33 (1974), p. 263. On certain Huntingdonshire manors, the period after the 1410s was characterised by a rapid decline in rents, E.B. DeWindt, *Land and people in Holywell-cum-Needingworth* (Toronto, 1972), pp. 145–6.

[8] Not all tenants paid the correct rent to manorial officials, and manorial officials sometimes failed to render all their cash to the seigneurial treasury, although this was true of all kinds of income, from court perquisites to corn and stock sales. For the problem of arrears elsewhere in East Anglia, see Britnell, *Colchester*, p. 257.

[9] This point is made by C.C. Dyer, 'A redistribution of incomes in fifteenth-century England?', in *Peasants, knights and heretics: studies in medieval English social history*, ed. R.H. Hilton (Cambridge, 1976), p. 211. For a discussion of fifteenth-century accounting procedures, see also J.S. Drew, 'Manorial accounts of St Swithun's Priory, Winchester', *English Historical Review* 62 (1947), pp. 20–41, and A.J. Pollard, 'Estate management in the later Middle Ages: the Talbots and Whitchurch, 1383–1525', *Ec.H.R.* 25 (1972), pp. 553–66.

[10] Indeed, it was precisely in the periods of particularly severe agricultural depression that rural dwellers were most likely to be attracted by high wages in the towns, Britnell, *Colchester*, p. 158.

Table 5.1. *Leasehold arable rents per acre, decennial means*
1400–1509

Decade	Ac/s	Total rent (d.)	Total area (acres)	Mean rent per acre	Indices
Lackford					
1350–9	2	3,978	485.3	8.20	100
1400–9	2	3,668	543.0	6.76	82
Lakenheath					
1300–99	14	11,832	1,712.8	6.91	100
1420–9	2	3,707	630.0	5.88	85
1430–9	2	4,278	735.3	5.82	84
1440–9	1	2,724	445.0	5.56	80
1450–9	4	10,643	1,930.0	5.51	80
1460–9	2	5,712	1,025.0	5.57	80
1480–9	1	2,844	505.5	5.63	81
Hilborough					
1350–99	2	442	101.0	4.38	100
1410–19	3	5,208	1,253.0	4.16	95
1470–9	1	2,276	612.3	3.72	85
Chippenham[+]					
1350–99				7.25	100
1424–9				6.50	90
1434–46				6.75	93
1477–83				5.00	69
1509–23				6.50	90
Fornham (A)					
1350–99	10	16,437	1,264.3	13.00	100
1400–9	8	16,290	1,719.3	9.47	73
1410–19	5	10,053	994.3	10.11	78
1420–9	5	9,120	900.3	10.13	78
1430–9	4	6,608	649.3	10.18	78
1440–9	2*	2,526	269.0	9.39	72
1460–9	1*	2,153	245.8	8.76	67
Methwold					
1350–99	1	8	1.0	8.00	100
1400–9	1	8	1.0	8.00	100
1410–19	1	904	145.0	6.23	78
1420–9	4	3,616	580.0	6.23	78
1430–9	2	1,808	290.0	6.23	78
1440–9	2	1,589	241.5	6.58	82
Mildenhall					
1300–99	6	83,077	3,907.3	21.26	99
1400–9	7	118,377	6,227.3	19.01	88

Table 5.1. (cont.)

Decade	Ac/s	Total rent (d.)	Total area (acres)	Mean rent per acre	Indices
1410–19	7	138,595	7,792	17.79	83
1420–9	2	37,993	2,141.3	17.74	83
1440–9	2	31,335	2,121.3	14.77	69
1460–9	1	15,882	1,138.5	13.95	65
1500–9	1*	17,528	1,288.3	13.61	64
Risby					
1350–99	12	6,310	676.3	9.33	100
1400–9	3	2,997	367.5	8.16	87
1410–19	3	3,190	422.3	7.55	81
					1350–1399 = 100

+ *Source:* Spufford, 'Chippenham', p. 35.
* Includes material culled from rentals.

abruptly abandoned, and the genuine shortage of tenants offered little hope of securing an immediate replacement. Hence rent collectors claimed that some lands were 'not occupied and it is not possible to lease them for want of hirers', and this was normally sufficient to secure an allowance for the rent. Another problem was the low market price of Breckland's staple products, which created recurrent cash shortages for the region's farmers. This happened to John Cowherd, who was described as a pauper despite holding several acres in Mildenhall, and probably to Henry Chapman, who paid arrears on four years' rent in a lump sum in 1413.[11]

Yet whatever the prevailing personal circumstances, there was an increasing tendency in the fifteenth century for tenants to refuse bluntly to pay their rents at all, a feature of many parts of England as well as Breckland.[12] In part this drastic sanction suggests an increasing rebelliousness amongst the peasantry, but in the main it reflects a sure knowledge of their strength in a buyer's land market. Landlords tried to resist these moves but ultimately realised that a reduced rent was better than none at all. In 1463 John Sparhawk was ordered to attend Mildenhall court on a charge of withholding rents and farms from the collector, but little more appears to have

---

11 BL Add.Roll 53138 (1464–5), and WSROB E.18/455/3 (account of Twamhill manor, 1412).
12 Dyer, 'Redistribution of incomes?', pp. 204–14. In *Lords and peasants*, p. 280, he suggests that such refusals were underlain by a sense of a 'fair rent'.

happened.[13] Similarly, where high rents had been renegotiated in the tenant's favour, we might also suspect the threat of rent refusal and seigneurial appeasement. The scribe might record the payment of '*iii s. de parte iiii s. . . . et non plures pro defectu conductorum*', a poignant reminder of the alternative to maintaining high rent levels.[14]

Manorial officials encountered similar, if not greater, problems when trying to raise court amercements. They often claimed that these simply 'are not possible to levy', an ubiquitous but unspecific phrase which generally satisfied the auditors. From Breckland comes a rare explanation of *why* amercements could not be levied, when in 1414 the Mildenhall collector pointed out that many debtors were outsiders whilst others were paupers.[15] At least most rent-payers tended to reside locally, whereas offenders in the manorial courts were sometimes itinerant peddlars, merchants or poachers from other villages who simply refused to pay court dues.[16] The poverty of tenants was sometimes explicit in the collector's failure to secure all the expected court revenues, as at Brandon in 1496–8 when a remarkable 47 per cent of potential court receipts were excused because of poverty.[17] Occasionally, however, peasants refused outright to pay amercements in a display of unprecedented indifference to seigneurial authority. Thomas Stonham of Mildenhall – with moral support from other villagers – had the audacity to argue that the charge against him was '*iniuste et sine causa et noluit solvere*'.[18]

The information recorded in table 5.2 indicates that refusals did not seriously reduce the overall level of seigneurial income. On most manors the auditors granted more allowances than in the fourteenth century, although at Brandon and Fornham these still never amounted to more than 5 per cent of expected income. At

13 WSROB E.18/451/5, court held March 1463. The same collector complained that 2s. 4d. rent '*detenet per Isabell Gaylon quia clamat esse suam propriam terram*', BL Add.Roll 53138; she was evidently using the slack land market to force concessions from the lord over the status of her land. In 1463, John Gerard of Thompson detained a number of rents and amercements from the lord with similar intentions, NRO WLS XIX/1.
14 A number of excellent examples of this are to be found in BL Add.Roll 53138.
15 BL Add.Roll 53131, collector's petition.
16 For example, 8s. 8d. was written off as uncollectable at Brandon in 1467–8 because it represented the 'amercements of outsiders', Bacon 666. At Mildenhall in 1411–12, the collector was allowed amercements owed by men from Barton, Exning, Isleham, Wangford and Worlington, BL Add.Roll 53129.
17 Bacon 689–91: 22s. 2d. was allowed in 1496–7, 34s. 10d. in 1497–8, and 33s. in 1498–9. One suspects there might have been a temporary cash shortage in the village.
18 BL Add.Roll 53129.

Lakenheath however around one-tenth of rent and court perquisites was written off as uncollectable. So refusals were definitely a growing problem for fifteenth-century landlords, but hardly an acute one. Yet this evidence only records those refusals ratified by the accountants, and many more unpaid rents and amercements were merely included in the arrears section until either payment was received or until the auditors finally accepted that it was uncollectable. How far did rents contribute to mounting arrears?

Arrears were a growing problem on many manors in fifteenth-century England, but historians have concentrated mainly on their size rather than their nature.[19] In fact this line of inquiry has been dictated by the documents themselves, which often record arrears as a lump sum rather than itemising the cause of debt. Fortunately, some fifteenth-century Breckland accounts are informative about the nature of arrears.[20] An analysis of these (table 5.3) indicates that rent arrears were not a significant problem on most manors. They hardly feature at Brandon and in ten Fornham accounts in the period 1400–29 they totalled around 47s. per annum, or *c.* 5 per cent of mean net income. At Fornham a greater problem was a failure to pay for demesne produce, notably wool.[21] Refusals to pay amercements created a far more serious problem than land rent arrears, and were a constant headache to the Bishopric of Ely at Brandon in the 1460s and 1470s. Between 1463 and 1499 almost one-quarter of court perquisites was cancelled at the audit, excluding that accumulating in arrears. In 1475 £25 9s. 1d. of amercements were struck from arrears as uncollectable, so that in reality at

---

[19] See, for instance, Raftis, *Ramsey abbey*, pp. 292–3.

[20] In fourteenth-century Breckland accounts, arrears were normally broken down – if at all – into the debts of manorial officials ('and on the bailiff, *x* shillings and on the reap-reeve, *y* shillings'), and so their exact cause remains unknown. Yet the increasing problems of the fifteenth century resulted in a move away from personal liability of manorial officials towards a specific breakdown of arrears with a list of individual debts and debtors. This marks a subtle change in the accounting system on many manors. In the fifteenth century, the incoming reeve/bailiff/rent collector was not *personally* charged with the debts of his predecessor, for these were listed separately at the audit. It was rare for the debts of an outgoing official to be eliminated on his departure, and they were often recorded in the accounts for years afterwards. Hence at Fornham (A) at the end of the 1422–3 account, arrears totalled £16 15s. 6d. (after allowances etc.), of which Robert Berold – a former collector of rents – owed 76s. 7d., and the incumbent bailiff, John Skarp, owed 30s. 9d., WSROB E.3/15.6/2.52.

[21] In 1410 Adam Woolman of Bury was charged £9 3s. 4d. for 400 fleeces, but at Michaelmas 1411 he still owed £4 13s. 8d. The debt was still outstanding a year later, although he did pay a float of 47s. 4d. *super compotum* to the auditors. In 1415 he still owed 7s., and by 1421 this had either been paid or written off as a bad debt, WSROB E.3/15.6/2.45–2.51b.

Table 5.2. *Allowances and respites granted at the audit on land rents and court perquisites on selected manors, 1350–1509*

Decade	A/cs	Land rent and court income*		Allowances and respites				Mean decennial net income
				Rent		Court dues		
		s.	d.	s.	d.	s.	d.	s.
Brandon								
1360–9	6	1,782	0½	1	0	14	6	294
1370–9	4	1,543	1½	8	6	—		384
1380–9	5	2,050	8¼	53	4	82	6	383
1390–9	9	3,340	7¾	13	2	8	8	369
1460–9	4	1,360	3	17	4	10	10	333
1470–9	6	2,018	2	—		68	6	325
1480–9	7	2,313	2½	—		39	5	325
1490–9	10	3,579	3	5	1	216	0	336
1500–9	1	375	9½	—		7	0	369
Lakenheath								
1360–9	2	1,124	7	101	7¾	180	8½	421
1370–9	2	1,025	6½	252	2¼	76	7	348
1380–9	2	1,094	0¾	210	7	161	4	365
1390–9	1	702	2	—		151	8	550
1420–9	2	906	11	24	2	78	4½	402
1430–9	2	946	11¼	58	5	61	8	413
1440–9	1	500	4¾	20	2	15	2	465
1450–9	3	1,758	8¼	—		124	5	545
1460–9	2	1,565	1¼	5	0	145	11	707
1480–9	2	1,319	11¼	42	1	170	1	553
Fornham								
1350–9	2	539	10¾	5	4	3	3	265
1360–9	6	1,938	5	2	5½	—		323
1370–9	2	754	7½	3	0		6	375
1390–9	1	380	11¼	—		42	0	338
1400–9	7	2,668	3½	118	6	67	3	355
1410–19	5	2,022	5½	29	4	5	0	398
1420–9	5	1,873	6¼	4	6	3	10	373
1430–9	4	1,408	11½	11	10	19	4	344
1440–9	2	653	11	12	8	2	5	319
1450–9	2	950	8½	64	2	2	5	442
1460–9	5	2,334	6½	165	11	6	4	432
1470–9	4	2,078	11½	152	11	4	9	480
Risby								
1350–9	5	401	0	—		2	3	80

Table 5.2. (*cont.*)

Decade	A/cs	Land rent and court income* s. d.	Allowances and respites				Mean decennial net income s.
			Rent s.	d.	Court dues s.	d.	
1360–9	2	147 7¼	—		—		74
1370–9	3	382 1¾	6	2	11	2	127
1380–9	1	132 8½		4	.	6	133
1390–9	1	136 8½	—		15	9	137
1400–9	3	421 8½	—		3	10	141
1410–19	2	298 11	—		—		149

Note:
* Rents of assize and leaseholds plus court perquisites, minus decays of rent.

least half of potential court income never reached the lord.[22] The reasons for this have been discussed elsewhere, but at Brandon poachers created a particular problem. In the 1460s four poachers from Downham and Thetford owed an amercement of £21, an enormous sum which the lord cannot have realistically expected to levy.[23] In fact it was never paid, suggesting that it was imposed as a deterrent and maintained in arrears for a suitable period of time as a constant reminder to other poachers of the penalty for their transgression.

Arrears continued to be a problem at Lakenheath, remaining just below £30 per annum for the first half of the century but rising to £106 8s. 6d. in 1481.[24] As on other manors, the preference was to isolate those defaulting on payments and to make them personally responsible for their debts rather than transfer the debit onto manorial officials. Peasant rent payments constituted only a very small percentage of arrears, and most rent arrears related to the leasing of the warren or the dairy. The Lakenheath evidence demonstrates most clearly that the accumulation of arrears was more a reflection of accounting policy than an indication of economic contraction on a manor. The Prior and Convent of Ely

[22] Bacon 671.
[23] The poachers were named as Richard Hayhowe of Downham, John and Richard Albon, and Robert Sterlyng of Thetford, Bacon 668. Unpaid court fines and amercements were also the chief source of arrears at Cressingham: in 1439–40, the arrears of £10 5s. 1d. were comprised entirely of amercements, NRO DCN Supplement (R187A).
[24] CUL EDC 7/15/I/47.

Table 5.3. A breakdown of some arrears, 1340–1509

Decade	A/cs	Total arrears £	s.	d.	Manorial officials (%)	Rents (%)	Court dues (%)	Demesne rent (%)	Stock (%)	Warren (%)	Others (%)
Brandon											
1360–9	6	2	10	0	100						
1370–9	5		16	1¾	100						
1380–9	4	13	11	7	44	35					21
1390–9	9	46	15	7½	44	9		24		17	6
1460–9	4	120	16	8		1	85	1		10	4
1470–9	6	91	6	7	1		95				3
1480–9	7	95	4	9			5			94	1
1490–9	10	531	14	2½			6			94	
1500–9	1	78	3	4	5					95	
Lakenheath											
1360–9	2	29	19	7	100						
1370–9	2	26	5	2¾	100	(32% on rent collector)					
1380–9	2	10	19	4¾	100	(14% on rent collector)					
1390–9	2	90	7	1¾	65				17	18	
1420–9	2	30	16	3	46	8	5		14	27	
1430–9	1*	14	6	4	8	11	10		71		3
1460–9	2	150	2	10¼	1		77		19	3	

Fornham

1340–9	3	52	12	8¼	10	90			
1350–9	2	30	18	7	29	71			
1360–9	3	14	18	8	37	63			
1400–9	4	14	0	13¾	74	26			
1410–19	5	56	16	1¼	7	18	12		63
1420–9	4	64	13	11	9	15	17	2	57

Notes:

★ 1431–2

Fornham accounts used are: 1347–9, 1351, 1353, 1361, 1364, 1367, 1400, 1402, 1406, 1409, 1410–12, 1414–15, 1421, 1423, 1425, 1427.

proved determined and intransigent creditors, recording debts which had long since become uncollectable, and this largely explains the amassing of arrears there. For instance, in 1481 gross income exceeded expenditure by £103 3s. 10d., but much of this 'income' constituted unpaid amercements and debts of men long since dead.[25] Some of these amercements dated back forty years,[26] and it was clearly unrealistic to expect exaction of these fines from such luminaries in the first instance, let alone after such a long period of time. The Prior had more justification in expecting payment for stock purchased on credit from the manor by various merchants, a serious problem in 1431–2 when debts on demesne wool and sheep sales represented 71 per cent of arrears.[27] However it was hardly realistic to expect Henry Trewe of Bungay's arrears of £10 4s. 0d. to be paid in 1482 when the debt had been incurred in 1422.[28]

Any assessment of changing levels of arrears tells the historian more about seigneurial expectations of income from a manor than about the level of economic activity there. In Breckland, arrears grew as seigneurial power was eroded and unrealistically large amercements were imposed in an attempt to coerce tenants into compliance; they grew as merchants assumed or were granted credit for demesne produce and as warreners struggled to meet warren rent levels in years when disease decimated their stock.[29] There is little indication that default on land rents was ever a serious problem, probably because Breckland landlords were increasingly prepared to renegotiate leasehold rents at a favourable level. This being the case, then the figures for net income from rents and perquisites (table 5.2) represent a passable indication of the money actually received by the lord each year.

We might therefore conclude that the chronology of decline varied from manor to manor, but that the lowest incomes were generally recorded between 1420 and 1470. The depth of decline

[25] For instance, £72 12s. 10d. represented accumulated fines on prominent feudal lords for their failure to maintain fenland water channels, such as the £23 13s. 4d. on a former bishop of Ely and the £20 on the bishop of Rochester.
[26] See, for instance, the accumulated amercements on the villagers of Downham, Littleport and Ely for illegal fishing in 1482, which were first recorded in 1437–8, CUL EDC 7/15/I/39 and 47.   [27] CUL EDC 7/15/I/36.
[28] The 1427–8 account noted that Trewe's debt had been owed since the first year of Henry VI's reign, CUL EDC 7/15/I/35.
[29] For the accumulation of arrears on the Bishopric of Worcester's estates, see Dyer, *Lords and peasants*, pp. 179–90.

Decline and recovery

Table 5.4. *Income from land rents at Lackford in the fifteenth century*

	Income			
Year	£	s.	d.	Indices
n.d., *c.* 1420	24	10	7	100
n.d., *c.* 1440	18	12	5	76
1487	14	6	10	59

Sources: WSROB E.3/15.52/3.1; E.3/
15.12/3.6; E.3/15.12/3.8.[30]

also varied, but on most manors the lowest decennial income levels were only around one-quarter to one-fifth lower than their fourteenth-century peaks. Only at Lackford did income from land rents decline drastically in the fifteenth century (table 5.4). Breckland's overall experience certainly compares favourably with the Percy estates in northern England, where rent income dropped by between 20 and 50 per cent in the fifteenth century.[31] There is no evidence that the decline in land values and rent income in Breckland was more severe than that experienced in many other areas of England.[32]

Whilst declining rent income provides one important indicator of the falling demand for land, a more direct approach is to calculate the area of land abandoned in the century after 1349. Unfortunately, this is impossible to do with any claim to exactness: rentals do not record the amount of arable which had reverted to pasture simply because such reversion was an integral feature of a region practising convertible husbandry. Yet there are indications that the bounds of village open-fields were shrinking from earlier limits. The recorded demesne arable at Culford rose from 254 acres in 1302 to 296.25 acres in 1435, probably because it had absorbed some redundant peasant land.[33] There were also a further 17.25 acres of land *in manibus domini*, and so it seems that 59.5 acres of arable had been permanently withdrawn from cultivation. In 1435 the total

[30] The dating for these documents given in R.M. Thomson, *The archives of the abbey of Bury St Edmunds*, Suffolk Records Society 21 (1980), is incorrect.

[31] J.M.W. Bean, *The estates of the Percy family 1416–1537* (Oxford, 1958), pp. 27–41.

[32] Hatcher, *Plague, population*, pp. 36–44.

[33] The 1302 extent is transcribed in E. Powell, *A Suffolk hundred in 1283* (1910), pp. 68–70; the 1435 extent is to be found in BL Add.Ms 42055 ff.23–46. The increase was obviously for the benefit of demesne pastoral – not arable – operations.

arable in the manor was officially given as 514 acres, yet we can assume that – for the purposes of arable farming – 12 per cent of this was now redundant, and in practical terms the arable comprised 454.5 acres. However, the area of land actually sown each year had fallen even further, as recuperative fallows increased and cropping intensity declined. This drop is impossible to measure exactly, but evidence of cropping on other manors suggests that only *c.* 35 per cent of arable was sown in any one year in the 1440s (see also table 4.3):

Year	Total arable (acres)	Area sown each year (%)	Estimated sown area (acres)
1340	514	60	310
1440	454	35	160

In the space of one century, the area sown each year had probably dropped by up to a half in many central Breckland villages.

In the late fourteenth century there had been a definite retreat from Breckland's poorest and least accessible arable, a process which continued into the early fifteenth. A few acres of sandy soil were absorbed into rabbit warrens, and at Lakenheath in 1419–20 'six acres of arable lie between the brecks and are not possible to lease because of the debility of the soil'.[34] However, this shedding of land at the physical margin of cultivation had definitely slowed down, and from the second quarter of the fifteenth century there are firm indications that tenants were lured into taking up land by falling rent levels. On all manors the area at leasehold continued to rise, although this is largely explained by the leasing of more demesne parcels and the conversion of former barley and customary rents to leasehold. However, some new leases were drawn up at attractively low rents. At Lakenheath in 1427–8, for instance, two full-lands 'formerly abandoned [*weyvo*] in the lord's hands' were

---

[34] CUL EDC 7/15/I/34, '*vi acras terre iacent inter les brakes et non possunt dimitti propter debilitatem soli eiuisdem terre*'. At Risby in 1413, 9 acres in Westfeld valued at 4d. per acre (mean rent that year was 7.14d.) were abandoned by William Ocle, WSROB E.3/15.13/2.26.

leased to two tenants, as were three more in 1442–3.[35] By this method landlords could at least maintain some stability in rent incomes whilst the value of that land (expressed per acre) continued to decline.

Whilst there are unmistakable signs of increased demand for land throughout Breckland, the rate and extent of increase varied between manors, and was nowhere great enough to constitute a 'recovery' before the last decades of the fifteenth century. For instance, expected income from assize and leasehold rents at Lakenheath rose from £25 14s. 3d. in 1487 to £28 9s. 3d. in 1541–2, but land values were still declining at Lackford in the 1480s and any recovery at Mildenhall was patchy.[36] The stirrings of recovery are best illustrated by evidence from Brandon and Feltwell. In 1437, Richard George leased three full-lands in Brandon which had previously been unoccupied, and subsequently there was a slow but steady stream of tenants willing to relieve the lord of unoccupied lands and buildings.[37] The analysis of completed land transactions in Brandon courts (table 4.1) shows that *inter vivos* transactions became proportionally much more important after 1450, a sure sign of renewed interest. Similarly, after almost a century of stagnation, the number of transactions per court rose sharply in the early sixteenth century, and some courts at this time record little else but tenurial activity. The land market's recovery is confirmed by a genuine increase in rent income from the 1460s.

The information in table 5.5 shows that rent income began to recover in the late fifteenth century, but it was neither rapid nor continuous. The difficulties at Feltwell in the 1490s might have been administrative, or perhaps caused by cash shortages in the village.[38] The recovery is much clearer at Brandon, and

---

[35] CUL EDC 7/15/I/35 and 39. The dates of abandonment are rarely given, although the previous tenant is invariably named. One suspects that these full-lands had been abandoned in 1349, but that the lord had only managed to lease small parcels of them subsequently. The lord's inability to lease them as composite holdings before the 1420s was a function of the disagreement over rent levels and land tenure on the manor. Compare this with the bishop of Ely's success in persuading his Brandon tenants to take up full-lands in the 1360s and 1370s.

[36] CUL EDC 7/15/I/48 and CUL EDC 1.C.3. For Lackford see table 5.4, and for Mildenhall see Bailey, 'At the margin', p. 289.

[37] Bacon 296/31, court held October 1437.

[38] In this decade, many of the surviving Feltwell accounts are in a confused state, with no income or expenditure totals recorded, and no indication of the bailiff's financial liability. See, for instance, NRO Ms 10009 mm.7, 9–11, 17.

Table 5.5. *Decennial mean income from land rents at Brandon and Feltwell, 1460–1509*

Decade	No. of accounts	Gross income s.	d.	deductions* s.	d.	Net income s.	d.	Mean net income s.	d.
Brandon									
1460–9	4	1,150	5	68	3	1,082	2	270	7
1470–9	6	1,784	3	69	6	1,714	9	285	10
1480–9	7	2,081	8	58	0	2,023	8	289	1
1490–9	10	2,977	1	19	5	2,957	8	295	9
Feltwell									
1480–9	4	1,587	6	32	10	1,554	8	388	8
1490–9	2	799	1	65	2	733	11	366	11
1500–9	4	1,580	2	28	4	1,551	10	387	11

Note:
* allowances, decays and respites.
Sources: Bacon 664–91; NRO Ms 10009 mm.1–6, 8, 12–16.

represented an increase in rent income of 10 per cent over the years, with the most appreciable gains in the 1470s.[39] It is tempting to see in this the stirrings of demographic recovery, especially as it substantiates Gottfried's supposition that East Anglian population began to rise in this decade.[40] However, as Blanchard has argued, increased rents may reflect renewed economic activity but not necessarily demographic growth, particularly in a region of commercialised agriculture like Breckland.[41] Nevertheless, the very fact that some degree of economic revival had occurred in Breckland by the late fifteenth century runs contrary to the prophecies of the population-resources model.

ARABLE FARMING

As the profitability of grain farming declined drastically in the later fourteenth and early fifteenth centuries, so landlords reduced the

[39] Unfortunately the Brandon rents are given as a lump sum and not itemised, so it is uncertain whether the recovery is due to the taking up of new lands or to the rising value of the old rents.
[40] R.S. Gottfried, *Epidemic disease in fifteenth century England: the medical response and the demographic consequences* (Leicester, 1978), pp. 213–22.
[41] I.S.W. Blanchard, 'Population change, enclosure and the early Tudor economy', *Ec.H.R.* 23 (1970), pp. 433–4.

scale of their demesne arable farming. A common policy was to
lease the demesne for a fixed annual rent, but, where direct exploitation continued, the area under cultivation often declined substantially. On one Berkshire manor, the demesne cultivated area fell by
75 per cent between 1316 and 1421, and in Devon the fall was as
much as 60 per cent between 1290–9 and 1450–9.[42] A similar
situation prevailed on most East Anglian demesnes in the early
fifteenth century, and a decline of up to 40 per cent was not
uncommon.[43] The area under cultivation also fell in Breckland (see
table 4.2). It was most prominent on demesnes in central villages,
notably at Lakenheath where there was a decline of 63 per cent
between 1300–49 and 1420–9; at Mildenhall the demesne cultivated area dropped by 54 per cent (1320–9 compared with 1420–9)
and by 48 per cent at Hilborough (1370–9 compared with
1410–19). Only at Methwold, Cressingham and Fornham (A) was
the decline closer to the East Anglian norm.[44] Demesne arable
farming suffered severely on the poorest soils of central Breckland,
and the balance of farming shifted even further towards pastoral
activities.[45]

The decision whether to lease demesnes was a fine one in the late
fourteenth century, but by the early fifteenth century there was a
decisive movement towards the security of rentier farming on
many estates.[46] The main barrier to profitable demesne farming
was the combination of sagging grain prices and a persistent rise in
wages, particularly those of the famuli. Famulus employment was

[42] R. Faith, 'Berkshire: the fourteenth and fifteenth centuries', in *The peasant land market in medieval England*, ed. P.D.A. Harvey (Oxford, 1984), p. 171, (Coleshill); Finberg, *Tavistock abbey*, p. 100.

[43] The demesne cultivated area fell by 8 per cent at Martham (1300–24 and 1400–24), and by 28 per cent at Hevingham (1327–8 and 1417–18), Campbell, 'Agricultural progress', p. 38 and 'Field systems', table 4.1. Between the 1340s and the early fifteenth century, the acreage sown on a number of north Essex demesnes fell by between 15 and 40 per cent, Britnell, *Colchester*, pp. 143–4.

[44] The sown area on the Methwold demesne fell by 17 per cent (1360–9 and 1440–9), 16 per cent at Cressingham (1290–1329 and 1410–19), and 27 per cent at Fornham (1340–9 and 1400–19)

[45] However, it is worth noting that some manors on good soils also suffered considerable decline in the fifteenth century. At Writtle (Essex), for instance, the area under cultivation fell by 56 per cent between 1361 and 1440, K.C. Newton, *The manor of Writtle: the development of a royal manor in Essex, 1086–1500* (London, 1970), pp. 56 and 75–7.

[46] This process is well documented. See, for instance, R.A. Lomas, 'The priory of Durham and its demesnes in the fourteenth and fifteenth centuries', *Ec.H.R.* 31 (1978), pp. 347–49; Britnell, *Colchester*, p. 147; Dyer, *Lords and peasants*, p. 167.

secure and rather attractive in the conditions of thirteenth-century land hunger, but when land and employment were widely available in the fifteenth century its unpopularity forced landlords to entice workers with higher wages.[47] At Fornham (A) the number of famuli was kept to a minimum, which occasionally necessitated the hiring of extra ploughmen at piece-rates, but total labour costs still rose sharply.[48] Furthermore, as customary labour services were commuted or fell into decay, so demesnes lost an important labour force capable of performing the basic farming tasks cheaply. By 1420–1 there were no works owed by peasants on the Fornham (A) demesne, and they were vastly reduced at Lakenheath and Mildenhall.[49] By 1417 only 8 per cent of the demesne crop at Hilborough was reaped by customary services.[50]

Changes in the economic climate also induced a change in the balance of crops grown. The proportion of oats sown fell everywhere, but especially at Fornham (A), Lakenheath and Methwold (see table 4.10). Rye was relatively more important in the 1410s at Cressingham and Hilborough, but showed a consistent decline on most manors as the century progressed. Wheat increased its relative importance, but the main gains were made by barley which came to occupy over half the sown area in many places. These trends are particularly striking when the sown acreages are considered. Oats, rye, and, to a lesser extent, legumes all bore the brunt of contraction, but barley even managed to hold its own in absolute terms on some contracting demesnes. Despite a drop in overall sown area of 17 per cent at Methwold between 1360–9 and 1440–9, the area under barley rose by 62 per cent. At Lakenheath an annual average of 80 acres of barley was sown in 1300–9 and 88 acres in 1440–9, and 118 acres at Fornham (A) in 1340–9 and 111 acres in 1440–9 (see table 4.2). Barley also appears to have maintained its popularity

---

[47] This unpopularity is suggested by a court case at Lakenheath, where Roger Outlawe, famulus, was presented for not performing his job, CUL EDC 7/15/II/Box 3/HV m.7, court held December 1415.

[48] For instance, in 1419–20 a ploughman and his plough were hired to help the famuli for 22 days costing 18s. 4d., and another man and his dung cart were hired for four days (4s.), WSROB E.3/15.6/2.51a. In 1404–5, two carters, four ploughmen and a dairyman were paid an average of 9s. 6d. each for the year's work, but in 1443–4 four ploughmen and two shepherds received 19s. each and also shared an extra 30s. clothes allowance, WSROB E.3/15.6/2.42 and 2.60.

[49] WSROB E.3/15.6/2.51b. At Mildenhall in 1400–1, of 2,420 winter and summer works owed, 98 per cent were either decayed or sold. Under full employment, reaping works alone could reap 330 acres of demesne corn, but in the same year only 18 acres were reaped in this way, and 306 acres were in manibus domini, BL Add.Roll 53120.

[50] NRO Hilborough Deposit Box T (Daleth), vii m.7.

among the peasantry. When John Archer's lands were seized in Brandon in 1418, of 42 sown acres 62 per cent were barley, 14 per cent oats and 24 per cent rye, and similarly when the bishop of Ely gained custody of 5 acres of peasant land in 1443, 3 acres were sown with barley.[51] In Mildenhall courts between 1520 and 1532 there were 53 debt and damage cases where the grain involved was specified, of which 83 per cent concerned barley, 9 per cent rye, 4 per cent malt and 4 per cent maslin and wheat.[52] Similarly, mid-fifteenth-century Northwold courts reflect the continuing popularity of barley.[53] The corn market as a whole might have contracted, but Breckland strengthened rather than weakened its commitment to barley production.

The explanations for these changes are best found in the data presented in tables 4.11 to 4.13. The fall in oats production is attributable to the reduction in the number of cattle on demesnes as dairy herds were sold and fewer plough beasts were required to till the land. Similarly, as the number of famuli on most manors declined in the fifteenth century, so rye became less important, and at Lakenheath and Fornham any surpluses were channelled into the local market.[54] Wheat production was still a difficult business on the sandy soils, but its higher value and quality enhanced its attractiveness, and on peripheral manors it ousted rye as the most important winter grain. However, with the exception of Cressingham, wheat was rarely sold to market and on most manors an increased proportion was sent to the seigneurial household for domestic consumption. Market sales of barley maintained their relative importance in the fifteenth century, although at Mildenhall the proportion sold fell by 12 per cent, and that sent to Bury abbey as malt rose by 14 per cent compared to the late fourteenth century. At Risby the proportion sold to market remained stable, although it rose by 8 per cent at Fornham, by 11 per cent at Hilborough and by 36 per cent at Cressingham.

A perceptible rise in the thickness of seed sown, together with the

---

[51] Bacon 294/11, court held October 1418, and Bacon 295/37, court held September 1443.
[52] WSROB E.18/459/69. The Mildenhall tithe returns presented in table 3.13 are based largely on fifteenth-century material and so suggest there was no weakening of barley's dominance.   [53] NRO Ms 18630.
[54] The average quantity of rye disposed of annually by manorial officials fell in the late fourteenth century from 84 qu. to 51 qu. at Lakenheath, from 63 qu. to 34 qu. at Fornham (A), and from 43 qu. to 14 qu. at Mildenhall. On the few manors where the quantity disposed of remained constant or even rose, such as at Cressingham and Hilborough, market sales increased.

adoption of less demanding cropping sequences, might suggest that productivity was raised above fourteenth-century levels. Yet these positive steps were undermined by the reduction of labour inputs as labour services declined and wage bills soared.[55] Consequently, demesnes became more dependent upon the famuli to perform the basic agrarian chores. Yet the famuli themselves were often unable to manage all of the basic requirements of ploughing and harrowing. It is therefore probable that marling, manuring and weeding was substantially reduced, and indeed after 1402 the Mildenhall demesnes began to hire men to spread dung on the fields at no little cost.[56] It is impossible to calculate exactly whether the dissolution of labour services and reduction in the number of famuli caused a fall in manpower capacity greater than the fall in the area under cultivation in the fifteenth century. Yet the need to hire expensive additional labour to perform basic tasks in a period of falling grain prices suggests that arable land was less intensively prepared than previously.

Whilst the leasing of demesnes became the norm on many estates in the fifteenth century, it did not guarantee landlords a stable income. The rental values of demesnes were sensitive to prevailing economic conditions, and lessees were frequently able to secure financial concessions from the landlord.[57] On many English estates, the 1420s and 1430s were a period of severe contraction in the value of demesne leases. During this time, demesne rents on many manors of the Bishopric of Worcester fell by up to 40 per cent, and on some Westminster abbey manors the fall was as high as 66 per cent.[58] The farm of two demesnes in east Bedfordshire fell by 40 per cent between the 1440s and the 1470s, and there was also a considerable decline in north Essex.[59] England as a whole suffered from a severe agricultural depression in the early fifteenth century. Most Breckland demesnes had undergone some piecemeal leas-

[55] This was also a feature on eastern Norfolk demesnes, Campbell, 'Agricultural progress', p. 39.

[56] There were no such payments between 1400–2, but in 1409–10, 18s. 5d. was paid to carry dung, 54 men were hired to spread it on the fields, and another 234 'rengs' were spread for 16s. 6d. These payments were necessitated by a prevailing shortage of famuli, BL Add.Roll 53126.

[57] See Dyer, *Lords and peasants*, pp. 180–3.

[58] *Ibid.*, pp. 168–70; Harvey, *Westminster abbey*, pp. 157–8.

[59] A. Jones, 'Bedfordshire: the fifteenth century', in *Peasant land market*, ed. Harvey, p. 182; Britnell, *Colchester*, pp. 256–7, 259. Once again, the Writtle demesne was in serious difficulties in the mid-fifteenth century. In 1419 it was leased for £146 13s. 4d, and for £113 6s. 8d. in 1442, the level at which it remained in 1487, Newton, *Writtle*, p. 73.

ing since the Black Death. However, the cumulative effect of this process was not substantial, for most demesnes were still largely intact in the early fifteenth century. Account rolls invariably record the rent for the demesne arable land separately, and so provide a rough indication of the profitability of large-scale arable farming in the fifteenth century (see table 5.6).[60] These figures represent the sums actually paid each year rather than the money due, and so are an accurate reflection that the depression in Breckland's grain farming was of a similar depth and duration to that in the rest of England. Only at Hilborough is there evidence of serious difficulties. The lord had ceased cultivating the manor directly by 1469, but lessees could only be found for 37 per cent of the demesne arable and a further 21 per cent had been abandoned to the rabbit-warren.[61] In total, these piecemeal leases were worth a mere 41s. 4d. to the lord, compared with the £13 6s. 0d. fetched by the lease of sheep pastures and the warren. A shortage of willing lessees explains the drop in rent at Fornham and Methwold in the 1420s, and a continuing shortage may explain why both manors were directly exploited by the lord in occasional years in the 1430s and 1440s. In 1456–7 two lessees were found for the Fornham demesne, Thomas Edward taking one share at £12 and Henry Winde the other at £8. Yet by 1460 Winde's rent arrears totalled £12 19s. 0d., which prompted Bury abbey to relieve him in mid-lease and sell off his crops to local merchants in 1461. Thereafter, the whole demesne was leased for £20 to Edward, who farmed it effectively and without debt for at least 16 years.[62] The location of demesne was undoubtedly an important consideration for potential lessees, and this largely explains the stability of the Thetford lease throughout the century: the Duchy of Lancaster simply let the arable, foldcourses and warren to the town's Cluniac priory, who then employed it as a home farm.[63]

The Fornham example suggests that large-scale arable farming was manageable in the fifteenth century, as long as rents were kept

---

[60] There is no evidence that the demesne arable was then sub-let by lessees.

[61] NRO Hilborough Deposit Box T (Daleth), vii m.9 records the lease of 177.5 acres of demesne to various tenants, together with the inclusion of 100 acres in the warren lease; m.8 gives the demesne area as 480 acres.

[62] WSROB E.3/15.7/2.11–2.19.

[63] The rent paid by Thetford priory for the lease of the Duchy's manor remained stable throughout the fifteenth century; it stood at £28 6s. 8d. in 1413–14, 1440–1, 1479–80, and 1513, PRO DL29.290/4765, 292/4808 and 295/4847, and CUL Add.Ms 6969 f.112.

Table 5.6. *Annual rents
paid for demesne arable land
('gaynor') in selected years,
1398–1542*

Demesne	Rent		
	£	s.	d.
Brandon			
1398–9	22	0	0
1463–4	13	6	8
1480–1	16	13	4
1529–30	23	0	0
1541–2	18	13	4
Cavenham			
c. 1440	13	6	8
c. 1490	11	6	8
Lakenheath			
1467–8	7	0	0
1487–8	7	10	0
1540–1	20	0	0
Fornham (A)			
1429–30	13	6	8
1461–2	20	0	0
1476–7	20	0	0
Mildenhall			
1444–5	21	0	0
1467–8	21	0	0
1539–40	42	0	0
Methwold			
1403–4	46	13	4
1413–14	42	0	0
1424–5	40	0	0
1451–2	32	0	0
1464–5	28	0	0
1479–80	30	0	0

Sources: Brandon, Bacon 663,
664, 675, 695 and 696;
Cavenham, PRO SC6.1117/12
and SC12.27/32; Lakenheath,
CUL EDC 7/15/I/46 and 48,
EDC.I.C.3; Fornham, WSROB
E.3/15.6/2.55, E.3/15.7/2.14 and

2.19; Mildenhall, BL Add.Rolls
53137 and 53139, and L.J.
Redstone, ed., 'First minister's
account of the possessions of the
abbey of St Edmund', *P.S.I.A.*
13 (1909), pp. 347–8;
Methwold, PRO DL29.289/4754,
291/4776, 293/4817, 295/4844
and 295/4847.

at a reasonable level and the land was carefully managed.[64] It also required a financial commitment from the landlord to keep the demesne granges, sheds and outhouses in good condition. Hence the abbot of Bury agreed to pay for maintenance at Fornham, and between 1456 and 1477 Thomas Edward was pardoned 15 per cent of his lease in order to effect such repairs.[65] Wherever landlords were negligent in maintaining manorial buildings, income from demesne leases was likely to suffer. The poor performance of the Methwold lease was largely due to the dilapidation of the demesne buildings. In 1523 a jury considered the manor house 'and scyte gretly ruynous and must nedefully be repayred', and warned that without prompt action 'no fermor may comy new in the seid manor, but the same manor . . . growe to fether decay than it is now'. The cost of repairs was estimated at nearly £100, and the extent of the neglect was such that the great barn 'can not be amendyd the tymber therof is so dispent and roten'.[66]

The falling value of land rents and the abandonment of peasant holdings indicates that peasant grain production also contracted sharply in the quarter-century after *c.* 1390. In some places a period of stability then ensued, for tithe farm rents at Mildenhall were fairly static in the later fifteenth century, falling from £30 13s. 4d. in 1425–6 to £29 1s. 4d. in 1467–8.[67] Yet the overall fall in output is also reflected in the value of manorial mills, which fell consistently throughout England. There was a spectacular decline in mill values

64 This relatively health state of affairs in Breckland contrasts with some areas of England where many lessees encountered severe financial difficulties. See R.B. Dobson, *Durham priory 1400–1450* (Cambridge, 1973), pp. 273 and 284–5, where lessees sometimes ended up '*impotentes*' as a result of their activities; and Searle, *Battle abbey*, pp. 368–9.
65 WSROB E.3/15.7/2.11–2.19.   66 PRO DL43/28.
67 BL Add.Rolls 53135 and 53139. The tithe rent recorded in the second account includes a valuation for demesne tithes which is omitted from this calculation.

on the Duchy of Cornwall's estates soon after the Black Death, and many mills around Colchester fell into disuse even before the end of the fourteenth century.[68] Breckland corn mills seemed to survive for longer, although many eventually disappeared by the mid-fifteenth century. Rent for the Lakenheath mill fell from £1 in 1394–5 to 6s. 8d. in 1437–8.[69] Valued at £2 in 1396–7, the Brandon mill stood vacant and in need of repair in 1442, although it was back in use for 20s. rent in 1463–4; by 1474–5, however, it had been abandoned, a fate which befell the millhouse at Hengrave.[70] On the other hand, the Fornham mill underwent substantial repairs in the early fifteenth century, with the result that its rent value almost doubled.[71] Unfortunately, none of this evidence can be used to prove that demand for grain remained higher in Breckland than elsewhere. The value of demesne mills was determined more by the landlord's ability to enforce millsuit than by the overall demand for grain. The collapse of milling at Lakenheath and Brandon was exacerbated by a growing peasant refusal to grind corn at the seigneurial mill, and the appearance of new private mills.[72] At Brandon in 1454 Thomas Smyth kept 'one new communal water mill in his messuage' for the express purpose of milling corn and malt.[73] At Fornham the demand generated by the Bury market probably helped the lord to ensure that his tenants performed their feudal dues.[74]

[68] Hatcher, *Duchy of Cornwall*, pp. 176–7, and Britnell, *Colchester*, p. 143. See also Dyer, *Lords and peasants*, pp. 172–3.

[69] CUL EDC 7/15/I/32 and 37.

[70] Bacon 661, 664 and 671; 295/35, court held August 1442. WSROB 449/2/345. In June 1443, the Hockham court noted that the old wood from the manorial windmill had been sold off, presumably after its demolition, NRO Ms 13849.

[71] In 1402–3, £12 19s. 3d. was spent overhauling the mill, and its value then rose from £2 18s. 4d. per annum to £4 4s. 0d., WSROB E.3/15.6/2.40 and 2.41. There is no indication that it had been converted to a fulling mill. Similarly, the mill at Buckenham Parva maintained a high value throughout the fifteenth century, and constant references to its millstone indicate that it too was still employed for corn rather than for fulling. In 1412–13 it was valued at £5 6s. 8d., dropped to £4 13s. 8d. soon afterwards, but returned to £5 6s. 8d. by 1483, NRO Hilborough Deposit Box T (Daleth), vii mm.6, 9, 17.

[72] See also Hatcher, *Duchy of Cornwall*, pp. 176–7.

[73] Bacon 295/57, court held May 1454; *'custodit j novum communem molendinum aquum in messuagio suo'*.

[74] There are no references to illegal milling in the Hilborough courts of the fifteenth century. On the contrary, Thomas Colvyle, the mill lessee, was amerced for charging peasants excessive tolls at the mill, NRO Hilborough Deposit Box T (Daleth), iii, court held February 1440. This evidence suggests that the coercive power of lordship could still be an important factor in maintaining corn mill rents in the fifteenth century.

PASTORAL FARMING

As sheep rearing possessed relative cost advantages over grain farming in the later fourteenth century, we might expect a continuing interest in sheep in the fifteenth century. Indeed, historians have noted a sharp increase in pastoral activities in places as widespread as Cornwall and Berkshire, and arable land in some regions was enclosed for sheep pastures in the third quarter of the century.[75] Yet, after the early part of the century, the harsh reality was that sheep farming also suffered periods of depression, and in many places the swing to pastoral farming was no more than an attempt to use land which would otherwise have laid idle.[76] Widespread investment in sheep farming in the late fourteenth century ultimately created a condition of over-supply in the wool market, with the result that some farmers ran down their activities in the fifteenth century. Consequently pastoral farming in north Essex was unable to compensate for the continuing decline in arable farming, and from mid-century some estates abandoned direct sheep farming entirely.[77]

Fleece prices in Breckland slumped in the 1390s,[78] and invariably resulted in a reduction in flock size (see table 4.14). Local prices then recovered until around 1415, and corresponded with an expansion in some flocks. Six shepherds from nearby villages were amerced for illegally grazing a total of 1,300 sheep on Lakenheath pastures in 1415, and 600 were still there in 1422.[79] By 1420–9 there were as many sheep on the Lakenheath demesne as there had been over a century before, and the flock was only 25 per cent smaller than it had been at its recorded zenith in the 1340s. At Hilborough the expansion of sheep farming in the early fifteenth century was certainly enough to compensate for the contraction in arable production, and the manor made large purchases of wethers and lambs in 1409–10 in order to increase its operations more rapidly.[80] The peasantry was also eager to exploit the prevailing boom, and

[75] Hatcher, *Duchy of Cornwall*, pp. 170–1; Faith, 'Berkshire', pp. 171–3.
[76] Lloyd, *Movement of wool prices*, pp. 22–4 and 29; Bolton, *Medieval English economy*, pp. 219, and 228–9.
[77] Britnell, *Colchester*, p. 255; Dyer, *Lords and peasants*, pp. 150–1.
[78] Bailey, 'At the margin', table 4.21.
[79] CUL EDC 7/15/II/Box 3/HV mm.5 and 19, courts held March 1415 and January 1422.
[80] NRO Hilborough Deposit Box T (Daleth), vii m.4.

in 1409 William Baketon paid the hefty sum of 26s. 8d. for a licence to increase his flock in Lackford by 200 sheep for twelve years.[81]

Yet the optimism was shortlived, and by 1420 prices for Breckland wool had dropped sharply, ultimately reaching a low of 1.5d. per fleece in the 1450s.[82] Some manors extended credit facilities to encourage buyers as wool prices fell, although even then full payment was often delayed for many years. Robert Stubbard paid promptly for 303 fleeces bought at Fornham (A) in 1415, but in 1422 he owed £7 13s. 1d. for wool purchased at least three years earlier, and the debt was still outstanding in 1427.[83] Worst of all, the 1452 Lakenheath clip remained unsold 'for want of merchants', and at Lackford in 1454 John Saddington was not bothering to maintain the hurdles and fencing of the demesne fold in his lease.[84] Faced with this fall in prices, some Essex manors attempted to bolster their incomes by fattening sheep for local urban markets, but this was not an important feature of Breckland flocks.[85] So even when wool prices were depressed, most demesne flocks in Breckland continued to be reared primarily for their wool clip or for domestic requirements, a remarkably conservative approach.

Despite the mid-century depression in wool prices, and despite the general movement towards rentier farming, few Breckland landlords were sufficiently discouraged to abandon sheep rearing entirely; indeed, the sheep and the rabbit were their best chances of bolstering flagging incomes. Thetford priory maintained an active interest in sheep farming by acquiring the use of other landowners' foldcourses, notably the Duchy of Lancaster and Rushford college.

[81] WSROB E.3/15.12/1.14, court held October 1409. In May 1402, John Flempton had 73 sheep in his fold over the allotted number, and in August 1403 overstocked the common land with 200 sheep.

[82] Throughout much of south-east England, fleece prices fell to a low of 1½d. in the 1440s and 1450s, M. Mate, 'Pastoral farming in south-east England in the fifteenth century', *Ec.H.R.* 40 (1987), pp. 525–7. She attributes the collapse of prices to poor stock caused by murrain, and to a deterioration of trading relations abroad. See also Rogers, *History of agriculture and prices*, vol. IV, p. 328.

[83] WSROB E.3/15.6/2.49, 2.52 and 2.54. William Barbour owed the Lakenheath demesne over £6 for wool in 1468, and had still not paid in 1482, CUL EDC 7/15/I/46 and 47.

[84] CUL EDC 7/15/I/41; WSROB E.3/15.12/1.4, court held April 1454. Such an inability to sell fleeces was not unusual for this period, Mate, 'Pastoral farming', p. 527.

[85] Britnell, contribution to *Agrarian history of England*, vol. III (forthcoming). There were a few sheep sold to market from Risby and Lakenheath, but this was exceptional, WSROB E.3/15.13/2.25; CUL EDC 7/15/I/34. Both Fornham and Hilborough began to send more regular supplies to the seigneurial household, WSROB E.3/15.6/2.49 and 2.60; NRO Hilborough Deposit Box T (Daleth), vii m.5.

In the late fifteenth century it had at least 2,000 sheep on various pastures around Thetford and its adjacent villages, and had also extended its operations to Lynford and Bodney.[86] Unfortunately, the leasing of demesne arable lands often meant that manorial accounts no longer recorded information about seigneurial flocks, although direct sheep farming certainly did continue. For instance, sheep totals ceased to be recorded after the 1390s in the Brandon accounts, but fifteenth-century courts still detailed annual sheep deaths due to murrain. In June 1454 the court recorded the deaths of 119 hoggs, 107 wethers and 75 ewes, which suggests there was a bigger flock here than in the 1390s, but that its details were now accounted centrally.[87] No sheep account was kept at Hilborough after 1417, although the manorial court continued to record large numbers of sheep deaths until at least the mid-1440s.[88] Two of the demesne foldcourses were at lease for over £11 by 1469–70, but another demesne fold did exist and the manor was still expending money on shepherds and other pasture grounds, indicating that its direct interest in sheep farming was not yet over.[89]

When Bury abbey restructured sheep farming on its estates in the early fifteenth century, Breckland was ideally placed to benefit from the administrative change.[90] Whenever the Fornham (A) demesne was at lease after the 1430s no flocks are recorded in the accounts, but there are clear indications that the abbot continued to rear sheep directly.[91] Sheep vanished from the accounts only because the abbot's operations were now recorded centrally and were concentrated on large sheep farms at nearby Culford and Coney Weston.[92] The abbey's flocks were no longer widespread across its estates, but were now almost exclusively centred on

---

86 IESRO HD 1538/92 f.16.
87 Bacon 295/57.
88 NRO Hilborough Deposit Box T (Daleth), iii, and vii m.6.
89 *Ibid.*, mm.8 and 9. This administrative procedure became widespread in the fifteenth century, and so it is difficult to be certain whether many landlords had abandoned direct sheep farming or not. Norwich Cathedral Priory certainly had at Cressingham by 1485, NRO DCN 64/1.
90 The restructuring was presumably an attempt to eliminate the administrative inefficiencies which hampered large-scale rearing on other ecclesiastical estates during the same period. See, for example, Raftis, *Ramsey abbey*, p. 291.
91 For instance, in the 1453–4 account under decays of rent it was noted that the lord had occupied a peasant foldcourse, WSROB E.3/15.7/2.10.
92 A. Simpson, *The wealth of the gentry* (Cambridge, 1961), p. 184 notes that there were over 2,000 sheep on the Culford farm in this period.

Breckland pastures.[93] The same was true on the cellarer's estates.
Operations were gradually run down and then abandoned at
Mildenhall by the 1430s, but, despite leasing the demesne arable at
Elveden, Ingham, Fornham (C) and Risby, flocks were still directly
maintained there.[94] These were the cellarer's chief breeding
grounds, whence stock was then sent to the lusher Bury pastures for
fattening before it reached the monastic tables.[95] Flocks were
maintained on these manors until their sale to the Bacon family in
1537.[96]

The declining profitability of wool production affected many
landlords throughout England and not just those in Breckland.[97]
The first half of the fifteenth century was a period of contraction in
most sectors of the economy, and falling population and a tendency
to over-supply were central to the decline.[98] It is probable that
wool prices were further depressed by deteriorating yields and
disruption to foreign trade,[99] and depressed prices were accompanied by rising wage payments to shepherds.[100] It is impossible to
be certain whether demand for Breckland wool fell more severely
than for the wool of other regions, although East Anglian textile
manufacturers continued to look to local suppliers for at least some
of their wool: indeed, the thriving worsted industry of Norfolk
depended upon coarse wool such as that of Breckland.

The low costs of sheep rearing relative to arable farming still
gave it a relative advantage in the depressed years of the fifteenth
century, and after mid-century its attractiveness was enhanced by

[93] This explains the remarkable appearance of over 1,500 sheep at Fornham (A) in the
1440s. At Michaelmas 1427 there had been 580 sheep at Fornham, of which 391 were in
one fold tended by John Charyte, and the remainder were in another under the care of
Robert Polle, WSROB E.3/15.6/2.54. By 1443 there were 555 wethers at Fornham All
Saints and a further 1,691 sheep in three other local folds, WSROB E.3/15.6/2.60.
[94] BL Add.Ms 7096 f.36; WSROB A.6/1/13.
[95] Out of 575 wethers received at the Bury grange in 1480–1, 192 or 33 per cent were sent
for slaughter to the monastic kitchens, WSROB A.6/1/13.
[96] IESRO HD 1538/92 f.29.   [97] Bolton, *Medieval English economy*, pp. 228–9.
[98] Hatcher, *Plague, population*, pp. 35–47; Lloyd, *English wool trade*, p. 28.
[99] Mate, 'Pastoral farming', pp. 525–6.
[100] The old practice of remuneration by 'sheepcorn', which had been employed on some
estates, was eventually scrapped and replaced by cash payments, WSROB E.3/15.13/
2.26. On those manors where cash stipends had always been the norm, wages rose
appreciably, from 5s. to 7s. per annum at Lakenheath between 1419 and 1455, and from
5s. 4d. to 10s. at Mildenhall between 1400 and 1425, CUL EDC 7/15/I/34 and 42; BL
Add.Roll 53120 and 53135. Again, such rapidly rising wage rates are explained in terms
of a declining population and the unattractiveness of famuli employment.

the gradual recovery of wool prices.[101] There was a distinct revival
in sheep farming from the 1460s, even in predominantly arable
regions such as the Midlands, where former open-fields were now
enclosed to create large sheep pastures.[102] Although Breckland's
convertible husbandry militated against permanent conversion to
grass in this manner,[103] miscellaneous evidence reveals that the
foldcourse system underwent gradual but distinct changes during
the same period. The late fifteenth and early sixteenth centuries
were marked by a perceptible increase in presentments for illegal
commoning and overstocking with sheep, and certainly a greater
seigneurial concern to tighten control over peasant activity. These
developments enabled lords and the wealthier peasants to increase
their operations at the expense of the smallholder, and landlords
took the first major steps towards re-securing a monopoly of
foldcourses.[104] There can be no doubting the renewed activity
amongst the owners of the large foldcourses. At Risby their competing interests resulted in a string of amercements for illegal
commoning, most notably by a succession of shepherds from the
surrounding villages of Flempton, Barrow, Saxham, Lackford and
Hengrave. In June 1498 it was established that the lessee of Hakkes
tenement possessed a foldcourse for 320 sheep, but that it was
illegally stocked with 520 sheep; in 1500 there were 500 sheep in the
fold, and even in 1530 a subsequent lessee still overstocked it by 40
sheep.[105] Similarly, a number of Methwold residents owed
amercements totalling over £5 for constant commoning transgressions in Feltwell in 1488.[106] Rushford must have resembled one
large sheepwalk by the early sixteenth century; Thetford priory
kept flocks totalling 1,800 sheep there and Rushford college had
sufficient pasture for 1,000 sheep.[107] Indeed, by the 1530s Thetford
priory held flocks totalling 4,200 sheep in nine Breckland
manors.[108]

101 The revival of the wool and cloth trades in the 1460s was partly stimulated by monetary
     devaluation and the resumption of foreign trade, Mate, 'Pastoral farming', pp. 531–2.
102 M.W. Beresford, *The lost villages of England* (Lutterworth, 1954), pp. 178ff, and
     Beresford and Hurst, *Deserted medieval villages*, pp. 12ff.
103 Allison, 'Lost villages of Norfolk', pp. 131–4.
104 See above chapter 2, pp. 74–6.
105 WSROB E.3/15.13/1.1 and 1.2, courts held June 1498, October 1500, and June 1530.
106 NRO Ms 10009 m.2.   107 IESRO HD 1538/92 ff.14 and 17.
108 *Valor ecclesiasticus*, vol. III, p. 310. In the manors of Halwyke and Westwyk (Thetford),
     Illington, Thompson, Croxton, Kilverstone, Brettenham, Snareshill and Rushford
     were a total of 35 (long) hundred sheep.

The new feature of this renewed interest was that it largely excluded the mass of the peasantry, and even a cursory comparison between early fourteenth- and early sixteenth-century courts reveals a drastic change in the extent of peasant involvement in sheep farming.[109] This inevitably reflects a fall in the aggregate number of peasant sheep in Breckland. This fall was partly due to declining population and the contracting demand for wool in the early fifteenth century, but it also reflects a proportionate decline in the small peasant's contribution to the region's sheep farming. Instead, sheep farming in Breckland was becoming concentrated into the hands of the landlords and other substantial flockmasters, such as John Croft of West Stow, who was taxed at £5 in 1524 and who leased Bury abbey's Culford sheepfarm in 1525.[110] This fall is reflected in the number of peasant sheep at Lakenheath (table 5.7).

This declining peasant involvement in sheep farming was not entirely self-motivated, for manorial lords deliberately sought to accelerate the tendency. Falling numbers of peasant sheep removed the need to maintain the large, separate *falda de collecte*, and the absence of references to these in sixteenth-century documents suggests that they had been absorbed into the demesne folds. Custom still demanded that peasant sheep be folded with those of the lord, but this was increasingly obstructive and inconvenient to a lord seeking to extend his own activities. Hence there are firm indications from the late fifteenth century that landlords were imposing restrictions on the number of sheep which each peasant could keep in the demesne fold.[111]

Sheep farming continued to play a substantial part in the fifteenth-century Breckland economy, but how did dairy farming fare? Indeed, the demand for beef and dairy products was likely to have remained buoyant in the fifteenth century relative to grain farming. Despite this, demesne herds in Breckland were gradually

[109] Earlier courts could each contain at least a dozen amercements for a variety of peasant grazing irregularities involving anything from two to two hundred sheep. By the late fifteenth century, not only are the number of sheep transgressions fewer in each court, but each transgression invariably concerns the large flocks of individual foldcourse owners.

[110] Simpson, *Wealth of the gentry*, p. 187; S.H.A. Hervey, ed., *Suffolk in 1524: being the return for a subsidy granted in 1523*, Suffolk green books 10 (1910), p. 62.

[111] Hence the peasant right to keep a small and fixed number of sheep (cullet) in the lord's fold, which Allison believed to be an integral feature of the foldcourse system, was only initiated in Breckland in the late fifteenth century. See above, p. 66. For the subtle but important changes in the foldcourse system in the late fifteenth and sixteenth centuries, see M.D. Bailey, 'The evolution of the foldcourse system in the fifteenth and sixteenth centuries' (forthcoming).

Decline and recovery

Table 5.7. *Peasant sheep in Lakenheath, decennial means 1400–1500*

Decade	A/cs	Fleeces	Lambs	Total tithes	Mean flock size
1300–49	11	1,650	378	2,028	1,659
1350–99	12	1,845	494	2,339	1,754
1420–9	2	181	66	247	1,112
1430–9	2	176	117	293	1,319
1440–9	1	115	61	176	1,584
1450–9	4	343	126	469	1,055
1460–9	2	88	37	125	563
1480–9	2	124	c. 50	174	783

reduced and then sold off altogether, and those manors which did maintain a herd invariably had trouble collecting the full rents each year.[112] In part this reduction in the number of cows reflects a streamlining of the manorial economy as a prelude to demesne leasing, but it must also indicate a response to falling demand for Breckland's dairy produce. At both Lakenheath and Mildenhall the stability of the fourteenth century was succeeded by retrenchment and, after an initial reduction in the early 1400s, both herds had been sold off by mid-century.[113] In 1400 there were no cows at Fornham and a brief revival between 1404–6 brought 70s. per annum, after which dairy farming was abandoned entirely.[114] The 19-strong herd at Cressingham in 1381 had been reduced to 7 by Norwich Cathedral Priory in 1417, and by 1428 it had been sold off entirely.[115] Evidence for peasant dairy farming is extremely limited. Peasants certainly continued to keep cows, particularly in those villages on the edge of Breckland, and perhaps the contraction of demesne herds reflects an increase in the peasantry's own operations.[116] Otherwise, the decline is best explained in terms of a saturated market for dairy produce. Breckland's poor-quality pastures were not ideal for dairy farming, and in an over-supplied market it was likely to suffer the brunt of contraction.

---

[112] This was certainly the case at Lakenheath, where 51s. 9d. rent was in arrears in 1394, and 26s. 8d. in 1432, CUL EDC 7/15/I/31 and 36.

[113] CUL EDC 7/15/I/32, 34, 36 and 40. At Mildenhall in the 1380s, the cow herd was around 35-strong, but there were only 24 in 1400, BL Add.Rolls 53116–8, 53120, 53129, 53134–5.   [114] WSROB E.3/15.6/2.38, 2.42, 2.43 and 2.45.

[115] NRO DCN Supplement (R187A).

[116] Cows appear to have remained an important part of the peasant economy in Hockham, although its overall prominence was not as great as it had been in the late fourteenth century. See NRO Ms 13849, courts held February 1447, October 1449, August 1450.

In general terms, the definite shift in emphasis from arable to pastoral farming is evident from various documents. In 1443 the Lackford bailiff received £7 10s. income, of which 69 per cent was specifically for agistment or leases of meadow.[117] In Lackford and Flempton courts between 1354 and 1412, around 50 per cent of all damage/trespass amercements by animals concerned the destruction of corn, yet between 1435 and 1487 27 per cent were in corn and 54 per cent in meadow or pasture.[118] Rents for quality pastures in Mildenhall remained buoyant in the early fifteenth century, in direct contrast to rent from arable land; the leases for the pastures of Cowshepyerd, Westyndych, Holmseye and Stockmedwe totalled £5 in 1402–3, and £5 2s. 3d. in 1444–5.[119]

Whilst warren output may have started to fall in the 1390s, the fifteenth century certainly saw a decline in the commercial profitability of warrens. Landlords were no longer prepared to exploit warrens directly and leased them out as part of the general movement towards rentier farming. Underpinning this was a tendency to over-supply on the English market,[120] and the continuing rise of wages.[121] Prices, on the other hand, were reasonably stable at just under 2d per rabbit for much of the fifteenth century, although they did sag slightly in the 1450s. This stability is remarkable in a period when prices of agricultural produce in general fell considerably, and reflects the relatively high demand for the rabbit.[122] However, it could not offset the increased costs of trapping, skinning and transporting the rabbit, and the result was a drop in profit margins on the late fourteenth century (see table 5.8).

These rents might suggest that rabbiting, along with most other sectors of the English economy, suffered its worst depression around mid-century. Lakenheath and Brandon warrens fell to around two-thirds their earlier value, and a small warren at Cavenham was untenanted for want of a hirer.[123] The figures then appear to suggest recovery as early as the 1450s–60s, although it is doubtful whether this was really the case, as the stated rents were

---

[117] WSROB E.3/15.12/5.2. Some of the lessees were residents of Bury St Edmunds, who were using the abundant Breckland pastures to bolster their incomes.

[118] WSROB E.3/15.12/1.1–1.8, 1.12–1.16. [119] BL Add.Rolls 53121 and 53137.

[120] Bailey, 'Rabbit and East Anglia', pp. 13–14.

[121] For instance, the Lakenheath warrener received a flat rate of 30s. 4d. in 1355 but in 1470 he was paid 60s. 8d. and an additional sum for trapping the rabbits, CUL EDC 7/15/I/16 and 34. In 1420 he was paid an extra 2s. 6d. for every 120 rabbits culled. At Brandon in 1392–3, the warrener was paid an extra 3s. for the long hundred, Bacon 657.

[122] Bailey, 'Rabbit and East Anglia', table 2. [123] PRO sc6.1117/12.

Table 5.8. *Warren lease valuations, selected years*

Warren	Rental values £	s.	d.
Brandon			
1398–9	20	0	0
1463–4	13	6	8
1480–1	20	0	0
1494–5	20	13	6
1541–2	20	13	6
Hilborough			
1412–13	8	0	0
1469–70	12	0	0
1485–6	12	0	0
Lakenheath			
1427–8	15	0	0
1442–3	12	0	0
1455–6	15	0	0
1481–2	10	0	0
1487–8	18	0	0
1540–1	20	0	0
Mildenhall			
1400–1	4	13	6
1407–8	5	0	0
1412–13	4	0	0
1444–5	2	6	8
1467–8	4	0	0
1539–40	5	0	0

Sources: Brandon, Bacon 663, 664, 675, 687 and 696; Hilborough, NRO Hilborough Deposit Box T (Daleth) vii, mm.5, 9 and 18 – the 1412–13 rent was actually 53s. 4d. 'for the farm of a third part of the warren'; Lakenheath, CUL EDC 7/15/I/35, 39, 42, 47 and 48, and EDC 1.C.3; Mildenhall, BL Add.Rolls 53120, 53124, 53130, 53137 and 53139, and Redstone, 'First minister's account', pp. 347–8.

seldom paid in full. For instance, Lakenheath warren rose in value to £15 in the 1450s, but the farmer actually paid only £7 in 1451 and £11 in 1459.[124] Arrears were particularly troublesome at Brandon. Robert George, the lessee, paid the full rent during the 1470s, which encouraged the Bishopric of Ely to increase it in 1480. George promptly defaulted on payment, running up substantial arrears by the 1490s, and as late as 1530 a different lessee still only paid half the required annual rent.[125]

Yet, despite these difficulties, the rabbit constituted a large proportion of seigneurial revenue on those manors where it had become well established. Excluding arrears, the warren lease comprised 33 per cent of potential manorial income at Brandon between 1400 and 1550, 21 per cent at Lakenheath in 1487, and 35 per cent at Methwold in 1480.[126] In absolute terms the rabbit was unable to generate the same levels of income as in the late fourteenth century, but its relative importance remained undiminished on some manors. There is an obvious paradox here. The rabbit was still an expensive and therefore rare commodity, whose steady price in a deflationary period reflects the development of new and wider markets for its fur and meat.[127] Yet the continuing fall in warren income in the fifteenth century would suggest that the opposite was true, and that opportunities for rabbit rearing had contracted drastically. How do we explain this conflicting evidence?

As there is no doubt that the market for rabbit remained reasonably buoyant in the fifteenth century, then the most likely explanation for this paradox is that the warren as a means of rabbit production fell in value. The drop in warren rents can partly be explained in terms of the general contraction of rents in the fifteenth century. As the tenant position grew stronger relative to the landlord in the fifteenth century, and as rental opportunities increased and diversified, so there occurred a general slippage of rents, which would have affected warren values. These values were further depressed by the rabbit population's slow but inexorable rise. For much of the fourteenth century, nearly all of Breckland's rabbits lived within the seigneurial warrens, but after the 1370s their demographic increase inevitably led to the colonisation of a

[124] CUL EDC 7/15/I/41 and 43.   [125] Bacon 657–90, and 695.
[126] *Ibid.*; CUL EDC 7/15/I/48; PRO DL29.295/4847.
[127] Bailey, 'Rabbit and East Anglia', pp. 13 and 15.

wider habitat, and this broke the warrens' monopoly of supply and consequently undermined their value.

'Wild' colonies became more common throughout Breckland in the fifteenth century, although they still failed to penetrate into the boulder clays of central East Anglia or the fens. Where rabbits had colonised land close to the original warren boundary, landlords sought to absorb it within the warren area. In 1425 William Gaylon was granted 18 acres by Bury abbey in recompense for his own arable lands *'que iacent infra warrenam'* of Mildenhall.[128] At Lakenheath in 1458 10.25 acres of long abandoned molland were officially absorbed within the warren area, and a similar fate befell an undisclosed amount of tenant land in Brandon in the 1490s.[129] Such a trend is significant, for not only does it indicate an attempt to preserve the warren's monopoly, but it reveals a seigneurial willingness to forego tenant rents and convert land to more productive use.

As rabbits continued to settle outside the warrens in the fifteenth century, so the warren values slipped further. Why should lessees pay substantial rents for warrens, when the warrens themselves were no longer the exclusive sources of rabbit supply? The wild colonies were still theoretically protected by the free-warren charter, but in practical terms it was almost impossible for the lord to impose his rights outside the protection of the warren, and so peasant access to the animal became much easier. The Duchy of Lancaster tried to charge 10s. for the right to take rabbits from a wild colony in Weeting (presumably spawned from Methwold warren) in 1414, but abandoned the idea soon afterwards.[130] Elsewhere, the spread of rabbits was causing increasing damage to crops. In 1404 the vicar of Tottington complained that the value of his tithes had been impaired by the spread of rabbits from John FitzRauf's warren.[131] Such protestations should be treated with some reservation, although even the sceptical auditors at Lakenheath conceded that 21 per cent of the demesne seeded area was destroyed by rabbits in 1420.[132] Yet there is no doubt that the problem had become worse by the early sixteenth century. An

[128] WSROB E.18/451/4, court held May 1425.   [129] CUL EDC 7/15/I/43; Bacon 687.
[130] PRO DL29.290/4765 and 4774. See Bailey, 'Rabbit and East Anglia', p. 14.
[131] Blomfield, vol. 1, p. 618.
[132] Of 155 acres sown that year, 24 acres of oats and 9 acres of rye were destroyed by rabbits, CUL EDC 7/15/I/34. In the same year, a Brandon tenant was pardoned his *relevio* on 40 acres of arable land because of the damage caused by rabbits, Bacon 294/15, court held June 1420.

inquisition at Methwold in 1522 declared that there were '7 or 8 score acres lond of late yeres past tylled and sowen and now enhabitt with conyes . . . they be so gretly encresid', and in 1563 Kennett warren and heath was 'well replenished with Coneys'.[133] At Freckenham in 1549 the warren lessee was ordered 'to destroy the rabbits that have burrowed in the common' and two years later the rabbits were described as *crescentes et multiplicantes in communa*.[134]

Another factor which undermined the value of the warren was the increasing popularity and sophistication of poaching. In response to this, the poaching statute of 1389 was reiterated in 1419.[135] Not only are court rolls much more explicit about the methods of poachers, but by mid-century the size of amercements levied on them had risen appreciably, sometimes to remarkable levels. In the 1460s the Bishopric of Ely amerced four Thetford and Downham men a total of £21 for their activities in Brandon warren, and Thomas Church of Risby was fined £10 by the Lackford court 'as an example to other malfactors' in 1516.[136] Other poachers increasingly preferred to operate in large gangs. These gangs were not merely a haphazard collection of individual poachers, but represented a deliberate and conscious pooling of experience and resources. They were well organised and ruthless, used their own nets, ferrets and dogs and were armed with an impressive array of weaponry.[137] Court officials of the Duchy of Lancaster tried to clamp down on the activities of two gangs in Methwold and Thetford in 1425 by raiding a number of local houses. They were evidently well informed, because the next court presented that a variety of nets and poaching accessories had been found.[138] Many members of these gangs were also engaged in specialist occupations, such as the bakers, weavers, fishermen, 'warners', shepherds and hostelers operating in Downham warren

---

[133] PRO DL43.7/28; WSROB 339/5. Indeed, Rogers, *History of agriculture and prices*, vol. IV, p. 717, comments that the price of rabbit rose more slowly than those of other goods in the sixteenth century, indicating that it had become more common.

[134] *'Facere destructionem cuniculorum habent foramina in communa ibidem ubi tenentes debent habere communicam suam pro averiis suis'*, WSROB 613/686/1, courts held October 1549 and October 1551.   [135] *Rotuli parliamentorum (1278–1503)*, vol. IV, pp. 121–2.

[136] Bacon 668; WSROB E.3/15.12/1.17.

[137] One Thetford gang operating in Downham warren in the 1440s was armed *'cum jakkis et salettis arcibus et sagittis'* whilst others poached *'cum fustibus et baculis'*, WSROB 651/31/4.

[138] PRO DL30.103/1423. At Thetford they found *'pursnettes furettes et alia ingenia ad capiend' cuniculos'*. Searches of this kind were still commonplace in the eighteenth century, Hay, *Albion's fatal tree*, p. 241.

in the 1440s.[139] The role of hostelers as co-ordinators of poaching operations should not be underestimated, for the contacts established in their trade enabled them to recruit strangers to work with the gangs. In most cases, certain members of each gang were known to court officials, but they were nearly always accompanied '*cum pluriis aliis ignotis*'. By drawing upon strangers, gangs gained not only an element of anonymity which reduced their chances of capture, but also a number of widespread and distant dispersal points for the stolen rabbits to reduce suspicion.[140]

It is possible to perceive in the formation of these gangs an element of Hobsbawm's social banditry, where criminal activities are regarded as an expression of social grievance.[141] Indeed, the rabbit was a very tangible reflection of the lord's legal and social superiority and would therefore appear an ideal object for this expression. John of Gaunt, an unpopular figure who was sought by the London rebels in 1381, was also Duke of Lancaster, and his East Anglian warrens were attacked in 1363.[142] They were again the target of violent assault during the 1381 uprising, when numerous rabbits were taken.[143] Indeed, a rabbit was strung up on the abbey gates at St Albans to signify the end of seigneurial privilege in 1381, and rabbit damage was cited as a source of friction in Kett's rebellion in 1549.[144] The connection between social protest and poaching is also evident in the case of Richard Shrogger, who detained rents and services at Methwold, and was a known poacher.[145] Yet the strong economic motivation of these gangs is apparent from the records, and rivalry between gangs was sometimes more powerful than emnity towards the warren owners. An Elveden gang operated extensively in Brandon and Downham warrens in the 1440s, but on 19 September 1445 clashed with a Thetford gang in Downham warren. The Thetford gang attacked three of the Elveden group 'and wounded them and led them

139 WSROB 651/31/3 and 4. In August 1440, Robert Myot of Brandon, weaver, Richard Alvon, shepherd, and John Howes, hosteler, were poaching. In Brandon, Robert Starlyng, barker, was caught poaching, Bacon 295/64.
140 There is no doubt that poaching gangs could be very effective. Four men from Thetford, Hargham and Ashby congregated with an unknown mob in Hockham warren on the night of 10 October 1448, and escaped with no less than 600 rabbits, NRO Ms 13849, court held February 1449.
141 E.J. Hobsbawm, *Bandits* (London, 1969), pp. 13–23. For the social role of game in the eighteenth century, see Hay, *Albion's fatal tree*, pp. 244–53.
142 *CPR*, 1361–4, p. 373.   143 *CPR*, 1381–5, p. 144.
144 Bailey, 'Rabbit and East Anglia', p. 18.
145 PRO DL30.104/1469 mm.3 and 4.

without licence to the town of Thetford and there unjustly impris-
oned them'.[146]

The accumulation of substantial arrears on the payment of
warren leases does not necessarily reflect depressed demand for the
rabbit. The large annual rents demanded for some warrens were
undoubtedly justified in normal years, but the rabbit population
could fluctuate enormously, even over short periods. So there was
no guarantee that a lessee could cull enough stock to raise the price
of the lease, and a run of bad years could prove disastrous.[147] The
problem was illustrated at Methwold warren, where in 19 years
between 1431 and 1467 it was only possible to cull rabbits on eleven
occasions.[148] Disease was a perennial problem, and although most
accounts are frustratingly silent about its nature and incidence,
references to murrain are more common in the late fifteenth
century. It certainly appears to have been an important factor in the
accumulation of arrears at Brandon in the 1480s and 1490s. In 1483
the warrener was pardoned his rent arrears because of murrain
amongst his stock, and in 1491 a further £11 1s. 5d. was allowed,
due to 'a great mortality in the winter'.[149] Hence landlords could
not take too severe an attitude towards arrears, for an intransigent
creditor might force a desperate lessee to cull dangerously large
amounts of stock to meet his debts, and thus threaten the very
existence of the colony. Indeed, in 1455–6 the Methwold auditors
explained that no rabbits were culled because of the need to
maintain the warren's stock.[150] Even as rentier farmers, landlords
had to manage their warrens with great care.

The fishing industry suffered from drastically declining fortunes
for much of the century, although this was equally true of a growth
centre like Bury and not a characteristic unique to Breckland.[151] In
1419–20, nine fishery leases at Lakenheath remained in the lord's

---

146 WSROB 651/31/4; '*verberaverunt et vulneraverunt et eos ab inde sine licencia duxerunt usque
ad villam de Thetford et ibidem eos iniuste . . . imprisonerunt*'. Two of the Elveden gang, John
Downing and William Fleming, had been amerced £4 for similar offences in Brandon
warren, Bacon 295/35, court held August 1442.
147 For instance, the bitterly cold winter of 1434–5 killed off many rabbits, and some
warrens had to be entirely restocked, Bailey, 'Rabbit and East Anglia', p. 9. Even in the
large Methwold warren, no rabbits could be culled until 1438, NRO NRS 11336; PRO
DL29.292/4798.
148 Accounts in series PRO DL29.291/4790 to DL29.295/4846.
149 Bacon 677 and 683. At Lakenheath in 1458–9 the warren lessee was allowed £4 because
of murrain, CUL EDC 7/15/I/43.
150 PRO DL29.294/4831.   151 Gottfried, *Bury and the urban crisis*, p. 114.

hands for want of a hirer.[152] By 1427 the Prior and Convent of Ely
had at least managed to find tenants for most of them, but only at
vastly reduced rents.[153] Annual income from fisheries averaged a
paltry 65s. during the century, a mere 20 per cent of the income
received between 1355 and 1376. At Brandon the fishery maintained its late fourteenth-century valuation of 53s. 4d., but by
1478–9 the manorial auditors accepted that lessees were in fact only
prepared to pay 40s. each year, and this had dropped further to 26s.
8d. in 1541–2.[154] Gottfried's explanation for the collapse of fishing
at Bury is that the intensive activities of fullers and dyers polluted
the waters of the Lark.[155] A more plausible explanation might be
that demand for local fish fell faster than demand for fish in general,
although this is difficult to prove. The abject collapse of the breck-
fen leases is surprising and contrasts with evidence from other
regions,[156] which may suggest that in Breckland demand for
fisheries themselves fell faster than demand for the fish in them.
Indeed there were two distinct processes serving to undermine the
value of fisheries in the fifteenth century, both of which were based
on declining seigneurial authority. Court rolls from all breck-fen
villages contain persistent references to illegal fishing in demesne
waters, and reveal the use of a wide range of sophisticated fish-nets
and traps.[157] Secondly, both commoners and fishery lessees were
increasingly amerced for failing to maintain fen drainage channels
and fisheries adequately. In 1415 John Geve was accused of not
scouring his Lakenheath fishery during the previous eight years and
in the following year all lessees were ordered to scour their fisheries

---

[152] They included the fisheries of Millemarche, Blakmore, Crouchstamp, Reedfen,
Saxwarp, Plantslode, Rovenee and nine botesgangs, CUL EDC 7/15/I/34.
[153] For instance, Saxwarp had fetched 16s. in the 1360s, but only 2s. for much of the
fifteenth century, whilst Crouchestamp fetched 30s. in the 1360s, 8s. in 1431–2, 4s. in
1451–2 and was abandoned four years later, CUL EDC 7/15/I/36, 40 and 42.
[154] Bacon 674 and 696.   [155] Gottfried, *Bury and the urban crisis*, p. 114.
[156] Demand for fish grew in the west Midlands in the fifteenth century, Dyer, *Lords and
peasants*, pp. 344–5.
[157] In November 1417, a number of Hockwold men were fishing illegally in Lakenheath,
and in 1455–6 the same village was amerced £6 13s. 4d. for similar offences, CUL EDC
7/15/II/Box 3/H.V m.9 and 7/15/I/42. At Northwold, the Bishopric of Ely struggled to
prevent regular incursions to its fisheries by men from Didlington, NRO Ms 18630,
court held December 1425. At Mildenhall, fishermen were constructing dams within
the fisheries and depositing 'leepes' (probably sedge baskets lowered into the
water), WSROB E.18/451/5, court held July 1462 and E.18/451/6, court held July 1481.
Brandon men were using 'hyves' to catch fish, and at Mildenhall Nicholas Willis '*trahit
cum rethe voc' a drake*', Bacon 295/24, court held December 1434 and WSROB E.18/451/
69, court held August 1525.

before 24 June, and in 1421 fifteen men were urged to remove overgrown grass from fisheries;[158] by this time few fisheries were leased without extensive wastage clauses. So the value of fisheries fell not just because of falling market demand for local fish, but because the fisheries themselves were increasingly ill-kept and overgrown, and because peasants were illegally plundering stocks.

TRADE

Declining production inevitably resulted in a fall in trade to levels below that of the later fourteenth century. Sales of turves and sedge in particular were still important, but no longer occupied large numbers of cottars and landless. In one Lakenheath court in 1328, fourteen men had been amerced for illegally selling turves, but in the whole of Henry V's reign only four men were thus indicted.[159] Brewing became concentrated into fewer hands (see table 4.17), and in many villages there were seldom more than one or two regular brewers: fewer people now resorted to brewing for subsistence purposes. Victualling remained important in the larger villages, and consumers were increasingly accustomed to drinking their ale and beer in designated ale-houses. Gambling grew in popularity in many of these establishments, emphasising the potential impact of high real wages on leisure pursuits. There were, however, some attempts to regulate this, and ale-houses in Brandon were scrutinised in the later fifteenth century as part of a wider concern over public order and the behaviour of the poor.[160]

The number of stalls at leasehold in Mildenhall market recovered temporarily in the early fifteenth century, rising from 11 in 1386 to 13 in 1410 after the cellarer of Bury abbey had ordered the construction of 7 new stalls at a cost of 10s. 8d. (table 5.9).[161] By mid-century, however, the numbers had fallen off sharply, and in 1465 it was noted that five stalls yielded no rent 'because they had been thrown down and were unoccupied'.[162] There might well have been a slight recovery in Breckland's trade in the 1410s, for

---

[158] CUL EDC 7/15/II/Box 3/H.V mm.7, 8 and 18, courts held December 1415, June 1416 and June 1421.

[159] CUL EDC 7/15/II/Box 1/8 m.16, court held November 1328; and Box 3/H.V.

[160] Bacon 297/12 and 14. See also McIntosh, 'Local change and community control in England', pp. 230–3.

[161] The new stalls were constructed in 1409–10, BL Add.Roll 53126.

[162] BL Add.Roll 53138. This was a familiar experience in many English markets around this time, see below, p. 307.

Table 5.9. *Leases of stalls in Mildenhall market, 1385–1465*

Year	Number of stalls	Total rent		Mean rent per stall
		s.	d.	d.
1385–6	11	10	7	11½
1400–1	11	9	8	10½
1410–11	13	16	10	15½
1417–18	7	8	5	14⅓
1444–5	3	4		16
1464–5	2	2		12

Sources: BL Add.Rolls 53118, 53120, 53127, 53133, 53137 and 53138.

Table 5.10. *The farm of tolls at Thetford, decennial means 1410–89*

Decade	Total farm received		Number of accounts	Decennial mean	
	s.	d.		s.	d.
1410–19	240	0	1	240	0
1420–9	663	9	5	132	9
1430–9	848	6	6	141	5
1440–9	560	0	4	140	0
1450–9	380	0	3	126	8
1460–9	646	8	5	129	4
1480–9	133	4	1	133	4

Sources: accounts in series PRO DL29.290/4765 − DL29.295/4847.

£12 was received for the farm of tolls over various Thetford bridges in 1414, which was 16 per cent higher than it had been in 1360.[163] The level of these tolls corresponds broadly to the volume of trade passing through Thetford, although rising administrative costs undermined the attractiveness of the farm to potential lessees and also contributed to its declining value during the century (table 5.10).[164]

---

[163] PRO DL29.288/4720 and 290/4765.
[164] There were similar tolls levied at Colchester, and these too slumped in the later fourteenth century. For a discussion of the causes behind this, see Britnell, *Colchester*, p. 249.

The Duchy of Lancaster continued to rebuild some stalls which had fallen into disrepair in the fifteenth century,[165] but it was not enough to offset the overall decline of Thetford market. There was also a fall in revenue from the market court; in 1434–5, 42 courts were held during the year and produced 43s. 2d., but in 1479–80 just 5 courts rendered 16s.[166] The root cause of this decline in income was undoubtedly the general contraction of trade, but at Thetford the problem was exacerbated by the town's location. The Little Ouse was only just navigable beyond Brandon, and, with less incentive to dredge the river in the fifteenth century, the passage of boats to the town became more difficult, so that even a moderate drought like that of 1462–3 could disrupt its trade.[167] Under such circumstances, it appears that Brandon, lying nine miles downriver, began to capture an increasing proportion of Thetford's trade. The Duchy of Lancaster possessed tollage rights over Brandon bridge, but in 1433 its officials tried to levy a wider range of tolls on 'diverse men from Bury St Edmunds' and 'diverse men of the countryside [*de patrie*]' trading in Brandon market.[168] In 1475 the bailiff of Thetford was again indicted in Brandon's court rolls for illegally collecting 'tolls and customs' from traders there, presumably in an attempt to recoup lost business.[169] None of these efforts were likely to have met with any success, and by the early sixteenth century much of Thetford's market activity involved the servicing of its ecclesiastical houses.[170]

This is not to argue that the breck-fen edge was immune from the general slump. As the overall level of trade receded, so many staithes became surplus to requirements, and in 1470 'lordstathe' in Brandon lay abandoned in the lord's hands because no tenant could be found.[171] Furthermore, the failure to maintain fenland ditches and waterways noted earlier also affected the network of lodes, and many became increasingly overgrown and inaccessible. Some of the smaller village markets must have become defunct in this period, although there are indications that both Hilborough and

---

[165] See, for example, PRO DL29.294/4844, when 2s. was spent on repairing two fish stalls.

[166] PRO DL29.292/4793 and DL29.295/4847.   [167] PRO DL29.294/4842.

[168] Bacon 295/22, court held August 1433.

[169] Bacon 296/25, court held March 1475. By the early seventeenth century, Brandon was an important inland port serving west Suffolk and Norfolk. In 1624, for instance, 2,880 stones of high-quality wool were shipped into Brandon from Boston via Lynn: P.J. Bowden, *The wool trade in Tudor and Stuart England* (London, 1962), p. 65.

[170] Thetford priory, for instance, regularly contracted local craftsmen to dye, full and shear cloth, Harvey, 'Thetford priory', pp. 18–19.

[171] Bacon 295/57, illegible date in 1470–1.

Hockham markets were still functional in mid-century.[172] Such manifest signs of contraction were inevitable given the considerable demographic decline of the later Middle Ages, but it is important to establish whether Breckland's decline was more pronounced than in other areas, and if trade per capita fell in the fifteenth century. Once again it seems that although there was decline in aggregate terms, Breckland fared no worse than many other English markets.[173] It was by no means uncommon for markets to become redundant, which happened throughout Norfolk, and even trading activity in cloth towns such as Sudbury and Clare fell rapidly in the early fifteenth century.[174]

Unfortunately, extant documentation offers no direct indication whether per capita trade declined, but it is perhaps significant that Breckland's trading links did not weaken. Intercourse between central villages and the principal markets continued, and merchants from more distant places continued to regard a trip to Breckland markets as worthwhile, for there was no weakening of links with Lynn merchants.[175] The Thetford bridge tolls also suggest that trade began to pick up slowly after a mid-century nadir, a suggestion reinforced by profits of the Mildenhall fair which fell from 27s. 3d. in 1412 to 22s. 2d. in 1464, but were valued at 30s. in 1539.[176]

The resilience of Breckland's trading links at once encouraged and sustained the regional specialisation in wool, rabbits and malting barley, but another factor was the continued success of the East Anglian textile industry. The fourteenth-century production boom had certainly been checked by the early fifteenth century, but thereafter output rose to new heights in many villages by the sixteenth century.[177] Whilst Gottfried may have overstated the demand for food and raw materials in Bury, it still remained a

---

[172] An unknown merchant was the victim of a theft at Hilborough, NRO Hilborough Deposit Box T (Daleth), iii, court held March 1434. A house in Hockham was identified as 'lying in the market' in October 1462, NRO Ms 13850.

[173] See, for instance, Reynolds, *English medieval towns*, chapter 7.

[174] Dymond, *Norfolk landscape*, p. 162; Britnell, *Colchester*, p. 190.

[175] There are numerous examples of Lynn merchants operating in Brandon market throughout the fifteenth century. In 1452 John Styflin *'de Lynn Episcopi, marchant'* is mentioned, as is John Lister of Lynn, Bacon 295/55 and 56. See also John Stevenson and Robert Leystocke of Lynn, Bacon 295/19 and 296/6, courts held October 1431 and August 1465.

[176] BL Add.Rolls 53130 and 53128; Redstone, 'Minister's account of St Edmunds', pp. 547–8.

[177] For the check in production at Colchester, see Britnell, *Colchester*, chapter 3. See also Pilgrim, 'The cloth industry in East Anglia', p. 253; Dymond and Betterton, *Lavenham*, pp. 6–8.

Table 5.11. *Annual rental value of the Lackford fulling mill, 1396–1512*

	Rental value		
Year	£	s.	d.
1396–7	6	6	8
1400–1	4	5	8
n.d., c.1420	5	0	0
1487–8	6	13	4
1512	7	6	8

Sources: WSROB E.3/15.12/2.2 and 2.3; E.3/15.52/3.1; E.3/15.12/3.5; 449/2/336.

lucrative market for Breckland produce in a difficult period, and the interest in sheep farming indicates continued demand for local wool. The fortunes of Breckland's own cloth producers are impossible to establish. Textile workers are certainly mentioned more frequently in fifteenth-century documents, but this might reflect the scribes' greater attention to personal details rather than a genuine rise. Although output was unlikely to have risen as rapidly as in the late fourteenth century, there are indirect signs that production continued to flourish. Whereas the rental value of fulling mills fell in many areas of England, demand for the mill at Lackford recovered strongly after slipping early in the century (table 5.11).[178] A number of Flemish and Brabantine workers also settled in the region in the fifteenth century, notably at Brandon, Fornham, Hengrave, Swaffham and Thetford, locations which strongly suggest that the immigrants were involved with the textile industry.[179] Many of the aliens recorded as living in Suffolk in 1440–1 had settled in the cloth villages of Babergh hundred or in the coastal ports, but there were also a number in Breckland. James Webster of Fakenham, Dutchman, and James Dutchman of Coney Weston were almost certainly weavers, whilst Henry Dutchman of

[178] Compare these fortunes with the fulling mills on the Percy estates at Cockermouth, where rents fell by 50 per cent between 1437 and 1470, Bean, *Percy estates*, p. 23. Fulling mills in Derbyshire underwent decline after 1380, I.S.W. Blanchard, 'Industrial employment and the rural land market 1380–1520', in *Land, kinship and life-cycle*, ed. Smith, p. 231. [179] *CPR*, 1429–36, pp. 561, 569, 573 and 575.

Mildenhall was explicitly designated as such.[180] Likewise, John Wolfe 'ducheman' of Northwold, was implicated in the theft of linen cloths in the village in December 1431.[181] It would appear that the production of linen remained popular in the fifteenth century. For example, Richard Tanne of Illington and five other men were amerced for retting hemp and linen in special pits in Hockham in 1442.[182]

THE CONTRACTION OF VILLAGES

The agricultural recession, and the continuing fall in population, inevitably meant that fifteenth-century villages became physically smaller, although this was true of all villages regardless of the quality of their soil.[183] By 1544 Chippenham had 'empty crofts and shrunken streets', and in Culford 13 out of 43 probable house sites were described as '*quondam edificatum*' in 1435.[184] In Forncett much of this decay had occurred before 1420 but in many Breckland villages the later fifteenth century was the period of greatest contraction.[185] Lackford courts between 1402 and 1412 dealt with an average of around 2.5 cases of wasted tenements per court, and nearer 4.5 cases in courts held between 1438 and 1487. Many of these cases were presentments threatening hefty fines if decayed buildings were not amended, but the court's bark was louder than its bite and heavy penalties were not often imposed. Landlords attempted to enforce maintenance of peasant buildings because decayed tenements inevitably reduced the capital value of the manor, but the harsh reality was that tenants could allow their houses to dilapidate with impunity, for a tenant failing to maintain his buildings was better than no tenant at all.

Direct action on dilapidated houses through the courts proved largely in vain, and so landlords adopted more practical inducements to maintain buildings. The most successful method was to provide financial aid, and at Fornham in 1402–3 a carpenter

---

[180] PRO E179.180/92.   [181] NRO Ms 18630.
[182] NRO Ms 13849, court held January 1442.
[183] For instance, of those houses standing in the late thirteenth century at Walsham-le-Willows, over half had disappeared 250 years later, Dymond, 'Walsham-le-Willows', p. 200. See also P. Warner, 'Greens, commons and clayland colonization: the origins and development of green-side settlement in east Suffolk', *Occasional papers, Department of Local History, Leicester University*, fourth series, 2 (1987), pp. 38–43.
[184] Spufford, 'Chippenham', p. 31; BL Add.Ms 42055 ff.39–41.
[185] Davenport, *Development of a Norfolk manor*, p. 104.

received 34s. to repair a house on Gunne's tenement and to rebuild one on Move's tenement.[186] By this time it was common for most land transactions involving buildings to contain waste clauses where landlords offered to provide thatch and timber if tenants promised to undertake regular repairs. On other occasions landlords were prepared to waive entry fines if the tenant guaranteed to repair buildings within an agreed period.[187] However, not all these inducements were successful, for the Brandon jurors complained that Thomas Noteman possessed a dilapidated tenement in 1421 despite having received 30s. and some timber from the bailiff for its repair.[188]

Despite seigneurial efforts, cases of wastage became ever more numerous in the fifteenth century and houses continued to fall into disuse, to be replaced by empty tofts.[189] To quantify and locate the exact areas of contraction in many villages is an impossible task from documentary evidence, but they all bore the scars of recession.[190] At Lackford four tenements were utterly decayed and abandoned in 1467 and four others were in urgent need of repair.[191] The April court of 1486 was dominated by nine wastage cases, including one that involved John Fletcher who was now keeping cows on the site of his cottage.[192] Dymond believes that house losses incurred in this period are still discernible in Icklingham, and indeed in 1459 Walter Owghey used a part of a ruined tenement as pasture.[193] The Mildenhall rental of 1500–1 is littered with references to 'empty places', including a number of empty plots in the market-place.[194] The decay of buildings was not restricted to peasant houses, for the extensive manorial complexes constructed in the heyday of direct farming were inappropriate to the economic conditions of the fifteenth century. A deed of 1426

---

[186] WSROB E.3/15.6/2.39b.

[187] John Warlworth was pardoned the entry fine on a Brandon cottage on condition that he rebuild it within two years, Bacon 296/22, court held September 1474. This was common enough in England: see, for example, Jones, 'Bedfordshire', p. 174, and Faith, 'Berkshire', p. 186. [188] Bacon 294/16, court held June 1421.

[189] When John Hobet entered a Brandon holding in 1448 he complained that the original cottage had disappeared, and so a new rent was negotiated for the vacant plot where it had once stood, Bacon 295/48, court held September 1448.

[190] Although Alan Davison is presently field-walking many Breckland sites, and his published results should prove instructive. [191] WSROB E.3/15.12/1.7.

[192] WSROB E.3/15.12/1.8.

[193] Dymond, 'Suffolk landscape', p. 22; WSROB E.3/10/9.8 f.2.

[194] WSROB E.18/400/1.3. Nor was this the end of the contraction, for in 1528 fourteen men were under penalty to repair five ruined tenements in Millestrete, two in Calklane, three in Eststrete and four in Westende, E.18/451/69 f.76.

reveals that the manor house at Flempton had disappeared leaving a vacant plot, and a similar fate befell Lackford manor.[195] In 1467 the court reported '*per inspectionem et considerationem*' that the manorial centre was totally devastated as in 'halls, chambers, granges, hedges, ditches and houses'.[196]

How much did the migration of peasants contribute to the contraction of Breckland villages, and is there evidence from the fifteenth century that they were now moving in search of more responsive soils? A house in Lakenheath certainly collapsed because its last tenant, Peter Everard, had abandoned it and moved to Bury St Edmunds, but other references linking dilapidation with migration are rare.[197] The decay of buildings in Breckland was more a function of demographic and agricultural decline than of peasant migration.[198] Permanent migration from manors continued to be a problem throughout East Anglia, and, although it was still no worse in Breckland than anywhere else, officials must have found difficulty keeping track of migrants and perhaps even failed to record their departure.[199] This might explain why many fifteenth-century Breckland courts are rather uninformative about the migration of tenants and their destination. Yet the available information indicates that migrants were still lured by the pull of urban centres. Bury apparently sustained its population by absorbing rural immigrants, and the town was undoubtedly a magnet for Breckland residents.[200] In the 1460s three Kilverstone women settled there, one of whom, Katherine Sadde, married a successful fuller.[201] Two Downham men even moved as far afield as Norwich in 1448, and from Lakenheath Alice Snype and William Dod settled in Lynn, and two others in Ely.[202]

The pattern of fifteenth-century migration was similar to that of the fourteenth, in that movement to other Breckland villages was more common than to villages outside the region. For instance, one inhabitant of Kilverstone had moved to Carbrooke (Norfolk) in the early 1460s, but others had settled in Bridgham, Cressingham

---

[195] WSROB 449/2/76.   [196] WSROB E.3/15.12/1.7.
[197] CUL EDC 7/15/II/Box 3/H.V. m.13.
[198] Changes in agriculture were certainly an important factor in the dilapidation of buildings — as the average size of peasant holdings rose and aggregate agrarian output declined, so fewer houses and farm buildings were required.
[199] This is implicit in a Fornham court order for the homage to draw up a list '*de aliis nativis fugativis*', WSROB E.3/15.7/1.11, court held October 1395.
[200] Gottfried, *Bury and the urban crisis*, pp. 67–70.   [201] NRO Ms 15166 m.1 and 4.
[202] WSROB 651/31/5, court held September 1448; CUL EDC 7/15/II/Box 3/H.V. mm.1 and 15.

Parva, Mildenhall and Thetford.[203] Many of the named emigrants were related to one another, and so it would appear that personal or family reasons were important motives for migration in Breckland. Thus, five members of the Ferthing family of Hilborough had all left to settle in nearby Holme Hale and Soham Toney.[204] However, the movement of people was not just in one direction, and a number of men were repeatedly amerced for settling in Brandon and Mildenhall without joining a tithing.[205] In fact Breckland's main problem was the seasonal – not permanent – migration of labour, presumably in search of higher wages. At Brandon in 1407 two men were amerced 6s. 8d. because they 'procured various labourers out of the demesne during the harvest when it was possible to occupy them in the same demesne', and at Mildenhall jurors complained that carpenters, thatchers and labourers resident in the village were accepting work 'in other villages when the men of the same village of Mildenhall wished to have them in their employment'.[206]

The view that Breckland did not suffer mass emigration in the later Middle Ages is substantiated by documentary research into its 'lost villages', which suggests that the case for fifteenth-century desertion has been overstated: villages contracted, but it was rare for them to disappear from the landscape entirely. This conclusion is drawn, not from any explicit, written evidence of village disappearance in the fifteenth century, but from the rather negative knowledge that villages continued to exist in later centuries. Archaeological research may eventually reveal more detailed evidence about the extent of village depopulation in this period, but meanwhile it is impossible to date desertions with certainty. There is some circumstantial evidence that a few villages were depopulated to the point of extinction in this century, particularly in those parts of Norfolk Breckland which had sustained the most rapid expansion in the late Saxon period. Hence it might appear that

---

[203] NRO Ms 15166 mm.1–2.

[204] NRO Hilborough Deposit Box T (Daleth), iii, court held November 1434.

[205] There were six men in Brandon in December 1434, but not in a tithing, Bacon 295/23. See also Bacon 295/7, 296/2 and 296/5, where one such man was Thomas Clerk, 'wever'. Amongst those similarly amerced at Mildenhall in October 1425 were three men with suggestive surnames of Fuller, Barker and Smith, WSROB E.18/451/3. See also E.18/451/5, court held July 1467.

[206] Bacon 293/17, court held November 1407 states '*procurant diversos laboratores extra dominicum tempore autumpnum dum possunt occupari infra istud dominicum*'. At Mildenhall, '*in aliis villis . . . dum homines eiusdem ville de Mildenhall voluit ipsos habere in suis operibus*', WSROB E.18/451/5, court held July 1462.

Buckenham Parva, Cleythorpe, Colveston, Hockham Parva, Lynford, Snarehill, Santon and Thorpe suffered such a fate.[207] In Suffolk Breckland, where settlement was altogether less dense than in Norfolk, the only possible example of medieval desertion is at Eriswell, where a small hamlet to the north of the present village's site was abandoned.[208]

The desertion of a medieval village is often taken as the most comprehensive sign of economic recession, a confirmation that agricultural output has reached its nadir. In some cases this is so, but historians may have paid too much attention to the fate of a settlement and not enough to that of its agriculture. For instance, evidence from seventeenth- and eighteenth-century Breckland (detailed in chapter 2) has shown clearly that the disappearance of a village does not always herald the demise of agricultural activity, but is often a symptom of agrarian reorganisation. The same could also be true for the Middle Ages. For instance, in 1551 it was recorded that 'ther is nether Church nor Chappell' at Santon, which would seem to strengthen the case for its desertion.[209] Yet neither the community nor its economy was defunct, for the same document admitted that 'neverthelis the sayed Bartillimew dothe yerely receave the tythe of certeyne pasture grounde ther in the tenure of Petre Role', and a Thetford account of 1480 noted that one Roger Calecross 'de Saunton' held a fish stall in the market.[210] This point is also relevant for other villages supposedly 'lost' in this period. Thetford priory kept 840 sheep on Lynford's pastures in the late fifteenth century, there was a sizeable rabbit-warren at Snarehill, and the corn mill at Buckenham was still at lease in 1486 for the healthy rent of £5 6s. 8d.[211]

---

[207] Allison, 'Lost villages of Norfolk', pp. 145, 152, 157–8.

[208] Even here, the case for medieval desertion is implied rather than conclusively proven, J.T. Munday, 'The topography of medieval Eriswell', *P.S.I.A.* 30 (1965), pp. 201–9.

[209] PRO DL43.7/32. This is Santon in Norfolk, and should not be confused with modern Santon Downham, which lies just across the Little Ouse in Suffolk. Downham acquired the prefix in later centuries.   [210] PRO DL29.295/4847.

[211] IESRO HD 1538/92 ff.16 and 17; NRO Hilborough Deposit Box T (Daleth), vii m.18. From documentary evidence it is impossible to date any of Breckland's lost villages to the fifteenth century with any certainty. The evidence presented by Allison would date Lynford's desertion with precision to the early/mid fifteenth century. However, a rental of Lynford reveals that there were at least 16 tenants in the village in 1406–7 (NRO DCN Supplement (R187A)), and so it might be possible that the site was still occupied in the early sixteenth century. Further research on Hockham Parva has indicated that the village survived the fifteenth-century crisis, only to be depopulated some time during the sixteenth century, A. Davison, 'Little Hockham', *Norfolk Archaeology* 40 (1987), pp. 84–92. Houses and residents of the village are specifically named in mid-fifteenth-century court rolls, NRO Ms 13849, court held July 1445.

Amidst the uncertainty, it is possible to draw some conclusions. A few Breckland villages did disappear at some stage between the Black Death and the mid-sixteenth century, but this did not necessarily entail the complete abandonment of the village lands; most continued to be used, even if it was only as sheep or rabbit pasture. Furthermore, the actual number of desertions in this period was small, and it is doubtful whether more than one-fifth of Breckland's 'lost villages' can be attributed to the Middle Ages; the rest disappeared in later centuries. So, despite unfavourable soil and climatic conditions, late medieval desertion was no more prominent here than in other areas of East Anglia (notably the Norfolk Goodsands). This conclusion should not surprise us unduly, for it supports evidence from Buckinghamshire and the west Midlands which indicates that desertions took place on a variety of soil types and were not noticeably confined to marginal land.[212]

Although there were few complete desertions in medieval Breckland, the weakening and contraction of its villages is reflected in a fall in aggregate village wealth as assessed for tax purposes. Declining wealth is known to have been a common feature of most English villages. In 1449–50 the collectors of the Lay Subsidy pressed for a permanent reduction in the amount due from each village, and the Exchequer considered these claims and duly granted them a relief '*villarum et burgorum desolatorum vastorum et destructorum . . . et depauperatorum*'.[213] It is doubtful whether the relief represented an exact attempt to assess the actual drop in village wealth between 1334 and 1449, but the sums conceded display enough variation to suggest that each one was at least considered on its own merits. Central Breckland villages suffered the greatest decline in wealth, presumably because of their particular disadvantages in grain production, but only Culford fared very badly, perhaps because it became the centre for Bury abbey's sheep-farming activities. However, Icklingham, Barnham and Euston were relatively successful, perhaps indicating involvement in textile production; certainly occupational specialism and marketing

---

[212] M. Reed, *The Buckinghamshire landscape* (London, 1979), pp. 147–51; C.C. Dyer, 'Deserted medieval villages in the west Midlands', *Ec.H.R.* 35 (1982), p. 33; Dyer, *Lords and peasants*, pp. 257–9.

[213] PRO E179.180/100. This has been produced as D. Dymond and R. Virgoe, 'The reduced population and wealth of early fifteenth-century Suffolk', *P.S.I.A.* 36 (1986), pp. 73–100.

opportunities explains why the breck-fen edge performed well.[214]
Suffolk Breckland's overall tax relief amounted to 16.4 per cent of
the 1334 assessment compared with 15.7 per cent for the county as a
whole, which hardly reflects an area bearing the brunt of economic
decline. On the contrary, it compares well with many parts of
Cambridgeshire which were granted 20 per cent relief, and with
Exning hundred (Suffolk) at 29.8 per cent.[215] It even compares
reasonably with the textile producing hundreds of Babergh,
Risbridge and Cosford in south Suffolk, which were granted relief
of 13.6 per cent, 15.6 per cent and 13 per cent respectively.

A direct comparison between the Lay Subsidies of 1334 and 1524
would appear to be the best method of ascertaining whether
Breckland maintained its regional wealth relative to other areas of
East Anglia, but unfortunately this is beset by problems. First, the
region's 1524 returns are incomplete, particularly those relating to
Blackbourne hundred, and so a representative comparison between
Breckland and high Suffolk villages would be impossible. Secondly, the sixteenth-century subsidies were essentially a graduated
tax and not a simple, fixed tax on goods which had been the case in
1283 and 1334, and so direct and detailed comparisons between
them are not entirely meaningful.[216] But more damaging to such
an approach are the changes in sheep ownership which had occurred between 1334 and 1524. Per capita wealth had been high in
Breckland in 1334 because extensive sheep rearing was a prominent
feature of peasant farming. Yet by 1524 ownership of Breckland
sheep had become concentrated into the hands of a few landlords,
many of whom were not assessed in the subsidy. For instance, the
inhabitants of Downham were assessed at £1 18s. 2d. in 1524, and
yet Ixworth priory and Bury abbey, who had monopolised sheep

---

214 Culford was granted relief of 58 per cent, compared with 10 per cent at Euston, 3 per
   cent at Icklingham, and none at Barnham.
215 In comparison, the relief granted in 25 Buckinghamshire settlements, including towns,
   averaged 18.6 per cent in 1446–7, Chibnall, *Sherington*, p. 151.
216 The 1334 Subsidy assessed the value of moveable goods in each village, and then taxed
   them at a fixed rate. In 1523–4 each individual's moveable goods were valued, but then –
   depending on the value – were taxed at different rates. In addition, aliens paid at double
   the rate. Thus it would be possible to have two villages in 1524 which were equally
   wealthy in terms of moveable goods, and this would be clearly represented if they were
   taxed at a fixed rate. However, if one of those villages possessed a number of wealthy
   aliens, then – under the new system – it would appear much wealthier than its
   neighbour.

farming in the village, were exempt from the subsidy.[217] Similarly, Thomas Lucas owned extensive foldcourses in Flempton, Lackford and Risby, but was resident in Saxham Parva and taxed in London.[218] Most of Flempton and Lackford's inhabitants were labourers, and presumably involved in running Lucas' extensive operations. These men were taxed at the fixed rate of 4d. each, thus giving the two villages the low combined assessment of 26s. 1od., but this in no way reflected the actual wealth in the village: what it did reflect, somewhat imperfectly, was a change in the distribution of that wealth. As there is no evidence that sheep farming had become monopolised to the same extent in areas of central Norfolk and Suffolk, then inter-regional comparisons from the 1524 returns would be misleading and unrepresentative.

The 1524 subsidy is likewise unreliable as a back marker for direct estimates of late medieval demographic changes. Campbell has argued that in East Anglia the returns are representative of the number of adult males resident in a village, but evidence from Essex suggests otherwise.[219] Their completeness and hence their usefulness for demographic purposes would depend upon the efficiency and honesty of local assessors and collectors, although their task would certainly have been harder in Breckland where market opportunities and the importance of the carriage trades resulted in a particularly mobile population. So what then happened to the region's population trend between 1400 and the early sixteenth century? Work on East Anglia (including Breckland material) by both Thrupp and Gottfried has suggested that the heavy losses of the late fourteenth century were succeeded by gentle demographic decline, or at best stagnation, until at least the 1470s, a view substantiated by an increasing volume of local studies.[220]

The extent of the decline is more difficult to calculate owing to

---

[217] Hervey, *Suffolk in 1524*, p. 227.   [218] *Ibid.*, p. 345.

[219] B.M.S. Campbell, 'The population of early Tudor England: a re-evaluation of the 1522 Muster Returns and 1524 and 1525 Lay Subsidies', *Journal of Historical Geography* 7 (1981), pp. 152–4, argues that these records are 85 per cent accurate as to the male population resident in each village. However, a comparison between tithing evidence and the Lay Subsidies of two Essex villages suggests a much wider divergence, L.R. Poos, 'Rural population of Essex', pp. 528–9.

[220] S. Thrupp, 'The problem of replacement rates in late medieval English population', *Ec.H.R.* 18 (1965), p. 118, draws evidence from both Brandon and Northwold and concludes that the 'period from 1349 to the 1470s, if it was a golden age, was the golden age of bacteria'. Gottfried, *Epidemic disease in fifteenth-century England*, represents an ambitious attempt to cull demographic data from testamentary evidence, and concludes that infectious disease was responsible for maintaining at best a stagnant population in

the paucity of direct evidence, but in certain Essex villages population fell by around one-third between 1380 and *c.* 1460.[221] This could well be true of Breckland. In 1381 there were approximately 650–700 people in Mildenhall, yet by 1535 the muster rolls record only 124 adult men, which indicates a minimum population of 415.[222] Similarly there had been a total of around 300 living in the four central villages of Euston, Fakenham, Knettishall and Wordwell in 1381, and in 1524 there were 60 males recorded there, which at a minimum estimate suggests 222 residents.[223] In all, it would seem that Breckland's population fell by around one-third in the fifteenth century, a figure also suggested by indirect indicators such as land values.

Despite imperfect evidence and its attendant pitfalls, it is tempting to try and reconstruct the long-term demographic trend in Breckland. It would seem that any population losses in 1315–22 were recuperated within a generation, so that on the eve of the Black Death there were more people in Breckland than at any time in the Middle Ages. Mortality was high in 1349, although for the next century some villages fared worse than others, even within an apparently homogeneous region such as this. Those with a flexible and sympathetic lordship and those offering a greater variety of non-agrarian occupations would have fared best. In all, the evidence suggests that between the 1340s and the 1460s Breckland's population fell by around 60 per cent, which was probably normal by East Anglian standards.[224] It is likely that such prolonged decline was partly a product of depressed fertility rates, but the impact of recurrently high mortality is particularly evident in Breckland.[225]

East Anglia between 1430 and 1470, see pp. 225–30. See also Gottfried, *Bury and the urban crisis*, pp. 58–63 for a rough estimate of the population trend on some rural manors in west Suffolk in this period.

[221] Poos, 'Rural population of Essex', fig. 2.

[222] There were 399 recorded inhabitants of Mildenhall in the 1381 Poll Tax, Powell, *Rising in East Anglia*, appendix. The extant Suffolk Breckland Muster rolls are described in E. Powell, 'The Muster rolls of the territorials in Tudor times', *P.S.I.A.* 15 (1915), pp. 113–43. The Poll Tax lists all adults over 14 years, whilst the Musters list all males between 16 and 60 years. Assuming there was no exemption or evasion, the actual population is found by dividing the Poll Tax figure by 0.6 and the Muster figure by 0.3: for this methodology, see J. Cornwall, 'English population in the early sixteenth century', *Ec.H.R.* 23 (1970), pp. 33–7.

[223] Powell, *Rising in East Anglia*, appendix; Hervey, *Suffolk in 1524*.

[224] See DeWindt, *Land and people*, pp. 166–71, and J.A. Raftis, *Warboys: two hundred years in the life of an English medieval village* (Toronto, 1974), p. 68.

[225] Thrupp, 'The problem of replacement rates', pp. 110–11; Gottfried, *Epidemic disease in fifteenth-century England*, pp. 134–5.

CONCLUSION

Economic activity in medieval Breckland was at its lowest in the fifteenth century. Grain production fell, land values and rent incomes declined, and villages contracted as landlords had difficulties finding tenants for their land. The emphasis in agriculture shifted further towards pastoral activities, although even income from sheep farming and rabbiting could not always compensate for the drop in arable production. Without doubt, Breckland's economic performance comes closer to fulfilling the predictions of the population–resources model in the period 1390–1470 than it does in the preceding era, but crucial differences between the region and the model still remain. First, there was no mass abandonment of Breckland in favour of more rewarding soils elsewhere; land values and rent income declined, but not noticeably more steeply than in the rest of East Anglia, and certainly *less* steeply than in other areas of England. Secondly, the timing of economic recovery in Breckland was very similar to that in other areas, and displayed none of the sluggishness expected of marginal regions: land rents, sheep farming and trade all showed signs of recovery after the 1470s and gathered pace in the early sixteenth century. Lastly, there is no evidence to suggest that the region's specialisation in agricultural production or its extensive trading links were undermined by the depression: markets certainly contracted, but the demand for Breckland's staple products of wool, barley and particularly rabbits fell less than the demand for other produce. In sum, there is no sign that economic depression in Breckland was exacerbated unduly by the infertility of its soils, nor that the depression was a specific product of the region's marginal status.

CONCLUSION

The study of a single region is not sufficient of itself to demand a complete reappraisal of what constituted a 'marginal' region in medieval England. In the orthodox model, Breckland is classified as marginal because of its poor soils and its peculiarly adverse climate. It was not, however, marginal in a locational sense, for medieval East Anglia was a prosperous and densely populated region. Infertile soils meant that large areas of Breckland were not cultivated in the Middle Ages, but this did not condemn the region to economic under-development. Indeed, in the two centuries after Domesday its development was integral, and not simply incremental, to developments in the wider economic nexus. The incidence and virulence of disease was severe in the century after 1349, but the subsequent depopulation and agrarian contraction was no worse in Breckland than in many other areas of lowland England. Breckland's economy certainly declined in absolute terms, but not as severely as historians had predicted, and there is no indication that peasants migrated from the region on any great scale.

As arable cultivation remained limited in Breckland, its economy responded in other ways to the growing pressure of population in the twelfth and thirteenth centuries. The resources of heath, river and fen presented opportunities in non-arable employment, and this diversification helped to raise peasant incomes. Another feature was the emergence of some specialised traits in agriculture, notably in sheep and rabbit rearing, and in the production of a fine malting barley. This specialisation became particularly pronounced after the Black Death, partly because demand for these products remained relatively buoyant, but also because rising costs forced regions to concentrate on those products to which they were best suited. Hence, the separate processes of diversification and specialisation bolstered Breckland's resilience to demographic decline, and created a buffer against the potentially disastrous effects of a contracting grain market. As a consequence, Breckland's performance is neither a reliable nor a sensitive indicator of changes in English agriculture as a whole.

The failure of a region of such intractable soils to conform to the orthodox model warrants some reassessment of conventional views on the margin. The assumption that inherent soil fertility, coupled with the prevailing level of population, was the prime determinant of regional growth and development requires some revision. The Breckland evidence shows only too clearly that the profitability of land depended as much upon its location, and upon institutional factors, as it did upon its quality. Nor was the land productivity of poor soils *bound* to decline after a few years' cultivation. It has been argued that 'the stored fertility of the soil would be mined out, and the land would lie exhausted. This may well have been the natural history of the East Anglian Brecklands . . . [these lands] were also those most likely to suffer from insufficient manuring, and . . . presumably predominated among the lands abandoned by the plough.' The consequences of this exhaustion are assumed to be calamitous: 'the proper way of accounting for [late medieval decolonisation] is to present it as the growing inability of the new lands to redress the balance of the old'.[1] Yet our evidence clearly demonstrates that flexible cropping arrangements could evolve in regions of poor soil, no less than on good soils. Indeed, Breckland's vast heathlands sustained a large sheep population, which provided a good supply of manure. As a result, land productivity was more constant under high population pressure than Postan had assumed. In contrast, we might argue that areas of limited pasture and rigid communal controls in agriculture – such as the 'champion' regions of England – were those most likely to suffer shortages of animal manure, and thus declining land productivity. This being the case, we should be wary of placing too much emphasis upon arable exhaustion at the margin as a primary cause of a Malthusian crisis in the early fourteenth century.

The response of Breckland's economy, first to sustained population growth and then to sustained population decline, was a positive one. But how typical is Breckland's experience to that of other so-called marginal regions? Its abilty to cope with such dramatically changing demographic circumstances was undoubtedly enhanced by its location, by its trading and marketing links.

---

[1] Postan, 'Agrarian society in its prime', p. 559; *Medieval economy*, p. 73.

Conclusion

Not all regions of medieval England enjoyed similar advantages, and so it remains likely that areas which were marginal in terms of soil, climate *and* location, such as the highland zone of Westmoreland, would probably have conformed to the classic model. Indeed, recent research has shown that the economy of the North Yorkshire moors fulfilled the predictions of the population-resources model almost exactly.[2]

Although Breckland's location was important, it is only a partial explanation of how the region overcame the disadvantages of its poor soils. In order to exploit this location, and in order to develop alternative sources of income, Breckland's peasants must have enjoyed relative freedom of time and action. Similarly, in order to adapt to prevailing economic conditions and to facilitate the development of specialised production, its agrarian system must have been relatively free of strict communal controls. We have established that this was indeed the case: although the bonds of feudalism in Breckland were not as loose as in eastern Norfolk, they were certainly more flexible than those in the 'champion' area of Midland England. Hence the nature of property relations is crucial to understanding how Breckland overcame the limitations of its environment.

Yet this is not to argue that social structures and property relations were the prime determinants of economic change in the Middle Ages. Such a conclusion would be misleading, for any attempt to isolate one presiding factor behind economic change is a gross over-simplification of a complex and intricate process. Regional development in medieval England was the product of many inter-related factors, and it is almost impossible to unravel those factors and lay them bare as if they operated in some independent and mutually exclusive fashion. For instance, the loosening of feudal bonds was most prominent in areas of high population density such as East Anglia, but it seems likely that demographic forces were as much a cause as a consequence of this process. In East Anglia, these developments facilitated the commercialisation and specialisation of production, which in-creased economic efficiency and peasant incomes, and which in turn stimulated further changes in demography and property relations.[3]

---

[2] McDonnell, 'Medieval assarting hamlets'.

[3] For a useful discussion and an econometric analysis of this general process, see G. Persson and Peter Skott, 'Growth and stagnation in the European medieval economy' (duplicated, London School of Economics).

A marginal economy?

In general terms, this book has tried to demonstrate that there are many different factors making for marginality, just as there are many different kinds of margin. A region is marginal for cultivation for a mixture of locational, environmental and institutional reasons, and only further research can establish how much weight to give to these three elements in a particular case. Nor is it certain that regions marginal for grain production are therefore marginal in economic terms. Economic development, even in agrarian-based economies, is determined by a complex interaction of property relations, demographic pressure, resource endowment, access to markets, and the extent of commercialisation.

APPENDIX. VILLAGE OF ORIGIN OF ALIENS RECORDED IN BRANDON, LAKENHEATH AND METHWOLD COURT ROLLS

BRECKLAND VILLAGES

Barnham, Barton Parva, Bromehill, Cavenham, Chippenham, Colveston, Cranwich, Cressingham Magna, Cressingham Parva, Croxton, Culford, Didlington, Downham, Elveden, Eriswell, Fakenham, Fakenham Parva, Feltwell, Flempton, Fouldon, Herringswell, Hilborough, Hockwold, Icklingham, Illington, Ingham, Livermere, Lynford, Methwold Hithe, Mildenhall, Mundford, Northwold, Oxborough, Quiddenham, Roudham, Rushford, Santon, Stanford, Stow (Bedon/West?), Sturston, Timworth, Thetford, Thompson, Tuddenham, Wangford, Weeting, Wilton, Worlington, Wretham.

Ampwyk (N), Appleton (N), Ashfield (S), Beachamwell (N), Bodney (N), Brockford (S), Bury St Edmunds (S), Cambridge (C), Carbrooke (N), Chevington (S), Combes (S), Denver (N), Diss (N), Earith (H), East Dereham (N), Ely (C), Emneth (C), Fincham (N), Fordham (C), Fransham (N), Gaytonthorp (N), Gedney (L), Gislingham (S), Gooderstone (N), Hadleigh (S), Hales (N), Hawkeden (S), Hessett (S), Heydon (N), Hilgay (N), Holmsey (N), Lavenham (S), London, Lynn (N), Massingham (N), North Tuddenham (N), Norwich (N), Oakley (S), Old Buckenham (N), Pakenham (S), Peterborough (H), Pulham (N), Rampton (C), Rattlesden (S), St Ives (H), Shipdam (N), Soham (C), Shouldham Thorp (N), Southery (N), Stanhoe (N), Stoke Ferry (N), Sutton (L), Sudbury (S), Swaffham (N), Titteshall (N), Walpole (N), Walton (N), Wells (N), Wereham (N), West Dereham (N), Wiggenhall (N), Wisbech (C), Wittingdon (N), Woolpit (S), Wyverstone (S).

C = Cambridgeshire, H = Huntingdonshire, L = Lincolnshire, N = Norfolk, S = Suffolk

BIBLIOGRAPHY

MANUSCRIPTS

Note: For purposes of brevity, this bibliography records the location and range only of primary material used in the book. For full details concerning the documents, the reader is referred to the catalogues of the relevant repositories and, wherever possible, to the catalogue of Bury abbey's archives published as Thomson, *Archives of the abbey of Bury*. However, where this or other cataloguing has proved unclear, confused or incorrect, full details have been included.

ESTATE RECORDS

Bury abbey:
   Werketone register   Thomson Ms No. 1281
   Lakenheath register   Thomson Ms No. 1283
   Unnamed register   Thomson Ms No. 1287
   Curteys register I   Thomson Ms No. 1289
   Curteys register II   Thomson Ms No. 1290
   White book   Thomson Ms No. 1293
   Unnamed customary   Thomson Ms No. 1294
   Cellarer's register I   Thomson Ms No. 1299
   Cellarer's register II   Thomson Ms No. 1300
Ely abbey:
   Coucher book   CUL EDR G3/27
   Registers   CUL EDR G2/3
                               CUL EDC 1.c.3
                               CUL EDC 1.c.4
Norwich cathedral priory: NRO DCN 40/13
Rushford college: IESRO HD 1538/92
Thetford priory: CUL Add.Ms 6969

INDIVIDUAL MANORS

Barnham
Terriers   WSROB HA513/30/1–3

Barton Parva
Accounts
  1273–1312   IESRO HD 1538/88
Court rolls
  1377–85   WSROB E.7/24/1.3
  1462–98   Bodleian Suffolk Rolls 1
  1521–32   WSROB E.18/451/69
Brandon
Accounts
  1343–1542   Bacon 644–696
  1341–75   PRO SC6.1304/23–36
Court rolls
  1317–1540   Bacon 289–97
Field book
  1566   IESRO V11/2/1.1
Brettenham
Extent
  1324   NRO Ms 15170
Cavenham
Accounts
  n.d.   PRO SC6.1117/12
Extents   PRO C134.42/1
                          PRO C135.87/27
                          PRO C136.47/27

Coney Weston
Evidences   Thomson Ms No. 1309
Cranwich
Court rolls
  1342–3   NRO NRS 18476 m.82
Cressingham Magna
Accounts
  1308–1429   NRO DCN Supplement (R187A)
Culford
Evidences   Thomson Ms No. 1310
Downham
Accounts
  1322–3   BL Add.Roll 9159
  1336–7   BL Add.Roll 9168
  1345–56   WSROB 651/35/2–6
  1362–3   WSROB 651/35/7
Court rolls
  1417–1455   WSROB 651/31/1–6
Elveden
Evidences   WSROB J515
Fakenham
Accounts
  1329–30   BL Add.Roll 9100

Court rolls

  1491–1500   WSROB E.7/14/1201

Feltwell

Accounts

  1337   NRO Deeds Box T

  1349–50   Christ's, Cambridge

  1396–1427   NRO Phi/472/1–3

  1485–1507   NRO Ms 19592 and 10009

Extent

  1539   NRO Ms 10030

Fornhams

Accounts

  1261–1470   Thomson Ms No. 332–49

  1342–1476   Thomson Ms No. 434–53

  1265–1315   Thomson Ms No. 463–80

Court rolls

  1276–1387   Thomson Ms No. 332–49

  1335–1423   Thomson Ms No. 417–33

  1263–1510   Thomson Ms No. 455–62

Cartulary   Thomson Ms No. 1311

Foulden

Rental

  n.d.   NRO Phi/474

Freckenham

Courts

  1547–53   WSROB 613/686/1

Gasthorpe

Account

  1417–18   J. Rylands Library, Phillipps charter 19

Courts

  n.d.   NRO DS 493(10)

Harling, West

Accounts

  1328–78   J. Rylands Library, Phillipps charters 9–16

Hilborough

Accounts

  1367–1485   NRO Hilborough Deposit Box T (Daleth), vii

Courts

  1311–1444   NRO Hilborough Deposit Box T (Daleth), i–v

Hockham Magna

Accounts

  1380–5   NRO Ms 13853–4

Courts

  1337–1525   NRO Ms 13848–13852 and 2522

Bibliography

Ickburgh
Courts
  1526–77   NRO WLS XXVI/1
Icklingham
Accounts
  1329–46   NRO Ms 13190–13200
  1342–3   BL Add.Roll 25810
Courts
  1386   NRO Ms 13187
Extent
  1459   WSROB E.3/10/9.9
Kennett
Accounts
  1270–1301   PRO sc6.768/5–21
Kilverstone
Courts
  1361–1517   NRO Ms 15165–8
Langford
Accounts
  1402–3   NRO NCC(Petre) Box 8/22
Courts
  1360–1422   NRO NCC(Petre) Box 8/21
Lackford
Accounts
  1368–9   WSROB E.3/15.12/2.1
  1396?   WSROB E.3/15.12/2.2
  1400–1   WSROB E.3/15.12/2.3
  1442 bailiff's receipts   WSROB E.3/15.12/5.1
  1443 bailiff's receipts   WSROB E.3/15.12/5.2
  1444 bailiff's receipts   WSROB E.3/15.12/5.3
  1449 bailiff's receipts   WSROB E.3/15.12/5.4
Courts
  1327–1553   Thomson Ms No. 677–95
                     WSROB E.3/15.12/1.18

Rentals
  early 14th cent.   WSROB E.3/15.12/3.7
  1397–7   WSROB E.3/15.12/3.3
  1399–1400   WSROB E.3/15.12/3.1
  1402–3   WSROB E.3/15.12/3.2
  temp. Hen.V   WSROB E.3/15.12/3.4
  early 15th cent.   WSROB E.3/15.52/3.2a
  early 15th cent.   WSROB E.3/15.52/3.1
  mid-15th cent.   WSROB E.3/15.12/3.5
  mid-15th cent.   WSROB E.3/15.12/3.6
  mid-15th cent.   WSROB E.3/15.12/3.8
  1487–8   WSROB E.3/15.12/3.5

Lakenheath
Accounts
  1290–1488   CUL EDC 7/15/I/1–48
                       PRO sc6.1001/5–6

Courts
  1310–*temp*.Ed.III   CUL EDC 7/15/II/Box 1
  Ed.III–R.II   CUL EDC 7/15/II/Box 2
  H.IV★, H.V, H.VI★ CUL EDC 7/15/II/Box 3
  H.VII★, H.VIII★   CUL EDC 7/15/II/Box 4
★deteriorating rolls, unable to be viewed

Methwold
Accounts
  1358–1480   In series PRO
                       DL29.288/4719 to DL29.295/4847

Courts
  1271–1502   In series PRO
                       DL30.104/1469 to DL30.104/1483

Rentals/surveys
  1523   PRO DL43.7/28
  1575   PRO DL43.7/29
Mildenhall
Accounts
  1323–1468   Thomson Ms No. 719–45
Courts
  1299–1533   Thomson Ms No. 712–18
Rentals
  1538, Aspals   Thomson Ms No. 747
  1500–1   WSROB e.18/400/1.3
Northwold
Courts
  1413–1508   NRO NRS 18629–18631
Quiddenham
Account
  1388–9   NRO Phi/493
Risby
Accounts
  1298–1415   Thomson Ms No. 1187–1213
Courts
  1491–1546   Thomson Ms No. 1185–6
Rushford
Extent
  1271   NRO Ms 2680
Thetford
Accounts
  1358–1480   In series PRO DL29.288/4719 to DL29.295/4847

Courts
1435–6 PRO DL30.105/1489
1467 PRO DL30.105/1490
1480, 1486 PRO DL30.105/1491
Rentals/surveys
1551 PRO DL43.7/32
Wangford
Terrier
1542 NRO Ms 4071
West Tofts
Account
1317–18 NRO Phi/500
Worlington
Extents
1321–2 PRO C134.89/21
1390 PRO DL43.14/3
Wilton
Account
1357–8 BL Add. Chtr. 67873
Wretham
Accounts
1303–1441 Eton College records vol. 30, no. 43–9
NRO Ms 18017

Court
1459 NRO Ms 18018

MISCELLANEOUS RECORDS

Hengrave Hall Collection WSROB 449/2
Rentals, groups of manors Thomson Ms No. 1252–9
Lay Subsidy
1332 PRO E179.149/7
Lay Subsidy relief
1449 PRO E179.180/100
Ulnage accounts
1403 PRO E101.342/18
1465–6 PRO E101.342/23
1466–7 PRO E101.342/25
1467–8 PRO E101.343/4
Schedule of aliens
1439–40 PRO E179.180/92
Poll Tax
1379 PRO E179.242/27
1379 PRO E179.149/51
1379 PRO E179.149/53
1379 PRO E179.149/55

Bibliography

PRINTED SOURCES

Calendar of the charter rolls, 6 vols., London, 1903–27.

Calendar of the close rolls, 1272–1509, 62 vols., London, 1902–55.

Calendar of inquisitiones post mortem, 14 vols., London, 1904–52.

Calendar of the patent rolls, 54 vols., London, 1891–1916.

Cartulary of Blythburgh priory, ed. C. Harper-Bill, Suffolk Charters Series 3, vol.II, Woodbridge, 1980.

'Customs of Hardwick in the early thirteenth century', unnamed editor, *P.S.I.A.* 1 (1850).

'Documents of Eriswell cum Coclesworth', ed. J.T. Munday, duplicated, WSROB.

Feudal documents from the abbey of Bury St Edmunds, ed. D.C. Douglas, London, 1932.

The field book of Walsham-le-Willows 1577, ed. K.M. Dodd, Woodbridge, 1974.

'First minister's account of the possessions of the abbey of St Edmund', ed. L.J. Redstone, *P.S.I.A. 13 (1909)*.

Inquisitiones and assessments relating to feudal aids, 1284–1431, 6 vols., London, 1899–1920.

Inquisitiones nonarum, London, 1807.

Kalendar of abbot Samson of Bury St Edmunds and related documents, ed. R.H.C. Davis, Camden Society, third series, vol. 84, 1954.

Lay subsidy of 1334, ed. R.E. Glasscock, London, 1975.

'The muster rolls of the territorials in Tudor times', ed. E. Powell. *P.S.I.A.* 15 (1915).

Pinchbeck register of the abbey of Bury St Edmunds etc., 2 vols., ed. F. Hervey, Brighton, 1925.

Reyce's breviary of Suffolk, ed. F. Hervey, London, 1902.

Rotuli hundredorum temp. Hen. III et Edw. I, 2 vols., ed. W. Illingworth and J. Caley, London, 1812–18.

Rotuli parliamentorum (1278–1503), 6 vols., London, n.d.

Statutes of the realm, 11 vols., ed. A. Luders *et al.*, London, 1810–28.

Suffolk in 1327: being a subsidy return, ed. S.H.A. Hervey, Suffolk green books, 9, vol. II, Woodbridge, 1906.

Suffolk in 1524: being the return for a subsidy granted in 1523, ed. S.H.A. Hervey, Suffolk green books 10, Woodbridge, 1910.

A Suffolk hundred in 1283, ed. E. Powell, Cambridge, 1910.

Valor ecclesiasticus, 6 vols., London, 1810–34.

Walter of Henley, ed. D. Oschinsky, Oxford, 1971.

West Stow and Wordwell parish registers with notes, ed. S.H.A. Hervey, Woodbridge, 1923.

SECONDARY WORKS

Abel, W., *Agricultural fluctuations in Europe from the thirteenth to the twentieth centuries*, London, 1980.

Allison, K.J., 'The lost villages of Norfolk', *Norfolk Archaeology* 31 (1955), pp. 116–62.

Bibliography

'Sheep corn husbandry of Norfolk', *Ag.H.R.* 5 (1957), pp. 12–31.

'Flock management in the sixteenth and seventeenth centuries', *Ec.H.R.* 11 (1958), pp. 98–112.

Allison, K.J., Beresford, M.W., and Hurst, J.G., 'The deserted villages of Oxfordshire', *Occasional papers, Department of Local History, Leicester University*, 17 (1965).

Armstrong, P.H., 'Changes in the land-use of the Suffolk Sandlings: a study in the disintegration of an ecosystem', *Geography* 58 (1973), pp. 1–8.

The changing landscape, Lavenham, 1975.

Aston, T.H. and Philpin, C.H.E., eds., *The Brenner debate: agrarian class structure and economic development in pre-industrial Europe*, Cambridge, 1985.

Bailey, M.D., 'The rabbit and the medieval East Anglian economy', *Ag.H.R.* 36 (1988), pp. 1–20.

'The evolution of the foldcourse system in the fifteenth and sixteenth centuries', (forthcoming).

Baker, A.R.H., 'Evidence in the *Nonarum Inquisitiones* of contracting arable lands in England during the early fourteenth century', *Ec.H.R.* 19 (1966), pp. 518–32.

Barber, M., McNulty, P. and Noble, P., eds., *East Anglian and other studies: essays presented to Barbara Dodwell*, Reading Medieval Monographs 3.

Bean, J.M.W., *The estates of the Percy family 1416–1537*, Oxford, 1958.

Bennett, H.S., *Life on the English manor: a study of peasant conditions 1150–1400*, Cambridge, 1937.

Beresford, M.W., *The lost villages of England*, Lutterworth, 1954.

The new towns of the Middle Ages: town plantation in England, Wales and Gascony, London, 1967.

Beresford, M.W. and Hurst, J.G., *Deserted medieval villages*, London, 1972.

Beveridge, W., 'The yield and price of corn in the Middle Ages', in *Essays in Economic History*, vol. 1, ed. E.M. Carus-Wilson, London, 1954.

Biddick, K., 'Medieval English peasants and market involvement', *Journal of Economic History* 45 (1985), pp. 823–31.

Birrell, J., 'Peasant craftsmen in the medieval forest', *Ag.H.R.* 17 (1969), pp. 91–107.

'Common rights in the medieval forest', *Past and Present* 117 (1987), pp. 22–49.

Blanchard, I.S.W., 'Population change, enclosure and the early Tudor economy', *Ec.H.R.* 23 (1970), pp. 427–45.

'The miner and the agricultural community in later medieval England', *Ag.H.R.* 20 (1972), pp. 93–106.

Blaug, M., *Economic theory in retrospect*, third edition, Cambridge, 1983.

Blomefield, F., *An essay towards a topographical history of the county of Norfolk*, 5 vols., London, 1739–75.

Bolton, J.L., *The medieval English economy*, London, 1980.

Boserup, E., *The conditions of agricultural growth: the economics of agrarian change under population pressure*, London, 1965.

Population and technology, Oxford, 1981.

Bowden, P.J., *The wool trade in Tudor and Stuart England*, London, 1962.

Brandon, P.F., 'Demesne arable farming in coastal Sussex during the later Middle Ages', *Ag.H.R.* 19 (1971), pp. 113–35.

Bibliography

Bridbury, A.R., *Economic Growth: England in the Later Middle Ages*, London, 1962.
  'The Black Death', *Ec.H.R.* 26 (1973), pp. 577–92.
  Medieval English clothmaking: an economic survey, London, 1982.
Briscoe, T., 'Anglo-Saxon finds from Lakenheath and their place in the Lark
  valley context', *P.S.I.A.* 34 (1978), pp. 161–70.
Britnell, R.H., 'Production for the market on a small fourteenth-century estate',
  Ec.H.R. 19 (1966), pp. 380–8.
  'Agricultural technology and the margin of cultivation', *Ec.H.R.* 30 (1977),
  pp. 53–66.
  'Minor landlords in England and medieval agrarian capitalism', *Past and Present*
  89 (1980), pp. 3–22.
  'The proliferation of markets in England 1200–1349', *Ec.H.R.* 34 (1981),
  pp. 209–21.
  Growth and decline in Colchester, 1300–1525, Cambridge, 1986.
Britton, E., *The community of the vill: a study in the history of the family and village life
  in fourteenth century England*, Toronto, 1974.
Bruce-Mitford, R.L.S., 'A late medieval chalk-mine at Thetford', *Norfolk Archae-
  ology* 30 (1947–52), pp. 220–2.
Burkett, M.E., *The art of the feltmaker*, Kendal, 1979.
Butcher, A.F., 'Rent and the urban economy: Oxford and Canterbury in the later
  middle ages', *Southern History* 1 (1979), pp. 11–43.
Butcher, R.W., *Report of the land utilization survey, parts 72–3: Suffolk*, London,
  1941.
Callard, E., *The manor of Freckenham*, London, 1924.
Campbell, B.M.S., 'Population change and the genesis of commonfields on a
  Norfolk manor', *Ec.H.R.* 33 (1980), pp. 174–92.
  'The regional uniqueness of English field systems? Some evidence from eastern
  Norfolk', *Ag.H.R.* 29 (1981), pp. 16–28.
  'The population of early Tudor England: a re-evaluation of the 1522 Muster
  Returns and 1524 and 1525 Lay Subsidies', *Journal of Historical Geography* 7
  (1981), pp. 145–54.
  'The extent and layout of commonfields in eastern Norfolk', *Norfolk Archae-
  ology* 38 (1981), pp. 5–32.
  'Agricultural progress in medieval England: some evidence from eastern Nor-
  folk', *Ec.H.R.* 36 (1983), pp. 26–46.
  'Population pressure, inheritance and the land market in a fourteenth-century
  peasant community', in *Land, kinship and life-cycle*, ed. Smith, pp. 87–134.
  'The complexity of manorial structure in medieval Norfolk: a case study',
  Norfolk Archaeology 39 (1986), pp. 225–61.
  'Towards and agricultural geography of medieval England', *Ag.H.R.* 36 (1988),
  pp. 87–98.
Chadwick, L., *In search of heathland*, Durham, 1982.
Chambers, J.D., *Population, economy and society in pre-industrial England*, Cam-
  bridge, 1972.
Chartres, J.A., *Internal trade in England 1500–1700*, London, 1977.
  'Road carrying in England in the seventeenth century: myth and reality',
  Ec.H.R. 30 (1977), pp. 73–94.

Bibliography

'On the road with Professor Wilson', *Ec.H.R.* 33 (1980), pp. 96–9.

Chibnall, A.C., *Sherington: fiefs and fields of a Buckinghamshire village*, Cambridge, 1965.

Chisholm, M., *Rural settlement and land use: an essay in location*, third edition, London, 1977.

Clark, C.G., *Population growth and land use*, London, 1967.

Clark, P., *The English alehouse 1200–1830*, London, 1983.

Clarke, R.R., 'The Breckland', in *The Cambridge region* ed. H.C. Darby, Cambridge, 1938.

Ancient peoples and places, vol. 14: East Anglia, London, 1960.

Clarke, R.R. and W.G., *In Breckland wilds*, second edition, Cambridge, 1937.

Clarke, W.G., 'The Breckland sand pall and its vegetation', *Transactions of the Norwich and Norfolk Naturalists' Society* 10 (1914–19), pp. 138–48.

In Breckland wilds, Cambridge, 1926.

Cole, L.G., 'The Black Death in East Anglia', *East Anglian Magazine*, 18 (1958–9), pp. 554–7.

Cook, O., *Breckland*, second edition, London, 1980.

Copinger, W.A., *The manors of Suffolk*, 7 vols., London, 1905.

Cornwall, J., 'English country towns in the 1520s', *Ec.H.R.* 15 (1962–3), pp. 54–69.

'English population in the early sixteenth century', *Ec.H.R.* 23 (1970), pp. 32–44.

Cromarty, D., 'Saffron Walden 1381–1420: a study from the court rolls', *Essex Journal* 2 (1967), pp. 104–13.

Crompton, G., 'The history of Lakenheath warren: a historical study for ecologists', *Report to the Nature Conservancy Council* (1972).

Crompton, G. and Taylor, C.C., 'Earthwork enclosures on Lakenheath warren, west Suffolk', *P.S.I.A.* 32 (1971), pp. 113–20.

Crosby, A., *A history of Thetford*, Chichester, 1986.

Darby, H.C., ed. *The Cambridge region*, Cambridge, 1938.

The medieval fenland, Cambridge, 1940.

A Domesday geography of eastern England, third edition, Cambridge, 1971.

ed., *A new historical geography of England before 1600* Cambridge, 1976.

Darby, H.C. and Maxwell, I.S., *A Domesday geography of northern England*, Cambridge, 1962.

Davenport, F.G., *The economic development of a Norfolk manor 1086–1565*, Cambridge, 1906.

'The decay of villeinage in East Anglia', *Transactions of the Royal Historical Society*, second series 14 (1900), pp. 123–42.

Davison, A., 'Some aspects of the agrarian history of Hargham and Snetterton', *Norfolk Archaeology* 35 (1970), pp. 335–55.

'West Harling: a village and its disappearance', *Norfolk Archaeology* 37 (1980), pp. 295–306.

'The distribution of medieval settlement in West Harling', *Norfolk Archaeology* 38 (1983), pp. 329–35.

'Roudham: the documentary evidence', *East Anglian Archaeology* 14 (1982).

'Little Hockham', *Norfolk Archaeology* 40 (1987), pp. 84–92.

Bibliography

Davy, D.E., *A journal of excursions through the county of Suffolk 1823–1844*, ed. J.M. Blatchly, Suffolk Records Society 24 (1982).

Denny, A.H., ed. *The estates of Sibton abbey*, Suffolk Records Society 2 (1960).

DeWindt, E.B., *Land and people in Holywell-cum-Needingworth*, Toronto, 1972.

Dobson, R.B., *Durham priory 1400–1450*, Cambridge, 1973.

Dodgshon, R.A., 'Land improvement in Scottish farming: marl and lime in Roxburghshire and Berwickshire in the eighteenth century', *Ag.H.R.* 26 (1978), pp. 1–14.

Dodwell, B., 'The free peasantry of East Anglia in Domesday', *Norfolk Archaeology* 27 (1939), pp. 145–57.

'Holdings and inheritance in medieval East Anglia' *Ec.H.R.* 20 (1967), pp. 53–66.

Dolman, P.C.J., 'Windmills in Suffolk: a contemporary survey', duplicated, Ipswich, 1978.

Donkin, R.A., 'Changes in the early Middle Ages', in *A new historical geography of England before 1600*, ed. H.C. Darby, Cambridge, 1976, pp. 75–135.

Douglas, D.C., *The social structure of medieval East Anglia*, Oxford, 1927.

Drew, D., *Man-environment processes*, London, 1983.

Drew, J.S., 'Manorial accounts of St Swithun's Priory, Winchester', *English Historical Review* 62 (1947), pp. 20–41.

Duby, G., *Rural economy and country life in the medieval west*, London, 1968.

Dyer, C.C., 'A redistribution of incomes in fifteenth century England?', in *Peasants, knights and heretics: studies in medieval English social history*, ed. R.H. Hilton, Cambridge, 1976, pp. 192–215.

Lords and peasants in a changing society, Cambridge, 1980.

'Deserted medieval villages in the west Midlands', *Ec.H.R.* 35 (1982), pp. 19–34.

'English diet in the later Middle Ages', in *Social relations and ideas: essays in honour of R.H. Hilton*, eds. T.H. Aston, P.R. Cross, C.C. Dyer and J. Thirsk, Cambridge, 1983.

'The social and economic background to the rural revolt of 1381', in *The English rising of 1381*, eds. R.H. Hilton and T.H. Aston, Cambridge, 1984, pp. 9–42.

'Changes in diet in the late middle ages: the case of harvest workers', *Ag.H.R.* 36 (1988), pp. 21–38.

Dymond, D.P., 'The Suffolk landscape', in *East Anglian Studies*, ed. L. Munday, Cambridge, 1968, pp. 17–47.

'The parish of Walsham-le-Willows: two Elizabethan surveys and their medieval background', *P.S.I.A.* 33 (1974), pp. 195–211.

The Norfolk landscape, London, 1985.

Dymond, D.P. and Betterton, A., *Lavenham: 700 years of textile making*, Woodbridge, 1982.

Dymond, D.P. and Virgoe, R., 'The reduced population of early fifteenth-century Suffolk', *P.S.I.A.* 36 (1986), pp. 73–100.

Ekwall, E., *English place names*, Oxford, 1960.

Erskine, A.E., 'The accounts of the fabric of Exeter Cathedral, 1279–1353', part II, *Devon and Cornwall Record Society* 26 (1983).

Evans, N., *The East Anglian linen industry: rural industry and local economy, 1500–1800*, Aldershot, 1985.

Bibliography

Everitt, A., 'The marketing of agricultural produce', in *Agrarian history of England and Wales*, vol. IV, ed. J. Thirsk, Cambridge, 1967, pp. 466–592.

Faith, R., 'Berkshire: the fourteenth and fifteenth centuries', in *The peasant land market in medieval England*, ed. P.D.A. Harvey, Oxford, 1984, pp. 107–77.

Farmer, D.L., 'Some grain price movements in thirteenth-century England', *Ec.H.R.* 10 (1957–8), pp. 207–20.

Farrow, E.P., *Plant life on East Anglian heaths*, Cambridge, 1925.

Finberg, H.P.R., *Tavistock abbey: a study in the social and economic history of Devon*, Cambridge, 1951.

Finn, R.W., *Domesday studies: the eastern counties*, London, 1967.

Forrest, A. J., *Masters of flint*, Lavenham, 1983.

Fox, H.S.A., 'Outfield cultivation in Devon and Cornwall: a reinterpretation', in *Husbandry and marketing in the south west 1500–1800*, ed. M. Havinden, Exeter papers in economic history 8 (1973).

Gage, J., *A history of Thingoe*, Bury St Edmunds, 1838.

Gilpen, W., *Some observations on several parts of Cambridgeshire, Norfolk, Suffolk and Essex made in 1769*, London, 1805.

Glasscock, R.E., 'The distribution of wealth in East Anglia in the early fourteenth century', *Transactions of the Institute of British Geographers* 32 (1963), pp. 113–23.

'England circa 1334', in *A new historical geography of England*, ed. H.C. Darby, pp. 136–85.

Gonner, E.C.K., ed., *Ricardo's economic essays*, London, 1923.

Gottfried, R.S., *Epidemic disease in fifteenth century England: the medical response and the demographic consequences*, Leicester, 1978.

Bury St Edmunds and the urban crisis 1290–1539, Princeton, 1982.

The Black Death: natural and human disaster in medieval Europe, London, 1983.

Gowers, W.R., 'The cultivation of flax and hemp in Suffolk in the fourteenth century', *The East Anglian: notes and queries* 5 (1893–4), pp. 180–3 and 200–2.

Gras, N.S.B., *The evolution of the English corn market*, Harvard, 1915.

Gray, H.L., *English field systems*, Harvard, 1915.

Grigg, D.B., *Population growth and agrarian change*, Cambridge, 1980.

The dynamics of agricultural change: the historical experience, London, 1982.

An introduction to agricultural geography, London, 1984.

Grimwood, C.G. and Kay, S.A., *A history of Sudbury, Suffolk*, Sudbury, 1952.

Haggard, L.R., ed., *I walked by night: being the life and history of the king of the Norfolk poachers*, Woodbridge, 1974.

Hall, P., ed. *Von Thunen's isolated state*, London, 1966.

Hallam, H.E., 'Some thirteenth century censuses', *Ec.H.R.* 10 (1957–8), pp. 340–61.

'Population density in the medieval fenland', *Ec.H.R.* 14 (1961–2), pp. 71–81.

Settlement and society: study of the agrarian history of south Lincolnshire, Cambridge, 1965.

Rural England 1066–1348, London, 1981.

'The climate of eastern England 1250–1350', *Ag.H.R.* 32 (1984), pp. 124–32.

Hargreaves-Mawdsley, W.N., *A history of academical dress in Europe until the end of the eighteenth century*, Oxford, 1963.

Harvey, B.F., 'The population trend in England between 1300 and 1348', *Transactions of the Royal Historical Society*, fifth series, 16 (1966), pp. 23–42.

Westminster abbey and its estates in the middle ages, Oxford, 1977.

Harvey, J.H., 'The last years of Thetford cluniac priory', *Norfolk Archaeology* 27 (1938), pp. 1–28.

Hatcher, J., 'A diversified economy: late medieval Cornwall', *Ec.H.R.* 22 (1969), pp. 208–27.

Rural economy and society in the Duchy of Cornwall 1300–1500, Cambridge, 1970.

Plague, population and the English economy 1348–1530, London, 1977.

'Mortality in the fifteenth century: some new evidence', *Ec.H.R.* 39 (1986), pp. 19–38.

Hay, D., *et al.*, *Albion's fatal tree: crime and society in eighteenth century England*, London, 1975.

Heard, N., *Wool: East Anglia's golden fleece*, Lavenham, 1970.

Hervey, J., 'Extent of Hadleigh manor, 1305', *P.S.I.A.* 11 (1903), pp. 152–72.

Hewitt, H.D., 'Chalk mines at Thetford', *Norfolk Archaeology* 31 (1955–7), pp. 231–2.

Hilton, R.H., *The economic development of some Leicestershire estates in the fourteenth and fifteenth centuries*, Oxford, 1947.

The decline of serfdom in medieval England, London, 1969; second edition, 1983.

Bondmen made free: medieval peasant movements and the English rising of 1381, London, 1977.

Medieval society: the west Midlands at the end of the thirteenth century, second edition, Cambridge, 1983.

'Small town society in England before the Black Death', *Past and Present* 105 (1984), pp. 58–78.

Hobsbawm, E.J., *Bandits*, London, 1969.

Holmes, G.A., *The estates of the higher nobility in fourteenth-century England*, Cambridge, 1957.

Holt, H.M.E. and Kain, R.J.P., 'Land use and farming in Suffolk about 1840', *P.S.I.A.* 35 (1981), pp. 123–39.

Holt, R., 'Whose were the profits of corn milling? The abbots of Glastonbury and their tenants, 1086–1350', *Past and Present*, 116 (1987), pp. 3–23.

Homans, G.C., *English villagers of the thirteenth century*, Cambridge, Mass., 1941.

'The Frisians in East Anglia', *Ec.H.R.* 10 (1957–8), pp. 189–206.

'The explanation of English regional differences', *Past and Present* 42 (1969), pp. 18–34.

Hoskins, W.G., *The making of the English landscape*, London, 1955.

Old Devon, Newton Abbot, 1966.

The age of plunder, London, 1976.

Jenkins, J.G., ed., *The wool textile industry in Great Britain*, London, 1972.

Jessopp, A., *The coming of the friars and other historical essays*, London, 1889.

Jones, A., 'Bedfordshire: the fifteenth century', in *The peasant land market in medieval England*, ed. P.D.A. Harvey, Oxford, 1984, pp. 178–251.

Jones, G.P., 'Building in stone in medieval western Europe', in *The Cambridge economic history of Europe*, vol. II, *Trade and industry in the Middle Ages*, eds. E. Miller, C. Postan and M.M. Postan, Cambridge, 1987, pp. 763–86.

Bibliography

Jones, P.E., *The worshipful company of poulters of the city of London*, London, 1939.

Keene, D., 'A new study of London before the Great Fire', *Urban history yearbook* (1984), pp. 11–21.

Kerridge, E., *Agrarian problems in the sixteenth century and after*, London, 1969.

Kershaw, I., 'The great famine and agrarian crisis in England, 1315–1322', *Past and Present* 59 (1973), pp. 3–50.

Bolton priory: the economy of a northern monastery 1286–1325, Oxford, 1973.

King, E., *Peterborough abbey, 1086–1310: a study in the land market*, Cambridge, 1973.

England 1175–1425, London, 1979.

Kirkham, G., 'Economic diversification in a marginal economy: a case study', in *Plantation to partition: essays in Ulster history in honour of J.L. McCracken*, ed. P. Roebuck, Belfast, 1981, pp. 64–81.

Kosminsky, E.A., *Studies in the agrarian history of England in the thirteenth century*, Oxford, 1956.

Lamb, H.H., *Climate, history and the modern world*, London, 1982.

Langdon, J., 'The economics of horses and oxen in medieval England', *Ag.H.R.* 30 (1982), pp. 31–40.

'Horse hauling: a revolution in vehicle transport in twelfth- and thirteenth-century England?', *Past and Present* 103 (1984), pp. 37–66.

Horses, oxen and technological innovation: the use of draught animals in English farming from 1066 to 1500, Cambridge, 1986.

LeGear, R.F., 'Three agricultural chalk mines in north-west Kent', *Archaeologia Cantiana* 99 (1983), pp. 67–72.

Leveritt, A.E., 'Country, county and town: patterns of regional evolution in England', *Transactions of the Royal Historical Society*, fifth series 29 (1979), pp. 79–108.

Levett, A.E. and Balland, A., *The Black Death on the estates of the See of Winchester*, Oxford, 1916.

Livett, R.G.C., 'Some fourteenth-century documents relating to Herringswell', *East Anglian* 10 (1904–9), pp. 121–4, 253–5, 330–2 and 386–8.

Lloyd, T.H., 'The movement of wool prices in medieval England', *Ec.H.R. supplement* 6, Cambridge, 1973.

The English wool trade in the Middle Ages, Cambridge, 1977.

Lobel, M.D., 'A detailed account of the 1327 rising at Bury St Edmunds and the subsequent trial', *P.S.I.A.* 21 (1933), pp. 215–31.

Lomas, R.A., 'The priory of Durham and its demesnes in the fourteenth and fifteenth centuries', *Ec.H.R.* 31 (1978), pp. 339–53.

Long, W.H., 'The low yields of corn in medieval England', *Ec.H.R.* 32 (1979), pp. 459–69.

Lucas, H.S., 'The great European famine of 1315, 1316 and 1317', *Speculum* 5 (1930), pp. 343–77.

McCloskey, D., 'English open fields as behaviour towards risk', in *Research in Economic History*, 1 (1976), ed. P.J. Uselding, pp. 154–62.

McDonnell, J., 'Medieval assarting hamlets in Bilsdale, north-east Yorkshire', *Northern History* 22 (1986), pp. 269–79.

McIntosh, M.K., *Autonomy and community: the royal manor of Havering, 1200–1500*, Cambridge, 1986.

Bibliography

'Local change and community control in England, 1465–1500', *Huntington Library Quarterly* 49 (1986), pp. 219–42.

McKinley, R.A., *Norfolk and Suffolk surnames in the Middle Ages*, London, 1975.

Maitland, F.W., *Domesday book and beyond: three essays in the early history of England*, Cambridge, 1897.

Makings, S.M., *The economics of poor land arable farming*, London, 1944.

Mander, R.P., 'The Black Death and other plagues in East Anglia', *East Anglian Magazine* 7 (1947–8), pp. 292–8.

Manly, G., *Climate and the British scene*, London, 1952.

Marshall, W., *Rural economy of Norfolk*, 2 vols., London, 1787.

Martelli, G., *The Elveden enterprise*, London, 1952.

Mate, M., 'Agrarian economy after the Black Death: the manors of Canterbury Cathedral Priory 1348–91', *Ec.H.R.* 37 (1984), pp. 341–54.

'Medieval agrarian practices: the determining factors?', *Ag.H.R.* 33 (1985), pp. 22–31.

'Pastoral farming in south-east England in the fifteenth century', *Ec.H.R.* 40 (1987), pp. 523–36.

May, P., 'Newmarket 500 years ago', *P.S.I.A.* 33 (1974), pp. 253–74.

Mayhew, N.J. 'Numismatic evidence and falling prices in the fourteenth century', *Ec.H.R.* 27 (1974), pp. 1–15.

Miller, E., *The abbey and bishopric of Ely*, Cambridge, 1951.

'The English economy in the thirteenth century: implications of recent research', *Past and Present* 28 (1964), pp. 21–40.

'The fortunes of the English textile industry in the thirteenth century', *Ec.H.R.* 18 (1965), pp. 64–82.

Miller, E. and Hatcher, J., *Medieval England: rural society and economic change, 1086–1348*, London, 1978.

Mingay, G.E., *Enclosure and the small farmer in the age of the industrial revolution*, London, 1968.

Miyoshi, Y., *A peasant society in economic change: a Suffolk manor 1279–1437*, Tokyo, 1981.

Morgan, M., *The English lands of the abbey of Bec*, Oxford, 1946.

Mosby, J.E.G., *Report of the land utilization survey*, part 70: *Norfolk*, London, 1938.

Munday, J.T., 'The topography of medieval Eriswell', *P.S.I.A.* 30 (1965), pp. 201–9.

'Eriswell notebook', dupicated, WSROB.

'Lakenheath 600 years Ago', duplicated, WSROB.

Newton, K.C., *The manor of Writtle: the development of a royal manor in Essex, 1086–1500*, London, 1970.

O'Flanagan, P., 'Markets and fairs in Ireland 1600–1800: an index of economic development and regional growth', *Journal of Historical Geography* 11 (1985), pp. 364–78.

Owen, D.M., ed. *The making of King's Lynn: a documentary survey*, London, 1984.

Page, F.M., *The estates of Crowland abbey*, Cambridge, 1934.

Paine, C., 'Wordwell, west Suffolk', duplicated, WSROB.

Parry, M.L., *Climatic change, agriculture and settlement*, Folkstone, 1978.

Bibliography

Paterson, J.H., *Land, work, and resources: an introduction to economic geography*, London, 1972.

Pelham, R.A., 'Fourteenth century England', in *An historical geography of England before 1800*, ed. H.C. Darby, Cambridge, 1936.

Persson, G. and Skott, P., 'Growth and stagnation in the European medieval economy' (duplicated pamphlet, London School of Economics, no date).

Pilgrim, J.E., 'The cloth industry in East Anglia', in *The wool textile industry in Great Britain*, London, 1972.

Pizer, N.H. 'The soils of Breckland', in *An ecological flora of Breckland*, ed. P.J.O. Trist, Wakefield, 1979.

Pollard, A.J., 'Estate management in the later Middle Ages: the Talbots and Whitchurch, 1383–1525', *Ec.H.R.* 25 (1972), pp. 553–66.

Poos, L.R., 'The rural population of Essex in the later Middle Ages', *Ec.H.R.* 38 (1985), pp. 515–30.

Postan, M.M., 'Agrarian society in its prime: Part 7, England', in *Cambridge economic history of Europe*, vol. I: *The agrarian life of the Middle Ages*, ed. M.M. Postan, second edition, Cambridge, 1966, pp. 548–632.

Fact and relevance: essays on historical method, Cambridge, 1971.

Essays on English agriculture and general problems of the medieval economy, Cambridge, 1973.

Medieval trade and finance, Cambridge, 1973.

The medieval economy and society: an economic history of Britain in the Middle Ages, Harmondsworth, 1975.

Postgate, M.R., 'Field systems of the Breckland', *A.g.H.R.* 10 (1962), pp. 80–101.

'Field systems of East Anglia', in *Studies of field systems in the British Isles,* ed. A.R.H. Baker and R.A. Butlin, Cambridge, 1973, pp. 281–324.

Postles, D., 'Markets for rural produce in Oxfordshire, 1086–1350', *Midland History* 12 (1987), pp. 14–26.

Powell, E., *The rising in East Anglia in 1381*, Cambridge, 1896.

A Suffolk hundred in the year 1283, Cambridge, 1910.

Power, E., *The wool trade in English medieval history*, Oxford, 1941.

Prigg, H., *Icklingham papers*, Woodbridge, 1901.

Rackham, O., *The history of the countryside*, London, 1986.

Raftis, J.A., *The estates of Ramsey abbey*, Toronto, 1957.

Tenure and mobility: studies in the social history of the medieval English village, Toronto, 1964.

Warboys: two hundred years in the life of an English medieval village, Toronto, 1974.

Rainbird, H., 'On the farming of Suffolk', *Journal of the Royal Agricultural Society* 9 (1848), pp. 261–329.

Rainbird, W. and H., *The agriculture of Suffolk*, London, 1849.

Ravensdale, J.R., *Liable to floods: village landscape on the edge of the fens, 450–1850*, Cambridge, 1974.

'Population changes and the transfer of customary land on a Cambridge manor in the fourteenth century', in *Land, kinship and life-cycle*, ed. R.M. Smith, pp. 197–226.

Ravensdale, J.R. and Muir, R., *East Anglian landscapes past and present*, London, 1984.

Bibliography

Razi, Z., *Life, marriage and death in a medieval parish*, Cambridge, 1980.

Redstone, V.B., 'Early Sudbury clothiers', *P.S.I.A.* 14 (1910), pp. 99–104.

Reed, M., *The Buckinghamshire landscape*, London, 1979.

Reynolds, S., *English medieval towns*, Oxford, 1977.

Richmond, C., *John Hopton: a fifteenth-century Suffolk gentleman*, Cambridge, 1981.

Ritchie, C., 'The Black Death at St Edmunds abbey', *P.S.I.A.* 27 (1955), pp. 47–50.

Roberts, S.C., trans., *Duc de la Rochefoucauld: a Frenchman in England in 1784*, Cambridge, 1933.

Roden, D., 'Desmesne farming in the Chiltern hills', *Ag.H.R.* 17 (1969), pp. 9–23.

Rogers, J.E.T., *A history of agriculture and prices in England 1259–1793*, 7 vols., Oxford, 1866–1902.

Rowell, T.A., 'Sedge in Cambridgeshire: its use, production and value', *Ag.H.R.* 34 (1986), pp. 140–8.

Roxby, P.R., 'East Anglia', in *Great Britain: essays in regional geography*, ed. A.G. Ogilvie, Cambridge, 1930.

Rubin, M., *Charity and community in medieval Cambridge*, Cambridge, 1987.

Russell, E.J., 'The reclamation of wasteland: the scientific and technical problems', *Journal of the Royal Agricultural Society* 80 (1919), pp. 112–32.

Russell, J.C., *British medieval population*, Albuquerque, 1948.

Ryder, M.L., 'The history of sheep breeds in Britain', *Ag.H.R.* 12 (1964), pp. 1–12 and 67–82.

   Sheep and man, London, 1983.

   'Medieval sheep and wool types', *Ag.H.R.* 32 (1984), pp. 14–28.

Saltmarsh, J.A., 'Plague and economic decline in England in the late Middle Ages', *Cambridge Historical Journal* 7 (1941), pp. 23–41.

Saltmarsh, J.A. and Darby, H.C., 'The infield-outfield system on a Norfolk manor', *Economic History* 3 (1935), pp. 30–44.

Saul, A., 'The herring industry at Yarmouth *c*.1280–*c*.1400', *Norfolk Archaeology* 38 (1981), pp. 33–43.

Saunders, H.W., 'A bailiff's roll for the manor of Lawshall, 1393–4', *P.S.I.A.* 14 (1910), pp. 111–46.

Scarfe, N., 'Markets and fairs in medieval Suffolk', *Suffolk Review* 3 (1965), pp. 4–12.

   The Suffolk landscape, London, 1972.

Schober, E., *Das Breckland*, Breslau, 1937.

Searle, E., *Lordship and community: Battle abbey and its banlieu*, Toronto, 1974.

Sheail, J., *Rabbits and their history*, Newton Abbot, 1971.

   'Rabbits and agriculture in post-medieval England', *Journal of Historical Geography* 4 (1978), pp. 349–55.

Shrewsbury, J.F.D., *The history of bubonic plague in England*, Cambridge, 1970.

Simpson, A., 'The East Anglian foldcourse: some queries', *Ag.H.R.* 6 (1958), pp. 87–96.

   The wealth of the gentry, Cambridge, 1961.

Smith, A., 'Regional differences in crop production in medieval Kent', *Archaeologia Cantiana*, 78 (1963), pp. 147–60.

Bibliography

Smith, C.A., 'Examining stratification systems through peasant marketing arrangements: an application of some models from economic geography', *Man* 10 (1975), pp. 95–112.

Smith, R.M., ed., *Land, kinship and life-cycle*, Cambridge, 1984.

'Families and their land in an area of partible inheritance: Redgrave, Suffolk 1260–1320' in *Land, kinship and life-cycle*, pp. 135–96.

Spratt, J., 'Agrarian conditions in Norfolk and Suffolk, 1600–1650', *Bulletin of the Institute of Historical Research* 15 (1937–8), pp. 113–16.

Spufford, M., 'A Cambridgeshire community: Chippenham from settlement to enclosure', *Occasional papers, Department of Local History, Leicester University* 20 (1965).

Steers, J.A. and Mitchell, J.B., 'East Anglia', in *Great Britain: geographical essays*, ed. J.B. Mitchell, Cambridge, 1962.

Taylor, J.A., ed., *Weather and agriculture*, Oxford, 1967.

Thirsk, J., 'The common fields', *Past and Present* 29 (1964), pp. 3–25.

'The farming regions of England', in *Agrarian history of England and Wales*, vol. IV, ed. J. Thirsk, Cambridge, 1967.

'Seventeenth-century agriculture and social change', in *Land, church and people: essays presented to H.P.R. Finberg*, ed. J. Thirsk, Reading, 1970, pp. 148–77.

England's agricultural regions and agrarian history, 1500–1750, London, 1987.

Thomas, A.S., 'Chalk, heather and man', *Ag.H.R.* 8 (1960), pp. 57–66.

Thomson, R.M. *The archives of the abbey of Bury St Edmunds*, Suffolk Records Society 21, 1980.

Thornton, G.A., *A history of Clare, Suffolk*, Cambridge, 1928.

Thrupp, S., *The merchant class of medieval London 1300–1500*, Chicago, 1948.

'The problem of replacement rates in late medieval English population', *Ec.H.R.* 18 (1965), pp. 101–19.

Titow, J.Z., *English rural society 1200–1350*, London, 1969.

Winchester yields: a study in medieval agricultural productivity, Cambridge, 1972.

Tittensor, A.M. and R.M., *The rabbit warren at West Dean near Chichester*, published privately, 1986.

Trist, P.J.O., *The agriculture of Suffolk*, London, 1971.

ed., *An ecological flora of Breckland*, Wakefield, 1979.

Veale, E.M., 'The rabbit in England', *Ag.H.R.* 5 (1957), pp. 85–90.

The English fur trade in the later Middle Ages, Oxford, 1966.

Victoria county histories, Norfolk and Suffolk.

Wade-Martins, P., 'Field-work and excavations on village sites in Launditch hundred, Norfolk', *East Anglian Archaeology* 10 (1980).

Warner, P., 'Greens, commons and clayland colonization: the origins and development of green-side settlement in east Suffolk', *Occasional papers, Department of Local History, Leicester University*, fourth series 2 (1987).

West, S., 'West Stow: the Anglo-Saxon village', 2 vols., *East Anglian Archaeology* 24 (1985).

White, W., *History, gazetteer and directory of Suffolk*, Ipswich, 1844.

Whittington, G., 'Field Systems of Scotland', in *Field systems of the British Isles*, ed. A.R.H. Baker and R. Butlin, Cambridge, 1973, pp. 530–79.

Bibliography

Wickham, W.A., 'Nonarum inquisitiones for Suffolk', *P.S.I.A.* 17 (1921), pp. 97–122.

Willan, T.S., *The inland trade: studies in English internal trade in the sixteenth and seventeenth centuries*, Manchester, 1976.

Willard, J.F., 'Inland transportation in England during the fourteenth century', *Speculum* 1 (1926), pp. 361–74.

'The use of carts in the fourteenth century', *History* 17 (1932), pp. 246–50.

Williamson, J., 'Norfolk: thirteenth century', in *The peasant land market in medieval England*, ed. P.D.A. Harvey, Oxford, 1984, pp. 31–106.

Wilson, C.H., 'Land carriage in the seventeenth century', *Ec.H.R.* 33 (1980), pp. 92–5.

Wrigley, E.A., 'A simple model of London's importance in a changing English society and economy', in *Towns in societies: essays in economic history and historical sociology*, eds. P. Abrams and E.A. Wrigley, Cambridge, 1978, pp. 226–43.

Young, A., *A general view of the agriculture of the county of Suffolk*, London, 1804.

A general view of the agriculture of the county of Norfolk, London, 1804.

Zeigler, P., *The Black Death*, Harmondsworth, 1969.

UNPUBLISHED DISSERTATIONS

Bailey, M.D., 'At the margin: Suffolk Breckland in the later Middle Ages' (Ph.D., Cambridge, 1986).

Blanchard, I.S.W., 'Derbyshire in the late Middle Ages' (Ph.D., London, 1967).

Campbell, B.M.S., 'Field systems in eastern Norfolk during the middle ages: a study with particular reference to the demographic and agrarian changes of the fourteenth century' (Ph.D., Cambridge, 1975).

Postgate, M.R., 'An historical geography of Breckland 1600–1800' (M.A., London, 1960).

Ridgard, J.M., 'The local history of Worlingworth, Suffolk, to AD 1400' (Ph.D., Leicester, 1984).

Smith, R.M., 'English peasant life-cycles and socio-economic networks: a quantitative geographical case study' (Ph.D., Cambridge, 1975).

Warner, P.M., 'Blything hundred: a study in the development of settlement, 400–1400' (Ph.D., Leicester, 1982).

Williamson, J., 'Peasant holdings in medieval Norfolk: a detailed investigation into the holdings of the peasantry in three Norfolk villages in the thirteenth century' (Ph.D., Reading, 1976).

INDEX

Agricultural Land Classification Survey, 35–6

agriculture: cropping and rotations, 56–65, 95, 208–20, 236–7, 283–4; pasturing arrangements, 65–85, 208–20; technology in, 85–96, 218–19; yields, 86–7, 95, 99–108, 204, 219, 224

ale: *see* brewing

ale-houses, 169–70, 260, 304

Ampton, 35, 44, 61, 80n, 196

animal ratios, 93–4, 219–22

arrears, 267–76, 298

Ashby (Norf.) 301n

Ashfield Magna (Suff.) 118, 120, 138n

Babergh hundred (Suff.), 116, 194, 198, 308, 315

Babwell priory, 233

Bacon family, 39, 52, 292

Badmondsfield (Suff.), 151n

Baltic, 147

Bardwell, 151n

barkers, 183–4

barley: 59, 64n, 90n, 91–3, 99–100, 122, 136–42, 146–9, 155, 168–9, 192, 194, 201–3, 208, 218, 237–45, 263–4, 282–3, 307, 318; leaseholds, 142, 226, 234; yields of, 101–4

Barnham: 28–30, 35, 89, 119–21, 141, 174, 193, 197, 314; field-systems, 41, 44, 61, 63, 68–9, 71, 81, 83–4

Barrow (Suff.), 293

Barton Magna (Suff.), 44, 50n, 91n, 157

Barton Parva: 36, 55, 67, 73, 78, 196, 234n, 249, 258, 270; occupations in, 163, 177, 184, 187

Bury abbey manor: 37, 89; arable farming, 98, 102, 104, 107, 139, 211, 214, 239–44; pastoral farming, 128, 221, 247

Beachamwell (Norf.), 36

Beccles, 149

Bedfordshire, 199, 284

Berkshire, 281, 289

Billingford (Norf.) 72n

Black Death, 222–7, 245

Blackbourne hundred: 29, 98, 112, 206, 223, 314; crops in, 85, 136–40; sheep in, 117–22; wealth in, 100, 145–6, 191–9

boats: 153–5, 157, 306; *see also* transport

Bodney, 35, 80, 291

Bolton priory, 200n

Boston (Lincs.), 155, 306n

bracken, 27, 55–6, 62

Bradfield (Suff.), 151

Brancaster (Norf.), 157n

Brandon: 31, 35–6, 55, 112, 115, 134, 140, 142n, 147, 156–7, 197, 258–9, 270, 283, 288, 304, 310, 312, 316n; field-systems, 41, 44–5, 49n, 51, 59, 60–2, 69–71, 78–9, 83; land market, 51, 205–7, 223–4, 226–31, 236, 266n, 279–80; market, 144, 150–1, 306; occupations in, 161–70, 173–6, 179–80, 182–7, 260–2, 300–3, 308; port, 151–5; warren, 131–2, 150, 152n, 183, 236, 252–5, 296–302

Bishopric of Ely manor: 37–8, 157, 234–5, 270–5; arable farming, 86, 101, 103, 105, 139, 209, 214, 224, 238–45; leasing, 203, 235, 286; pastoral farming, 124–5, 127–8, 217–18, 220, 246, 257, 291

Breckland: delimitation, 34–6; breck-fen edge, 36, 66, 98, 109–10, 121, 147, 150, 152–5, 157, 165, 195–7, 303, 315; central villages, 35–6, 60, 82–5, 121, 147, 151, 195–7, 227, 281, 307, 314; peripheral villages, 36, 44, 51, 59–60, 82–6, 121, 151, 195–7, 227

343

Index

Index

Forncett (Norf.), 229, 226n, 309
Fornham All Saints: 36, 47–8, 97, 113,
135–6, 140, 142, 151, 196, 227,
232–3, 249n; field-systems, 45, 68,
74, 79, 81; land market, 205, 222–9,
231, 266, 268, 270; occupations in,
168, 184, 187, 189, 190, 308
  Bury abbey manor (Fornham (A)): 39,
63, 150, 157, 168, 204n, 208, 253,
271–2, 274–5, 309–10, 311n; arable
farming, 88–9, 98, 102, 105, 107,
139, 203–5, 208, 211–12, 214–17,
219, 236n, 239–44, 281–3; leasing,
203, 258, 285–7; pastoral farming,
90, 91, 123–5, 128, 217n, 221, 247,
251n, 290–2
Fornham St Genevieve: 36, 45, 48, 54,
174, 182, 196, 251; field-systems, 44,
64, 70
Fornham St Martin: 36, 129, 146, 151,
196, 205, 207, 249; field-systems, 44,
77–8n, 83–44; occupations in, 168,
176–8
  Bury abbey manor (Fornham (C)): 37,
64, 142, 203–4, 225, 258; arable
farming, 102–3, 105, 107, 139,
201–2, 240–5; leasing, 235, 251;
pastoral farming, 90, 127–8, 201,
221, 245, 250, 257, 297
Foulden, 36
Freckenham, 36, 69, 89n, 127, 132, 136,
149, 181–2, 197, 300
free-warren, 129–30
fullers/fulling: see mills; textiles

Gasthorpe, 36, 76, 107, 163, 139, 197,
239–44
Gazeley (Suff.), 208n
Gooderstone (Norf.), 130, 144
Grimes Graves, 33, 165
Grimshoe hundred, 97, 99, 194n, 199
Guiltcross hundred, 99, 195, 197–8

Hadleigh (Suff.), 154n, 172, 179, 191,
262n, 263
Halesowen (Warks.), 38
Hampshire, 5
Happing hundred (Norf.), 198
Hargham, 36, 197, 301n
Harling, East, 36, 144, 190, 197
Harling, Thorpe, 35, 77, 197, 313
Harling, West: 35, 53, 110n, 138, 163,
175, 177, 190
  manor of: arable farming, 101, 104,

106–7, 139, 233, 237, 239–44;
pastoral farming, 76, 220, 245–6, 257
Harthill (Norf.), 84n
Havering (Essex), 170
Hawkedon (Suff.), 208
heathland: communal rights on, 54–6, 81,
113; ploughed for arable, 2, 57–8,
62–4, 91, 95, 112–14, 203, 205, 208;
see also brecks
hemp, 142, 181–2, 185
Hengrave: 36, 39, 54, 81, 98, 135, 150–1,
163, 196, 249, 288, 293; occupations
in, 174, 189–90, 308
Herringswell: 28, 35, 136n, 174, 196;
field-systems, 68n, 70n, 79
  Bury abbey manor, 37
Hevingham (Norf.), 232n, 281n
Higham, 34, 36, 81, 196
Hilborough: 35, 37, 39, 223, 232, 288n,
312; field-systems, 68, 78, 90n; land
market, 228, 266, 268; market, 144,
263–4, 306; occupations in, 183;
warren, 132, 134, 252, 254, 285
  manor of: arable farming, 94, 98, 101,
104, 106, 139, 214, 238–44, 281–3,
285; pastoral farming, 220, 246, 250,
289, 291
Hinderclay (Suff.), 190
High Easter (Essex), 191
Hockham, Magna and Parva: 35, 39, 149,
198, 205–6, 234n, 249, 253, 288n,
313; field-systems, 45, 70–1, 79;
market, 144, 146n, 263, 307;
occupations in, 163–4, 183, 260–2, 309
  Earl of Norfolk's manor: 37, 89, 94,
106, 139, 238–44; see also Kennett
Hockwold, 36, 152, 155n, 161–3, 188n,
303
Holkham (Norf.), 66
Holme Hale (Norf.), 312
Honington, 36, 76, 81, 119, 192n, 196
Hopton, 36, 119, 192, 196
horses, 20–1, 94, 156–7
Hunston (Suff.), 192n

Ickburgh, 35, 80, 81, 144, 188n
Icklingham: 31, 35, 37, 128, 142, 196,
208, 310, 314; field-systems, 59, 61,
80, 83, 89, 93, 94n; occupations in,
162n, 163, 165, 176, 177
  manor of: arable farming, 101, 104,
106, 139, 237–44; leasing, 203;
pastoral farming, 90, 117, 122,
124–7, 217, 220, 245–6

346

Index

Index

Index

Threxton, 36, 163
Thunen, Johann von, 12–14, 87
Tilney (Norf.), 150
Tiltey abbey, 121
timber, 151
Timworth: 35–6, 54, 89n, 135, 151n, 176, 184, 197, 222–3; field-systems, 44–5, 64, 68; land market, 49
Bury abbey manor, 37, 90
Tottington, 36, 89, 299
transport: 12, 14, 20–1, 150; in Breckland, 153–7, 218, 308–7
Troston: 36, 119–20, 141, 142, 176, 192, 193, 196; field-systems, 72, 81, 114
Tuddenham, 29, 36, 89, 175–6, 184, 196
turves, 163–4, 259, 304

Walpole, 150
Walsham-le-Willows (Suff.), 56, 131n, 309n
Walsingham (Norf.), 169
Walter of Henley, 86
Waltham (Essex), 191
Wangford: 26, 31–2, 36, 41, 44–5, 197, 270n; field-systems, 76; occupations in, 161, 164
warreners, 134–5, 184–5, 254–5
warrens: see rabbits
wealth, taxable of peasantry, 23–4, 100, 191–9, 315–16
weavers/weaving: see textiles
Weeting, 36, 160, 184, 188n, 299
Wells (Norf.), 155, 174
Westminster abbey, 284

West Stow, 29, 36, 45, 48, 56, 110, 119–21, 135, 141, 177, 193, 196, 294
West Tofts, 36, 107, 138, 170, 188n, 203n, 239–44, 139
wheat: 64n, 91–2, 138–41, 146n, 148, 150, 192, 194, 201–2, 209–17, 237–45, 282–3; yields, 99–108
Wilby, 36, 88n, 198
Wilton, 36, 139, 161–3, 188n, 139
Wiltshire, 5
Wisbech (Cambs.), 157
Wissey, river, 29, 135, 153–4, 163, 177
wool, 126–7, 147–50, 173–4, 245–8, 251, 264, 271–2, 276, 289–90, 292, 307, 318
woodland, 26, 151, 158, 163
Worcester, bishopric of, 276n, 284
Wordwell, 29, 36, 45, 55, 119–20, 135, 141, 190, 193, 196, 317
Worlington: 36, 44, 98, 144–5, 149, 152–3, 197, 270n; field-systems, 84n
Worlingworth (Suff.), 257n
Wretham, East and West, 36, 53, 57, 107, 126, 138–9, 190, 197, 201, 210–11; occupations in, 165, 177, 190
Ogbourne priory manor: arable farming, 203, 239–44; pastoral farming, 246, 248
Writtle (Essex), 281n, 284n

Yarmouth, Great, 151, 157
Yaxley (Suff.), 155
York, 150
Yorkshire, 3, 98–9, 116, 200, 229n